The Embrace of Eros

The Embrace of Eros

Bodies, Desires, and Sexuality in Christianity

Margaret D. Kamitsuka, Editor

Fortress Press

Minneapolis

THE EMBRACE OF EROS
Bodies, Desires, and Sexuality in Christianity

Cover image: Edna Bullock, Three Nudes on Dunes, 1990 © 1990/2010 Bullock Family Photography LLC. All Rights Reserved.
Cover design: Laurie Ingram
Book design: Hillspring Books

Library of Congress Cataloging-in-Publication Data

The embrace of eros : bodies, desires, and sexuality in Christianity / [edited by] Margaret D. Kamitsuka.
       p. cm.
Includes bibliographical references and index.
ISBN 978-0-8006-9667-2 (alk. paper)
Sex—History of doctrines. 2. Sex—Religious aspects—Christianity.
  I. Kamitsuka, Margaret D.
BT708.E43 2010
233′.5—dc22   2009042985

Manufactured in the U.S.A.

14 13 12 11 10   1 2 3 4 5 6 7 8 9 10

CONTENTS

PART II. CULTURE: BODIES, DESIRES, AND SEXUAL IDENTITIES

PART III. RECONSTRUCTION: EROTIC THEOLOGY

CONTRIBUTORS

Edward P. Antonio is associate professor of theology and social theory at the Iliff School of Theology in Denver, Colorado. In addition to his academic duties he also serves as Iliff's Diversity Officer. He edited *Inculturation and Postcolonial Discourse in African Theology* (Peter Lang, 2006) and has published articles on black theology, Kierkegaard and empire, environmental ecology, and African indigenous thought. He is a native of Zimbabwe.

Corey Barnes is assistant professor in the department of religion at Oberlin College, Ohio, where he teaches medieval religion and the history of Christianity. He holds an M.A.R. in historical theology from Yale Divinity School and a Ph.D. in historical theology from the University of Notre Dame. He is currently working on a monograph tentatively titled *'Not as I will': Christ's Two Wills in Scholastic Theology.*

Joy R. Bostic is assistant professor of religious studies at Case Western Reserve University in Cleveland, Ohio. Her scholarship focuses upon African American religions with a special emphasis on womanist theology and black women's spiritualities and religious practices. She received her Ph.D. in systematic theology from Union Theological Seminary in New York City in 2006 and is currently working on a book on activism, mysticism, and African American women.

Paul E. Capetz is professor of historical theology at United Theological Seminary of the Twin Cities and an ordained minister in the Presbyterian Church (U.S.A.). He is the author of *Christian Faith as Religion: A Study in the Theologies of Calvin and Schleiermacher* (University Press of America, 1998) and *God: A Brief History* (Fortress Press, 2003), as well as coeditor with James M. Gustafson, *Moral Discernment in the Christian Life: Essays in Theological Ethics* (Westminster John Knox, 2007).

Shannon Craigo-Snell is associate professor of religious studies at Yale University, specializing in modern Christian thought. She offers courses on feminist theologies, political and liberation theologies, and theology and theater.

She has published two books: *Silence, Love, and Death: Saying "Yes" to God in the Theology of Karl Rahner* (Marquette University Press, 2008) and *Living Christianity: A Pastoral Theology for Today* (Fortress Press, 2009), coauthored with Shawnthea Monroe.

Rebecca L. Davis is assistant professor of history and women's studies at the University of Delaware, where she specializes in the histories of sexuality, religion, and ethnicity in the modern United States. Her book, *More Perfect Unions: The American Search for Marital Bliss*, is forthcoming from Harvard University Press in 2010.

David H. Jensen is professor of constructive theology at Austin Presbyterian Theological Seminary. His research explores the interconnections of Christian theology and daily life. His most recent book is *The Lord and Giver of Life: Perspectives on Constructive Pneumatology* (Westminster John Knox, 2008). He is currently writing a book that develops a theology of human sexuality and editing a book series with Fortress Press on theological reflection on everyday practices such as cooking, parenting, and working.

William Stacy Johnson is the Arthur M. Adams Professor of Systematic Theology at Princeton Theological Seminary. He earned a Ph.D. in religion from Harvard University and has authored and edited a number of works, including: *H. Richard Niebuhr: Theology, History, and Culture* (Westminster John Knox, 1996), *The Mystery of God: Karl Barth and the Postmodern Foundations of Theology* (Westminster John Knox, 1997), and *A Time to Embrace: Same-gender Relationships in Religion, Law, and Politics* (Eerdmans, 2006).

Serene Jones is President of Union Theological Seminary and Roosevelt Professor of Systematic Theology, previously the Titus Street Professor of Theology at Yale Divinity School. Her publications include *Feminist Theory and Christian Theology: Cartographies of Grace* (Fortress Press, 2000) and *Calvin and the Rhetoric of Piety* (Westminster John Knox, 1995). Among her coedited works are: *Feminist and Womanist Essays in Reformed Dogmatics* (Westminster John Knox, 2006) and *Constructive Theology: A Contemporary Engagement with Classical Themes* (Fortress Press, 2005).

Mark D. Jordan is R. R. Niebuhr Professor at Harvard Divinity School. His interests include Christian ethics of sex and gender, the limits of religious language, medieval Latin theology, and the ethical or ritual creation of religious identities. His recent books include *Telling Truths in Church: Scandal, Flesh, and Christian Speech* (Beacon, 2003) and *Blessing Same-Sex Unions: The Perils of Queer Romance and the Confusions of Christian Marriage* (University of Chicago Press, 2005). He is currently writing on the rhetoric of American church controversies over homosexuality.

Laurie A. Jungling is assistant professor of religion and ethics at Augustana College in Sioux Falls, South Dakota. Her research centers around the theological concept of vocation as a positive ethical framework for engaging difficult moral issues, particularly issues surrounding sexuality and gender. She is the author of "Passionate Order: Order and Sexuality in Augustine's Theology," the *World and World* essay prize-winner for doctoral candidates for 2006–07.

Margaret D. Kamitsuka is associate professor in the department of religion at Oberlin College, Ohio, specializing in gender and religion. In addition, she serves on the advisory council of the Gender, Sexuality, and Feminist Studies Institute at Oberlin College. She earned her Ph.D. from Yale University and is the author of *Feminist Theology and the Challenge of Difference* (Oxford University Press, 2007).

Paul Lakeland is the Aloysius P. Kelley S.J. Professor of Catholic Studies and the director of the Center for Catholic Studies at Fairfield University in Connecticut. His most recent book is *Church: Living Communion* (Liturgical, 2009). Two of his publications, *Catholicism at the Crossroads: How the Laity Can Save the Church* (Continuum, 2007) and *The Liberation of the Laity: In Search of an Accountable Church* (Continuum, 2003), won awards from the Catholic Press Association.

James W. Perkinson is a longtime activist, educator, and recognized spoken-word poet from inner-city Detroit and professor of social ethics at the Ecumenical Theological Seminary. He also lectures in intercultural communication studies at the University of Oakland, Michigan. He holds a Ph.D. in theology and history of religions from the University of Chicago. He is the author of *White Theology: Outing Supremacy in Modernity* (Palgrave Macmillan, 2004) and *Shamanism, Racism, and Hip-Hop Culture: Essays on White Supremacy and Black Subversion* (Palgrave Macmillan, 2005), and has written extensively in both academic and popular journals on questions of race, class, and colonialism in connection with religion and urban culture.

Laurel C. Schneider is professor of theology, ethics, and culture at Chicago Theological Seminary in Chicago, Illinois. Her books include *Beyond Monotheism: A Theology of Multiplicity* (Routledge, 2007) and *Re-Imagining the Divine: Confronting the Backlash Against Feminist Theology* (Pilgrim, 1999). She is co-convener of the Constructive Theology Workgroup and serves on the Status of LGBTIQ Persons in the Profession of the American Academy of Religion.

John E. Thiel is professor of religious studies and director of the University Honors Program at Fairfield University, Connecticut. His most recent books are *Senses of Tradition: Continuity and Development in Catholic Faith* (Oxford University Press, 2000) and *God, Evil, and Innocent Suffering* (Crossroad, 2002). Twice a recipient of fellowships from the National Endowment for the Humanities, he sits on the editorial board of *Theological Studies* and is a member of the American Theological Society.

Mark I. Wallace is professor of religion and member of the Interpretation Theory and the Environmental Studies Committees at Swarthmore College. His books include *Green Christianity: Five Ways to a Sustainable Future* (Fortress Press, 2010); *Finding God in the Singing River: Christianity, Spirit, Nature* (Fortress Press, 2005); and *Fragments of the Spirit: Nature, Violence, and the Renewal of Creation* (Continuum, 1996). He is a member of the Constructive Theology Workgroup and active in the Philadelphia-area educational reform movement.

Tatha Wiley teaches at the University of St. Thomas in St. Paul, Minnesota. Her publications include *Original Sin: Origins, Developments, Contemporary Meaning* (Paulist, 2002), *Paul and the Gentile Women: Reframing Galatians* (Continuum, 2005), and *Creationism and the Conflict over Evolution* (Wipf & Stock, 2008). She edited *Thinking about Christ: Proclamation, Explanation, Meaning* (Continuum, 2003) and she is series editor for *Engaging Theology: Roman Catholic Perspectives* from Liturgical Press.

ACKNOWLEDGMENTS

I want to acknowledge a debt of thanks to the Workgroup on Constructive Theology, which under the leadership of Serene Jones and Paul Lakeland sponsored the April 21–23, 2006, conference on sex that planted the seeds for this anthology. At that conference, some of the authors in this volume presented papers that grew into these essays. Others subsequently contributed new material provoked by the lively conversations that took place throughout that Workgroup weekend. In addition, this anthology has been enriched by others who participated in the process in various ways: Rosemary Carbine, Mary McClintock Fulkerson, Esther Hamori, David Kamitsuka, Jean Kim, Kwok Pui Lan, Joy McDougall, Shelly Rambo, Geoffrey Rees, Kathleen Sands, John Thatamanil, and Emilie Townes.

Editor-in-chief at Fortress Press, Michael West, was instrumental in helping to conceptualize a volume that would present cutting-edge theological perspectives on eros in a readable and teachable format. I am grateful to acquisitions editor, Susan Johnson, and senior production editor, Carolyn Banks, for overseeing the production of the whole. My thanks go as well to the Oberlin College Office of Sponsored Programs for generous student assistant grants. Oberlin College religion major Sarah Gardner ('09) was funded to work as an editorial assistant and provided diligent and careful help at all phases of the project.

INTRODUCTION

Margaret D. Kamitsuka

The lover followed the paths of his beloved absorbed in thought.
He tripped and fell among the thorns, and it seemed to him that they
were flowers and that he lay on a bed of love.

— Ramon Llull, *The Book of the Lover and the Beloved*[1]

THE GENESIS OF *The Embrace of Eros: Bodies, Desires, and Sexuality in Christianity* was a 2006 conference attended by about fifty theologians and scholars of religion from across North America who came together to discuss how eros and sexuality have fared in Christianity historically and up to the present.[2] The papers presented brought into sharp focus how Christian texts and traditions can be implicated in many contemporary societal struggles and injustices related to human gendered and sexual embodiment. The presenters also emphasized that Christianity has had a nearly obsessive fixation on the dynamics of sexual desire. Whether through repression, spiritualization, or regulation, Christianity has made the body and its passions central to what is means to be human—and "saved." We in the Western world live, willingly or resistantly, in the ongoing wake of this legacy; therefore, it behooves us to know more about eros and the Christian tradition. After this 2006 conference, conversations continued with other scholars of religion, thus sowing the seeds for an anthology which would investigate the possibilities for and the shape of an embrace of eros in Christianity that would be enlivening not repressive, matter-of-fact not obsessive, plurivocal not uniform. This introduction presents to readers the principal themes of this text's critical interaction with the Christian tradition: eros, bodies, and sexuality.

WHOSE EROS? WHAT CHRISTIANITY?

Eros, from the name of the Greek god of love, understandably is associated for most people with pleasure, including sexual pleasure; few, no doubt, expect the Christian tradition to be its place of nurture. Christianity from its inception preached continence and eschewed pleasures of the flesh. Jesus' statement that people in heaven "neither marry nor are given in marriage, but are like angels" (Matt. 22:30) was applied to extol virginity and abstinence within marriage. When the apostle Paul directed Christians to think of their bodies as temples of the Holy Spirit (see 1 Cor. 6:19), they took this to mean that Christian faith requires elevating spiritual concerns over bodily desires. Paul's allowance of marriage and remarriage as an outlet for those who are "aflame" with sexual desires (1 Cor. 7:9) seems liberal in comparison to third-century church theologian Tertullian who declared, "We admit one marriage, just as we do one God," and who even advised widows not to remarry but to commit themselves to what is "nobler"—namely, "the continence of the flesh."[3] By the fourth century, sex even within marriage was spoken of as base, unclean, and dishonorable, as we see in Jerome's pronouncement that "in view of the purity of the body of Christ, all sexual intercourse is unclean" and his teaching to husbands: "If we abstain from intercourse, we give honour to our wives."[4] It is no hyperbole to say that Christianity, from its origins and in its formative years, was largely antierotic, casting aspersions even on those dimensions of human relations where sex was licit. Even Protestant reformer Martin Luther, who deemed celibacy so rare a gift as to be called a miracle, still thought along patristic lines that sexual desire was sinful, though permissible in marriage where "God excuses it by his grace."[5]

Does this mean that eros was completely absent from Christian writings? Many scholars would consider this claim to be too flat. Take, for example, the history of interpretation of the biblical Song of Songs, a book dripping with erotically charged energy between a yearning young woman and her virile lover. Early church theologians saw the dangers this text posed for monastic contemplation. How should monks at prayer interpret verses like these?

I slept, but my heart was awake.
Listen! My beloved is knocking.
"Open to me, my sister, my love,
my dove, my perfect one . . ."
My beloved thrust his hand into the opening;
and my inmost being yearned for him. (Song 5:2, 4)

Origen, a third-century Neoplatonic theologian, urged an allegorical reading of this poem: the young maiden represents the soul and the young man who calls out to her is the word of God.[6] From Origen in the Eastern church to twelfth-century mystic Bernard of Clairvaux in the West, the eroticism in the Song of Songs was alive and well in monastic piety—under the veil of allegory, of course.[7]

The effort to control and channel eros is not just an antique or a medieval Christian struggle. The church continued its vigilance through the early modern period. In the seventeenth-century North American context, sexuality was inextricably linked to the colonizing and missionizing of indigenous populations and to the economic entrenchment of slavery.[8] Passion and sexual incontinence was read onto the dark-skinned subjugated body in distorted ways that postcolonial and race theorists today are still unraveling.

Since the 1970s with the rise of the women's liberation and gay pride movements, various church and parachurch organizations have attempted to consolidate eros with traditional (read: heterosexual, patriarchal) "family values." For most church denominations, sexual activity within marriage is seen as blessed; all other forms of sexual expression are consigned to categories of abomination (homosexuality), fornication (premarital or adulterous heterosexual sex), and misguided uses of the body (masturbation). A parachurch organization called Exodus International, which bills itself as "promoting the message of *Freedom from homosexuality through the power of Jesus Christ,*"[9] organizes and offers referrals to programs for helping homosexuals "re-connect with [God's] original design and purpose for them as a man or woman"—that is, to covert to heterosexuality.[10] Evangelicals involved in this effort note the importance of providing a message not only of freedom from (homosexuality) but also freedom for (eros in marriage). In this regard, the conservative Protestant organization Focus on the Family runs an online marriage-counseling blog to answer questions couples may have about sex, in order to foster vibrant sexuality within the proper bounds of the husband-led Christian family.[11] There is a booming industry of how-to marriage and singleness guides from conservative Christian publishing houses. Titles include: *Sex and the Single Guy:*

Winning Your Battle for Purity; Real Questions, Real Answers about Sex: The Complete Guide to Intimacy as God Intended; and *Why Say No When My Hormones Say Go?*[12] The titles may strike some as prosaic or even humorous, but the burgeoning sales figures are real. The embrace of godly marital eros is felt all the way to the Vatican: Pope Benedict XVI's first encyclical, *Deus Caritas Est* (2005), calls for a unity of the "wordly" love of eros and *agape* ("love grounded and shaped by faith") in the intimacy of the conjugal act.[13]

Liberal theological reflection on the meaning of eros today is trying to break out of binary approaches that pit sexualized eros against nonsexual *agape* love.[14] Eros is not just about sexuality, so say many contemporary theorists. African American poet, essayist, and self-affirmed lesbian Audre Lorde spoke strongly for a broad understanding of eros. In her essay "Uses of the Erotic: The Erotic and Power," which has reached near-creedal status among contemporary liberal theologians commenting on this issue, Lorde defined eros principally as a "creative energy" and "lifeforce" that has the capacity for "providing the power which comes from sharing deeply any pursuit with another person. The sharing of joy, whether physical, emotional, psychic, or intellectual, forms a bridge between the sharers."[15] It may entail sexual or nonsexual sharing; it may be solitary. It is always "replenishing and provocative" in that it incites and empowers from the deep wellsprings of the self.[16] For contemporary theologians, the erotic is inextricably linked to spirituality as the source of human well-being.[17] Moreover, from this perspective, celibacy and erotic desires are not mutually contradictory terms. Celibacy, the most misunderstood of lifestyles especially today, should not properly be seen, its adherents claim, as a life of asexuality or sublimation of passion.[18]

Whether found in liberal or conservative Christian contexts, the issue of eros seems to be an increasingly central and contested issue in Christian discourse today. Most Christian circles seem to have surmounted the early church's disdain of eros, but now the battle is over "Whose eros?" and "What Christianity?" The embrace of marital eros by some conservative Christians has meant the exclusion of the erotic "other" (gays, bisexuals, etc.). Conversely, the embrace of eros for lesbian, gay, bisexual, transgendered, and questioning (LGBTQ) persons by the liberal wing of the church has provoked a splintering within Christianity of global proportions.[19] Eros, it seems, will shape Christianity worldwide for the twenty-first century.

THE EMBRACE OF BODIES—BUT NOT THEIR PLEASURES

Christianity has, from its origins, been intensely body focused. There are theological, ritual, and spiritual reasons for this. Theologically, the doctrine of the incarnation—the notion that God became human flesh in the person of Jesus of Nazareth—was affirmed as orthodox in the ecumenical church councils of the fourth and fifth centuries. Henceforth, anything other than belief in Christ's indivisible full divinity and full humanity was considered anathema. The Athanasian creed states: "Although He is God and man, He is not two, but one Christ." Creedal affirmations such as this precipitated in the early church a decisive anti-Docetic and anti-Manichean turn. Docetism, the viewpoint that God only appeared to take human form in Jesus of Nazareth, was rejected by the dominant patristic voices, which insisted that the "Son" really became incarnate in a human body. The early church's rejection of the Manichean dualism is seen starkly in the *Confessions* of Bishop Augustine of Hippo (354–430), who was at one time a follower of Manichean philosophy, which viewed the material world as evil. As a new convert, Augustine at first bristled at the notion that God would have deigned to be born of a woman, since how could he be thus "mingled with her flesh without being defiled"?[20] Notwithstanding their subsequent rejection of Docetism and Manicheanism, church fathers such as Augustine could not embrace the body's pleasures; rather, bodily appetites were associated with animal lusts arising from the "habit of the flesh."[21] Henceforth, regulating sinful "flesh" became an obsessive focus of the church.

Ritually, Christianity's central sacramental practices developed as revolving around the body. The Eucharist, the laying on of hands in rituals of healing, the giving of last rites—these and other practices of material religion consolidated bodies as central to Christian ritual. In many ecclesial rites, purification of the body is transacted or symbolized. Whether it involved infants or adult catechumens, baptism became a ritual for purifying the body from sin and consecrating the whole person as part of the church community. What occurs in the sacrament of baptism, sixteeenth-century Protestant reformer John Calvin says, is "the mortification of our sin. . . . For so long as we live cooped up in this prison of our body, traces of sin will dwell in us; but if we faithfully hold fast to the promise given us by God in baptism, they shall not dominate or rule."[22] Not surprisingly, gender often played a role in how the body was seen as in need of purification. For example, the now defunct rite called the "churching of women" (where postpartum women were readmitted to church after the sprinkling of holy water and priestly prayers) communicated—whether intentionally or not—that the bloody process of birth somehow rendered women's bodies impure.[23] Ancient proscriptions concerning menstruating women partaking the Eucharist or even entering a church confirm the notion that blood was seen as defiling female bodies, despite the effort to construe the prohibition otherwise.[24] The ritual embrace of bodies in Christianity is punctuated by images of the defiled, sinful, gendered body.

Spiritual practices in Christianity, especially with the rise of monasticism, put the body front and center with its practices of prayer. Marked by extreme asceticism (fasting, sexual continence, self-flagellation, denial of sleep, and so on), monastic life was extremely body negating. Nevertheless, the body was also seen as indispensable. Early seventh-century abbot John Climacus aptly captures this sentiment:

> [B]y what rule or manner can I bind this body of mine? . . . How can I hate him when my nature disposes me to love him? How can I break away from him when I am bound to him forever? How can I escape from him when he is going to rise with me? . . . He is my helper and my enemy, my assistant and my opponent, a protector and a traitor. . . . If I wear him out he gets weak. If he has a rest he becomes unruly. . . . If I mortify him I endanger myself. If I strike him down I have nothing left by which to acquire virtues. I embrace him. And I turn away from him.[25]

Spiritualities across the spectrum of Christianity show this tension regarding the body. The body is necessary for one's devotional life of bodily practices; yet the body's sin-prone inclinations are at odds with one's spiritual aspirations. Again, gender perceptions intersect with this tensive attitude toward the body resulting in a mix of misogyny and eroticism, as seen in the writings of the so-called desert fathers—ascetic men who often saw the devil coming to tempt them sexually in the form of a woman.[26] While medieval female mystics waxed eloquent about union with their bridegroom Christ, their embrace of his body did not translate into care of their own bodies, which they sometimes mortified to the point of "holy anorexia," as one scholar puts it.[27]

SEXUALITY AND SEXUAL DESIRES

Sexuality as an orientation or an identity is a very modern notion, foreign to theological and other writings predating the advent of modern psychology. Even in the contemporary age, theologians and religious ethicists have stumbled for terminology to describe sexualities outside of the heterosexual norm and gender expressions outside of the male-female binary. Three methodological developments have proved decisive for a breakthrough for contemporary theologies addressing the issue of sexuality.

First, gender analysis, borrowed from women's studies, began to figure prominently in religious studies from the 1980s.[28] Although women cannot be reduced to sexuality, there has been an entrenched historical linking of women to sexual temptation. Hence, discussing women in the Christian tradition not only caused the issue of sexuality to emerge, when before it had been relegated to narrow categories (e.g., marriage), but it also precipitated new methods of scholarly analysis. For example, Toinette Eugene's essay on black spirituality and sexuality in a 1985 anthology on feminist ethics exemplifies an approach that feminist, womanist, and other scholars of religion—including many contributing to this volume—would henceforth employ: an intersectional analysis that allows religious experience to be refracted in terms of intersecting cultural factors of embodiment: gender, sex, race, class, ethnicity, sexual orientation, and so on.[29]

Second, new modes of historical analysis are being explored and debated in religious studies, marked by the postmodern paradigm shift in intellectual thought. Many scholars are influenced by the way postmodern historians, like Michel Foucault, exposed the cultural codes, gestures, regulations, and "discourses" of sex for eras predating the term *sexuality*. Scholars have found that these discourses of sex turn out to be very diverse, culturally contingent, and multivocal. Moreover, when these discourses are most filled with religious diatribes about sin and debauchery, they ironically have the effect opposite to the intended one—that is, not repression but consolidation of the very desires they mean to stamp out, not eradication but "dissemination and implantation of polymorphous sexualities."[30] For example, Mark Jordan has investigated how the practices of the confessional elicited—in order to categorize, judge, and punish—accounts of male-male sex acts, or "sodomy" as it began to be called after the eleventh century. Paradoxically, in training confessors to root out tendencies toward sins of sodomy, church authorities instructed that "only very virile men, men excessively attached to women" should hear confession, because it became apparent from the flow of sexual narratives in the confessional that sodomy was "in fact not repulsive [but] . . . immensely attractive" to many men.[31] Foucault and other postmodern theorists have provided scholars one way to analyze the discursive production of sexualities—a mode of analysis that continues today, now with attention given to ever-expanding discourses of religion, psychology, law, medicine, psychiatry, pornography, global capitalism, virtual reality, and so on. Theologians today, including several in this volume, are employing aspects of postmodern modes of analyzing how cultural discourses and bodily practices invest bodies with sexual meaning, value, and power.

A third development that has had an impact on how theologians approach the issue of sexuality has been the methodological shift to experience as a valid and often preferred source and norm for theological reflection.[32] Whereas in the past theologians might have turned to normative Christian texts (Scripture, creedal documents, magisterial teachings, etc.) as primary sources and norms, the past three decades have seen a flood of theological texts whose starting point or primary criterion of validity is human experience, such as the experience of women, gays, lesbians, transgendered people, and so on, where gender, embodiment, and sexuality have come to the fore as lenses for doing theology.[33] Whether through phenomenological analyses of embodiment or ethnographic investigations of particular bodily practices, theological writing has been transformed by making concrete human experiences central for reflection about God, Christ, the church, and salvation. When combined with gender analysis and postmodern modes of reflection, the methodological focus on experience has made possible a growing theological embrace of the issue of sexual desire, revealing a vast uncharted territory of bodily practices, identities, and spiritualities waiting to be narrated, theorized, and theologized.

HISTORY, CULTURE, AND RECONSTRUCTION

The Embrace of Eros is divided into three parts: history, culture, and reconstruction. The historical section (part one) provides an overview of the persistent anxiety in Christianity regarding eros—from the writings of the early church fathers to modern papal encyclicals and Protestant denominational rulings. Given what the Bible and authoritative theological voices have said about sex historically, what possibilities exist to reengage the tradition in light of contemporary perspectives on eros? David Jensen surveys what the Bible is thought to say about sex and asks, Should the Bible be taken as a rule book on matters of sex or is there a possibility for a more eros-friendly hermeneutic? Against the backdrop of the early church's polemic against sexual desire, Mark Wallace proposes a theology of the erotic, tactile healing of bodies with a focus on Luke's narrative about a woman who engaged in intimate touching of Jesus' body. Tackling the apostle Paul's supposed invectives against homosexuality, William Stacy Johnson argues that Paul's writings are best understood as a critique of practices of slavery in the Roman Empire—not as a moral denunciation of Greco-Roman homoeroticism. Augustine of Hippo, arguably the pivotal thinker for Western Christendom, bequeathed to us an anthropology of denial that equated bodily desires with death, according to John Thiel, who explores why this viewpoint has been so resilient in the

Christian tradition. Corey Barnes introduces readers to the subtleties of the Scholastic theology of Thomas Aquinas (1225–1274) to show the extent to which Aquinas's views on bodily appetites could potentially provide some basis for affirming the goodness of passionate bodies. Tatha Wiley critically assesses the views on sexuality and contraception in the 1968 papal encyclical *Humanae vitae* and proposes an alternative approach to sexuality for Roman Catholic married couples. Do principles of the Protestant Reformation support homosexual ministers who will not comply with current denominational rules of self-imposed celibacy? This question guides Paul Capetz in his semiautobiographical essay as an ordained Presbyterian minister actively grappling with this current theological and existential issue.

Part two reflects theologically on bodies, desires, and sexual identities in the modern period. Five scholars use various critical theories (including theories of race, gender, queerness, and postmodernity) in order to analyze and reflect theologically on the construction of embodied eros in a range of modern cultural attitudes and practices. Shannon Craigo-Snell analyzes how female theologians such as herself find themselves attempting to "pass" as male in the academy by valuing masculine modes of rationality and by devaluing the embodied relationality that has marked women's cultural ways of knowing. Mark Jordan's essay tracks how church leaders from the post-WWII era and later struggled to label and religiously situate persons with male-male sexual desires. Rebecca Davis demonstrates how eros and gender were constructed for conservative Christian families based on one of the most widely read evangelical marriage manuals of the 1970s, Marabel Morgan's *The Total Woman*. Edward Antonio outlines the theological challenge of conceptualizing African sexual identities in light of the devastation of HIV/AIDS and the legacy of colonizing Western public-health discourses about sexuality in Africa. Theologian and spoken-word artist James Perkinson comments theologically and autobiographically on intersections of eros and white male fetishizing of hip-hop.

The guiding question for part three of *The Embrace of Eros* is, How can classic Christian doctrines be reformulated in light of more positive views of eros? The essays in this section offer theological reconstructions of five traditional doctrinal loci: creation, incarnation, ecclesiology, eschatology, and pneumatology. Laurie Jungling reinterprets the doctrine of creation as God's call to embodied relationality based not only on the freedom to seek erotic possibilities but also on the call to faithfulness appropriate to our creaturely finitude in time and space. In her reflections on the doctrine of the incarnation, Laurel Schneider uses the provocative term *promiscuous* to represent the refusal of divine exclusivity in God's choice for fleshly intimacy with humanity. Paul Lakeland's essay on ecclesiology employs the dialectic of presence and absence in order to compare Protestant and Catholic metaphorical representations of the church's love of and desire for God and to project a dynamic ecclesiology of desire. Is there sex in heaven? This question guides Margaret Kamitsuka's reflection on eros and the resurrection of the body in light of the Freudian psychodynamic theories of feminist philosopher Julia Kristeva. Joy Bostic reads Toni Morrison's iconic *Beloved* in relation to feminist and womanist pneumatologies in order to formulate a doctrine of the Holy Spirit who brings erotic justice to broken flesh.

All the authors in this anthology are academic scholars in religion. Some have ministerial standing or seminary teaching appointments and would situate their scholarship in terms of ecclesial commitments. Some see their theological scholarship as situated within the sphere of religious studies where the validity of doing theology as an academic discipline is an issue they often have to defend. All the authors share a commitment to engage critically and constructively with the historical and current textual sources and material practices of the Christian tradition. Although the authors tend toward liberal positions, this volume does not present a univocal view on eros. For example, Schneider calls for considering the eros of divine incarnation in terms of the metaphor of promiscuity, while Jungling challenges the implied literal sexual promiscuity in the call for freedom in many current erotic theologies. Even the arguably most central figure to shape the theology and ecclesial institutions of the early church, the apostle Paul, is variously interpreted. Wallace categorizes Paul as a leading and early proponent of sexual renunciation that distanced Christianity from it Jewish origins, while Johnson situates a very Jewish Paul in the context of Roman practices of sexualized violence imposed on the bodies of colonized peoples such as his fellow Jews.

The hoped-for consequences of *The Embrace of Eros* are several. It is hoped that readers will gain an appreciation for the constraints and possibilities of eros and Christianity. These essays show representative instances of how the Christian tradition's imposition of constraints on bodily passions have not only denigrated desires and normalized identities in marginalizing ways but have also inculcated a disciplinary ethics-as-rule-following. Attempting to regulate eros based on scripturally derived rules overlooks how Scripture itself can be seen as an extended narrative of desire (Jensen). To this day, the cultural effects of the church's disciplinary discourses on the body are widespread: female theologians are constrained to think and act as "male" in order to be recognized as rational (Craigo-Snell); sexually active gay ministers are constrained against their conscience to pretend publicly to be celibate straight men (Capetz); Roman Catholic couples are constrained to hide the fact that their 2.5 children are not a dead give-away of their surreptitious use of prohibited birth control (Wiley).

These essays also show the possibilities for reengaging the tradition to find submerged, untapped dynamics of desire and new questions about the power and limits of eros for frail flesh. The evangelical wife, by enacting sexual submission, thereby validates—and hence to some extent controls—her husband's gendered and erotic authority within the marriage (Davis). We might associate the message that sex is natural with modern pop psychology, but it was the medieval Scholastic theologian Thomas Aquinas who was part of an underappreciated sea change in theological views on eros when he argued that sexual desire is natural to, rather than a corruption of, human nature (Barnes). This is not to say that Christian views of eros will heal what ails our current consumerist, voyeuristic cultural infatuation with erotic titillation. Just the opposite is the case: the centuries-long Euro-Christian colonialist exploitation of bodies of color must first be analyzed in order to expose white racist fears and desires (Perkinson). We must add to this sociopolitical analysis a psychological analysis of eros as a product of often conflicted psychosexual human development. Only then can we allow ourselves the luxury of imagining eros in a heavenly key, though, even then, the deep psychosexual wounds we struggle with in this life may be carried into the next (Kamitsuka).

This volume does not settle the matter of eros and Christianity. Rather, *The Embrace of Eros* points to the need to continue to hear new voices and entertain new cultural challenges, while reengaging with the texts and practices that have formed Christian identities for two millennia. Christians have been taught to believe that God is love. The time has come to reflect anew on the plenitude and mystery of divine eros and risk falling among its thorns.

Further Suggested Readings

Burrus, Virginia, and Catherine Keller, eds. *Toward a Theology of Eros: Transfiguring Passion at the Limits of Discipline.* New York: Fordham University Press, 2006.

Nelson, James B., and Sandra P. Longfellow, eds. *Sexuality and the Sacred: Sources for Theological Reflection.* Louisville: Westminster John Knox, 1994.

Pinn, Anthony B., and Dwight N. Hopkins, eds. *Loving the Body: Black Religious Studies and the Erotic.* New York: Palgrave Macmillan, 2004.

Rogers, Eugene F., Jr. *Theology and Sexuality: Classic and Contemporary Readings.* Malden, Mass.: Blackwell, 2002.

PART I

History: Engaging Eros in the Tradition

CHAPTER 1

The Bible and Sex

David H. Jensen

FOR CENTURIES CHRISTIANS have argued about sex. The Bible figures prominently in this history of argument, perhaps more prominently than anything else in Christian traditions. Across the generations, Christians have cited biblical texts to endorse or prohibit various sexual behaviors, argued with those same texts, and attempted to place them within broader theological frameworks. In the history of Christian theology, biblical texts are summoned as truth, dismissed as irrelevant, cited in isolation, and woven together in broad tapestries. "What does the Bible say about sex?" many Christians ask. This seemingly simple question yields anything but a simple answer. The Bible says many sometimes conflicting things about sex, so in some regards this is the wrong question to be asking. Christians ought first ask, "What is the character of the book we call Scripture?" Attention to that question must precede discussion of the often thorny subject of the Bible and sex. With that in mind, this chapter surveys three approaches to the Bible and sex that broadly frame current debates: (1) an approach that focuses on the explicitly "sexual texts" and sees the Bible as a guidebook on sex; (2) an approach that deems the Bible an insufficient, outmoded, and even oppressive text on many issues, including sexuality, in the contemporary age; and (3) an approach, which I advocate, that views Scripture as itself a narrative of desire, situating sexuality as one moment within other expressions of relationship.

THE BIBLE AS A GUIDEBOOK FOR SEXUAL BEHAVIOR

Perhaps the most common way of reading the Bible with regard to sex is to view it as a guide for sexual behavior. The Bible, in this view, offers clear prohibitions of specific sexual behaviors and might be described as a "how-not-to" manual, though it also provides some general principles for conceiving "godly" sex. One assumption about sex in this approach is that sex is a gift in the proper context and dangerous in the wrong context. One of the fundamental guides for godly sex occurs near the beginning of the biblical canon, in the creation stories. "Therefore a man leaves his father and his mother and clings to his wife, and they become one flesh. And the man and his wife were both naked, and were not ashamed" (Gen. 2:24-25). Here, "one flesh" is taken both as a metaphor for the nuptial covenant and for the intertwining of bodies in sex as the seal of that covenant. Evangelical theologian Stanley Grenz offers one interpretation of this text, with an eye to sex in marriage: "Whenever the couple engages in sexual intercourse they are reaffirming the pledge made on their wedding day and are giving visual representation of the content of that vow."[1] The model of Adam and Eve becomes the pattern for rightly ordered sex: without shame, with restraint, shared with one other person (of the opposite sex) in marriage. Whatever departs from this pattern *ipso facto* is questionable. What is cause for the cry of elation within marriage, "This at last is bone of my bones and flesh of my flesh" (Gen. 2:23), is cause for lamentation anywhere else.

Once this norm—marriage between a man and a woman—has been established for godly sex, the sexual prohibitions within the Bible appear to make sense. Sex that occurs outside of marriage must be viewed as suspect, not merely because it undermines the marital covenant but because it also does injury to the body of Christ—that is, the extended Christian community of which the couple is a part. Paul's vice lists enumerate activities that inflict such injury. In 1 Corinthians, for example, Paul admonishes his readers for abusing the Lord's Supper in ways that marginalize the poor (11:17-34) and for engaging in power struggles (1:10-17). He also specifically condemns a man for living with his father's wife (5:1). This specific instance of illicit sex Paul names *porneia*, generally translated as "fornication" or "sexual immorality" in the New Revised Standard Version of the Bible, but a term that Paul himself never clearly defines.[2] Paul often constructs vice lists related to *porneia*. For readers who assume that Paul offers specific rules for sex in this and other passages, *porneia* has come to mean nearly any sexual behavior other than penile-vaginal intercourse within marriage: masturbation, oral sex, anal sex, sex practiced with inordinate passion or desire.[3] One problem with the understanding of these vice lists as a guide is that it is difficult to discern what Paul is actually condemning. In 1 Corinthians, Paul mentions *porneia* in reference to prostitution and illicit marriages; in Galatians 5:19 he seems to use it more generally, without connection to specific sexual behaviors. This vagueness has allowed each generation to redefine the meaning of *porneia* to be whatever departs from the supposedly self-evident mores of each era. Even the common, specific definition of fornication as "sexual intercourse between unmarried persons" admits of exceptions in most contemporary Christian ethics. As Anglican systematic theologian John Macquarrie writes, "the presence of a measure of commitment makes it undesirable to apply the word 'fornication' indiscriminately," particularly to persons in a "stable relationship."[4] Yesterday's fornication, in short, often becomes today's sexual norm.

The chief prohibition that often comes to the fore in the "guidebook" approach to sex is the condemnation of homosexuality, supposedly another instance of *porneia* that violates the conditions of godly sex. According to this view, the holiness codes of the Hebrew Bible can be applied to contemporary society. Leviticus 18, for example, is devoted exclusively to sexual holiness, prohibiting various degrees of incest, sex with women during menstruation, adultery, bestiality, and the oft-cited: "You shall not lie with a male as with a woman; it is an abomination" (v. 22). In Leviticus 20, this command is reiterated, this time with the stipulation that those who commit such acts shall be put to death (v. 13). These two verses are the only times the phrase, translated more literally as "the lying down of a woman," occurs in the entire Hebrew Bible. They appear within long lists of prohibitions meant to distinguish Israel's religious practice from other Near Eastern tribes. Certain behaviors, and the avoidance of certain behaviors, distinguish these people of the covenant from all others: from clothing, to diet, to rules for appropriate sacrifice. Prohibition of specific sexual behaviors occurs in the midst of these various other prohibitions. For the guidebook approach to reading Scripture, this context and concern are of little consequence, as the behaviors prohibited for Israel are taken as valid for our time as well. Hence, conservative Presbyterian theologian Robert Gagnon can write that anal intercourse

> constitutes a conscious denial of the complementarity of male and female found not least in the fittedness (anatomical, physiological, and procreative) of the male penis and the female vaginal receptacle by attempting anal intercourse (or other forms of sexual intercourse) with another man. Anal sex not only confuses gender, it confuses the function of the anus as a cavity for expelling excrement, not receiving sperm. . . . For one man to "lie with" another man in the manner that men normally "lie with" a woman was to defile the latter's masculine stamp, impressed by God and evident in both the visible sexual complementarity of male and female and in the sacred lore of creation.[5]

The "lying down of a woman," for Gagnon, means any male-male sexual intercourse, whether in the context of a committed partnership or in the midst of an orgy. Gagnon's approach, moreover, assumes to know what "the lying down of a woman" means: it means gay sex, which constitutes a violation of the created order. However, such extrapolation avoids the specificity of the text. Strictly speaking, even if one were to accept the correlation between the Levitical prohibition and gay sex, the prohibition would only extend to the partner who penetrates the other in instances of male-male anal intercourse.[6]

Contemporary rule-based understandings of sex, however, do not simply appeal to Levitical holiness codes. They often claim a broader framework for condemning homosexuality in Romans 1–3. Embedded in a sweeping indictment of Jew and Gentile are these phrases: "For this reason God gave them up to degrading passions. Their women exchanged natural intercourse for unnatural, and in the same way also the men, giving up natural intercourse with women, were consumed with passion for one another. Men committed shameless acts with men and received in their own persons the due penalty for their error" (Rom. 1:26-27). Among all scriptural references to same-sex acts, this is the only one that includes women. Again, determining what sexual behaviors Paul condemns here is difficult: temple prostitution? ritual sex? pederasty? While scholars have argued incessantly about what kinds of behavior are implied, Paul seems to be rather unconcerned with the specifics. His chief concern is idolatry, exchanging the glory of God for other images, serving "the creature rather than the Creator" (v. 24). Idolatry caused God to give the people up "to degrading passions" (v. 25). Despite the claims of contemporary rule-based theologies of sex, the condemnation is not against same-sex activity but idolatry that brings forth disorder in the body. This focus on idolatry is something that a rule-based approach tends to obscure.

The rule-based approach tends to enumerate extensive prohibitions. In the rightly ordered sexual universe, one simply says "no" to prostitution and homosexuality; extramarital and premarital sex; fornication and too much passion within marriage; bestiality and masturbation. Though most rule-based approaches distinguish between many sexual behaviors, with some practices being more serious violations of rules than others, the norm against which all behaviors are measured is a marriage between one man and one woman. As evangelical theologian Lauren Winner puts it, "Abstinence before marriage, and fidelity within marriage; any other kind of sex is embodied apostasy."[7]

To summarize the problems with the rule-based approach to the Bible and sex: passages that seem to talk about sex, or have come to mean sexual subjects, are primarily devoted to other matters. Romans 1–2, which routinely gets cited in condemnations of homosexuality, is instead concerned with demonstrating the need for the gospel; Sodom and Gomorrah, another oft-cited text (Gen. 19:1-29), is about hospitality and the denial of hospitality, not sex. Leviticus is concerned with idolatry first and only derivatively with sexual behaviors that are evidence of idolatry. Only recently have the so-called sexual meanings of these texts come to the fore. All these factors have led some to throw up their hands when it comes to the Bible and sex. Mark Jordan, for example, states this frustration baldly: "There are, in short, no self-evident lists of biblical passages about sexual matters."[8]

THE BIBLE AS INSUFFICIENT, OUTMODED, OR OPPRESSIVE ON SEXUALITY

Not only do some contemporary theologians deny that the Bible gives self-evident rules about sex, they furthermore argue that the Bible has problematic aspects that make it an insufficient, outmoded, or oppressive guide to sexual matters. From this perspective, the Bible must be read with a hermeneutic of suspicion regarding sex and sexuality. One glaring problem is the Bible's patriarchal assumptions. Take the paradigm of marriage as an example. The commandment against coveting a neighbor's wife (note the gender)—and by implication, the commandment against adultery—is couched in the language of property. Adultery becomes in this context less an affront to marriage than to the property rights of the male possessor: "You shall not covet your neighbor's house; you shall not covet your neighbor's wife, or male or female slave, or ox, or donkey, or anything that belongs to your neighbor" (Exod. 20:17). Scriptural rules of sexual behavior, moreover, tend to implicate women more than men. Some of the Pastoral Epistles are especially evident of this tendency, singling out younger widows as particularly prone to sins of the flesh: "But refuse to put younger widows on the list; for when their sensual desires alienate them from Christ, they want to marry, and so they incur condemnation for having violated their first pledge" (1 Tim. 5:11-12). The author here is urging his audience not to have younger widows make vows of perpetual chastity; instead he urges that they remarry. Women are singled out in this list as if they are more prone to sexual vice than men.

Given this perspective, it is not surprising that the pastoral epistles also suggest that women are more likely to be swayed by false teaching. For example, 2 Timothy refers to "silly women, overwhelmed by their sins and swayed by all kinds of desires, who are always being instructed and can never arrive at a knowledge of the truth" (3:6b-7). This correlation of women as more susceptible to sin is by no means restricted to Deutero-Pauline literature.[9] In 1 Peter, husbands are to "show consideration for your wives in your life together, paying honor to the woman as the weaker sex, since they too are also heirs of the gracious gift of life" (3:7). Texts like these pepper the New Testament and have affected many modern approaches to gender, sexuality, and marriage. In the eyes of some who would use these texts to frame an understanding of theology and sex, the approach is straightforward: be wary of sex, and be particularly wary of women who display their sexuality openly.

The majority voices in Scripture, in other words, assume male privilege and the secondary status of women. Within the broad swath of biblical narrative, women are blamed for sin (Gen. 3:12; 1 Tim. 2:12-15), enjoined to remain silent in assembly (1 Cor. 14:34), and assumed to belong to their husbands in a manner analogous to property (Exod. 20:17). More glaringly, the trope of the loose woman or harlot is used throughout Hebrew Bible and the New Testament to epitomize unfaithfulness, whether the whore of Hosea (chaps. 2–4), who is stripped naked and exposed, or the whore of Babylon who is burned and devoured (Rev. 17:16).

Even the more benignly sexual texts of the New Testament—such as the paeans for marriage—are soaked in patriarchy. In the Deutero-Pauline Epistles patriarchy is assumed and celebrated. Ephesians, for example, enjoins wives to be subject to their husbands, comparing a husband's "headship" to Christ who is "head of the church" (Eph. 5:22-23). Husbands, by contrast, are enjoined to love their wives, "as Christ loved the church" (Eph. 5:25). Subjection, in this view, is a decidedly one-way street (see Col. 3:18-19). Where mutual submission to one another is encouraged, marriage is connected to slavery and the problematic assumption of "owning" another person: "For the wife does not have authority over her own body, but the husband does; likewise the husband does not have authority over his own body, but the wife does" (1 Cor. 7:4). It is no coincidence that the exhortations to husbands and wives in Deutero-Pauline literature occur near injunctions toward slaves and masters. Paul simply makes this connection even more explicit—marriage itself is a kind of mutual slavery, by which one's bodily rights are given over to another.

For some contemporary theologians, texts with these patriarchal and hierarchical assumptions about women and sex cannot be taken at face value as guides for godly sex because the rules they appear to offer no longer apply. The connections between male headship, slavery, and even mutual submission, make the biblical framework for marriage nearly irredeemable:

> The institution of slavery with its attendant violence and injustice is accepted as part of the general world-view of the New Testament. The point to carry forward is that the theology of marriage is so integrated into the institution of slavery and the hierarchical order of social relations which slavery services that, once slavery has been repudiated by Christianity (after nineteen centuries), the theology of marriage based upon it must also be repudiated.[10]

Simply put, use of the Bible alone in constructing a view of sex and marriage is naïve and anachronistic at best, and dangerous at worst. It leads either to ignoring the patriarchal and hierarchical context in which these texts arise or to perpetuating these patterns without end. Reading the Bible literally and applying it for today "oppresses its victims and it undermines the gospel."[11]

In light of these difficulties, some feminist theologians argue that one needs to read against Scripture in the name of a more liberating understanding of sex. Anne Bathurst Gilson claims that the Christian tendency to prize disinterested agape at the expense of eros infects the history of the church and the canon itself. Better, in the tradition's eyes, to love another selflessly than to affirm the self (and other) through eros. Better to love without too much passion than to desire. Gilson claims that this preference for *agape* over eros reaps rotten fruit that we must cast aside, whether found in Scripture or elsewhere. Biblical prohibitions of specific sexual behaviors, for example, create a culture of compulsory heterosexuality among Christians, "the belief that the one-man, one-woman, one-flesh relationship in the context of lifelong marriage is not only God-given but God-*demanded*."[12] So entrenched is this belief within Christianity that the church generally abhors other expressions of sexual relationships. In the face of Scriptures that demean women and even foster violence against nonheterosexual persons, Gilson argues for the development of an erotic faith, a faith articulated less in scriptural narratives than it is in the power of an immanent God: "God is the power of eros, affirming bodyselves, yearning with us away from eroticized violence and into embodied justice and erotic mutuality. . . . God as the power of eros is She who is with us, who is moved and changed and touched by and with us."[13] In this vision, the Bible appears only on the margins, often as a foil to erotic justice.

THE BIBLE AS A NARRATIVE OF DESIRE

Another approach to the Bible focuses on reading it as what I am calling a narrative of desire. From start to finish, the Bible expresses relationships: of creation's relationship with God, of human persons' relationships with one another; of God's election of a nation for particular relationship with God in covenant and of the extension of that covenant to the world in Jesus Christ. As the Bible narrates these relationships, which are intimations of grace and incidents of sin, the reader glimpses divine desire that makes us participants in desire. Like a lover who longs for consummation, God desires human fulfillment in communion with God and one another. Read as a narrative of desire, the Bible's supposedly nonsexual texts have much to say about sex.

The first glimpse of God's desire occurs in the Genesis creation stories. The desire to create in the first narrative stems from God's delight, illustrated in the frequent recurrence of the phrase, "God saw that it was good," and the final phrase, "God saw everything that he had made, and indeed, it was very good" (Gen. 1:12, 18, 21, 25, 31). Everything in creation is contingent, made for relationship with God and the rest of creation. God creates not out of lack but out of the desire for others to be, a desire that is fulfilled by word and breath. The breath of God that stirs all to life in creation breathes through human beings. The opening word of divine desire in the Bible, then, can become the basis for reframing some contemporary understandings of desire. Most accounts of desire, especially sexual desire, conceive it as stemming from an internal hunger or emptiness, an absence that can only be filled by clinging to another to make one whole. This opening biblical account of desire, however, proceeds from fullness to fullness: "Creativity bespeaks fullness that overflows, that wants to give of its resources to express itself. The paradigm case is once again the creation of the world. As God is portrayed in the Hebrew Bible and Christian theology, God does not lack. The divine is in need of nothing. Yet God desires to create the world and desires to make it beautiful."[14] God desires out of abundance and creates in order to share that abundance with all that is.

In the second creation story, God's desire becomes intimately physical, as God forms the man from the dust of the ground and breathes into his nostrils the breath of life (Gen. 2:7). As human beings speak for the first time, they become partakers of God's desire, a desire expressed in the longing for companionship with another. After the creation of a partner, the man's exclamation in the garden rings with the satisfaction of desire and desire's intensification in sex, the sharing and mingling of flesh: "This at last is bone of my bones and flesh of my flesh" (Gen. 2:23). The approach of a companion does not extinguish desire but makes it flourish in togetherness.

Genesis also narrates the distortion of desire. Desire becomes a hollow shell of itself when it proceeds out of perceived lack, when one seeks to possess someone or something for oneself alone, apart from God. If divine desire proceeds from abundance and wanting to share in abundance, so that others might flourish, desire's shadow self stems from craving for possession. The first instance of this distortion is the multifaceted story of the tree, the serpent, and the first humans. Adam's and Eve's failure is not the desire for knowledge, not the breaking of a divinely given rule, but their perception that the tree has something that they lack which they simply must have for themselves: knowledge of good and evil apart from God. Their culpability is believing the serpent's lie that God wants to withhold something good from them. The "fall," read thus, is not about disobedience or the seeking of knowledge but about Adam's and Eve's refusal to partake in the abundance of the garden that allows desire to flourish, falsely believing that they can obtain a scarce resource outside God's provision by holding it and keeping it for themselves. Thus, the fruit of the tree becomes all the more desirable, a "delight to the eyes" (Gen. 3:6), that can only be satisfied by hoarding it. Almost as soon as human beings become participants in God's desire, they begin to think that it is meant for possession, not sharing. In its twisted form, desire turns in upon itself and becomes insatiable: for the fruit, in the end, does not satisfy, but only leaves the two ashamed, seeking satisfaction elsewhere, in work that degenerates into toil, in unjust relations between man and woman (Gen. 3:16-17). Begun in fullness, desire soon devolves into scarcity in human hands.[15]

God's response to this twisting of desire in the fall is to seek relationship more intensely, to pledge fidelity to a particular people even amid misdirected desire. God's expression of relationship takes the shape of a concrete pledge, or covenant, made to an otherwise insignificant people. Through this pledge to this people, God shows the world the fullness of God's desire. As the narration of covenant unfolds, God displays the shape of desire expressed in love and faithfulness to a covenant people and grief and anger when covenant is broken (Exod. 34:6-7; Num. 11:33; 32:13). Covenant becomes the shape of God's desire, the way God sinks an anchor of flesh into the world by making concrete promises to a particular people. Desire does not become diffuse but gathers intensity as it pledges fidelity and fruitfulness to a particular people. Covenant reveals a biophilic God, who desires that all might live into the fullness of relationship. Covenant teaches believers that they need not choose between a generalized love for the world and love for a particular beloved; rather, the two are inextricably intertwined. Reading divine desire in this way demonstrates that love for the world emerges in particular promises to a beloved.

The New Testament can be read as continuing the theme of desire, as it is personified in Jesus of Nazareth. The Gospel narratives portray Jesus as both the object of desire, the focus of those who seek him, and also as one who desires, who will not cease desiring until all partake in life's fullness. First, Jesus is the focus of desire, the one in whom the human desire for God finds its incarnational home. When he calls the disciples, Jesus awakens in them a desire for him: "And Jesus said to them, 'Follow me and I will make you fish for people.' And immediately they left their nets and followed him" (Mark 1:17-18). By his very presence and his word, Jesus kindles Simon's and Andrew's desire, so much that they drop their nets at the call. As Jesus finds them, their desire finds a home.

Jesus' touch also focuses desire. In most of the stories of healing, Jesus touches indiscriminately, without regard to a person's status in life. At times those who long for healing also reach out to touch him, as in the case of the unnamed hemorrhaging woman. She appears amid another crowd, approaches Jesus from behind, and touches the fringe of his cloak, saying, "If I only touch his cloak, I will be made well" (Matt. 9:20-21). The language here is delicate, as the fringe of a garment can also serve as a euphemism of sexual touch. The woman's bleeding, moreover, is related to her sexuality, because according to purity codes of the time, a blood flow that will not cease prevents her from sexual intimacy (Lev. 18:19). Her touch intimates sex and the desire to be healed. Jesus' touch imparts sexual healing and the gift of life. To touch him is to desire him.

This focus of desire does not evaporate in the resurrection accounts. Indeed, as the appearance narratives in John indicate, desire for Jesus' touch intensifies rather than abates after the crucifixion. Mary first mistakes the risen Christ for a gardener, then, upon having her eyes opened by hearing her name, also desires to touch Jesus' body. She reaches out in desire, longing to hold the risen rabbi, only to be told by him, "Do not hold on to me, because I have not yet ascended to the Father" (John 20:17). Mary longs for the consummation of her heart's desire, communion with her "Lord" (John 20:13). This communion expresses the life and touch of the body, the longing to embrace and be embraced; yet, this embrace will not occur until others have been told the news and invited to embrace him. Even in this intimate resurrection appearance, others are invited to touch.

Thomas sees the risen Christ after Mary does, and his desire to touch achieves consummation. Thomas, aggrieved with desire, despondent over the loss of his beloved,[16] not only touches his beloved but also enters his body through the wound in Jesus' side. Jesus invites Thomas in: "Reach out your hand and put it in my side" (John 20:27). Thomas reaches out and enters Jesus, both literally and physically. Thomas now "knows" Jesus in the knowledge of flesh touching flesh. This account of the interpenetration of flesh, which carries more than a hint of sex, is an invitation into communion with Jesus. Desire seeks communion with nothing less than the body and blood of the risen Christ.

What Jesus offers Thomas he also offers to all who believe: to receive his body at the communion table. To penetrate Jesus' flesh is also to taste him and be penetrated by him. Seen in this way, the institution of the Lord's Supper is itself a narrative of desire. Jesus took, blessed, broke, and gave the bread. Later, the disciples (and all subsequent believers, by invitation) recall how Jesus takes, blesses, breaks, and gives his life to all borne by desire. What Jesus establishes in this meal is also what he has established in his ministry and promises in God's coming reign. In this meal, Jesus both embodies and gives voice to desire: "I have eagerly desired to eat this Passover with you before I suffer; for I tell you, I will not eat it until it is fulfilled in the kingdom of God" (Luke 22:15-16). The meal is the fulfillment of Jesus' desire for communion, as well as the continual offer for communion with him in the taste of bread and wine. Taste, the intimate form of human touch, is a profound method of communion.[17] In the sacrament of Holy Communion, believers "taste and see that the LORD is good" (Ps. 34:8) by taking Jesus into their mouths, as lovers taste one another. The meal is meant to express Christ's desire for the believer, the believer's desire for him, and the desire for the whole earth to taste and see.

In the book of Revelation, desire displays a tortuous path. The book documents the distortion of desire: what happens when nations twist desire into greed, violence, and lust that make martyrs out of believers. This New Testament book depicts the nations' lust for power in the well-worn image of the "great whore" of Babylon (Rev. 17:1), the woman who personifies the Roman state and captures the gaze of the nations. As the whore becomes "drunk with the blood of the saints and the blood of the witnesses to Jesus," the kings of the earth who have grown rich in her empire commit "fornication with her and the merchants of the earth [grow] rich from the power of her luxury" (Rev. 17:6; 18:3). This luxury is short lived, however, as the whore's body is laid in waste. The imagery here is horrifying and inherently problematic: vice symbolized in a woman, who is ultimately consumed in the fire of God's judgment (Rev. 18:8-9). These "texts of terror"[18] locate vice upon a woman's body, products of a male gaze that glimpses greed, treachery, unfaithfulness, and lust in the "other." This trope has unleashed its share of disaster, from blaming rape on victims, to the commercial sexualization of girls at increasingly younger ages, to domestic and sexual abuse that can make the home the most dangerous place in society for women. Much of Revelation locates the distortion of desire upon the female body. The whore image, in short, may be irredeemable, suggesting that the idolatry that the author sought to shake is evident in his own interpretation of the female figure. Desire in Revelation displays a distorted and tortuous course.

The tortured weave of the Bible's closing pages hardly presents a template for desire's flourishing. The text's concern with purity yields anything but a pure description of desire, tainted as it is with misogyny and violence. Revelation is not an easy text to read, understand, or stomach. Readers should struggle with it, just as the early church struggled with whether to include it in the biblical canon and as feminist theology struggles with its meaning and legacy.[19] Yet a struggle with the text can yield surprising riches, for embedded amid its problematic imagery is another shape of desire and its flourishing, depicted in images of the renewal of heaven and earth and the re-creation of Jerusalem, the heavenly city. In this narrative, Christ comes as the bridegroom of humanity, and the faithful are commanded to prepare for that marriage (Revelation 21). When Babylon falls, the "Lamb" emerges to take the church as his bride, making a new covenant where death and tears no longer reign, where the home of God appears among mortals

(21:3-4, 9). Traditional as the marriage image is for expressing desire, it also accomplishes queer things for the saints of the church since it makes all the faithful, both male and female, brides of Christ. In anticipation of this marriage, moreover, the erotic permeates the text.[20] In a tradition that supposedly bears the seeds of the condemnation of homosexuality, the marriage outlined in Revelation—nuptials in which Christ takes the inhabitants of the New Jerusalem, male and female, as his bride (19:7-8; 21:2)—betrays more than a hint of homoeroticism. In Revelation, if desire finds a home in marriage, that home is distinctly queer, for the male saints who populate the book of Revelation become, in the end, the brides of Christ.

Thus far, I have suggested biblical texts read as narratives of desire when the desire implied in those texts was at best oblique and at worst problematic. There is, however, one book of the Bible, the Song of Songs, that is redolent of sex. Even here, however, we need an interpretive lens. Throughout the ages this poem has been the subject of varying attention. Some Talmudic and kabbalistic traditions within Judaism deem it the "holy of holies" in the canon, "the erotic charge of the divine revelation of Torah to the people."[21] In medieval Christendom, the Song generated more commentaries than any other book among monastics. The twelfth-century Cistercian abbot, Bernard of Clairvaux, for example, preached eighty-six homilies on the Song and never finished his sermon series.[22] A sensual poem that lingers on the body, conveying touch and desire, the Song contains the voices of two unnamed lovers. The woman's voice, moreover, occupies significantly more space than the man's (a comparative rarity in patriarchal traditions) and speaks without reservation or restraint concerning sex. "O that his left arm were under my head, and his right hand embraced [made love to] me" (Song 2:6); "My beloved thrust his hand into the opening, and my inmost being yearned for him. I arose to open to my beloved, and my hands dripped with myrrh, my fingers with liquid myrrh, upon the handles of the bolt" (5:4-5); "My beloved is mine and I am his; he pastures his flock among the lilies" (2:16). In this text, bodies are relished and desired for their taste, compared with pomegranates, nectar, milk, and spices. These are bodies meant for lingering, touching, tasting, and feeding. Given the relative sexual explicitness of its cadences, it is no surprise that most Christian traditions have tended toward allegory: the primary theme is not the earthly love between lovers, their longing for one another, but the love between God and Israel (or God and the church). Otherwise the pomegranates appear too juicy.

While much of Christian tradition has interpreted the Song allegorically, much contemporary biblical interpretation focuses on the Song as a poem of sexual love. I suggest that this discrepancy represents a false dichotomy between two interpretations. The Song expresses desire in its earthy and divine fullness, "*rightly* [taking] human sexual love as an analogue of the love between the Lord and Israel."[23] The Song neither impels us to gloss over the sex that is dripping from the pages nor encourages us to understand sex only as an end in itself. The point here is comparison: God's desire for humanity is like a lover's desire for the beloved, body and soul: a desire to touch, commune, be close, enter into, make room for, taste.

Christian traditions have had a notoriously difficult time considering the sexual alongside the divine. Earthly love for a beloved, in most cases, is construed as in some way inhibiting the soul's communion with God—hence Paul's lukewarm defense of marriage, "For it is better to marry than to be aflame with passion" (1 Cor. 7:9)—and the church's fourth-century condemnation of those who taught the spiritual equality of marriage and celibacy.[24] Throughout much of the tradition, the implicit message is that desire for one's earthly lover obstructs one's desire for God, but the Song suggests otherwise. Without mentioning God at all, the imagery encourages the reader to linger over the beloved, to touch and to taste. This is the imagery of sex in all of its earthiness: the lovers on the pages of the Song are focused on one another, attend to one another, and delight in each other simply because they are present to each other. They know each other's skin as much as their own. This narration of knowing and being known, even without the mention of God's name, is an invitation to compare God's love with the beauty, pleasure, and taste of sex.

Here, in the most sexual text of the Bible, is an absence of the rules that have come to characterize much subsequent Christian discussion of sex. Instead what we find is desire, its intensification, and even its intoxication when focused on the beloved. Part of the Song's intent is, I suggest, to invite the reader to see and taste that desire. The desire of the Song is not an either/or—either my earthly beloved or God—but, rather, an exuberant both/and to the lover and to God as lover. The desire of the Song thus "spills out beyond the limits of the Song itself,"[25] finding expression in sex but not restricted to sex.

CONCLUSION

Controversy over sex has been a part of Christian traditions since the calling of the disciples. Amid this controversy, the church has turned routinely to its Scripture for guidance. The New Testament records some of these controversies: Paul's letters, for example, document arguments within the early

Christian communities over sexual behaviors. Though the particulars of these New Testament controversies have receded from light, the rhetoric that Paul employs to address them abides. Though the terms of controversy over sex have changed over the centuries (with marriage ultimately gaining a status as legitimate as celibacy), the controversy remains. Even though the amount of space devoted in the Bible to sexual behavior is relatively small—especially in comparison to economic behavior—Christians still turn to Scripture for clarity about sex in tumultuous times.

The default position for reading about sex in the Bible is to discern in the text rules to govern behavior. Though explicit rules about sex are generally absent even in Paul's enumeration of vices and *porneia*, the church has had no difficulty extrapolating rules from disparate texts: sex is made for the marital bond and procreation; all other sex is inherently sinful; sexual desire must be bridled even in marriage; homosexuality is wrong, period. Even today when arguments over sex surface in the churches—typically concerning homosexuality—the same texts surface: Paul's vice lists, Levitical purity codes, perhaps an allusion to Sodom and Gomorrah. Rules, rules, and more rules: Sex must fit within these rules and the church must clarify and police them. Yet, as I have attempted to show in this essay, the rule-based approach to Scripture is fraught with problems. First, it reads Scripture in a strikingly nonnarrative manner as a handbook for behavior. Conversely, when the Bible is read as a story of God and God's beloved, it can shape the reader by the tenor and trajectories of the characters within it: God's covenant with Israel, Israel's stumbling in maintaining covenant, the extension of covenant to the world in Jesus Christ, and his rejection by those he loved. In this approach, the Bible encourages the reader to become a part of the narrative itself, to allow the biblical world to absorb the universe,[26] so that it shapes Christians not by its codes but by the story that unfolds on its pages. If believers comb the text merely for rules about sex, they not only miss the Bible as narrative but also close their eyes to its narratives of desire among beloveds, who reflect in some small manner God's desire for the world.

A second problem with combing the text for sexual rules is its invariable selectivity and refusal to acknowledge the problematic contexts within which one finds the rules. For example, the lukewarm endorsements of marriage in the New Testament assume a patriarchal view of male headship in the household. Adultery, as prohibited in the Hebrew Bible, is connected to property rights. Even when rules seem specific in the Bible, the circumstances surrounding them are morally abhorrent for contemporary readers, whether in regard to slavery or the status of women.

No wonder that the contemporary period has witnessed so many voices claiming that biblical rules regarding sex are oppressive and can no longer apply. In diagnosing the patriarchal baggage of the circumstances surrounding sexual rules in Scripture, these critics hit the mark. Yet some of their readings of the Bible, surprisingly, also reflect rule-based assumptions—namely, that the Bible supplies rules about sex that are inappropriate and antigospel for Christians today.

The alternative that I have attempted to illustrate in this chapter is to read the Bible as a narrative of desire: of God's desire for humankind and of humankind's desire for communion with God and for relationship with one another. Sex is one dimension and expression of the desire for communion and connection, intimacy and relationship. This approach to the Bible invites the reader to see how desire intensifies in its focus: God's desire for relationship with a people expresses itself in covenant; and God's love for the world is expressed in particular relationship in the incarnation—that is, God's revelation of God's very self in one human being. In each case, desire for the world gets expressed in particularity, in a focused intensification of God's love.

Contemporary culture often tells us that the focusing of desire invariably smothers it. Stay in any sexual relationship long enough—whether marriage, partnership, or otherwise—and the flames eventually fade. The jaded view of sexual relationships in contemporary culture is that intimacy quickly becomes banal; as time goes by with the beloved, mystery evaporates as people take each other increasingly for granted. Irritation rather than discovery characterizes the relationship as the years pass. The more I know about my beloved, the less there seems left to know, and thus familiarity breeds laziness and dissipation. Sex becomes, as it were, old hat, unless desire finds a new home with someone else while the old love is left behind. In Western consumer economies, sex is meant for consumption—rather rapid consumption—as desire roams from place to place in search of new loves. The commercialization of sex in American culture encourages the rapid movement of getting what we can.

If Christians read Scripture as a narrative of desire, they are encouraged to linger: to linger over the body of Christ, to linger over the history of God's desire for the world, to linger over Holy Communion, to linger in the presence of their beloved. In this context, the beloved becomes all the more enticing and desirous along the way, as Christ and Christians come to know each other. Such is the journey of sex, when conceived in light of covenant and incarnation, God's desire for humankind. Sex becomes a passage to deeper knowing of our beloved, discovery, and the yearning of desire.

This focusing of sexual desire results in neither the smothering nor containment of desire but in a growth stronger than death: "Set me as a seal upon your heart, as a seal upon your arm; for love is strong as death, passion fierce as the grave" (Song 8:6).

The church has often preached that sexual desire has to be contained and restricted, lest it become dangerous; hence, the only place to channel sexual desire is in marriage—never outside marriage, never with the same sex. The narrative of desire as it unfolds in the biblical text suggests something different: not the bottling up of desire, but its growth and increase, where "flashes are flashes of fire, a raging flame" (Song 8:6). God's desire for communion does not dissipate with the establishment of covenant with Israel or the incarnation of Jesus; rather, it continues to kindle desire until all creation finds a home in the new creation, a desire that will not find satisfaction and reward until the end of the days (Dan. 12:13).

Further Suggested Readings

Gagnon, Robert A. J. *The Bible and Homosexual Practice: Texts and Hermeneutics*. Nashville: Abingdon, 2001.

Guest, Deryn, Robert E. Goss, Mona West, and Thomas Bohache, eds. *The Queer Bible Commentary*. London: SCM, 2006.

Jenson, Robert W. *Song of Songs*. Interpretation, a Bible Commentary for Teaching and Preaching. Louisville: John Knox, 2005.

Martin, Dale B. *Sex and the Single Savior: Gender and Sexuality in Biblical Interpretation*. Louisville: Westminster John Knox, 2006.

Newsom, Carol A., and Sharon H. Ringe, eds. *The Women's Bible Commentary*, exp. ed. Louisville: Westminster John Knox, 1998.

Rogers, Jack. *Jesus, the Bible, and Homosexuality: Explode the Myths, Heal the Church*. Rev. and exp. ed. Louisville: Westminster John Knox, 2009.

CHAPTER 2

Early Christian Contempt for the Flesh and the Woman
Who Loved Too Much in the Gospel of Luke

Mark I. Wallace

AT ITS ORIGINS, Christianity was deeply troubled about the role of the body and sexual expression in spiritual life ("It is well for a man not to touch a woman," 1 Cor. 7:1). Today, however, many Christians are moving into a joyous space where sexual pleasure and intimacy are valued as a primary site of God's presence in human community.[1] This emergence into what I would call carnal spirituality is nourished by the endearing scriptural narratives of sexual and nonsexual touching that challenge the soul-deadening disregard for bodily pleasure in some of the central teachings of ancient Christianity. The biblical celebration of erotic pleasure reaches a crescendo in the Song of Solomon ("Oh, may your breasts be like clusters of the vine . . . and your kisses like the best wine," 7:8-9 RSV) and continues with canonical stories about Jesus' scandalously fleshly, transgressive acts of sexually nuanced touching and being touched. The exegesis of one of these ancient stories in the New Testament around the theme of erotic hospitality is the focal point of this essay.

After a brief introduction to early Christian attitudes toward bodily desire, my focus falls on the "sinful woman"—or better, the "woman who loved too much"—in Luke 7:36-50 who lovingly massages, wets, and kisses Jesus' feet, perhaps preparing them for his burial. This unnamed woman wets Jesus' feet with her tears, rubs them with her hair, kisses them with her mouth, and anoints them with a sweet-smelling lotion. Noting the importance of this story for biblical erotics, I focus on how Jesus embraces the scandal this robustly sensual encounter generates ("from the time I came in she has not stopped kissing my feet," 7:45) in order to articulate his message of welcoming the body as central to his mission. Next, I compare this Lukan story of deep touching with the healing intimacies between Ruth and Boaz, a widowed Gentile and her Hebrew kinsman in the book of Ruth, and Sethe and Paul D, two former slaves in Toni Morrison's novel *Beloved*. The ancient practice of arranged marriage, along with the modern slave trade, generally trafficked in flesh as a market commodity; nevertheless, against the greatest of odds, Ruth and Boaz, on the one hand, and Sethe and Paul D, on the other, develop their own rituals of erotic play and healing. The enfleshed sensuality of biblical and Morrisonian touching celebrates, welcomes, and heals flesh as sacred gift. Through the Lukan woman's and Jesus' passion for intimacy, and echoing the book of Ruth and *Beloved*, I conclude with the outlines of a biblically inflected "haptology" (Gk., *haptos*)—a theology of touching—with the potential to heal our culture of its abuse of one another's flesh and to teach us to love our own and others' innermost desires for pleasure, intimacy, friendship, and love.

WAR AGAINST THE FLESH

Much of early Christianity is a sustained polemic against bodily instincts, sexual desire, and even the institution of marriage itself. The three loci for these arguments are (1) Jesus' valorization of voluntary, self-imposed celibacy in Matthew 19:12 ("For there are eunuchs who have been so from birth, and there are eunuchs who have been made eunuchs by others, and there are eunuchs who have made themselves eunuchs for the sake of the kingdom of heaven. Let anyone accept this who can"); (2) Jesus' proposal in Matthew 22:30 that married couples, postmortem, will be angel-like, single people again ("For in the resurrection [spouses] neither marry nor are given in marriage, but are like angels in heaven"); and (3) Paul's ascetic ideal in 1 Corinthians 7:8-9 that marriage, while not a model state for Christians, is sometimes necessary as a prophylactic to fend off uncontrollable lust ("To the unmarried and the widows I say that it is well for them to remain unmarried as I am. But if they are not practicing self-control, they should marry. For it is better to marry than to be aflame with passion").

Privileging celibacy allowed early Christians to position themselves as religiously superior to their "fleshly" cousins in the Jewish world of the first and second centuries C.E. As a celibate who put under control his sexual desires, Paul distinguished between the Gentile Christian "children of the promise," who are the true heirs of God's covenant with Israel, and the Jewish "children of the flesh," whose covenant with God, while not abrogated, is now expanded to include Jewish and non-Jewish followers of Jesus (Rom. 9:1-13). Paul and his patristic successors became masters of allegorical biblical hermeneutics in which the "living spirit" of the Christian gospel supersedes the "dead letter" of Jewish law. Sexual renunciation and spiritual circumcision became tangible signs of this new figurative reading of Torah. In the writings of Paul and other early church leaders, the old observance of the law relied on outward, physical signs of obedience to Torah (especially having children and being circumcised), whereas the new fidelity to Christ takes leave of the body in favor of the inner faith of the believer. Procreation and circumcision were basic to Jewish observance based on the Genesis commands to "be fruitful and multiply" (1:22) and "Every male among you shall be circumcised" (17:10). These corporeal covenants are spiritualized and set aside by Paul in favor of his proposal that "he who marries his fiancée does well; and he who refrains from marriage will do better" (1 Cor. 7:38) and his notion that "true circumcision" is not "external and physical" but "a matter of the heart—it is spiritual and not literal" (Rom. 3:28-29). True covenantal life with God is a spiritual exercise of the heart, not a product or a mark of the flesh. Inward fidelity to Jesus and the gospel now supplants outward duty to Torah.

Paul's move away from the outward activities of procreative sex and circumcision to the inner life of the Spirit marked a sea change in the evolution of early Christianity from its Jewish origins.[2] The physical reality of Israel and the sexualized, circumcised Jewish body were now supplanted by the "new Israel" of the church and the holy Christian body, which had taken leave of the flesh (read: sexuality, procreation, and circumcision) in order to realize the ideal of pure, sexless, unmarried life in the Spirit. Virginal purity was now the insignia of genuine Christianity—a cultural oddity in antiquity that opened up an unbridgeable rift between early Christianity and formative Judaism: "in spite of the enormous variations within both Christianities and rabbinic Judaism, the near-universal privileging of virginity, even for

Christian thinkers who valorize marriage, produces an irreducible difference between that [Christian] formation and rabbinic Judaism, for which sexuality and procreation are understood as acts of ultimate religious significance and for which virginity is highly problematic, as Christian writers in antiquity correctly emphasized."[3]

Over and against formative Judaism, the New Testament's deprecation of the body and sexual desire rendered many subsequent early Christian leaders "athletes of God," in historian of antiquity Peter Brown's phrase, who made war against their flesh in order to cultivate their spiritual natures.[4] Origen, the third-century Christian allegorical theologian, literally interpreted Jesus' blessing regarding those who "[make] themselves eunuchs for the sake of the kingdom of heaven" (Matt. 19:12) and at age twenty castrated himself. As a virgin for Christ no longer dominated by his sexual and physical drives, Origen graphically appropriated Jesus' counsel about celibacy and became a perfect vessel for the display of the Spirit.[5] Origen's celibate athleticism is further underscored by the extracanonical fifth-century text, Pseudo-Titus, which offers a sustained exhortation to celibacy and monastic rigor as a badge of purity and holiness.[6] The author calls on young men to be like the mythological phoenix, a paradigm of virginal solitude, and achieve holiness by avoiding female temptation:

> Above all the ascetic should avoid women on that account and see to it that he does (worthily) the duty entrusted to him by God. . . . O man, who understands nothing at all of the fruits of righteousness, why has the Lord made the divine phoenix and not given it a little wife, but allowed it to remain in loneliness? Manifestly only on purpose to show the standing of virginity, i.e., that young men, remote from intercourse with women, should remain holy.[7]

In the Christian West, Augustine appears most responsible for early Christian antagonism toward sex and the body. Extending Paul's dictum that "what the flesh desires is opposed to the Spirit, and what the Spirit desires is opposed to the flesh" (Gal. 5:17), Augustine maintains that human beings are ruled by carnal desire (concupiscence) as a result of Adam's fall from grace in the garden of Eden. All people are now "in Adam," as it were, since Adam's sin is transferred to his offspring—the human race—through semen, what Augustine calls the "seminal substance from which we were to be propagated."[8] As historian of early Christianity Elaine Pagels puts it, "That semen itself, Augustine argues, already 'shackled by the bond of death,' transmits the damage incurred by sin. Hence, Augustine concludes, every human being ever conceived through semen already is born contaminated with sin."[9] In their fleshly bodies, seminally generated infants are tainted with "original sin" communicated to them through their biological parents' sexual intercourse. To put this point bluntly, the fetus is damned at the moment of conception—even before birth—because it is contaminated by Adam's primordial transgression through the transmission of semen during the conjugal act. Augustine further asserts that physical weakness, bodily suffering, and sexual desire (*libido*) itself are signs that the corporeal, material world is under God's judgment. "Ever since Eden, however, spontaneous sexual desire is, Augustine contends, the clearest evidence of the effect of original sin."[10] Thus, without the infusion of supernatural grace, all of creation—as depraved and corrupted—is no longer amenable to the influence of God's love and power. Augustine's division between spirit and sex, religion and desire, God and the body is an ugly splitting that survives in our own time—an era, often in the name of religion, marked by deep anxiety about and hostility toward human sexuality, the body, and the natural world in general.

Jesus' elevation of celibacy, Paul's proscriptions against marriage, and Augustine's linkage between original sin and erotic desire continue to cast a long shadow over the church's teachings about sexuality. Many scholars today regard Paul's and Augustine's sexual theologies as bedrock to contemporary Christians' negative attitudes toward sex and the body:

> Paul and Augustine are two theologians who stand at the headwaters of the Christian religion. They have bequeathed to Christianity an anti-sexual legacy that lingers to this day. Or to express the matter colloquially, traditional Christianity had deliberately chosen to take a dim view of sex. Take, by way of example, the church's veneration of celibacy (the state of having no sex by having no spouse). With its commitment to the concept of the divided self and with its veneration of Saint Paul, who wished that all people were unmarried like him (1 Cor 7:7), the church over the centuries has applauded celibacy. Prior to Christianity's emergence, perpetual celibacy was practiced in neither the Gentile nor Jewish worlds (an exception was the Essene community at Qumran). To be unmarried and childless was—especially for Jews—a disgrace. But Christianity introduced a new way of viewing perpetual celibacy.[11]

It is against the backdrop of this sort of sexless spirituality in early Christianity—an ideal that divided Christianity from Judaism in antiquity— that the erotic hospitality of Luke's Jesus is sketched. Alongside the early church's "majority report" concerning noncorporeal Christian existence, I analyze Luke's "minority report" of Jesus' and the anonymous woman's transgressive and erotically charged interactions as a counterpoint to the mainstream ideal.

THE UNNAMED WOMAN AND EROTIC CARE OF BODIES

The sexual body is a privileged site of divine encounter in the Lukan story of the unnamed woman who washes Jesus' feet. At Simon the Pharisee's dinner party, an anonymous woman enters Simon's home and lovingly wets Jesus' feet with her tears and hair. Uninvited, she approaches Jesus from behind, lets down her hair and begins to wash and anoint his feet with a jar of perfume, her hair, and her many tears. Throughout this initial encounter, significantly, Jesus does not speak. Simon wonders to himself how Jesus, claiming to be a prophet, could allow this sort of woman, perhaps a prostitute, to touch him. As if reading Simon's thoughts, Jesus tells a parable about two debtors and how the one who owes the most, once forgiven his debts, now loves the most. Simon understands the meaning of the parable, and Jesus, in one of his classic man-bites-dog reversals of the social order, publicly rebukes Simon for not fully welcoming him to his home and then praises the kissing woman for her "great love" (7:47). Like many of Jesus' narratives, the story inverts established expectations. Who is the real sinner, the true lover, the authentic follower of Jesus in this account: Simon, the established religious leader, or the notoriously sinful woman? At the end, Jesus forgives the woman her sins and offers her God's peace, which provokes much questioning and likely criticism among Simon's dinner guests.

As with many biblical narratives, the scandal and irony of this story is lost to many of us today. Like other scriptural texts, this story has been domesticated by some commentators' appeal to the putative religious message of divine forgiveness at the story's end and a general disregard of the shock and discomfort the story was intended to generate among its hearers and readers.[12] Using a feminist hermeneutic, I argue that the story is an exercise in erotic performance art that intends to liberate readers into a new relationship with Christ that is body- and pleasure-affirming. I examine how Luke 7:36-50 functions as a model of female agency that subversively challenges certain structures of oppression in antiquity. From this perspective, the text can be read as valorizing a particular transgressive practice (the unnamed woman's sexualized foot washing) in order to realize emancipatory possibilities for identity formation against the social and religious distortions of its time.

To begin to make this case, let me offer here a retelling of the story in contemporary terms in order to imagine how the story might speak afresh to the present-day reader.

A Disturbing Incident at Local Minister's Home

Something astonishing took place last week in the home of the Reverend and Mrs. J. Josiah Alexander IV of First Presbyterian Church of Smithtown. As is their custom, the Alexanders invited this year's theologian-in-residence, the Reverend Ian Cameron, to a formal lunch after the morning worship service. A local unemployed woman, reportedly charged this past summer with solicitation, gained access to the house and approached Rev. Cameron just as the Alexanders and guests were sitting down for supper. Appearing emotionally unstable and crying profusely, the woman (her name was not disclosed) unloosened her long hair and proceeded to take off Rev. Cameron's socks and shoes. She then wet his feet with her tears, rubbed them with her hair, and kissed them incessantly, or so it appeared. The woman was wearing a vial of perfume, or similar substance, around her neck that she also used in her attentions to Rev. Cameron's feet. To everyone's dismay, Rev. Cameron allowed these theatrics to continue for quite a while, and then, shockingly, rebuked Rev. Alexander (and presumably Mrs. Alexander) for not properly welcoming him to their home, and contrasting them unfavorably to this overly wrought woman.

"I entered your home," he said, "and you did not shake my hand or offer me a hug or kiss, whereas this woman placed my tired feet in her own hands and has not ceased to kiss me since I sat down. You did not take my coat, buy she took my socks and shoes and thoughtfully put them aside for me. You did not offer me a drink, but she continues to massage my feet, refreshing my body and spirit and welcoming me to your home in the way you should have done. See this woman? She loves me, but what about you?"

Understandably, the Alexanders and guests were stunned into silence by Rev. Cameron's reprimand, not expecting a respected member of the clergy to sanction the behavior of this uninvited intruder. Equally shocking, Rev. Cameron concluded the woman's visit by telling her that God had forgiven her sins—a rather remarkable claim for a woman who has a reputation as a person of ill repute. The event has generated considerable controversy in Smithtown, where members of the Mayflower-descended and Princeton-educated Alexander family have been respected pillars of the community for generations. Younger residents are referring to the scene at the Alexander home as a "happening," while Rev. Alexander and elders at First Presbyterian are considering initiating a formal ecclesiastical review of Rev. Cameron's behavior during the incident.

With this contemporary retelling as a backdrop, I read the Lukan story as a countertestimony to mainstream Christian anxiety about the body and sexuality. In this vein, I see two crucial issues: the question of the woman's identity as an urban sinner, and the quality of her amorous encounter with Jesus as the basis of God's forgiveness and peace in her life.

Who is the anonymous woman? Much has been written about the phrase in verse 37 that the unnamed woman was "of the city, a sinner," when she learned about Jesus' presence in Simon the Pharisee's house and came to minister to him. It is possible, but by no means certain, that the woman was a prostitute. Feminist biblical scholar Elisabeth Schüssler Fiorenza writes that the appellation "sinner" was reserved in antiquity for criminals or those persons who worked in disreputable jobs such as tax collectors, servants, domestics, swineherds, tanners, prostitutes, and so on. Many of these professions were not available to women (though certain service jobs and prostitution were options for women). As well, female prostitutes, as has been the case historically, lived in brothels in urban areas in the first century. Circumstantially, it is possible that this "woman of the city, a sinner" was a prostitute, but to make this claim with any certitude is a mistake.[13]

While this woman in Luke may or may not have been a prostitute, it is also a mistake to identify her with Mary Magdalene who, erroneously, was often read as a prostitute herself in the exegetical history of this narrative. The story of how Mary Magdalene—a steadfast follower of Jesus who bankrolled his early preaching tours (Luke 8:1-3) and was the first eyewitness to the resurrection (John 20:11-18)—became a prostitute has been carefully analyzed by exegetes.[14] In part, the conflation of the anonymous woman in Luke and Mary of Magdala—the "harlot-saint" of early Christian mythology—likely stems from the confusing number of Marys within the New Testament (e.g., Mary the mother of Jesus, Mary Magdalene, and Mary of Bethany, to name just three of the most prominent) that led to a composite "Marian" picture.[15]

Confusion about the woman's identity in the Lukan story is further overdetermined by another layer of misunderstanding in the reception history of this text—namely, the harmonizing of this account with the similar story of the woman who anoints Jesus' head at Bethany in the other Gospels. At first glance, Luke 7:36-50 bears a number of formal similarities with Matthew 26:6-13, Mark 14:3-9, and John 12:1-8. Some commentators think a "single gospel memory" animates each account, but it is especially clear in Luke's narrative that a different message is being advanced.[16] On the one hand, in all four accounts, a woman appears with Jesus in a home environment and uses a costly jar of ointment on his body, perhaps in gesture of anointment. In each case, this act provokes a negative reaction by onlookers that is complemented by Jesus' defense of the woman. In many regards, however, the differences between the four narratives are more striking than the similarities. Matthew and Mark locate the woman in the house of Simon the leper, and John locates her in the house of Mary, Martha, and Lazarus. Luke puts the woman in the home of Simon the Pharisee. In the non-Lukan accounts, the disciples complain that the ointment should not have been used on Jesus but sold with the proceeds given to the poor. As well, the Matthean and Markan accounts place the anointing on Jesus' head, not his feet, explicitly associating the anointing with preparing Jesus' body for burial (as does John). On the other hand, however, all three of these versions make no mention of what is central to the story's scandal in Luke's version: the woman's excessive love of Jesus symbolized by her tears and kissing of his feet, and Jesus' forgiveness of the woman's sins.

What is refreshingly distinctive about Luke's story is how its sexually nuanced details foreground the loved and nurtured body as central to Jesus' message of healing and forgiveness. Jesus and the woman engage one another's flesh in tenderness and affection. It is precisely because they perform this, as it were, erotic theatre of the senses that God's power is realized—namely, the woman's sins are forgiven. Note that the relationship between the woman and Jesus is one of mutuality and reciprocity. She approaches him and reaches for his feet, and he welcomes her touch, her tears, her kisses. The "Son of God" enjoys being fondled by this woman and, in turn, he offers her God's forgiveness and peace. God's hospitality is actualized by the woman's deep welcoming of Jesus' needy body: "the *mutual* exchange of hospitality between Jesus and the woman is characteristic of the divine visitation."[17]

The power of God's love made manifest in this excessive display of affection is made clear in Simon's initial dismay with Jesus' enjoyment of the woman's stroking of his body. "If this man were a prophet," he says to himself, "he would know what sort of woman is touching him." The buried assumption in Simon's logic is that a true prophet would not allow such a boundary transgression by a woman of such bad reputation. Luke provocatively reverses Simon's logic, a point no reader could miss: it is precisely because this woman is engaging in publicly forbidden behavior and Jesus knows exactly who she is that his identity as a prophet is confirmed. Jesus' divine prophethood is established on the basis of what society regards as sexually polluting behavior, which Jesus now shows to be a privileged site of divine presence and power. At a meal with a Pharisee, where women were likely not welcomed, and in a first-century culture where women were viewed as property or worse, the woman shreds the social order with her bold physicality. As François Bovon notes, "The woman comes into the midst of a dinner reserved for men, carries a bottle of perfume, unlooses her hair (a particularly erotic action for Jewish perceptions), repeatedly kisses Jesus' feet, and finally in the presence of all the guests does something that belongs in the realm of intimate behavior or even of perverse practices: she anoints his feet."[18] The woman enters a male space with brio and courage, presumably unfastens and lets down her hair, which is long enough to be used as a makeshift towel, and commences a prolonged wiping, kissing, and anointing of Jesus' feet.

Consider the parallelism between her actions in verse 38 and Jesus' endorsement of the same in verses 44-46. Luke writes that the woman wet Jesus' feet with her tears, wiped them with her hair, kissed them, and anointed them with perfume (7:38). Jesus then replies to Simon that she has wet his feet with her tears, wiped them with her hair, kissed them (continually, he adds), and anointed his feet with perfume (7:44-46). The four verbs employed to describe these actions (*brecho*, Gk., to wet; *ekmasso*, to wipe; *kataphileo*, to kiss; *aleipho*, to anoint) and the actions themselves as recounted by Jesus are the same. The parallelism drives home the text's central theme: Jesus' and the woman's amorous performance art signals that excessive desire for the well-being of another's flesh is the grounds for salvation and forgiveness in God's new order of being. "The kingdom of God is among you," says Jesus in Luke 17:21. God's new order is not "out there" waiting to arrive; it is "here and now" as modeled in this parable of erotic intimacy.

Commentators on Luke are often uncomfortable with the unabashed sensuality in the passage. Far from the text being an exercise in biblical *ars erotica*, traditional readers hyped the "sinful" adjective for the woman, assumed she was a prostitute, interpreted her weeping as repentance, and basically saw her as immodest and shameful. As feminist exegete Teresa Hornsby writes, the woman in Luke 7 was not read as a strong, independent agent of her own spiritual and carnal desires for Jesus but as a sexually suspect, immoral penitent whom Jesus deigns to forgive.

> The image of a woman being so lavishly physical with no apparent fear of reprisal and without any shame associated with her act made me glad . . . because I could finally identify with a character in the biblical text, a character who in my initial reading acts independently in blending together the movements of her body with an expression for raw emotion. . . . But when I looked at the interpretation of Luke's passage, I could not find

the woman I had read. I was disappointed to discover that this figure has been used since the earliest interpretations as a symbol of every woman's lewdness, as a symbol of a woman's physicality that stands over and against what is "good" and "proper." With very few exceptions, especially in any work prior to the mid-1980s, scholars either call her a prostitute or they claim that the label the narrator gives her of "sinner" (*hamartolos*) surely indicates that the anointing woman is a carnal transgressor; her effusive weeping, they write, must be indicative of sexual, shame-inspired remorse and repentance; her ointment must have come from her prostitute's tool-box; and the fact that she is kissing a strange man can only mean that she is sexually immoral.[19]

Hornsby is correct. In the history of mainstream biblical theology, the woman is not a model of bold love but an object lesson of immorality. Earlier English translations of the Bible use various deprecating subtitles in order to define the text in this way: The New American Bible titles Luke 7:36-50 "The Pardon of a Sinful Woman," while the Revised Standard Version calls it "The Woman Who Was a Sinner."[20] These editorial subtitles miss the point of the pericope. The story is not about the woman's sinfulness but about her great love for Jesus; it is not about how bad she was, or how promiscuous she now supposedly is, but about how her lavish care of Jesus' flesh overflows "proper" boundaries and realizes God's love; it is not about shameful sexual transgression but about Jesus' and the woman's shameless license to pleasure and heal the body. The passage, then, would be better subtitled as "The Woman Who Loved Too Much," "The Woman Who Could Not Stop Kissing the Lord," or "The Woman Who Loved Jesus with Complete Abandon." In her lavishly erotic relationship with Jesus, the unnamed woman pushes the boundaries of social convention by massaging Jesus' feet with her hair and bodily fluids, leading to her forgiveness and opening to readers then and today new possibilities for sexually charged spiritual and bodily relations.

JESUS' AND BOAZ'S FEET

A cursory reading of the Lukan focus on Jesus' feet reminds readers today, as it has throughout Christian history, of the story of Ruth and Boaz. The book of Ruth is a postexilic Hebrew love story that celebrates the inclusion of outsiders within the changing demography of Israel in the third or fourth century B.C.E. Ruth, a Moabite, lives with her mother-in-law, Naomi, outside of Israel when both Ruth's husband and Naomi's husband die. In mourning, Ruth and Naomi decide to relocate to Bethlehem, Naomi's family home, where Ruth meets a member of her extended family, on older man named Boaz. Naomi tells Ruth to wash and perfume herself and after Boaz has had a meal to go and lie down, unannounced, in Boaz's bed, at his feet, "So [Ruth] went down to the threshing floor and did just as her mother-in-law had instructed her. When Boaz had eaten and drunk, and he was in a contented mood, he went to lie down at the end of the heap of grain. Then she came stealthily and uncovered his feet, and lay down" (Ruth 3:6-7). Ruth climbs into bed with Boaz, uncovers his "feet" (i.e., his genitals) and when he awakens at midnight, she asks him to "spread your cloak over your servant [i.e., have sexual relations], for you are next-of-kin" (Ruth 3:9). Boaz agrees and says he will marry her. To avoid embarrassment, Ruth leaves his bed early the next morning before anyone learns of their encounter the night before. Boaz soon thereafter marries Ruth, and they subsequently have a son name Obed.

Traditional commentaries regard the message of the story to be that Ruth, a non-Jewish foreigner, preserved the family line through which King David emerged by marrying a Hebrew man, Boaz: "The women of the neighborhood gave him [Ruth's son] a name . . . Obed; he became the father of Jesse, the father of David" (Ruth 4:17).[21] On this telling, the importance of Ruth is essentially patriarchal and political: she is a placeholder in the Davidic line that preserves the traditional monarchy. In this vein, she is the legal property of whoever becomes her husband, as Boaz makes clear to Ruth's nearest kinsman regarding the twin purchase of a field owned by Naomi and the person of Ruth: "The day you acquire the field from the hand of Naomi, you are also acquiring Ruth the Moabite" (Ruth 4:5). While the bare facts of this reading are accurate, it misses another line of emphasis in the story—namely, that Ruth, like the Lukan woman, is a highly capable and bold agent of her own desires who courageously transgresses social boundaries in order to welcome the body of her lover. She does not define herself as a passive object to be bought and sold; rather, she is an active agent of her desires and hopes.[22]

Consider one example that illustrates the agency and resourcefulness of both women. While the anonymous woman uses what she has at hand—her hair—to care for Jesus' body, so also does Ruth rely on her own assets—in this case, her rhetorical skills—to claim Boaz as her kinsman, even though she had a nearer kinsman (unnamed in the story) who should have been her more likely partner. Like the Lukan woman who follows through on her desires for Jesus, Ruth prefers Boaz and goes after him, not her closer cousin. In both cases, eros's arrow follows its own logic.

The role Boaz's feet play in the account further illuminates the narrative artistry at work in the Lukan story. Readers of Ruth have long understood Ruth's action of uncovering Boaz's feet as another way of speaking about sex. With the exception of the Song of Solomon, in general, the Bible does not use explicit language to describe sexual activity or genitalia but relies instead on pointed, conventional euphemisms to communicate these ideas (e.g., "loins" or "feet" for genitalia, "nakedness" or "knowing" for sexual union).[23] In light of these stylistic devices, new vistas of meaning are opened in Luke 7 when this narrative is read against the backdrop of the book of Ruth. As Hornsby writes,

> Luke's heightened attention to the feet of Jesus may also suggest to read-ers various sexual images. That "feet" is a euphemism for male genitals not only in Hebrew texts but also in the Septuagint as well as other Hellenis-tic and Greco-Roman literature has been convincingly argued. Chapter 3 of the book of Ruth, a plausible intertext to Luke's pericope, offers one of the strongest examples of the euphemism. . . . I am not arguing that Luke presents the anointing woman as attending to Jesus' genitals; I am merely suggesting that to any reader, first century or present day, familiar with the book of Ruth, Luke's attention to a woman at a man's feet sexually nuances a narrative that portrays a woman in an active role.[24]

Ruth's story and Luke's text can be read as tender portraits of warm-hearted haptology. Beyond the taboos and prohibitions of their respec-tive cultures, both narratives are about hands touching "feet," arousing the appreciation of the men who are the partners in their erotic adventures, and climaxing in enriched experiences of God's presence and power (i.e., the preservation of the Davidic line in Ruth, and the forgiveness of the woman's sins in Luke). Just as Luke's unnamed woman ceaselessly kisses Jesus' feet and makes real possibilities of carnal intimacy that shatters the prohibitions con-cerning public space and public familiarity in antiquity, so also Ruth may be seen as following her heart's yearnings and actively shaping her relationship with Boaz, shattering postexilic Israel's definition of women as chattel.

TONI MORRISON'S GOSPEL OF FLESH

Toni Morrison's *Beloved*, published in 1987, is a gripping fictional retelling of the true story of the infanticide of a little girl by her grief-stricken mother in 1850. Sethe, the protagonist of the novel, is a runaway slave who is almost recaptured, along with her children, at a time when escaped slaves could be hunted like animals across state lines and taken into custody by their masters or bounty hunters. Sethe kills one of her daughters, the "crawling-already? girl" Beloved—so the title of the novel—in a frantic attempt to prevent her from being returned to slavery by her nemesis, a man referred to as School-teacher. In part, the novel is a series of flashbacks to the antebellum and Civil War years in which Sethe, now with her other daughter, Denver, is literally haunted by the unspeakable memories of Beloved's death and related events at the Sweet Home plantation where she was housed. Sethe's good friend from the Sweet Home years, Paul D, comes to live with her, Denver, and Beloved, the half-woman, half-child ghost of the infant Sethe had killed ear-lier. Sethe remembers how Schoolteacher's plantation boys assaulted her at Sweet Home, stole her breast milk, and cut open her back with beatings. Paul D recalls life on the chain gang and the humiliation of wearing a horse's bit in his mouth, contorting his face into a painful grimace.

Beloved tells a story of indescribable physical suffering, on the one hand, and of bodies being healed through hair combing, back touching, breast feeding, foot rubbing, and hand holding, on the other. Readers encounter bodies that are broken beyond repair and souls crushed without mercy or remorse. Heal-ing seems impossible, but Morrison uses religion—a certain kind of African-derived, body-loving, nature-based religion—as the medicine the slaves and ex-slaves in the novel use to heal themselves. In particular, she profiles Baby Suggs, Sethe's mother-in-law and itinerant evangelist, whose message, "which transforms the Christian message of self-abnegation and deliverance after death, is meant to heal the broken and suffering bodies of those who endured slavery."[25] Nine years after Baby Suggs's death, Sethe remembers her sermons and dancing in the Clearing, an open space deep in the woods outside Cincin-nati where slaves and fugitives would gather to hear Baby Suggs, sitting on a large rock in the trees, preach her new gospel of flesh:

"Here," she said, "in this here place, we flesh; flesh that weeps, laughs; flesh that dances on bare feet in grass. Love it. Love it hard. Yonder they do not love your flesh. They despise it. They don't love your eyes; they'd just as soon pick em out. No more do they love the skin on your back. Yonder they flay it. And O my people they do not love your hands. Those they only use, tie, bind, chop off and leave empty! Love them. Raise them up and kiss them. Touch others with them, pat them together, stroke them on your face 'cause they don't love that either. *You* got to love it, *you*! . . . This is flesh I'm talking about here. Flesh that needs to be loved. Feet that need to rest and to dance; backs that need support; shoulders that need arms, strong arms I'm telling you."[26]

Sethe recalls Baby Suggs's healing services as "fixing ceremonies" that enable her to recover—somewhat—from the physical and psychological wounds suffered under slavery and its aftermath. Sethe's broken recovery sets the stage for readers today to mend from the toxic effects caused by the transatlantic slave system in its time and other systems of oppression in our own time. Baby Suggs's sermons in the Clearing allow present-day readers to regard the whole novel itself as an extended fixing ceremony— "a prayer," as literary critic Barbara Christian writes, "a ritual grounded in active remembering which might result, first of all, in our understanding why it is that so many of us are wounded, fragmented, and in a state of longing. Then, perhaps, we might move beyond that fracturing to those actions that might result in communal healing and in a redesigning of the contemporary world called the 'New World.'"[27] This sort of "spiritual" reading of *Beloved*—but spiritual in the sense of world affirming, not world denying—is a counterperformance that staves off the debilitating effects of pathological, anticorporeal religion. In their worst moments, Christianity and its antebellum henchmen despise the flesh, but Baby Suggs teaches us to love our flesh. They tell us to hate our bodies, but she tells us to raise up and kiss our bodies and tenderly touch our bodies and others' bodies as well. Baby Suggs's gospel of flesh is a fixing ceremony that grounds readers' desires to perform rituals of healing and renewal in the face of institutional systems, including the Christian church, that inculcate disgust and derision toward this beautifully enfleshed world, God's gift to all of us and to ourselves.

In the novel's chronology, Sethe has another healing encounter with Paul D around the time of Baby Suggs's ministry in the Clearing. She tells Paul D the chilling story of the Sweet Home assault when the plantation boys extracted Sethe's breast milk and then whipped her after she complained to Mrs. Garner, mute and powerless, the proprietress of Sweet Home (so named, horrifically and ironically). She says "Schoolteacher made one [of the boys] open up my back, and when it closed it made a tree. It grows there still."[28] Sethe says this as she is bending over a hot stove, at which point Paul D reaches

[b]ehind her, bending down, his body an arc of kindness, he held her breasts in the palms of his hands. He rubbed his cheek on her back and learned that way her sorrow, the roots of it; its wide trunk and intricate branches. Raising his fingers to the hooks of her dress, he knew without seeing them or hearing any sigh that the tears were coming fast. And when the top of her dress was around her hips and he saw the sculpture

her back had become, like the decorative work of an ironsmith too passionate for display, he could think but not say, "Aw, Lord, girl." And he
would tolerate no peace until he had touched every ridge and leaf of it
with his mouth, none of which Sethe could feel because her back skin
had been dead for years. What she knew was that the responsibility for
her breasts, at last, was in somebody else's hands.[29]

Sethe and Paul D's love story is a sensual tale of renewal and pleasure
that counterbalances the scenes of unbearable cruelty in the novel. Paul D's
hands are an artist's painting a work of beauty over a canvas of flesh crying
out for life and deliverance. Sethe's breasts have come home, nestled in the
hollows of Paul D's hands, hands that show her that the care of her breasts,
at last, are in someone else's hands, and breasts that show him the delight
and wonder of intimacy with a woman of fortitude and passion. When Paul
D thinks but cannot say, "Aw, Lord, girl," he and Sethe are making a nest for
God to inhabit, a beautiful place for the Spirit to indwell, a setting where the
Lord—"Aw, Lord, girl"—is present and alive and beating in the rhythm of
the two hearts that are now one, the two bodies that are now one flesh. Erotically charged, sexually inflected, this scene, like the scene of Baby Suggs in
the Clearing, offers readers a fixing ceremony, a gospel of flesh, which they
can enter into for their own restoration and repair.

BIBLICAL HAPTOLOGY FOR OUR TIME

The scandal of Luke's narrative of the woman who loved too much is that
a certain type of woman had the temerity to violate sacrosanct boundaries of appropriate public conduct by touching (*haptos*) and kissing (*kataphileo*)
Jesus. The thrust of the story is revealed in Simon's comment *sotto voce* that
if Jesus were a prophet, he would know what sort of woman this is and, by
implication, not allow her to touch him. However, Jesus not only permits
the woman's touches and kisses, he relishes in them; indeed, he luxuriates
in them to the point of upbraiding and, likely, humiliating Simon and his
guests by honoring the woman as a lover—his lover?—a woman who shows
to everyone what real hospitality, even affection, is. Quiet at first as she wets
and wipes his feet with her tears and hair, Jesus eventually speaks and offers
to forgive the woman her sins and offers her God's peace. Wetting, wiping,
kissing, anointing, touching—this "sinful" woman from the city, like Ruth and
Sethe, has presumably suffered greatly and is now transforming her suffering
by seeking carnal joy in her beloved. The Lukan woman, Ruth, and Sethe
self-actualize by seeking pleasure and healing in the face of large-scale structures of social and political subjugation. In these transgressive performances

of desire and love, God becomes real and is made present to the actors and their readers alike.

Nietzsche lamented that Christianity's greatest sin is to despise life, drive underground one's innermost drives and passions, and teach contempt for the body.[30] But in the cracks and along the margins of Christianity's erstwhile ambivalence and sometimes hostility toward sensual pleasure there emerges many extraordinary celebrations of erotic delight and embodied existence in Scripture and elsewhere. Christianity will always be in travail with itself, but might it be possible one day that the gospel of flesh would trump the Christian ideal of sexual renunciation? Biblical stories and modern fiction alike offer an antidote to so much *contemptus corpus* nonsense in the annals of official Christian teaching. The logic and scandal of Christian faith has always been an exercise in the coincidence of opposites (i.e., divinity and humanity are one). This essay calls Christians to recover this ancient incarnational wisdom and renew the unity of spirit and flesh, the sacred and the body, God and humankind so that physical, erotic, sexual life can become a privileged site of divine power and love once again.

Further Recommended Reading

Bovon, François. *Luke 1: A Commentary on the Gospel of Luke 1:1—9:50.* Hermeneia. Trans. Christine M. Thomas, ed. Helmut Koester. Minneapolis: Fortress Press, 2002.

Brown, Peter. *The Body and Society: Men,° Women, and Sexual Renunciation in Early Christianity.* New York: Columbia University Press, 1988.

Burrus, Virginia, and Catherine Keller, eds. *Toward a Theology of Eros: Transfiguring Passion at the Limits of Discipline.* New York: Fordham University Press, 2006.

Jordan, Mark D. *The Ethics of Sex.* Oxford: Blackwell, 2002.

LaCocque, André. *Ruth.* A Continental Commentary. Trans. K. C. Hanson. Minneapolis: Fortress Press, 2004.

Levine, Amy-Jill, ed., with Marianne Blickenstaff. *A Feminist Companion to Luke.* Cleveland: Pilgrim, 2001.

Pagels, Elaine. *Adam, Eve, and the Serpent: Sex and Politics in Early Christianity.* New York: Random House, 1988.

Plasa, Carl, ed. *Toni Morrison, Beloved.* New York: Columbia University Press, 1998.

Rogers, Eugene F., Jr., ed. *Theology and Sexuality: Classic and Contemporary Readings.* Oxford: Blackwell, 2002.

CHAPTER 3

The New Testament, Empire, and Homoeroticism

William Stacy Johnson

A NEW ACCEPTANCE OF SAME-GENDER COUPLES is now dawning in Western countries. In the United States a number of jurisdictions have begun to allow gay marriages or civil unions, and many more are likely to do so in the years ahead. Elsewhere, I have offered a detailed argument that the exclusively committed relationships of gay and lesbian couples should be consecrated within our religious communities, validated within our legal system, and welcomed within the framework of our democratic polity.[1] I shall not repeat those arguments here. In this essay, I argue that references to homoeroticism in the New Testament are in significant measure a response to the sexual ethos of domination and submission that pervaded the Roman Empire. I make this argument not as a specialist in early Christian origins but as a theologian seeking guidance from the past to help reorient the church's protracted debate over same-gender relationships. I am by no means the first to suggest the obvious: that New Testament texts on homoeroticism derive their meaning from the specific Greco-Roman context in which they were written. However, scholars have been slow to recognize the theological and interpretive significance of the most important feature of this context—namely, in New Testament times, Roman views of sexuality were linked to a cruel ideology of conquest and empire.[2] Well-meaning New Testament scholars have led us down the wrong path by suggesting that the best backdrop for understanding these biblical verses is the ancient Greek practice of pederasty.[3] The problem with this argument is that pederasty was not especially prominent in the days of the New Testament.

The New Testament is best understood, so I shall argue, not in reference to classical Greece but against the background of imperial Rome. In contrast to the Greeks, the Romans used sexuality in general, and homoerotic sexuality in particular, as an instrument of state-sponsored terror. When seen through this lens, it is little wonder that the three isolated New Testament references to homoeroticism were negative. This essay examines Roman homoeroticism through the eyes of an occupied people, in order to show that the New Testament is referring to something very different from the committed same-gender couples who are seeking relationship equality in Western societies today. Conservative claims that the New Testament treats homoeroticism as intrinsically sinful will not hold up to scrutiny after learning more about the situation of slaves in the Roman Empire. In short, paying attention to the context of empire helps us see why the New Testament sayings on homoeroticism should have no bearing on contemporary ethical debates.

GETTING THE CONTEXT RIGHT:
FROM HOMOSEXUALITY TO HOMOSEXUALITIES

Those who use the Bible to reject gay sexuality usually make the ahistorical assumption that there is a single, monolithic reality called "homosexuality" that is the same yesterday, today, and always. It is true that in all times and places, and across all cultures, races, and religions, there have been people with homoerotic desires. Nevertheless, by paying attention to the particularities of context, we begin to see that it is not very helpful to speak of a singular abstraction called "homosexuality." Instead, there are many homosexualities, which differ profoundly according to time, place, social condition, and culture. Classifying three different types of homoerotic conduct helps us to see this more clearly.[4]

First, there is age-differentiated homoeroticism. This type was exemplified by the pederasty of the ancient Greeks. It also found expression in

Melanesian culture where all older males passed on virility from one generation to another through homoerotic acts. In Greece, pederasty was a practice
cultivated among elite families.[5] It was an institution in which a mature male,
often in his early twenties, known as the *erastēs* (lover), served as a model of
virtue for a younger male usually around age eighteen, the *eromenos* (beloved).
The younger male, who was undergoing a rite of passage to masculine matu-
rity, was expected to be the passive recipient of his mentor's sexual affections.
Contrary to popular misunderstanding, this was not the same as the predatory practice of "pedophilia." Not only was the sexual activity in pederasty
voluntary, but it also ceased when the younger party arrived at a more mature
age. Most of the men who engaged in these practices were not acting out of
an exclusive same-gender sexual orientation and almost all of them would
later go on to have wives and father children. The purpose of pederasty
in ancient Athens was to turn elite young men into educated, acculturated
citizens. Unlike pedophilia, pederasty was a socially accepted institution in
which most responsible male citizens participated.

Second, there are status-defined relationships in which one partner performs a sexual role that is active and the other a passive, usually stigmatized
role. This was the form of homoeroticism that prevailed in the Roman world.
It is not that pederasty disappeared entirely in the social world of the Roman
Empire, but it was not nearly as central as in ancient Greece. In the sexual
ideology of the Romans, male sex acts, whether heterosexual or homosexual,
were performed by social superiors upon social inferiors. The upshot was the
creation in Rome of a glaring double standard: for a freeborn Roman male
to allow himself to be sexually penetrated by another male was considered
shameful, even criminal; however, for him to gratify his own sexual urges
with a male slave or other social inferior was considered appropriate. Indeed,
it was even expected as part of the definition of Roman manhood. I shall
return to the example of Rome momentarily.

The third type of homoeroticism, egalitarian, is what Western societies
are being asked to approve today. In contrast to the asymmetrical way the
Romans conceived of sex, in which everything depends on who does what
to whom, in egalitarian homoeroticism the relationship is mutual. We cannot
assert dogmatically that there never were such egalitarian relationships in the
ancient world. After all, the pederastic relationship in ancient Greece was
supposed to bring mutual benefit to *erastēs* and *eromenos*, and their friendship
was often enduring. Nevertheless, because of the active/passive conceptual-
ity in pederasty, the sexual relationship itself was not conceived as mutual
and did not continue after the younger man reached adulthood. In other

words, what Western societies are debating today—voluntary relationships between loving peers—is something very different. Today, many gay and lesbian couples are giving themselves to each other in exclusively committed relationships, raising children, and caring for one another for better or worse, in sickness and in health, with the intention of maintaining a lifelong relationship.

Scholars have long pointed out that nowhere is this egalitarian type of homoeroticism explicitly mentioned among the condemnations in the New Testament.[6] It has been countered that since some egalitarian relationships may have existed from time to time in the ancient world, New Testament references should be read broadly to include them.[7] This essay argues that examining the particular Roman ethos of domination and exploitation which prevailed when the New Testament was written leads us to conclude that the second type, the exploitative, status-defined relationship, is what the earliest Christians witnessed on a widespread basis and chose to condemn.

THE ROMAN SEXUAL ETHOS
OF SUBMISSION AND DOMINANCE

Roman rule was synonymous with sexual humiliation, rape, and death. When the Romans conquered a city, it was standard practice to rape the women, humiliate sexually the defeated soldiers, and consign significant portions of the population to slavery. The Jews living in Palestine in Jesus' day were no strangers to these oppressive practices. For example, in 4 B.C.E., around the time that Jesus was born, a Jewish uprising against Roman power led the Romans to sack and raze the city of Sepphoris, which lay just a few short miles from Jesus' own village of Nazareth. Similarly, when Jewish revolt broke out again in 66 C.E.—during the very years when the earliest writings of the New Testament were being formulated—the Romans destroyed the city of Magdala (in which, presumably, Mary Magdalene was born), slaughtering many of the city's inhabitants and taking many more away into slavery. Imagine what it would be like if these atrocities had been committed in an American city today. Would not all our news stories, literature, poetry, and moral reflection be permeated with the memory of such things? We need only recall how the events of September 11, 2001, influenced American consciousness to see how events of violence can shape the worldview of a people.

In the context of Rome, acts of sexual humiliation were not mere isolated instances. They were part of Rome's construction of gender, enforcement of class boundaries and citizenship, and understanding of honor and eth-

ics. Extreme sexual aggressiveness and obscenity was even the hallmark of
Roman humor; yet, for the victims of Roman aggression, this was no laughing
matter.[8] Sexual humiliation was part of an active Roman campaign of psychological terror. It was no accident that Roman iconography portrayed defeated
peoples as women being sexually subdued. So widespread were these violent
practices that if a woman hailed from a conquered city, it was presumed
that she had been raped. Some have even wondered whether the situation
of widespread rape during this time period prompted the rabbinic rule that
no matter who the father, the child of a Jewish mother is considered to be a
Jew.[9]

In keeping with this ideology of dominance, all male Roman citizens
were expected to gratify their urges through both homosexual and heterosexual encounters. The famous Roman poet Catullus considered it normal
for a freeborn male to have sexual passion for both males and females. At the
same time, Catullus looked down on any citizen who allowed himself to be
sexually penetrated by another man. This was so because the male Roman
citizen was always expected to be the "doer" of the sexual act. For him to
become the passive partner of another male was considered shameful. On the
other hand, he was both permitted and expected to gratify his sexual urges
with social inferiors, including women, male prostitutes, and male slaves.

Hence, it was not unusual for a Roman soldier to demonstrate his dominance by sexually humiliating a defeated enemy. Similarly, for a Roman citizen to pleasure himself sexually by using a noncitizen slave was considered
to be normal and acceptable. Even though the act may have been humiliating
from the standpoint of the passive recipient, from the point of view of the
elite Roman perpetrating the act, it was considered a moral nonevent—a
mere release of energy and nothing more. It was typical for male citizens
to own slaves and to resort to these slaves for sexual favors. The pervasiveness of slavery is evidenced in the pages of the New Testament, for example,
the Roman centurion who comes to Jesus with his boy-slave (*pais*, Matt. 8:6;
doulos, Luke 7:2).

Though Roman homoerotic expression was commonplace and even
taken for granted, it was also circumscribed within clear legal limits, and
these limits are important to underscore as we read the New Testament.
According to the classics scholar Amy Richlin, in the Roman world, "there is
no [literary] trace of a real and established homosexual relationship between
men of the same age."[10] References to such relationships occur in the midst
of invective, making such evidence unreliable. Another classics scholar, Marilyn Skinner, observes that there were only two legitimate objects for homo-

erotic release available to the Roman citizen in New Testament times: male prostitutes and male slaves.[11] This we know not only from literary evidence but from artifacts such as the so-called Warren Cup, which depicts an elite Roman having sex with a slave boy on one side and another having sex with a male prostitute (or older slave) on the other.[12] Not surprisingly, these are the two categories—male prostitutes and slaves—that we find mentioned in New Testament vice lists that allude to homoeroticism.

A LIST OF VICES: 1 CORINTHIANS 6:9-10

In 1 Corinthians 6:9-10, male prostitutes and another category that I identify as elite "men-who-have-sex-with-men" (*arsenokoitai*) are mentioned together. Paul admonished his audience:

> Do you not know that wrongdoers will not inherit the kingdom of God? Do not be deceived! Fornicators, idolaters, adulterers, male prostitutes [*malakoi*], men-who-have-sex-with-men [*arsenokoitai*], thieves, the greedy, drunkards, revilers, robbers—none of these will inherit the kingdom of God. (1 Cor. 6:9-10)[13]

On the one hand, this list speaks in generalities. This is not surprising since the list is not specifically Christian in origin but is a standard enumeration of immoral actions. Many in the Greco-Roman world would have considered homoerotic sexuality to be morally shady, even if legally permissible. What is the purpose of a laundry list of vices? Authors in New Testament times cited such lists in order to "hook" their audience rhetorically. When New Testament authors employed these lists, they were making a general twofold appeal for the community to strive for upright conduct and to shun behaviors that would bring them shame (e.g., 1 Cor. 5:10, 11; 6:9-10; Rom. 1:29-31; Gal. 5:19-23; Col. 3:18; Eph. 5:21; 2 Tim. 3:1-5).

On the other hand, the mention of homoerotic conduct here is quite specific and refers to a particular kind of hedonistic sexuality that falls outside a committed, covenantal context. In 1 Corinthians the term translated by the New Revised Standard Version (NRSV) as "sodomites" is *arsenokoitai*, which literally means "males who go to bed with males." This term had a specific type of practice in mind.[14] The word translated by the NRSV as "male prostitutes" is *malakoi*, which literally means "soft ones." Although some rightly point out that the meaning of *malakoi* is obscure, many believe it refers to the receptive, penetrated partner in male-on-male sexual intercourse, probably in the context of male prostitution. The linking of *arsenokoitai* and *malakoi* here points precisely to the hedonistic homoerotic practices that were legally permissible and widespread in the Roman Empire. Such practices were almost always performed by social superiors upon social inferiors. That is, there was nothing essentially loving, exclusive, or covenantal about these encounters. They were premised on Roman understandings of class, power, and status.

In specifically linking "male prostitutes" (*malakoi*) and "men-who-have-sex-with-men" (*arsenokoitai*), Paul was referring to a situation where one man sold himself to another. The men who were selling themselves (or being sold by others) could have been slaves. They might also have been former slaves who, upon being freed, sold themselves to other men for money. To sell oneself in this way was considered demeaning for a freeman, underscoring the moral and social implications of the distinction between slave and free—a distinction to which I shall return shortly. Some scholars suggest that usage of the term *arsenokoitai* outside the New Testament occurs in contexts suggesting economic injustice.[15] Again, this is in keeping with my contention that the primary target of these New Testament vice lists was the Roman custom of dominance and exploitation.

SLAVERY IN THE ROMAN CONTEXT

The Roman legal system not only permitted male prostitution but also homoerotic sexuality with slaves. Slavery was part and parcel of the ethos of mastery and dominance at the center of the Roman way of life. Since Roman society was founded on a slave economy, slavery was the central reality shaping the economic and social world of the New Testament. Not to take account of this fact in exegesis is to miss what was really going on in the early Christian world. To put it another way, trying to understand sexuality in Rome as separate from slavery is like trying to understand sexuality in America without accounting for the availability of birth control and the pervasiveness of sex in entertainment and advertising. To ignore these things is to miss the way in which sexuality is socially constructed in a particular time and place.

Earlier scholarship considered Roman slavery to be fairly benign, since slaves could be freed around the age of thirty. Furthermore, some slaves could rise to positions of great responsibility and prominence in the master's domain. We must not ignore, however, the brutal conditions under which most slaves lived. Under Roman law a slave was defined as a "thing" (*res*), and this "thing" belonged to and owed absolute obedience to the master. A slave was regarded not as a person but merely as a "body" or *skeuos*. This body could be used in whatever way the master wished.

Harvard sociologist Orlando Patterson has identified humiliation as the hallmark of the slave's status. Patterson aptly describes the slave as living under a cloud of what he calls "social death." Defining slavery as the "permanent, violent domination of natally alienated and generally dishonored persons," Patterson contends that the condition of slavery is more than a mere legal or economic matter.[16] The domination that lies at the heart of slavery aims to be total. The slave is not only deprived of freedom but is also considered completely devoid of honor. To understand this, think of slaves who were captured by the Romans in war. These were persons who, in military terms, should have been dead. In a society rooted in honor, the fact that they were permitted to live, when death would have been an honorable end, only underscored their status as neither possessing honor nor deserving of any.

Slavery is seldom even mentioned in the various antigay books purporting to explain the Bible and homosexuality, even though the institution of slavery was one of the chief structures within which homoerotic activity occurred in the Roman world.[17] To be a slave was by definition to be a sex object. If the slave owed absolute obedience, this included complete sexual obedience. Since it was considered a morally neutral thing for a Roman citizen to release his sexual energy at the expense of his slave, the sexual resort to slaves was quite frequent. Even slaves who had won their freedom still found themselves granting sexual favors to the powerful as one way of fulfilling their duties. As Roman rhetorician Seneca the Elder quipped: "Unchastity is a crime for the freeborn boy; a necessity for the slave; and a duty for the freedman."[18]

Moreover, the fact that one was a slave meant that one's reproductive life was no longer one's own. A slave was not permitted to marry. If the slave cohabited with another, the offspring from this union belonged to the master. Just as in the antebellum American South, the slave family could itself be broken up, bought, and sold at the master's whim. The prospect of manumission did not protect one from these indignities.

In short, slavery and sexuality, just like power and gender, were intimately linked in the ancient world. They were so linked, in fact, that the connection is merely assumed in the New Testament rather than elaborated in any detail. Nevertheless, in New Testament passages such as 1 Timothy 1:10 we catch a glimpse of what was going on.

A SECOND LIST OF VICES: 1 TIMOTHY 1:10

The author of 1 Timothy sets forth a list of immoral practices that includes, in the same breath, "fornicators [*pornoi*], men-who-have-sex-with-men [*arse-*

nokoitai], and slave traders [*andrapodistai*]." The placing of these three types of disrespected persons together is far from arbitrary. It may seem that the first two terms, which pertain directly to sexual practices, differ from the third group of people, who traded in human beings. However, the slave trade in Rome was synonymous with the sex trade. People were bought and sold not only to provide masters with a source of physical labor but also to provide a body over which to exercise sexual dominance.

One pervasive feature of Roman sexual practice was the lively trade in young boy-slaves who had been captured as part of the spoils of war and sold into slavery. In order for these slaves to retain their youthful appearance, the slave traders castrated some of them before offering them on the auction block. This helps explain the matter-of-fact appearance of eunuchs in the pages of the New Testament (Acts 8:27-39). In Roman literature, it was commonplace to think of slave traders who engaged in the castration and sale of boys as social pariahs who habitually mistreated their merchandise and cheated their customers—much like a disreputable used-car salesman but on a more hideous moral scale.[19] This pariah status itself reflects an irony at the heart of Roman society. The trade in sexuality was widely practiced and widely accepted; yet, at the same time, it was the subject of ridicule and even disdain. It is not hard to imagine how elite Roman men might have harbored ambiguous feelings about this widespread practice of castration. In fact, this mutilation and sale of boys was such a rampant feature of Roman life that the Romans themselves became uncomfortable with the practice and on three occasions passed laws designed to ban it. That the boy-slave trade continued despite this legislation testifies to its lucrativeness.

The spotlight that 1 Timothy shines upon slavery and the slave trade is another strong piece of evidence that the situation of imperial violence and abuse was the primary horizon from which the New Testament writers viewed the world. Given that the Romans had carried tens of thousands of Jewish men, women, and children into slavery in their conquest and continual oppression of Palestine, it is no wonder that various forms of the sex trade would make it into the New Testament vice lists.

PAUL'S LETTER TO THE ROMANS

That New Testament statements against homoerotic behavior are best understood against the background of the imperial dominance and exploitation practiced by the Romans is true not only of 1 Corinthians and 1 Timothy but also of Paul's Epistle to the Romans. We gain a clue into reading Romans by first considering the earliest letter written by the apostle Paul, 1 Thessalonians, where Paul provides a statement of his understanding of sexual ethics, which anticipates and sheds light on what he will say about sexuality elsewhere in his corpus:

> For this is the will of God, your sanctification: that you abstain from fornication [*porneia*]; that each one of you know how to control your own body [*skeuos*] in holiness and honor, not with lustful passion [*epithumias*], like the Gentiles who do not know God; that no one wrong or exploit a brother or sister [*ton adelphon*] in this matter, because the Lord is an avenger in all these things, just as we have already told you beforehand and solemnly warned you. (1 Thess. 4:3-6)[20]

As we think about this passage in relationship to the argument over same-gender sexual relationships, three things need to be said.

First, Paul was a Jew and reasoned like a Jew. This means that law (Torah) is at the center of his thinking. This is crucial, because legal thinking is not a rigid adherence to rules but, rather, is always dynamic and ongoing. Legal reasoning deals in concrete cases and in drawing distinctions and similarities from one case to another. Even the most superficial acquaintance with rabbinic reasoning makes this clear. It is a general principle of legal and ethical analysis that we should always interpret specific prohibitions in light of the overarching goal for which they have been issued. So, then, what is the reason for the rule Paul articulates? Paul's teaching is in the service of promoting a positive spiritual goal—namely, that his hearers would become more holy or, in the language of the tradition, "sanctified." In other words, Paul is not issuing prohibitions for prohibition's sake; he is providing guidance aimed at correcting social ills and bringing holiness into sexual relations. It will not do simply to repeat one legal pronouncement in a very different context without determining whether this new application is faithful to the old or whether it requires change or emendation. Thus, if exclusively committed same-gender unions today actually help gay and lesbian people to live more holy lives, then arguably at least this much of Paul's vision for the ordering of Christian life has been satisfied.

Second, the prohibition of sexual immorality is framed as a task of knowing how to control one's own body and restrain unbridled passion. To this extent, Paul is combining his Jewish background with a healthy dose of Roman Stoicism. This should not be surprising to us at all, since the Stoics were stern critics of the cult of empire, which I am claiming was a chief concern of New Testament ethics.

Third, prohibited practices are connected with a practical test: Paul is concerned to promote a way of life that would keep people from being sexually exploited. The NRSV speaks of exploitation of a brother or sister; yet, literally, the Greek refers to men—and even more specifically still to the Christian brother (*ton adelphon*). This could be an admonishment not to offend another brother by taking that brother's wife. It could also conceivably contemplate not offending a brother by having sex with him. This would be addressing Christian masters who owned Christian slaves. In either event, the focus is sex that constitutes exploitation. That exploitation is a major focus of the apostle is hardly surprising when we keep in mind that so much of the sexual practice of the Roman world was exploitative by design. This insistence on sexual discipline and refusal to engage in exploitation gives us the key to interpreting Paul's remarkable Letter to the Romans.

One of the major theological themes of the Letter to the Romans is the reconciliation of Gentile and Jew, specifically, by extending to Gentiles the promise of sanctified identity and abundant blessings that came along with the Jewish covenant. Given the violent way that Gentiles had dominated the Jews, this is as radical and surprising a statement as one can imagine. Set within this general discussion of Jew and Gentile, Paul wrote his famous (or infamous) words about the pervasive homoerotic behavior of the Roman world. His discussion is not at all focused on homoerotically inclined individuals, as would be the case if his concern were with what we call "sexual orientation." Instead, he paints a general picture of Roman sexuality run amok. In other words, he does not characterize specific individuals but the Gentiles as a whole. Paul employs a familiar rhetorical convention here, using a sexual slur to elicit consent from his audience, many of whom would have agreed that sexual profligacy was rife within the ancient Roman world. While he lifts up homoerotic behavior as an example of how the Gentiles have departed from the ways of God, he does not elevate it above other vices, which he enumerates in detail (Rom. 1:29-32), and he makes clear in the very next chapter that the sins of the Jews are just as bad and that Jews are just as in need of God's grace (2:1-29).

The specific things Paul writes about homoerotic practices, especially his claim that such practices are "against nature" (*para phusin*), are mostly borrowed from the teachings of Roman Stoicism—in particular, Stoic criticism of the profligate exercise of sexual passion. Paul writes:

> For this reason God gave them [Gentiles] up to degrading passions. Their women exchanged natural intercourse [*phusikēn chrēsin*] for unnatural [*para phusin*], and in the same way also the men, giving up natural intercourse [*phusikēn chrēsin*] with women, were consumed with passion for one another. Men committed shameless acts with men and received in their own persons the due penalty for their error. (Rom. 1:26-27)

The debate over what this text means is important, since antigay advocates claim that here we have a clear New Testament reference, set specifically within a theological frame, that condemns all homoerotic acts of every sort, no matter what the context.[21] Is this true?

In declaring such acts to be unnatural, Paul reflects the typical view of his day that something is unnatural if it is unconventional or out of the ordinary. The term *unnatural* was used in the Greco-Roman world to refer to behavior ranging from extreme acts of courage to such things as the perceived unnaturalness of eating meat.[22] This may explain why in Romans Paul looks askance at people who "degrade" (*atimazō*) their bodies and do things that are unnatural. In another letter, Paul uses the very same language to criticize men who wear long hair: "Does not nature [*phusis*] itself teach you that if a man wears long hair, it is degrading [*atimia*] to him?" (1 Cor. 11:14). Few would claim that Paul's condemnation of this behavior should be applied today.

What about the mention of women giving up natural intercourse for passion with one another? Again, the language of "giving up natural intercourse" simply proves that Paul is thinking about heterosexual persons who are departing from their "natural" heterosexual nature. Paul gives no hint of referring to that small group of persons we know about today for whom a same-gender desire flows from a same-gender sexual orientation. As professor of early Christian history Bernadette J. Brooten has exhaustively demonstrated, Paul does not articulate a particularly new or distinctively Christian understanding of ethics but simply echoes Roman-period sources that looked askance at love between women.[23] Paul's concern about what we call lesbianism fits with his general and culture-bound assumptions about male dominance and female submission.

Beyond the first chapter of Romans, Paul makes another surprising reference to unnatural behavior when he depicts none other than God acting in a way that is *para phusin*.[24] God defies our ordinary religious categories in order to bless not only Jews but also Gentiles. Paul explains it this way:

> For if you [Gentiles] have been cut from what is by nature [*kata phusin*] a
> wild olive tree and grafted, contrary to nature [*para phusin*], into a culti-
> vated olive tree, how much more will these natural [*kata phusin*] branches
> be grafted back into their own olive tree. (Rom. 11:24)

Notice what is happening here. In the first chapter of Romans, Paul says that
the Gentiles have sexual habits that are unconventional or contrary to nature
(*para phusin*). In Romans 11, Paul uses the very language from chapter 1 to
describe how God acts contrary to what seems natural (*para phusin*) in order
to graft Gentiles into God's original covenant with the Jews.

Seen from this perspective, the noteworthy thing about the letter to the
Romans is not that it has a negative view of Gentile homoeroticism. Most
Jews held this view in those days, and the sexual violence of the Roman con-
querors only intensified this view. The unexpected thing is that this perception of Gentile impurity does not prevent Paul from reaching out to them.
His goal as an apostle, in fact, is to reach all the Gentiles (Rom. 1:5). In God's
mercy, all have been included: "There is no distinction between Jew and
Greek; the same Lord is Lord of all and is generous to all who call on him"
(10:12). Again, the amazing thing is not that Paul expresses a negative view
of Gentile homoeroticism. Given that, in the Roman context, homoeroticism
manifested itself predominantly in the practices of humiliation—slavery and
prostitution—this negative view is not surprising. What is shocking is the
way Paul understands the gospel to require him to embrace these very same
Gentiles, notwithstanding their sexual offenses, and to make them part of
God's covenant.

What the New Testament Does Not Say about Slavery and Homoeroticism

Sometimes the silence of the New Testament speaks more loudly than its
words. As already noted, the institution of slavery was pervasive in the
Roman world. On this subject, the silence of the New Testament is deafen-
ing. Nowhere in the New Testament is slavery as an institution denounced
or even called into question. Every time slavery is mentioned in the New
Testament—and this includes Paul's Letter to Philemon—it is accepted.
There is the baptismal formula in Galatians 3:28, which declares that in
Christ there is no longer "slave or free." The very idea of being a slave to
Christ could have had the revolutionary effect over time of calling into
question slavery to human powers (see 1 Cor. 7:23). Nevertheless, the early
church was not able to envision the full revolutionary potential of statements

such as Galatians 3:28 on slavery. Slavery as an institution and the rules for how slaves ought to behave were accepted. Slaves were admonished to obey their masters (Eph. 6:5; Col. 3:22). Paul advises them not to seek their freedom but to "remain as they are" (1 Cor. 7:6). In addition, we know that Christians in the early church sometimes owned slaves.[25]

This leaves us with two vital questions about slavery that have a bearing on how we assess the New Testament's treatment of homoerotic behavior. First, what were the sexual expectations for Christians in the early church who happened to be slaves? As mentioned before, slaves had no autonomy. They were not allowed to marry and were legally the sexual property of their masters. As such, slaves were expected to grant sexual favors on demand—whether to the master or to someone else at the master's bidding. This applied to both male and female slaves. Assuming that 1 Thessalonians 4:3-6 prohibits adultery with another man's wife and not homoeroticism, then there is nothing in the New Testament that speaks specifically to the issue of whether a male slave had to grant homoerotic favors to his master—no advice, no command, nothing. Why not?

Some antigay advocates have argued that the very act of homoerotic sexual practice is considered by the biblical writers to be an intrinsic violation of divine law—a rupture in the natural and social order and one that jeopardizes one's very salvation. This seems highly questionable. In light of the Roman background of sexual dominance and imperial violence, it seems much more plausible that New Testament writers were focused on particular ethical situations. Moreover, if homoerotic acts were considered to be an intrinsic offense, then the silence of the New Testament concerning whether a Christian slave should carry out his homoerotic duties is very hard to explain. It might be argued that the general admonitions against fornication (*porneia*) include an implicit ethical word of resistance to slaves. However, this argument ignores the fact that under the sexual mores of Roman culture, having sexual relations with a slave—whether male or female—was precisely not considered to be *porneia* at all but an act that was morally neither here nor there. This cultural context would render the need for an explicit word declaring homoeroticism to be *porneia* all the more necessary.

Even if it is assumed that the command against *porneia* included an implicit (and so unspoken) mandate directed to slaves, the question still remains how a slave could possibly be expected to follow such a mandate. How could a male slave refuse a master's homoerotic advances? To refuse one's master in any respect was considered to be an act of rebellion, deserving of death. If homoerotic practices were really thought to be intrinsically sinful, which would require a Christian male slave to resist under pain of death, would we not expect a clear New Testament teaching to that effect? Instead, the specific advice of the New Testament is one of passive obedience: slaves must obey their masters (Eph. 6:5). If slaves were admonished by Christian teaching to obey their masters in all things, what makes us think that this imperative included an exception for homoerotic advances?

To be sure, arguments from silence can be hazardous. We are not in a position to say with absolute certainty what advice was actually given to male slaves in specific cases regarding their vulnerability to unwanted homoerotic advances. Perhaps the advice varied from situation to situation. What we do know is that no New Testament writer felt a need to record any clear advice about such matters to slaves. What we also know is that no New Testament writer felt the need to set forth a clear and explicit commandment to Christian masters to refrain from such homoerotic activity.

So then how are we to interpret this silence? The best explanation is that the texts are silent about slaves as the passive recipients of homoerotic sexual advances for the very same reason the texts refrain from challenging slavery as an institution—that is, the early Christian community knew that homoerotic activity was occurring, that it occurred with regularity, and that it was simply accepted as inevitable. It might even be that many Christians accepted the Roman assumption that such acts were ethically neutral. In either event, the New Testament writers did not see fit to define homoerotic behavior as intrinsically sinful.

CONCLUSION

American culture has come a long way in its embrace of civil rights for gay and lesbian persons, but there is still a long way to go. The philosopher Martha Nussbaum sums the situation up this way: "American society appears willing to tolerate, somewhat grudgingly, the existence of lesbians and gay men, provided it does not have to put up with their happiness."[26] One obstacle to greater societal openness to the happiness of gay and lesbian couples is the traditional reading of the New Testament texts on homoeroticism. I have argued that when we read the New Testament texts in light of the Roman ethos of sexual dominance and exploitation, nothing in those texts says anything to prohibit the happiness of committed gay and lesbian couples. The New Testament says nothing about egalitarian homosexual relationships, and what it says (and does not say) about slavery undercuts the idea that homoeroticism was thought to be intrinsically sinful. Since slavery was the primary context of Roman homoerotic activity, and since the New Testament admonishes slaves to obey their masters, then there is a certain acquiescence to homo-erotic activity that belies the claim of some conservatives that homoeroticism is declared to be intrinsically sinful. Recognizing the ethos of dominance and submission that prevailed in Roman practices of sexuality enables us to see how New Testament denunciations of exploitative homoerotic practices have no bearing whatsoever on egalitarian same-gender relationships today. This recognition, in turn, should help Christians realize the wrong-headedness of centuries of church teaching on this subject and the untold damage this teaching has done to so many.

Further Suggested Readings

Brooten, Bernadette. *Love between Women: Early Christian Responses to Female Homoeroticism.* Chicago: University of Chicago Press, 1998.

Glancy, Jennifer. *Slavery in Early Christianity.* New York: Oxford University Press, 2002.

Johnson, William Stacy. *A Time to Embrace: Same-Gender Relationships in Religion, Law, and Politics.* Grand Rapids: Eerdmans, 2006.

Murray, Stephen O. *Homosexualities.* Chicago: University of Chicago Press, 2000.

Richlin, Amy. *The Garden of Priapus: Sexuality and Aggression in Roman Humor.* New York: Oxford University Press, 1992.

Skinner, Marilyn B. *Sexuality in Greek and Roman Culture.* Oxford: Blackwell, 2005.

CHAPTER 4

Augustine on Eros, Desire, and Sexuality

John E. Thiel

THE THEOLOGICAL CAREER OF AURELIUS AUGUSTINUS (354–430) has so influenced the Christian tradition that one could credibly argue that no person besides Jesus himself has had more of a hand in shaping its beliefs and practices. Augustine's views on the Trinity, creation, the nature of the church, grace and free choice, and the efficacy of the sacraments all molded the history of theological thinking on these topics and, in some cases, even set the course for what became Christianity's orthodox heritage. Even when the medieval Catholic tradition resisted the strong theology of grace of his later years by consigning it to oblivion, Augustine remained its undisputed authority whose name theological commentators invoked in order to justify their opinions on nearly every other Christian matter. No traditional thinker exceeded Augustine's measure in the minds of the great Continental Reformers, perhaps even to the point that the Reformation was as much a recovery of Augustine as it was a recovery of Paul. Although this history of Augustinian effects has been extensive at the level of belief, practice, and doctrine, it has been most consequential at the level of Christian attitudes toward and values concerning human desire, the yearning that our minds, hearts, and bodies experience for what they lack and wish to make their own. In this essay, I will explore Augustine's views on desire, assess their remarkable influence on Christian life throughout the centuries, and consider how Augustinian sensibilities are still very much engrained in the tradition, even as we have become critically aware of their deleterious effects.

A Brief Tour of Augustine's Thought

I would like to make an argument here that draws on Augustine's whole career and, for that matter, on the events of his entire life. The intelligibility of that argument requires a basic knowledge of that life and thought which some readers of this essay may not possess and which I would like to offer as a brief sketch. No doubt, the shorthand quality of this exposition will be subject to all sorts of criticism, though the presentation here claims to be no more than an orientation that serves the purposes of our more focused attention to the issue of desire in Augustine's thought.

Born in 354 in the North African town of Thagaste in present-day Algeria, Augustine from his youth demonstrated a keen intelligence that continued to prove itself throughout his life.[1] His intellectual ability first appeared in a facility for words that brought him boyhood honors in rhetoric. He studied the classical Latin poets, cultivating a breadth of literary knowledge on which he drew throughout his life. Around the age of twenty-six, he wrote a book on aesthetics that has since been lost, the first of many books and treatises that would be the issue of an extraordinarily prolific literary career. Even though Augustine was strikingly intelligent, he exhibited a certain rigidity of mind that appeared throughout his life in a proclivity to "either-or" thinking, an intellectual habit that would have telling consequences for the Christian tradition.

This disjunctive mind-set first appeared at the age of nineteen as Augustine troubled philosophically and, of course, emotionally about the problem of evil and sought comfort in the belief system of Gnostic dualism. For about ten years of his life, from his late teens to his late twenties, Augustine was a practicing Manichean, and, like all Gnostics, identified evil as material existence itself. In his early belief system, the physical universe, and particularly the body, imprisoned the divine spirit that committed Gnostics believed their inner self to be. This divine self, tragically lost in an ontologically evil world, could transcend its fallen state through the awareness of its self-divinity in this life or by escape from the body at death and return to the heavenly realm of the true God. For the young Augustine, this dualistic account of reality placed evil on one side of a metaphysical either-or. Existence was either good or evil, spirit or matter, metaphysically saved or metaphysically lost. There were many advantages to this Gnostic worldview, not the least of which was the clarity of its explanation of the age-old problem of evil. For the Gnostic, there was nothing mysterious about evil. Rather, evil was as clear and concrete as the material world with which it was identified, and as obviously distinguishable from the goodness of the divine spirit that the Gnostics claimed as their true self.

Ironically, we notice a second site for Augustine's disjunctive mind-set at the very point in his life that he abandoned the Manicheism of his youth. Both talented and ambitious, Augustine sailed to Rome in 383 in search of better students than those he had tutored in Carthage. By the following year, he was appointed professor of rhetoric in Milan and with the passing of just a few years had become a member of the emperor's inner circle as a valued advisor and speechwriter. Through the persistence of his mother Monica, who ever pressed his conversion to Christianity, Augustine befriended the Milanese bishop Ambrose, whose allegorical reading of the Bible convinced him that Christianity was an intellectually defensible religion at the very time that he was growing dissatisfied with Gnosticism. We know of this time in Augustine's life, the late 380s, largely through his report of it in his spiritual autobiography, the *Confessions*, written about thirteen years later. As we shall see in short order, there is good cause to be suspicious that the narration of the *Confessions* is an accurate rendition of the events it relates. Yet, we can probably trust the veracity of Augustine's account of his conversion to Christianity in one important respect. Augustine's decision for Christian baptism in 387 seems to have been premised from the beginning on a vocational commitment to the ascetical life, first as a *Servus Dei*, a layman devoted to the ascetical path, and then as a priest and bishop. Conversion to Christianity, of course, did not require the convert to embrace asceticism, since the renunciant life is always extraordinary and the way of the few. But for Augustine, the prospect of Christian conversion seemed to have entailed a choice either for the world or for the church, either for the pleasures of the flesh or for their renunciation, either for his early life in pursuit of fame or a new life devoted to the denial of the flesh for the sake of eternal life. It is this disjunctive definition of Augustine's vocational path that seems to have made his choice for Christianity so difficult, utterly life transforming, and, from all the symptoms that Augustine recounts in autobiographical detail, attended by nothing less than a mental and physical collapse.[2] The newly baptized Augustine put an end to his impending social marriage, made his way back to North Africa, and began practicing the ascetical life.

The third site for Augustine's disjunctive mind-set appears in a remarkable shift in his theological thinking that began to take place shortly after his consecration as bishop of Hippo in 395. At this time, through his study of Paul's Letter to the Romans, Augustine came to credit the divine will with all the power that brings believers to eternal life. A few years earlier, shortly after his conversion in 386, Augustine began to write treatises against the Manicheans. These early works, such as *On Genesis, Against the Manicheans* (389), and *On True Religion* (391), affirm the goodness of the created world against Gnostic dualism and explain evil as privation—a position Augustine brought to his new Christian worldview from his reading of the philosopher Plotinus. Evil, for the anti-Manichean Augustine, possesses no ontological status. It is a metaphysical absence, a lack of being, or, in the moral sphere, an aberrant, though freely chosen, act of the will that lacks proper conformity to the divine order. Free choice of the will is a theme throughout the anti-Manichean writings since this Christian belief challenged Gnostic fatalism, which locked spirit and body into respectively good and evil actions beyond any choice at all. One of the anti-Manichean writings, *On Free Choice of the Will* (388–395), explored this creaturely endowment in depth, with a very humanist-sounding Augustine touting the power of moral choice, reason's natural appetite for God and the will's receptivity to its guidance, the moral agent's responsibility before God, and the contributions of free choice to eternal salvation.[3]

By the time Augustine became bishop of Hippo Regius in 395, the early views had changed, and as the years passed the change became permanent. In a series of reflections penned in 396 and addressed to his friend Simplicianus, Ambrose's successor as bishop of Milan, Augustine explained Paul's Letter to the Romans by downplaying the value of freely chosen works for salvation and crediting God's grace entirely for the victory of eternal life.[4] The *Confessions*, written in the years 397–401, makes the same point narratively, in the way Augustine relates the event of his conversion. Augustine configured himself in the *Confessions* as a person enslaved by the pleasure of sex and pridefully resistant to the Christian life—a resistance which, in spite of himself, was broken finally by the irresistible power of divine grace. Augustine's account does not place conversion in his personal choice but in God's inexorable will. Even the literary presentation of the *Confessions* seems to reflect this theme, with each "book" or chapter of the text beginning and ending with searching prayers and scriptural citations that frame Augustine's story within the biblical story, as though his life achieves its meaning only by losing itself in the life of God.

Now, there is every reason to suspect that the events catalogued in the *Confessions* did not take place exactly as Augustine described them. As we have seen, shortly after his conversion, Augustine devoted his prodigious literary energies to treatises against the Manicheans in which he celebrated the integrity of free choice of the will. It seems likely that those early works, which date from the late 380s and early 390s, are more faithful renditions of his religious views at the time of his conversion, which would suggest that Augustine understood his conversion, when it occurred, as an exercise in free choice. This in turn would mean that the *Confessions'* narrative of conversion recounts past events in light of the changed understanding of grace and free will that Augustine had settled on by the time he wrote *Ad Simplicianum* (396). This is not to say that free choice of the will disappears in the *Confessions'* narrative of amazing grace. However, the choice that Augustine imagined there now seems to be a negative power exercised only in sinful resistance to grace and not the effective, empowered choice between good and evil that Augustine had championed in his anti-Manichean writing *On Free Choice of the Will.*

Augustine articulated this negative account of free choice with fine precision throughout the running theological battle he fought with the monk Pelagius and his supporters from the year 411 until his death in 430. Against the Pelagians' moral optimism and lofty confidence in the virtuous capacity of free choice, the late Augustine argued for a salvation so utterly within God's graceful power that it could only be described as predestined. In the anti-Pelagian writings, free choice remains a real power within the limitless scope of God's predestinating grace; yet, as a natural power, free choice is sinful through and through. For Augustine, "the human will is not taken away [by God's grace], but changed from bad to good, and assisted when it is good." God's grace "converts [good wills] from bad wills" and "directs [the divinely converted wills] to good actions and to eternal life." It was the Augustine of the Pelagian controversy who intensified Paul's strong notion of human sinfulness to the point of a theologically refined conception of original sin, which made human fallenness as inescapable as birth and made eternal condemnation God's righteous judgment on all humanity. Since all humanity deserves condemnation, God's benevolent decision to will the saved to eternal life is untouched by human merit or deservedness and determined "by a counsel most secret to [Godself], indeed, but beyond all doubt most righteous."[5] Augustine's death came as he was still defending these views, particularly in his final years, against his Pelagian-minded adversary, the Italian bishop Julian of Eclanum. For Augustine, faith in the power of God's predestinating grace to redeem a naturally irredeemable human nature was the very message of the gospel.

DISJUNCTIVE DESIRE

These three sites in Augustine's life and intellectual career—the either-ors of dualism, vocation, and volitional power—have something to say about the cast of his mind and his manner of negotiating events and circumstance. Augustine shows a proclivity to frame ideas and occurrences oppositionally, by imagining reality as a contest between alternatives to which he has assigned value. Dialectical thinking, of course, may simply capture something of the structural way in which human minds go about their business, however much the content of their thinking is acculturated. Thought systems as different as ancient Platonic philosophy (which exerted a profound influence on Augustine's conversion to Christianity) and modern liberal constitutional law, and practices as different as free-market investing and team-competitive sports, configure a slice of the world or all of it oppositionally in order to frame a context for human purpose. Even systems of thought that challenge this dialectical framework, like Mahayana Buddhist logic or poststructuralist philosophies, or practices such as Quaker consensus shaping and egalitarian forms of pedagogy, recognize the prevalence and power of the oppositional framework that they judge deficient. At some level, then, Augustine's either-or style of thinking and choosing is rather ordinary and unsurprising; yet, there are aspects of the Augustinian disjunctiveness that account for its preponderant influence on Christian sensibilities through the ages. Three characteristics are noteworthy. First, Augustine defines the alternatives in his oppositional framework in rather extreme ways. Second, these extremes are invested with religious value. Third, although there are many implications of his investment of dialectical extremes with religious value, the most consequential for the Christian tradition has been the way this oppositional imaginary frames Augustine's account of human desire. We can see early examples of this theological investment in the doxological language of the *Confessions* and in the way Augustine presents his decision for conversion.

Augustine's poetic description of the human desire for God in the *Confessions* became a paradigm for accounts of spiritual yearning throughout the tradition. The opening lines of Book 1 are as typical as they are moving. As a creature of God, the human person possesses an "instinct" to praise God, praise that is engendered by the very difference between creator and creature. The human person "bears about him [sic] the mark of death, the sign of his own sin, to remind him that you [God] thwart the proud." The contrast between human perdition and divine goodness, between human deathliness and the fullness of the divine life, seems to stir the desire for God: "The thought of you stirs him [the believer] so deeply that he cannot be content unless he praises you, because you made us for yourself and our hearts find no peace until they rest in you."[6] Augustine finds this desire to be so strong that he is at a loss to explain its intensity. "Why do you mean so much to me? Help me to find words to explain. . . . Tell me why you mean so much to me."[7] The narrative of the *Confessions* attempts such an explanation crafted along the lines of the work's opening lines quoted above.

The difference between God and creatures configures a space in which the yearning for God gathers its energy. "My God, how I burned with longing to have wings to carry me back to you, away from all earthly things, although I had no idea what you would do with me!"[8] Although this passage represents this emotion as negatively charged by everything creaturely, Augustine's finite point of focus is much more specifically defined by fleshly desire. Augustine understood himself to be gripped from the age of sixteen by the "frenzy" of a lust before which he could only "surrender."[9] Later, arriving in Carthage as a young man, he found himself in a "hissing cauldron of lust" that "muddied the stream of friendship with the filth of lewdness and clouded its clear waters with hell's black river of lust."[10] The middle-aged bishop who tells his story of conversion understands his sexual desire as an addiction beyond the power of the will, as a "state of bondage" endured by "a prisoner of habit, suffering cruel torments through trying to satisfy a lust that could never be sated."[11] Augustine returns to this bondage motif later in his narrative as he recounts the inspiring tale of the conversion of Victorinus, a public official who denounced his fear of social rejection to embrace the true faith. Inspired by the courage of Victorinus, Augustine feels all the more shame at his recalcitrant attachment to the flesh and his sinful resistance to the desire for God. "I longed to do the same [as Victorinus]," Augustine laments, "but I was held fast, not in fetters clamped upon me by another, but by my own will, which had the strength of iron chains." Augustine is utterly consistent in naming the nature of his bondage. "For my will was perverse," he states,

> and lust had grown from it, and when I gave into lust habit was born, and when I did not resist the habit it became a necessity. These were the

links which together formed what I have called my chain, and it held me fast in the duress of servitude. But the new will which had come to life in me and made me wish to serve you freely and enjoy you, my God, who are our only certain joy, was not yet strong enough to overcome the old, hardened as it was by the passing of time.[12]

Here we see so clearly the disjunctive dimensions of Augustine's account of desire, which he defines as either the desire for God or the desire for the flesh, and with the flesh all the ways of the world. Indeed, so disjunctively does Augustine represent desire that he concludes his account of desire's struggle by imagining it as two: "So these two wills within me, one old, one new, one the servant of the flesh, the other of the spirit, were in conflict and between them they tore my soul apart."[13] Disjunctive desire, it seems, is a function of a disjunctive self, rent by its conflicting desires for self and for God.

This disjunctively desirous self appears most starkly in Augustine's anti-Pelagian writings, especially in his rather bizarre account of sexual desire in Book 14 of the *City of God* (413–427). Here, the explicit theme is not the opposition between the desire of the flesh and the desire for God, though that contest is never far from Augustine's mind; rather, the spotlight in the *City of God* is decidedly on the desire for the flesh as a perverted consequence of the first sin. Augustine offers a remarkable reading of Genesis 1–3 that makes sexual desire and the pleasures of sexual intercourse postlapsarian miscarriages of an original state of grace in paradise.

Augustine does not think that sexual intercourse itself is a consequence of the fall. The biblical command to "Be fruitful and multiply" (Gen. 1:28) places the propagation of humankind in the will of God. Augustine assumes that had the first parents obeyed this divine command in paradise, the begetting of children would have transpired through the same biological act of sexual reproduction responsible for every human birth, save the Savior's. There were other opinions in the early Christian tradition. The second-century theologian Tatian the Syrian, for example, had argued that sexual intercourse itself was the first sin, and so never would have transpired had paradise endured.[14] Augustine, like a majority of Christian thinkers, held the view that sexual intercourse is God's plan for the propagation of the species and so, like all created things, good. Augustine, though, imagines that sexual intercourse before the fall of Adam and Eve would not have been instigated or attended by the passionate desire that now motivates postlapsarian persons, but instead by a reasoned choice to beget a child, in his judgment the only rational and authentic purpose of sexual intercourse. In a sinless human history that extended paradise, he asserts, "the man would have sowed the seed and the woman would have conceived the child when their sexual organs had been aroused by the will, at the appropriate time and in the necessary degree, and had not been incited by lust."[15]

We find sexual intercourse on either side of the first sin, but now it is sexual desire that becomes disjunctive. Absent before the fall, sexual desire rages after, itself a consequence of the first sin. As either absent or present, sexual desire marks the transition from innocence to guilt, from obedience to rebellion, and from freely chosen self-mastery to the chaotic passion of the sinful self. Augustine is not at all reluctant to describe the sinful side of this disjunction. In an interesting passage, he presents a phenomenology of sexual passion that presses all the way to a surprising judgment:

> We see then that there are lusts for many things, and yet when lust is mentioned without the specification of its object the only thing that normally occurs to the mind is the lust that excites the indecent parts of the body. This lust assumes power not only over the whole body, and not only from the outside, but also internally; it disturbs the whole man, when the mental emotion combines and mingles with the physical craving, resulting in a pleasure surpassing all physical delights. So intense is the pleasure that when it reaches its climax there is an almost total extinction of mental alertness; the intellectual sentries, as it were, are overwhelmed. Now surely any friend of wisdom and holy joys who lives a married life but knows, in the words of the Apostle's warning, "how to possess his bodily instrument in holiness and honour, not in the sickness of desire, like the Gentiles who have no knowledge of God"—surely such a man would prefer, if possible, to beget children without lust of this kind.[16]

Or, perhaps not! Augustine's expectation of unquestioned agreement would hardly be embraced by the vast majority of human beings who have found the completion of sexual desire in passionate pleasure to be a meaningful, enjoyable, and fulfilling dimension of their lives. Augustine's judgment that "any friend of wisdom and holy joys"—a Christian, in other words—would prefer that desire be actualized in the intellectual pursuit of a reasoned good and not at all in the pleasure of sexual passion is a rhetorical extension of his ascetical vows to the dimensions of common sense. As such, it becomes a symbolics of human fallenness in which the "tumultuous ardor of passion" marks the embodiment of sin.[17] Perhaps we can highlight the character of this symbolics by comparing a sexually passionate relationship with another kind of relationship that Augustine values highly.

Any reader of Augustine's writings can plainly see the importance of friendship in his life. Augustine narrates his life in the *Confessions* so that every significant event in his journey to God is attended by the company of friends. A dying friend who shares the young Augustine's skepticism for Christianity chides him for scoffing at his sickbed baptism and, by his change of mind and heart, forces Augustine to consider the power of the sacrament.[18] His friends Simplicianus and Ponticianus tell stories of Christian heroism that inspire Augustine and push him closer to conversion.[19] When he finally feels compelled to convert, his faithful friend Alypius follows his example just moments later.[20] The early dialogue *On Order* (386) makes the friends with whom he shared the Cassiciacum retreat in the winter of 386/87 his conversation partners and captures the camaraderie of all in a newfound spiritual purpose that charged their intellectual life. These friends, with the exception of his ever-present mother, are all men and, from the picture Augustine paints of their relationships, nothing sexual ensues between and among them. Indeed, in Augustine's judgment, the presence of sexual desire in a relationship makes it less than authentic, a reason in the *Confessions* for the anonymity in which Augustine keeps the woman with whom he had a common-law marriage of eleven years and who was the mother of his son.[21] In his anti-Pelagian writing *The Literal Meaning of Genesis* (401–414), Augustine even wonders why God fashioned a woman as Adam's companion if the man needed company and conversation. "How much more agreeably," Augustine claims, "could two male friends, rather than a man and a woman, enjoy companionship and conversation in a shared life together."[22]

Thus, we meet another portrayal of disjunctive desire: either the desire for a sexual other in which the desire itself is the embodiment of sin; or the desire for the nonsexual other, the friend, who, from Augustine's perspective and in his patriarchal and heterosexual assumptions, is a man. We noted how Augustine valued the spiritual companionship of the nonsexual other: his male friends and his mother. We might add God to the mix of nonsexual others with whom he desired to have a relationship. This is especially clear in the *Confessions* where Monica is portrayed throughout the narrative as the voice of God that Augustine first resists and then accepts. Noteworthy, too, is the spiritual climax to Augustine's personal narrative in Book 9 shortly before Monica's death when mother and son share a mystical vision of God.[23] This homology in the desire for the nonsexual other found in the relationships to God, mother, and friends is set in Augustine's mind over and against the desire for the sexual other, characterized by the tumultuous passion of which all are guilty and which all are obliged to resist, even those who have chosen the married life with its divine command to be fruitful and multiply.

Into this symbolics of human fallenness, we must also factor Augustine's willingness to follow Paul in understanding death itself as God's just punishment for sin, an explanation that both justifies God in the face of evil and denies the integrity of innocent suffering. For Augustine, all suffering, which finally culminates in the suffering of death, is guilty. Death is the deserved consequence of human sin, whose universality is causally aligned with the universality of death. Death and sexual desire, then, are dual bodily markers of sinfulness and so resemble each other in their bodily symptoms. Neither death nor sexual desire respects the human will, which cannot help but yield to both. The irresistible power of death, in this regard, possesses an analogue in the irresistible power of sexual passion, which, at least as desire if not as consummation, overwhelms the body, exposing the person's guilty and shameful powerlessness within the common sin of humanity.[24] Thus, for Augustine, erotic pleasure is saturated with deathliness. Logically in the Augustinian binary, freedom from erotic pleasure radiates the fullness of life, which flourishes only in relationship to the nonsexual other.

AN ANTHROPOLOGY OF DENIAL

Augustine's wisdom, insight, and creativity are renowned. Only the most myopic critic would question the power of Augustine's intellect, his erudition, or his inestimable contributions to what later Christians have esteemed in the tradition. Yet, many today would judge the Augustinian legacy to be very much a mixed bag and would find the very issue with which we are concerned here among its negative contents. Our modern discontent with Augustine centers on his influential account of human brokenness, which he represents in a theology of disjunctive desire. Parsed in the Augustinian mind-set of "either-or," death and eternal life square off as the work of sin and grace respectively. Death is equated with bodily desire, the physical dimensions of love, and passionate pleasure—all of which stand opposed to our fulfilled selves, the resurrected persons Christians hope to be in eternal life. The effect of this theological reasoning is that we understand ourselves as set against ourselves. Erotic desire, which motivates us, accompanies us, and through which we express and profoundly share ourselves with those closest to us, is judged, in this anthropology, to be not ourselves at all. Although Augustine imagined our bodies in the eschatological presence of the beatific vision, he imagined them as desireless to the same degree that he imagined them as sinless and deathless. An odd, but remarkably influential, interpretation of the fall thus sanctions an equally odd rejection of bodily desire and sexual pleasure as important dimensions of who we are in ourselves and in our relations to others. The desire for God entails the denial of bodily desires, which are never understood as love but only as personal or corporate sin.

This anthropology, which we can describe as an anthropology of denial, has been a mainstay of Western Christian consciousness throughout the centuries. Indeed, it has been so resilient that it has shifted shape in order to survive the confessional fragmentation of the Reformation era. In the medieval and Roman Catholic traditions, the anthropology of denial appears in the practice of a hierarchy of discipleship that valorizes the religious lives of ascetics over the religious lives of the laity. This vocational divide was disjunctively defined by the ascetical desire for spirit or the lay desire for bodies. It is not difficult to see the attractiveness of disjunctive desire for a celibate like Augustine.[25] Imagining the self as engaged in a struggle between flesh and spirit, sin and grace, sexual and nonsexual desire, and finally between death and life, allowed ascetics to place all of their commitments, promises, and goals squarely on the side of the angels and to configure reality itself in an utterly self-reifying way. The historical effects of this imaginary were such that all Christians—the few who were ascetics and the very many who were not—embraced its values, extending its anthropological denial of sexual desire into the self-understanding of the laity in the church as well. This version of the anthropology of denial supported the traditional assumption that saintliness was incompatible with sexual activity, a judgment that explains the paucity of canonized married saints in the Catholic tradition and, to the degree that women were prejudiciously associated with bodiliness, the preponderance of male over female ascetical saints.[26]

The Lutheran and Reformed traditions rejected the ascetical version of the Augustinian denial as incompatible with the doctrine of *sola gratia* ("grace alone") and indicted the ascetic on the charge of works righteousness, self-salvation by heroically virtuous deeds. However, the great Reformers affirmed the Augustinian denial in another form. Luther and Calvin, who resurrected the Augustinian doctrine of predestination to bolster the Pauline denial of natural virtue, despaired with Augustine that humanity after the fall and apart from grace was anything but spiritually dead. Here, in the Reformation theologies of justification, *gratia* and *quod in se est*, what one is by nature, are set off against each other, the *quod* now the concupiscent natural desire of all, understood not merely as inclination or temptation but rather as sin itself. The anthropology of denial in its Catholic style makes enacted sexual desire profane and makes ascetical celibacy a prerequisite of saintly virtue. The anthropology of denial in its Protestant style makes all natural, as opposed to graced, bodily actions profane. To paraphrase Paul in Romans 5:20, sin abounds, and we can only be grateful that grace, which is anything but us, abounds all the more.

AN ALTERNATE HISTORY OF THE AUGUSTINIAN TRADITION, OR THE POSSIBILITY OF A MORE DESIRABLE AUGUSTINE

A religious tradition is a function of the beliefs and practices of its members throughout the ages. What Christians hold in their hearts, profess in expressions of faith, and enact with their bodies in ways they judge to be truthful is what a tradition is. This means that the Augustinian anthropology of denial in its Catholic and Protestant styles is something of our own making. Why did we do this to ourselves? Why did the Christian tradition embrace this anthropology of denial so consistently? Perhaps historian of early Christianity Elaine Pagels's Freudian observation in *Adam, Eve, and the Serpent* captures something of an answer. We would rather feel guilty, she says, than helpless.[27] The guiltiness of the self set against itself in the anthropology of denial makes us actors in God's drama rather than bystanders to the otherwise random suffering that inevitably enters our lives and finally takes them. Guilty suffering is purposeful because its cause is so clearly identified as ourselves, thus placing our self-denial in the symmetry of the divine justice. Whether her answer is right or wrong, Pagels's mention of an alternative—that is, the acknowledgment of helplessness that may more truthfully describe our posture before death—reminds us of the simple fact that things need not be as they "Augustinianly" are. Dissatisfied with the Augustinian heritage, recent theology has shown that there are many theological directions to follow besides the tradition's main thoroughfare of sinful desire. An interesting exercise in alternate or hypothetical history might have us imagine what the consequences would have been had the young Augustine walked a different road suggested in his earliest work on desire, *On Free Choice of the Will*.

This early, anti-Manichean writing is Augustine's first foray into the theological construction of desire. Early in the text, he rejects any definition of evil that would measure it by its consequences in life or by appeal to conventional judgments, whether private or public. Rather, Augustine directs the reader to desire (*libido*) as the source of all evil.[28] Here, in the early Augustine, desire is false, but it is not particularly a function of sexuality or bodiliness itself. Desire is false because, when enacted, it values the lesser goods of creation over the supreme, uncreated goodness of God. We may be suspicious of the hierarchical worldview in which Augustine frames the workings of evil here, since we are aware of the history of effects of this mentality, especially when energized by religious values. However, Augustine's depiction of the hierarchy here only entails a valued distinction between the Creator and the creature, which I would take to be a basic belief. Moreover, his rendition of the hierarchy provides a framework for judging the idolatrous confusion of Creator and creature, which in itself still holds up as a respectable understanding of sin, especially for a culture likes ours, lost in the commodification of desire.

This earlier work could have made for a different Christian history because Augustine contrasts the false movement of the desiring will with its virtuous counterpart in order to illuminate the dynamics of free choice. Augustine does not use the language of desire to describe the experiential motivation that chooses God, portraying virtuous choice instead as guided by the natural inclination of reason toward the Creator.[29] Nevertheless, in another possible universe, he *could* have used the language of desire to describe virtuous inclination, and by doing so he *could* have valorized another kind of desire rooted in the mind, in the heart, and, if we really imagine wildly, in the body too. In this anti-Manichean work, Augustine makes every effort to affirm the goodness of all physical being, including of course the human body, and so might have affirmed a more holistic and integrated portrait of desire that did not deny the passionate body but instead claimed its natural desires as divinely created goodness. Had Augustine gone in this direction, then the result may very well have been an untragic account of the human condition that avoided the anthropology of denial and that, presuming Augustine's comparable influence on the tradition in this imaginary, might have led to a very different Christian history. In such an alternate history, sexual desire and the desire for God would not be disjunctive alternatives but would both be desires for the good whenever sexual desire truly pursues goodness and the desire for God is not mendacious idolatry. In such an alternate history, theological values would not support a hierarchy of discipleship, nor would bodily desire be configured as sin itself. In such an alternate history, guilt would not be a powerless desire to be self-importantly powerful in the long history of sin (as it is in Pagels's psychological diagnosis) but an authentic response to the failure of passionate desire's natural goodness.

I actually think that we can find pieces of this desirable Augustine in the pages of the *Confessions*, a work well on the way to Augustine's developed anthropology of denial. As we have seen, Augustine sews the seams of his autobiographical chapters with interludes of divine praise that powerfully express a deep yearning for God. Perhaps we can read again the text's opening lines, though now from the perspective of our brief experiment in alternate history, and with changes in the translation to make the desire it expresses more inclusive: "The thought of you stirs [one] so deeply that [one] cannot be content unless he [or she] praises you, because you made us for yourself and our hearts find no peace until they rest in you."[30] Divorced from the text's narrative of sinful bodily desire, this passage, and many like it, portray the desire for God in seemingly erotic imagery that both elevates the creature into the mysterious glories of the creator and fathoms God in the depths of the self. If Augustine's thought had imagined desire in this way and made room for two kinds of desire—one good and one evil, and both desires of the whole self— then the tradition would not have had to face the Augustinian either-or that gained authority in various disjunctive ways: ascetic or lay, nature or grace, the denial of self or the affirmation of God.

In my own desire to say something discussable about a great mind in a few pages, I am aware that I have passed over Augustine's account of history in the *City of God*. Extending my thought-experiment to that big book would not be difficult. The *City of God* is, in many respects, a politicization of the anthropology of denial. For Augustine, desire unleashed in history explains the violence that riddles the earthly city and that makes it so in need of divine rescue. Am I wrong in thinking that as much as contemporary theologians tend to disdain Augustine's anthropology as an account of the self, they are rather attracted to its political version as an account of the violence of history, in our own day specifically as the deleterious workings of globalization and empire? If so, is this because Augustine has explained history's habitual cycle of violence well or because we, as his theological heirs, have been seduced by his tragic vision to the point that we fail to see the ways in which erotic desire is at work in the body politic too, perhaps in some of the places that we only judge to be embodied fallenness, violently passionate, and absent of love? Like the great thinker he is, Augustine leaves us with more questions to ponder about the selves we are and the selves we might be.

Further Suggested Readings

Brown, Peter. *Augustine of Hippo: A Biography.* Berkeley: University of California Press, 1967.

—————. *The Body and Society: Men, Women, and Sexual Renunciation in Early Christianity.* New York: Columbia University Press, 1988.

Evans, G. R. *Augustine on Evil.* Cambridge: Cambridge University Press, 1982.

Fredriksen, Paula. *Augustine on Romans: Propositions from the Epistle to the Romans: Unfinished Commentary on the Epistle to the Romans.* Chico, Calif.: Scholars, 1982.

O'Donnell, James J. *Augustine: A New Biography.* New York: Ecco/HarperCollins, 2005.

Pagels, Elaine. *Adam, Eve, and the Serpent: Sex and Politics in Early Christianity.* New York: Random House, 1988.

CHAPTER 5

Thomas Aquinas on the Body and Bodily Passions

Corey Barnes

SCHOLASTICISM EXERCISED A PROFOUND INFLUENCE on Christianity in the medieval West, and Thomas Aquinas (1225–1274) was one of its foremost figures.[1] Aquinas's writings both reflect general trends in medieval Christian thought and display a brilliance of their own. Aquinas employed the methods and newly available sources of Scholasticism. At the same time, he broke from typical views in recognizing *concupiscentia* (concupiscence, sensual appetite) as a natural aspect of human nature rather than a corruption of that nature.[2] Aquinas's personal narrative lacks a dramatic conversion parallel to Augustine's own experience of struggling with concupiscence, but Aquinas's apparent relative freedom from such struggles should not be confused with ignorance of or unconcern about the body and bodily passions. Aquinas discussed the body and bodily passions in several contexts, ranging from questions on the soul to treatments of ethics to discussions of the afterlife. The task of summarizing Aquinas's views on the body and bodily passions requires much framing and exposition to avoid erroneous assumptions and to highlight the typical and the novel aspects of his thought. From a modern perspective, Aquinas could seem to harbor very negative views of the body and bodily passions; yet, compared to the standards of medieval thought, Aquinas viewed the body and bodily passions in a remarkably positive light. This essay will present various contexts where Aquinas discussed the body and bodily passions and gesture toward how Aquinas's approach might be recontextualized to apply, with limitations, to contemporary reflections on the body and sexuality.

A theme underlying many of Aquinas's theological works is the common medieval metaphor of life as a journey to God. This appears both on the grand level of structural organization and in Aquinas's detailed responses to specific questions. For Aquinas, God is the answer to the question of happiness every individual invariably asks. God as the supreme good (*summum bonum*) stands alone as the unchanging good capable of fulfilling the human yearning for happiness. After the fall and the diverse effects of original sin, human beings mire themselves in a futile pursuit of lesser, mutable goods. These goods are not necessarily bad or harmful, but preferring lesser goods to the supreme good cannot help but remain a self-defeating enterprise. Aquinas identified this as a basic truth of the human condition, but his theological vision stressed that the pessimistic reality of sin does not determine the story of humanity. Aquinas's reflections on the body and bodily passions offer a distant glimpse of the deeper optimism with which he views the unfolding human drama. At the same time, they reveal the subordinate status of the body and the provisional nature of the bodily passions and sensible goods.

INTELLECTUAL BACKGROUND

Scholasticism often has an ill-deserved reputation as a stagnant investigation of minutiae; however, this reputation ignores the fundamental dynamism of Scholastic thought. Aquinas taught, thought, and wrote in a Scholastic idiom representing the confluence of several factors, including the rise of universities, the use of dialectical procedures, and the acquisition of Greek and Arabic philosophical texts. These factors placed Scholastic thinkers at the center of an impressive intellectual movement open to new questions and new answers to perennial questions.[3] The most important of these factors for understanding Aquinas's intellectual background is the availability of new sources, most notably the writings of Aristotle. Arabic translations of Aristotle's works and Arabic commentaries on Aristotle became available to the

Latin West during the rise of Scholasticism. Use of Aristotelian philosophy, in varying degrees, became a hallmark of Scholastic thought.[4]

Prior to the Scholastic period, the dominant philosophical influence of Christian thought was Neoplatonism. This influence persisted due especially to the stature of Augustine (354–430) and the later fifth- or sixth-century theologian Pseudo-Dionysius the Aeropagite, both of whom learned much from Neoplatonic sources (Plotinus, Porphyry, and Proclus). Augustine and Pseudo-Dionysius were held in the highest regard throughout the Middle Ages. To this Neoplatonic inheritance were added the *libri naturales* (works on natural science and philosophy) of Aristotle and commentaries on Aristotle. These works quickly developed a following despite prohibitions to teaching them at the University of Paris. By the middle of the thirteenth century, the curriculum was largely Aristotelian. Thomas Aquinas began to study Aristotle with his teacher Albertus Magnus and later began his own commentaries on Aristotle using the new translations produced by William of Moerbeke.[5] Aquinas's commentaries indicate both his serious engagement with Aristotle's thought and his sense that students needed guidance to accept the truths conveyed by Aristotle while rejecting the errors. Many were, in Aquinas's opinion, being led astray on certain topics by the commentaries of Muslim scholars Avicenna (Ibn Sina) and Averroes (Ibn Rushd). Aquinas was commenting on Aristotle throughout the composition of his unfinished masterpiece, the *Summa theologiae* (1266–1273), which serves as this essay's primary source.[6] The *Summa*'s constant references to Aristotle or to Aristotelian ideas thus come as little surprise. Aristotle was particularly important for Aquinas's understanding of the body as a necessary constituent of a human being.

Another factor of Aquinas's intellectual background relevant to the present topic is his membership in the Dominican Order (*Ordo Praedicatorum*, Order of Preachers). The mendicant orders (Dominicans and Franciscans) were a thirteenth-century novelty that faced serious opposition at the University of Paris and elsewhere. These orders embraced a rigorous form of poverty, usually known as evangelical poverty, and devoted themselves to preaching and performing the sacraments. The mendicant lifestyle faced serious criticism from many professors at the University of Paris and several church officials. Aquinas rebutted challenges to the mendicant life during his first period of teaching in Paris and continued to articulate and defend the mendicant ideals in his *Summa theologiae*.[7] He began working on the *Summa* at a Dominican house of studies in Rome to provide his fellow Dominicans with a work covering moral theology embedded within a concise treatment of dogmatic theology.[8] He intended the *Summa* to provide a concise and coherent introduction to dogmatic and moral theology for friars preparing to fulfill their charge as mendicants. Thus, the context for Aquinas's treatment of ethical issues surrounding sexuality and the bodily passions was this: Aquinas was a celibate writing for other celibates who would preach to and hear the confessions of noncelibates.

The negative and gendered perceptions of the body common in medieval thought are well known. As a general rule, the body was associated with ignorance and sin while the soul was associated with knowledge and virtue. Women were identified with the body and its negative connotations; men were identified with the soul and its lofty connotations.[9] Scholars have also noted positive views and uses of the body in medieval Christianity. Belief in the resurrection of the body and debates about the mechanisms of such resurrection were standard features of medieval Christianity, indicating a positive appreciation of the body.[10] With the rise of *imitatio Christi* (imitation of Christ), which focused on Christ's humanity and on ascetic practices perfecting the penitent in Christ's image, the spiritual value of the body was highlighted.[11] Too much should not be made of these generalities, but they do provide a context for situating Aquinas's positive estimation of the body. Scholastic thought was not insulated from larger trends of medieval Christianity, nor were those trends immune to the influence of Scholastic thought.

BODY AND SOUL

Questions regarding the relationship of soul and body gained a new urgency in the thirteenth century with the recovery of Aristotelian texts. The spectrum of views responded differently to two main concerns. On the one hand, Scholastics sought to defend the immortality of the soul as a substance or a something and, on the other hand, sought to preserve the unity of the body and soul. A Platonic conception was thought better to preserve the former, while an Aristotelian conception was thought better to preserve the latter. Plato viewed the soul as a person and construed the unity of the body and soul as a unity of operation. In Plato's view, the soul functions as motor for the body but remains separate from and superior to the body. The standard example is that the soul uses the body as a sailor uses a ship. Prior to the introduction of an Aristotelian conception of the soul, some form of a Platonic understanding held sway in Christian thought. While Aquinas was familiar with Platonic views of the soul,[12] his anthropology rested largely on his Aristotelian understanding of the human being as a "hylemorphic" unity—that is, a human being is a unity composed of matter (Greek *hyle*) and form (Greek *morphe*).[13] Aquinas held that the soul is the substantial form of the body, meaning the soul gives the body being but also depends on the body for knowledge and perfection. This rigorous Aristotelianism distinguished Aquinas from his contemporaries.[14]

The *Summa*'s investigation of humanity begins with the soul. As the principle of a human being's "intellectual" operation (the processes of knowing and reasoning), the soul must be incorporeal and subsistent. The soul is a subsistent thing capable of surviving the body. As a spiritual substance, though of the "lowest grade," the soul does not depend upon the body for its existence and can continue its intellective operations when separated from the body.[15] However, the soul is not a complete thing. Aquinas refused to identify the human being with the soul alone and made clear the soul's perfection is realized only through informing the body. The soul is the substantial form of the human body, giving the body a share in its being. The soul has "an aptitude and natural inclination for union with the body" and finds its perfection in this union.[16] Aquinas stressed that the soul is not a person or a human being but, rather, a part of a human being.[17] A part finds the perfection of its nature in the whole. The soul without the body is partial and imperfect. Aquinas's insistence on the soul as the one substantial form of the body represents a departure from the dominant trends of Christian reflection on the soul.[18]

Aquinas presented the human body as informed by the intellectual soul, yielding the human being. This entails both a logical priority to the soul and the superiority of the soul to the body; yet, Aquinas assigned positive value to the body as a necessary constituent of the human being. The intellectual operation of the soul is proportioned to the perfection of its nature in union with the body.[19] Aquinas followed Aristotle in rejecting a Platonic theory of *anamnesis* (learning as reminiscence of innate knowledge) and in suggesting, to the contrary, that the human intellect must receive sense data as the foundation of the intellective process. Sense reality is preserved in the imagination as a "phantasm" or a likeness of a particular thing.[20] The intellect turns to the phantasms and abstracts from them. The process of turning to and abstracting from the phantasms lies at the heart of human cognition and depends upon the union of body and soul. For Aquinas, the principle operation of a human being is this intellectual understanding, and the ultimate happiness of a human being is the perfection of understanding. The ultimate happiness of a human being thus begins with the soul receiving from the body. In sum, Aquinas's presentation of the human being as a hylemorphic unity of body and soul granted a positive value to the body. The body, as an integral component of the human being, contributes to the perfection of the human being and so, also, to the perfection of the soul. According to Aquinas, the unity of operation between the body and soul must be founded upon a metaphysical unity.

BODILY PASSIONS AND HUMAN REASON

Exploring the role of the bodily passions or "sensitive appetites" (desires for things pleasing to the senses) leads us to a distinction fundamental to Aquinas's anthropology—namely, the distinction between the state of integrity and the state of sin. Before turning to the role of sensuality in each state, we must understand his views on the faculty of sensuality itself.

The "appetitive faculty" can be divided into the intellective appetite and the sensitive appetite. Sensuality designates the sensitive appetite, which inclines the person toward something desirable to the senses. A pressing question for Aquinas concerned whether sensuality is obedient to reason. He argued that the faculties of sensuality are moved according to a kind of judgment in which particular reason is directed through universal reason. In other words, universal principles are applied to individual cases. The sensitive appetite does not desire the universal good but, rather, particular goods. The faculties of sensuality thus obey reason by obeying the deduction of particular conclusions from universal principles.[21] The sensitive appetite is subject to the rule of the will in execution. Aquinas noted that human beings are not immediately moved according to the sensitive appetites but are only moved when the will consents. This differentiates human beings from non-rational animals.[22]

With these basic points of reference in mind, let us turn to the condition of human beings in the state of integrity or innocence, before sin and its diverse consequences. This state is marked by rectitude of order known as original justice. In the state of original justice, human beings were subject to God, sensuality was subject to reason, and the body was subject to the soul. The proper order of sensuality to reason and of the body to the soul most concerns us here. Aquinas argued that humanity was created in the image and likeness of God. Every aspect of creation displays some likeness to God insofar as it exists at all and so participates in the divine good. Human beings particularly image God in the rational soul or mind; yet, even the body participates in the image of God to the extent that it is properly ordered to the rational soul. Human beings were good but not perfect. The state of integrity represented the divine intention for humanity; it indicated the beginning of a journey according to which human beings, aided by grace, could merit ultimate beatitude. Grace elevated the natural good of human actions to the supernatural level, fulfilling the promise offered in human nature. It is in this sense that "grace does not undue nature but perfects it [*gratia non tollit naturam sed perficit*]."[23] Since Aquinas believed that human beings are intended to reach beatitude based upon their own merit and that merit requires elevation by grace, it follows that even in the state of integrity, human beings required grace to achieve their ultimate end. Aquinas argued that human beings were founded in grace in the state of integrity and that grace made possible the proper ordering characteristic of this state.

In the state of integrity, sensuality was subject to reason and the body was subject to the soul. The sensual appetite is characterized by certain passions of the soul, some directed toward goods and others toward evils. Aquinas held that the passions of the soul of human beings in the state of integrity were directed toward goods that were present or that would be enjoyed in their proper time but were not directed toward absent goods, toward goods that should not be possessed at that time, or toward evils. The lack of these passions depends upon the circumstances of innocence and provides for a harmony of passions under reason. Aquinas further argued that in the state of innocence the sensual appetite was wholly obedient to reason. He drew this out by contrasting the sensual appetite in the state of innocence and in the state of sin or corruption:

> [The passions of the soul in the state of innocence] were there otherwise than they are in us. The sensual appetite, where the passions reside, is not totally subject to reason in us. Sometimes the passions prevent or impede the judgment of reason in us; at other times, they follow the judgment of reason in as much as the sensual appetite obeys reason to some extent. In the state of innocence, however, the inferior appetite was totally subject to reason. In that state there were no passions of the soul unless they followed the judgment of reason.[24]

In the state of integrity, reason did not dominate sensuality.[25] No conflict arose between sensuality and reason, because the sensual appetite was wholly ordered by and to reason. This harmony was facilitated by the external conditions of the state of innocence and was aided by grace. This perfect ordering of sensuality to reason was not natural to humanity based upon its own structure but resulted from divine assistance. Again, concupiscence is natural to humanity, but in its natural state it is not perfectly or wholly subject to reason.

The proper unity and harmony between body and soul follows much the same lines. In the state of integrity, the soul was given a supernatural gift according to which it could preserve the body from all corruption as long as it remained properly subject to God.[26] By virtue of this gift, the soul preserved the body from corruption and undue passion. This does not imply, Aquinas was careful to note, that there were no bodily needs. For example, human beings in the state of integrity needed food. The supernatural power allowing for the preservation of the body and so for immortality did not remove the natural need for food.[27] Aquinas repeatedly mentioned that human beings constitute a medium between incorruptible and corruptible creatures since the soul is naturally incorruptible and the body is naturally corruptible. Because of this mediating position, it was fitting that generation of the human race in the state of integrity happen through sexual reproduction. In defending this position, Aquinas appealed to a principle crucial to his theological anthropology: "Those things that are natural to human beings were neither subtracted from nor given to human beings through sin."[28] He held that sexual reproduction is natural to humanity and was present in the state of innocence.

Aquinas elaborated the characteristics of sex in the state of innocence by contrasting it with sex in the state of sin or corruption. Sex in both states shares the function of generation through union of male and female. Sex in the state of corruption adds "a certain deformity of immoderate concupiscence," and when the "pleasure of sex and the fervor of concupiscence are not moderated by reason, a human being is made into a beast."[29] This seems to suggest that sexual pleasure is greater in the state of corruption than in the state of integrity and that this abundance of pleasure overwhelms reason; however, the opposite is the case. Aquinas argued for greater sensual pleasure in the state of innocence on account of the purity of human nature and the perfection of the bodily senses. The deformity of immoderate concupiscence that characterizes sex in the state of corruption results not from an increased magnitude of sexual pleasure but from the decreased moderation of reason over the sensual appetite. Aquinas provided an analogy with food. Someone who eats in moderation does not experience less pleasure in food than a glutton; the glutton cannot be satisfied with this pleasure and immoderately desires food beyond what is reasonable. The state of integrity did not restrict the fullness of pleasure but only "the ardor of immoderate passion and the disquiet of the soul."[30] Aquinas went beyond simply allowing for sexual reproduction in the state of integrity; he affirmed that sex in the state of integrity involved a fullness of pleasure reflecting the harmony of body and soul. That harmony is disrupted by sin, and so now attention must turn to the problem of concupiscence in the state of corruption.

Since the passions of the soul relate to the sensitive appetite, they depend not simply on the disposition of the soul but also on the disposition of the body, which raises the question of the relationship between reason and the sensitive appetite in the state of corruption. Absent from the state of corruption is that grace according to which the body was perfectly ordered by and to the soul. Consequently, the body is no longer wholly subject to the rule of reason. Aquinas was clear that the body's subjection to the rule of reason in the state of integrity was never a question of despotic or forced rule. There remains even in the state of corruption some rule of reason over the body and bodily passions. (Recall that the sensitive appetite depends upon a kind of judgment in which particular reason is directed through universal reason. Thus, insofar as the sensitive appetite is determined by a judgment, it is subject to the rule of reason.) In contrast, "the quality and disposition of the body are not subject to the rule of reason. . . . the movement of the sensitive appetite is impeded by rather than wholly subjected to the rule of reason."[31] In the state of corruption, the graced order and harmony of body and soul has been disrupted but not severed. The intimacy between sensitive appetite and reason enjoyed in the state of innocence has given way to some estrangement. This estrangement allows for immoderate passions to develop and even to overwhelm the judgment of reason. This state of tension and temptation is natural to humanity.

This brings us to the specific question of concupiscence in the state of corruption. Concupiscence illuminates the change from integrity to corruption with particular clarity since it involves the soul, the body, and the subjection of bodily passions to reason. Concupiscence relates to the good of the whole human being, body and soul, which locates it within the sensitive appetite. The passion of concupiscence occurs when an absent but desirable object of the senses draws the individual.[32] This passion can either be natural or unnatural. Natural concupiscence is directed toward what Aquinas labeled natural sensible goods or goods fitting to bodily nature, such as food and sex. Human beings share this natural concupiscence with other animals. Aquinas characterized this natural concupiscence as concupiscence of the flesh, which relates to the preservation of the individual or of the species.[33] Unnatural concupiscence is found in human beings alone and occurs when sensible goods fitting to bodily nature are desired beyond what is natural. A hungry person naturally desires food for the preservation of the body. A glutton unnaturally desires food in the excessive pursuit of pleasure focused upon a natural sensible good. The state of corruption, marked as it is by a disorder of body and soul, tends to foster this unnatural concupiscence. Human beings are born into this state, but their individual actions contribute to the formation of habits that dispose them to specific actions. As an individual repeats acts of unnatural concupiscence, the inclination to such acts develops into a steady disposition. Aquinas characterized unnatural concupiscence, whether directed at natural goods beyond the rational needs of the nature or at unnatural goods (e.g., wealth or ornaments), as concupiscence of the eyes.[34]

Aquinas also examined the connection between concupiscence and original sin. He considered original sin both in its formal and in its material aspects. Original sin is formally the privation of original justice, which provided the requisite grace for the soul to be subject to God and for the body to be subject to the soul. Original sin also involves a disordering of the soul's faculties most evident in the turn away from the supreme good to lesser, changeable goods. The common name for this disordering is concupiscence.[35] This identification concerns only unnatural concupiscence. Natural concupiscence follows the rule of reason in desiring those goods necessary for preservation of individual or species. Unnatural concupiscence exceeds any rational limits, and it is this concupiscence that must be identified with the self-destructive yearnings of a disordered individual. Aquinas could hardly have been clearer: concupiscence itself naturally desires the rationally validated sensible goods necessary or useful for the individual or the species. Far from being a base corruption of nature, concupiscence promotes the continuation and perfection of nature. Original sin represents a corruption of nature materially synonymous with unnatural concupiscence. This unnatural concupiscence perpetuates the soul's disorder, slowly but surely diminishing the good of human nature.

When reflecting on original sin's diminishment of the good of human nature, Aquinas distinguished three ways to consider that good. First, the good of human nature can be considered in terms of the properties naturally pertaining to the species. Second, it can be considered in terms of an inclination to virtue characteristic of the state of integrity. Third, it can be considered in terms of original justice. Original sin, Aquinas concluded, diminishes the good in the first sense not at all, diminishes the second good in part, and diminishes the third good entirely.[36] This provides a useful spectrum for investigating the bodily passions in the state of corruption, particularly in terms of the first two goods of human nature. Bodily passions relate to the intrinsic principles of human nature and are undiminished in their good from this perspective. The diminished inclination to virtue consequent to original sin combined with the disordered relationship of body to soul yields unnatural concupiscence. As original sin diminishes the inclination to virtue, reason can no longer moderate the sensual faculty's ordering of desirable objects. Aquinas characterized this disruption as the wound or injury of concupiscence.[37]

In summary, the hylemorphic nature of a human being grants positive value to the body and bodily passions. The faculty of sensuality is a natural and beneficial feature of humanity, providing the sense data necessary for cognition and fostering the preservation of the individual and species. Aided by original justice in the state of integrity, the body and the sensitive appetite are perfectly ordered to the soul and reason. This proper ordering guarantees not only the harmony of passions before sin but also the fullness of sensual pleasure in sexuality. Original sin disrupts this proper order with the result that the sensitive appetite immoderately desires mutable goods beyond any rational limits and without any proportioned relation to the preservation of the individual or the species. Original sin thus deforms concupiscence into an unnatural appetite for sensitive goods. This unnatural concupiscence must always be distinguished from natural concupiscence. Concupiscence relates to the good of the whole human being, the conjoined body and soul. The privation of original justice and the diminished inclination to virtue following original sin wound the whole human being, body and soul. These wounds do not erase nature, but they hinder the natural functioning of the body and soul. This disruption and disorder foster unnatural concupiscence, which affects the whole human being.

SEXUAL PLEASURE
Aquinas presented concupiscence as natural to humanity and argued for the fullness of sexual pleasure in the state of integrity. This positive evaluation of concupiscence distinguishes Aquinas from his contemporaries, but it does not imply an unequivocally positive evaluation of sexual pleasure. Aquinas noted the disorder of human beings after the fall and the consequent immoderate concupiscence that pursues sexual pleasure as an end in itself. To round out Aquinas's views on sexual pleasure, it is necessary to introduce a third and final state: beatitude. Beatitude is the direct vision of God and the corresponding felicity of this vision, and it is to this happiness that human beings ought to move. The scheme of life as a journey ends in beatitude and in the perfection of the whole human being, soul and resurrected body. Aquinas allowed no role for sex or sexual pleasure in this perfected state.

Aquinas never elaborated a complete or coherent theory of sexual pleasure. Reflecting on his views requires stringing together disparate contexts, which reveals positive views on the body and bodily passions along with an underlying subordination of sexual pleasure to the soul's intellectual enjoyment of God. This subordination is not limited to sexual pleasure but extends also to the parallel pleasures of food and drink. In other words, Aquinas cast in the same light pleasures relating to those acts that preserve the individual and the species. The individual is preserved through food, and the species is preserved through sexual reproduction. In both cases, the proper and rational end of the act is preservation rather than pleasure. Eating or sex should only be performed for their rationally appointed ends. Pursuing food or sex for pleasure contravenes reason and the body's proper subjection to reason and to the soul. Aquinas regarded the pleasures of food and sex as accompanying goods to the true goods of sustenance and reproduction. Pleasure is only a good as a subordinate and accompanying good to the true end of each action.

Aquinas made clear the subordinate nature of sexual pleasure when discussing the possibility of sex among the resurrected. He denied that there will be sex or the use of food among the resurrected. Given that Aquinas recognized sexual reproduction and concupiscence as natural to humanity, does their absence in the resurrected state constitute some diminishment of nature? Aquinas believed it does not constitute any diminishment of nature or of enjoyment. Exploring the reasons for this belief reveals the provisional nature of sensible goods and the subordination of the resurrected body to the beatified soul.

The licit and proper aim of sex is reproduction. Aquinas was clear on this point throughout his writings. This need not imply that sexual pleasure is in some sense corrupt; in fact, it is part of the original intention of human beings. Nevertheless, sexual pleasure should never by itself be the aim of sex. This renders sex among the resurrected problematic. There will be no need for sexual reproduction of human beings in the beatific state because the immortal life of the beatified will itself preserve the species. Since there will be no need for reproduction, the only aim of sex would be pleasure.[38] Pursuing sex solely for pleasure indicates a disorder within the individual, a lack of proper subordination of body to soul. Those enjoying the beatific vision will enjoy also a perfect order of body to soul, which precludes the pursuit of sensual pleasure as an end in itself. Aquinas was quite clear that sensual pleasures have no role in beatitude.[39] The felicity of beatitude relates to the soul and overflows to the body. Sensual pleasures contribute nothing to this felicity. In other words, the presence of sexual pleasure among the resurrected would not increase or complete their happiness.[40] Mistaking the absence of sensual pleasure for the absence of some degree or type of happiness represents a fundamental misunderstanding of the beatific vision as the fulfillment of human nature.

On the surface, Aquinas's denial of sexual pleasure or any sensual pleasure among the resurrected seems not to sit well with his affirmation of concupiscence and sexual reproduction within the original intention of humanity. What it actually reveals is the subordinate and provisional status of the body and bodily passions.[41] The body is an essential part of human nature and serves several essential functions. Without the body, a human being is incomplete. The full felicity of a human being requires not simply the soul's beatitude but also the soul's union to a perfected body. The soul's beatitude overflows into the body, allowing the body some share in the soul's felicity. For Aquinas, as for other medieval Scholastics, true happiness rests in the soul. The beatific vision provides a magnificent bliss surpassing any other enjoyment imaginable. Given this experience of unqualified joy, any lesser pleasure or enjoyment would merely distract one from happiness. When the body's order to the soul is perfected in beatitude, the body will complete the human being and receive the overflow of the soul's glorification. To whatever extent one can speak of bodily passion and pleasure in this state, it would simply indicate the body's reception of enjoyment from the soul.

LIMITATIONS AND POSSIBILITIES
OF A THOMISTIC APPROACH TO THE BODY

Aquinas viewed the body as fundamentally good and as a necessary constituent of a human being. From a modern perspective, this can easily seem a most unremarkable claim, but it is remarkable in the context of common medieval Christian views on the body. Beyond simply claiming that the body is good and a necessary component of a human being, Aquinas affirmed that the human person's identity depends on the body as well as on the soul. A human person is not simply or even primarily the soul or the mind. Personal identity is determined as well by the body. An individual is this particular individual due to the body and soul together.[42] Without the body, the soul loses the perfection of the species. More importantly, it loses its personal completion. A complete human being requires a rational soul informing a body. The body provides the sense data from and through which the soul acquires knowledge. The body and bodily pleasure are good but subject to misuse and corruption. Sin and the loss of original justice disrupt the proper order of body to soul and of soul to God. This state of disorder is marked by a confused preference for lesser, mutable goods to the true good.

Aquinas was the first medieval to recognize concupiscence as natural to humanity. This represents a fundamental shift away from the Augustinian association of concupiscence and sin. While fundamental, this shift is incomplete, and here we see the limitations in Aquinas's views on the body and its pleasures. The body is good, but the goods of the body are merely provisional. Sensual pleasures are goods accompanying the true good of an action's rational end. The removal of this rational end removes too the reason for the accompanying sensual pleasures. The resurrected body will contribute no pleasure to the beatified human being; rather, it will simply receive the overflow of glorification from the soul. The body and bodily passions are good but subordinate to the soul and to the goods of the soul. This is clear at every stage of a human being's journey but never clearer than in the beatific state. Aquinas's presentation of the afterlife makes clear that bodily goods are provisional goods and nothing more. Is the subordination of the body to the soul so complete as to undermine Aquinas's positive views on the body and bodily passions?

Aquinas's views on sensual pleasure in general and sexual pleasure in particular might be regarded as too narrow, negative, or limited for any contemporary application. To whatever extent his views can be recontextualized for contemporary aims, this recontextualization must begin with Aquinas's presentation of the human being as a hylemorphic unity. The basic stance of this notion outlives the Aristotelian metaphysics underlying its formulation by Aquinas.[43] Any attempt to take seriously the human condition and the role of sexuality and the erotic in that condition must offer some compelling response to any strictly articulated mind-body dualism. Aquinas initiated a fundamental shift by presenting concupiscence, even in its relative freedom from reason, as natural to humanity.

These two key aspects of Aquinas's thought, namely hylemorphism and concupiscence as natural to humanity, provide the requisite foundation for any adequate treatment of the body and its passions because they value the body as a necessary component of human nature and personal identity. Fostering a positive identification with the body represents a first step toward promoting the inherent worth of the body and its passions. This sense of inherent worth can be extended to and can be used to extend Aquinas's views on concupiscence and sensual pleasure. This extension requires a recontextualization of sensual pleasure in general and sexuality in particular. Aquinas restricted the rational end of sex to reproduction. This restriction denigrates the natural good of sexual pleasure by reducing it to an irrational and accompanying good. Removing this restriction opens new options for recognizing the inherent worth of the body and its appetites. Aquinas's hylemorphism and positive judgment of concupiscence can be developed to recognize sensual pleasure as not only a natural good but also as a rational good. This development would continue the shift begun by Aquinas in presenting concupiscence as natural to humanity and would provide a solid foundation for contemporary approaches to the body and sexuality.

Further Suggested Readings

Stump, Eleonore. *Aquinas.* New York: Routledge, 2003.

Torrell, Jean-Pierre. *Saint Thomas Aquinas.* Vol. 1: *The Person and His Work.* Trans. Robert Royal. Washington, D.C.: Catholic University of America Press, 1996.

Van Nieuwenhove, Rik, and Joseph Wawrykow, eds. *The Theology of Thomas Aquinas.* Notre Dame, Ind.: University of Notre Dame Press, 2005.

Wawrykow, Joseph. *The Westminster Handbook to Thomas Aquinas.* Louisville: Westminster John Knox, 2005.

CHAPTER 6

Humanae vitae, *Sexual Ethics, and the Roman Catholic Church*

Tatha Wiley

IN TWENTIETH-CENTURY DOCUMENTS on social, economic, and political matters, popes and the Second Vatican Council have spoken to the world with credibility and poignancy about the exploitation and oppression that fuel injustice for much of the world's population.[1] Addressing both contemporary socioeconomic configuration and the scientific worldview, the Roman Catholic Church has entered into dialogue with the modern world, contributing even research of its own scientists and the values of its social teaching. In many conciliar and papal documents, the world is dynamic and open, and truth is on the move in a constant formulation of insights and discoveries.

In the church's pronouncements on sexual ethics, however, this dynamic world disappears and the circumscribed one of neo-Scholasticism returns. Truth becomes permanent, absolute, and unchanging. Laws embedded in the intelligibility of the created order reveal the ends toward which the nature of each species is oriented. These laws, expressions of God's will for the universe, are known with certitude by the *magisterium*, the teaching office of the church. They are pronounced as normative to those who belong to the church. Emblematic of such teaching and instructive about the features and roots of its teaching have been Roman Catholic pronouncements on birth control.

The preeminent example is the 1968 encyclical, *Humanae vitae*, "On the Regulation of Birth" (hereafter *HV*). There Pope Paul VI reaffirmed the church's long-standing prohibition of any direct interference with the procreative capacity of sexual relations.[2] This had been a theme of earlier encyclicals, notably Pope Leo's encyclical on Christian marriage issued in 1880, *Arcanum divinae sapientiae*. Other twentieth-century encyclicals also specifically prohibited artificial birth control. Pius XI did so in *Casti connubii*, issued in 1930, which denounced it in the strongest of terms, calling contraception "intrinsically against nature" and a "sin against nature." By deliberately frustrating the reproductive capacity of the conjugal act, he wrote, the couple commits "a deed which is shameful and intrinsically vicious."[3] Papal documents were not the first to condemn contraception. In 1140 C.E., the influential moral theologian Gratian included a prohibition against contraception in his code of canon law, *A Harmony of Conflicting Canons*, known as the *Decretum*. He followed Augustine in emphasizing that marital sex is only to be used for procreation and not for pleasure, as did Pope Gregory IX in 1234 (the first pope to do so).[4] Pope Sixtus called contraception homicide in 1588. In *Humanae vitae*—despite explicit rejections of its moral necessity by his own study commission, convened after Vatican II—Paul VI reaffirmed this longstanding prohibition against any interference with the procreative potentiality of sexual relations.[5] John Paul II, who succeeded to the papacy in 1978, fully supported the presuppositions and method of *HV* during his long pontificate.

This essay conducts a critical assessment of sexual ethics in *HV* in light of popular Roman Catholic dissent, criticisms by Roman Catholic moral theologians, and the broader history of patriarchy in the Christian tradition within which it must be situated. This assessment will demonstrate that the moral teaching on sex of the Roman Catholic Church presupposes a particular concept of the purpose of sex and marriage in the created order. This conception is connected with God's intention, and there is no hint that this purpose could be any different than what the church teaches. Following this critical assessment, I propose an alternative Roman Catholic sexual ethics that, while drawing on the best of Catholic tradition, is more open and dynamic.

SEXUAL ETHICS IN *HUMANAE VITAE*

Citing the Second Vatican Council, *HV* stated that "Marriage and conjugal love are by their nature ordained toward the procreation and education of children" (#9). *HV* asserted that "procreative finality applies to the totality of married life" (#4). Indeed, these conceptions of sex and marriage taught by the *magisterium* are "established by God" and "written into the actual nature of man and of woman" (#12). In the end, Paul VI argued, man "has no dominion over his specifically sexual faculties, for these are concerned by their very nature with the generation of life, of which God is the source" (#13).

The church's sexual ethics makes biology absolute: procreative sex is moral, nonprocreative sex is immoral. The moral imperative is explicit: each and every "marital act must of necessity retain its intrinsic relationship to the procreation of human life" (#11). To have sex for any purpose other than that for which it was divinely created is, Pope Paul wrote, "repugnant to the nature of man and woman." Every couple must recognize, the pope wrote, that

> an act of mutual love which impairs the capacity to transmit life which God the Creator, through specific laws, has built into it, frustrates His design which constitutes the norm of marriage, and contradicts the will of the Author of life. Hence to use this divine gift while depriving it, even if only partially, of its meaning and purpose, is equally repugnant to the nature of man and of woman, and is consequently in opposition to the plan of God. . . . Sexual faculties . . . are concerned by their very nature with the generation of life, of which God is the source. (#13)

The sexual directives of *HV* followed many centuries of such assistance, beginning in the sixth century, when Irish monks initiatied the practice of confession and produced the penitentials, books that categorized sinful acts and determined appropriate penances.[6] With the Council of Trent in the sixteenth century, seminary manuals provided even more systematic guidance to sins and penances. Since the seventeenth century, all sexual sins have been characterized as grave—that is, serious sins that break one's relationship with God and require confession and penance. Contraception was considered grave—a mortal sin requiring confession—because it interfered with the two goods of marriage: the unitive good or the reciprocal self-giving of the spouses; and the procreative good, the transmission of life.[7] *HV* continued that judgment. This "inseparable connection, established by God," meaning the connection between the unitive and procreative ends, exists because "the fundamental nature of the marriage act, while uniting husband and wife in the closest intimacy, also renders them capable of generating new life" (#11). Interference with the procreative capacity of sexual relations cannot be justified. Paul VI wrote that "it is a serious error to think that a whole married life of otherwise normal relations can justify sexual intercourse which is deliberately contraceptive and so intrinsically wrong" (#14).

The practice of categorizing sins continues today. Thirty years after *HV*, the "*Vademecum* for Confessors Concerning Some Aspects of the Morality of the Conjugal Life," issued by the Vatican's Pontifical Council for the Family, reinforced its teaching. The document assisted priests in differentiating among sins and assigning appropriate penances. It condemned artificial birth control with even more force than had *HV*. Referring to its own teaching as "definitive" and "irreformable," which in Catholic circles suggests teaching that is "infallible" or unchangeable, the *Vademecum* accorded the moral prohibition of birth control the same status as such primary Christian beliefs as Christ's divinity. Characterizing contraception as intrinsically evil, the *Vademecum* reiterated that interference with the sexual act is a violation of both the unitive and procreative ends of marriage.[8]

RECEPTION OF *HUMANAE VITAE*
In the late 1960s, expectations among Catholics were high that the new spirit of change initiated by the Second Vatican Council would make its way even into the church's moral teaching on contraception. When Paul VI issued the encyclical maintaining the church's traditional position, a worldwide firestorm erupted in the popular press and theological journals. Widespread theological dissent mirrored popular disregard of the ban, generating a real crisis of authority in the church. Today polls of American Catholics report that 80 percent disagree with the church's teaching, while the Sunday pews, now accommodating families averaging 2.5 children, provide nonscientific evidence of actual Catholic sexual practice.[9] A corresponding decline in the practice of confession suggests that couples do not consider their lack of adherence to *HV* a matter for confession and repentance. I offer my sense of the popular Catholic reaction and then describe the theological dissent to *HV*.

The Popular Reaction. To married couples, the encyclical's direct addressees, the tone of the document and its assumptions about sex and marriage must seem from a different world than the one in which they live. An apt example is sexual desire. While popular culture acknowledges and even encourages sexual desire, *HV* seeks to minimize it. *HV* instructs couples to "acquire complete mastery over themselves and their emotions," "control their natural drives," and practice "self-denial" and "periodic continence" (#21). Hidden in *HV*'s footnotes but quite evident in its approach is the influence of Augustine, fifth-century bishop of Hippo, whose guilt over his adolescent promiscuity led to a lifetime of trying to overcome what he saw as the internal disorder created by sexual desire.

Augustine's moral teaching on sex has dominated Catholic thought for sixteen centuries.[10] The context for his discussion of sex and marriage was original sin. He saw Adam's sin as a failure at the beginning of history, specifically, a failure to obey. Adam knew God's command yet chose to disobey it. The punishment for original sin was the disorder—concupiscence—now experienced in human nature. That men had erections was shameful for Augustine; this inability to control one's body was a reflection of the fall (of Adam and Eve). Before the fall, he thought, the genitals would have behaved rationally. Sexual desire after the fall was dominated by lust, including sexual desire within marriage.[11] Augustine designated everything about sex as evil—sexual appetite, sexual pleasure, the desire for sex. Even the sexual act within marriage was evil, Augustine thought, unless its purpose was explicitly procreative. The agreement between Augustine and *HV* is straightforward: the only legitimate use of sex is for procreation.[12]

In contrast, my sense is that if married couples today find sexual desire a problem in their marriage, it is more likely an absence of desire that contributes to a marital crisis rather than an excess of sex. Even the characterization of desire for one's spouse as lust seems foreign to most Catholic couples I have encountered, as does thinking that original sin as the appropriate framework for understanding sex and marriage. For married couples themselves, sex is an avenue of fulfillment, not an evil consequence of the fall. Similarly, contemporary persons think of rape and other types of coercive and nonconsensual sex, not nonprocreative marital sex, as examples of intrinsic evil. In devoting an encyclical to the evil of nonprocreative sex, Pope Paul VI seemed oblivious to such sex-related evils as the global sex trafficking of women and children, the incidence of sexually predatory behavior of counselors and ministers, and the epidemic of HIV/AIDS, to name only a few of problems facing the world then and today.

In contemporary theories of human nature and psychology, by contrast, sexuality is understood as an intrinsic dimension of one's human existence and personality. Sexual relations are not just biological acts of sexual organs but are expressions of self-giving, commitment, and love. The thought that freedom from pregnancy would create a situation of abuse, as *HV* suggests, seems odd to most Roman Catholic couples I know. *HV* argues that if a man grows accustomed to the use of contraception, he might reduce his wife to being the object of his own sexual desires (#17). To use contraceptives, *HV* asserts, introduces a pernicious intentional habit into the conjugal life of the couple (#7). By using contraceptives to close their biological openness to procreation, the couple intends and does evil.

HV seems to presume, in particular, the worst of men—as if only the threat of pregnancy keeps the male sex drive within some kind of civilized bounds that otherwise would have no limit. But I would contend that being in love is expressed sexually. In relationships that do not suffer from dysfunctions, partners do not "use" one another or "use" sex but engage each other and engage in the intimacy of sexual intercourse. In my view, it is not openness to procreation that eliminates abuse but respect for the dignity of another and love for that person.

The Theological Reaction. If *HV* had been issued before Vatican II, it is likely that most Roman Catholic moral theologians in the United States would have accepted it with characteristic grace. While they did not all think alike, preconciliar moral theologians generally did not waver in their allegiance to official church teaching. They would have agreed with *HV* because the *magisterium* taught it. However, *HV* was issued in 1968 to a post–Vatican II church, and in the United States it occasioned widespread public dissent by theologians.[13] The encyclical continues to be a subject of debate today.

For some, engaging in public dissent was costly. Some theologians were prohibited from speaking about the encyclical. Charles Curran, a prominent moral theologian at Catholic University of America, was removed from his tenured position.[14] Along with the crisis of authority provoked by *HV*, dissenting theologians took on the hard work of trying to say exactly what was wrong with the church's argument. At the heart of the theological critique was the problematic character of three dimensions of the church's traditional ethics: natural law, acts analysis, and physicalism. We explore each in turn.

With the long-standing Catholic optimism about human reason, despite its darkening by original sin, *HV* presumes that human beings are capable of understanding the world that God has made, including human nature as part of that world. The church derives moral principles embedded in nature from the discernment of the purposes of nature. These principles reflect God's plan for human beings. This is the natural law. In grasping the natural law—what is true and good—humans also apprehend God's eternal law.

Traditional natural-law arguments typically work as syllogisms. The major premise is the formulation of the moral principle. The particular act to be evaluated is the minor premise. The conclusion is logically derived from the relation between the major and minor premises of the syllogism. So, the Roman Catholic argument against the use of contraception also follows this form:

- The natural and moral purpose of sex is generative.
- Contraception interferes with generative sex.
- Therefore, contraception is unnatural and immoral.

The church's condemnation of homosexual sex is derived from the same ethical argument that grounds heterosexual marital sex as either moral or immoral. From the definition of moral sex as procreative, nonprocreative relations of same-sex couples cannot be anything but immoral. The certainty with which the *magisterium* makes both the heterosexual and homosexual argument directly reflects the logical power of the syllogism. It enabled Paul VI to claim in *HV* that "the teaching of the Church regarding the proper regulation of birth is a promulgation of the law of God Himself" (#19).

It is this certainty that contemporary theologians highlighted as problematic.[15] The church presents moral and immoral sex as if its generative purpose were self-evident. Its argument "sees" the function of complementary heterosexual genitals and "knows" from the biology that the moral purpose of sex is procreative. However, this assertion is not knowledge but a hypothesis that stands in need of verification. It is as yet merely an idea about the purpose of biology and physical acts, not a verified judgment. The *magisterium* is very confident that the purpose it sees in sexual intercourse is what is written into nature, but change assumptions about anthropology or gender or about scientific judgments about purpose in nature, and the idea is less obvious.

The difficulty lies in part in the syllogistic method itself. A syllogism puts propositions in logical relation to one another. However, human meaning is also historical and contextual; it is dialectical as well. It may express genuine insights but it expresses oversights too. Syllogisms cannot accommodate ambiguity or ideology, two primary features of moral reality. The certainty projected by the syllogism may be misplaced, and the moral situation may be more complex and ambiguous. What is projected as true may be a formulation driven instead by ideological vested interests, bearing little connection to what is in fact the case.

The confidence with which the *magisterium* portrays its knowledge of the natural law and the will of God is stated quite clearly. For example, *HV* states that "No member of the faithful could possibly deny that the Church is competent in her *magisterium* to interpret the natural law. . . . For the natural law, too, declares the will of God, and its faithful observance is necessary for men's salvation" (#4). The relation between the church and God is even closer in this remark: "The teaching of the Church regarding the proper regulation of birth is a promulgation of the law of God Himself" (#20).

In the tradition, natural law was understood as reason discerning what was proper to human nature. In grasping what should or should not be done, reason grasps the eternal law, God's plan for human nature. The problem, however, is confusing what one thinks or assumes with what is so. Judgments that appear certain or necessary may, in fact, be shaped by personal or cultural interests or presuppositions. Androcentrism makes it appear absolutely true, for example, that women are less fully human than men and that social, legal, and religious discrimination against them is justified. Male domination is conceived as fundamental to the order of creation. These propositions seem self-evident. There is a kind of conceptualism involved that identifies the concept with truth "out there." Truth, however, resides in verified judgments.

The natural-law assertions that the encyclical makes are clear, but moral theologian Joseph Komonchak argues that they are not verified with evidence.[16] That every sexual act must be open to procreation is asserted rather than demonstrated, as is the idea that sexuality and marriage are intrinsically ordered toward procreation. These positions are said to be derived from natural law, but the encyclical offers no reasons to demonstrate them. The encyclical does not make clear what the moral difference is between the intentional use of natural family planning (the so-called rhythm method) and the use of artificial birth control and why the former is acceptable and the latter not. In a strongly worded conclusion, Komonchak says that the problem with the *magisterium's* argument from natural law is "in the inadequacy of that understanding and in the consequent incoherence in application."[17]

Along with Roman law as a model for theology, with the consequent understanding of sin as crime, moral theology in the tradition focused on the individual to the exclusion of consideration of the whole person in his or her social and historical context. "Acts analysis" is the method of reasoning from acts to ends. Attention here is put on the minor premise of the syllogism: the act is to be evaluated in light of the major premise, the moral principle. Purposes or ends are built into nature. To grasp the ends proper to nature is a capacity of reason. To understand these purposes is to understand what God wills for this nature. Acts that conform with the purposes built into nature are moral. Acts that violate or interfere with these purposes are immoral.

The focus of the medieval church's confessional guides and of the manuals of moral theology after the Council of Trent was almost exclusively on individual sinful acts—not on what one should do but what one should not do. Contemporary theologians, however, place acts in the context of persons, their development, circumstances, and relationships. One person's acts affect others directly and indirectly. Acts analysis does not attend to situations or admit ambiguity or allow for moral complexity.

Most moral theologians concur that a chief problem with *HV* is its physicalism—that is, the way it derives its central moral principle from the body. The procreative capability of the sexual organs dictates their moral use. For a sexual act to be moral, intercourse must be open to procreation, and nothing may be used that would interfere with that function for any reason. *HV* states that persons "are not free to act as they choose in the service of transmitting life, as if it were wholly up to them to decide what is the right course to follow"; rather, they must conform to "the will of God the Creator," which the church spells out (#10). A blanket moral injunction follows. The natural law teaches, *HV* asserts, that "each and every marital act must of necessity retain its intrinsic relationship to the procreation of human life" (#11), and thus deliberately contraceptive relations are intrinsically wrong (#14).

The church's sexual ethics has come under much scrutiny for its negativity not about extramarital sex but marital sex itself. For example, the desire for sex is negative, counsel is given to limit sexual relations, sex open to procreation is the only legitimate use of sex, and contraception is imagined to lead to excessive demand for sex on the part of husbands. The scrutiny is not only on the negativity in the church's treatment of sex but the very assumptions about sex. Is it self-evident that the meaning and purpose of marriage and marital sex is procreation or that nonprocreative sex is evil? Is it self-evident that interference with the physical aspect of procreative capacities is intrinsically evil or that the use of contraception should constitute a mortal sin?

Many questions come up, too, about the method by which the church reaches its conclusions. Among these are questions about the certainty with which the church asserts that its knowledge of natural law is knowledge of God's will and about the exclusive concentration on sexual acts isolated from persons, relationships, and real-life situations. Much attention has been put on the way in which the church's sexual ethics derives moral principles from biological structures.

WOMEN, PATRIARCHY, AND *HUMANAE VITAE*

The three philosophical elements of the traditional approach discussed above (natural law, acts analysis, and physicalism) have received much attention from Roman Catholic moral theologians; however, understanding the church's sexual ethics requires reconstructing the broader historical and cultural framework within which it fits. I argue that *HV* must be situated within the church's patriarchal historical assumptions about women's subordination and about women's God-given maternal vocation.

In the ancient world, the primary identification of "body" is with "woman." An androcentric gender anthropology (that is, a male-centered concept of being human) conceives of human nature dualistically, with the higher capacities of humanness ("mind") being assigned to male nature and the lower capacities ("body") identified with femaleness. Men *have* bodies. Women *are* bodies. In the dominant androcentric understanding, women's function in creation—reproduction—follows from her identification with body. Her body is a vessel for male seed.

Patriarchal law secures the subordination of women by defining them as the property of men. Persons and property are different under the law and in moral theory. While persons have rights or obligations, property does not.[18] Persons possess freedom and have the capacity for self-determination. Without freedom, property has no means of self-determination. Consequently, ancient moral principles are formulated for men. The Decalogue command on coveting provides a good example. "You shall not covet your neighbor's house; you shall not covet your neighbor's wife, or male or female slave, or ox, or donkey, or anything that belongs to your neighbor" (Exod. 20:17). The "you" in the command refers to males, as does "your neighbor." Both are male heads of households, meaning owners of property. The command has to do with the way one man approaches another's property.

Even though viewing women as property effectively eliminated their moral agency, moral commands—at least what were portrayed as such— were heaped upon them, as in this New Testament mandating of subordination, written in the apostle Paul's name: "Let a woman learn in silence with full submission. I permit no woman to teach or to have authority over a man: she is to keep silent" (1 Tim. 2:11-12). The author here realigns women's salvation with reproduction: "Yet she will be saved through childbearing, provided they continue in faith and love and holiness, with modesty" (2:15).[19] Until the Second Vatican Council, it was routine for papal documents on marriage to refer to 1 Timothy and other texts that instruct women to be subject to male rule.

After the New Testament period, the Christian tradition carried the ancient patriarchal and androcentric notions further. Male theologians identified women with body, body with sex, and body and sex with sin. Christian theologians in the first five centuries C.E. transposed the cultural sexism of their patriarchal world into a theological anthropology of gender inequality. Following 1 Timothy, theologians blamed Eve for bringing evil—and as a consequence, death—into the world. Irenaeus wrote, "Having become disobedient, [Eve] was made the cause of death, both to herself and to the entire human race." Ambrose wrote that Eve "was first to be deceived and was responsible for deceiving the man."[20] John Chrysostom put the matter bluntly: "The woman taught once, and ruined all."[21]

Augustine put subordination into creation itself. He argued that women were subordinate to men even prior to the fall. Augustine wrote: "For we must believe that even before her sin woman had been made to be ruled by her husband and to be submissive and subject to him."[22] In his *Decretum* Gratian wrote, "the woman has no power," summing up the status of women in a patriarchal world, "but in everything she is subject to the control of her husband."[23] Later, at the height of medieval theology in the thirteenth century, Thomas Aquinas followed Augustine in holding that female subjugation to male rule was part of the order of creation. Subordination preceded sin and was not a result of the fall.[24] He accepted as well Aristotle's biological theory that women were defective or incomplete males.[25] Aquinas agreed with the long-standing androcentric tradition that associated women with reproduction, writing that woman was "included in nature's intention as directed to the work of generation."[26]

Some theologians went beyond thinking of women as being the origin of sin to regarding them as sin itself, crossing the line from androcentrism to misogyny. Clement of Alexandria, a late-second-century theologian, surely did so in his remark that "every woman should be filled with shame by the thought that she is a woman."[27] Another early theologian, Tertullian, famously speaking directly to women, wrote:

> You are the devil's gateway: you are the unsealer of that (forbidden) tree: you are the first deserter of the divine law: you are she who persuaded him whom the devil was not valiant enough to attack. You destroyed so easily God's image, man. On account of your desert—that is, death, even the Son of Man had to die.[28]

These early church and medieval theologians were celibate males who viewed sexuality through the experience of people who were not in love, not married, presumably not engaged in sexual relations, not experiencing the burdens of family, nor dealing with the personal challenges of bringing children into the world. They inculcated in the Christian tradition a distrust of the body, distrust of sexuality, and a distrust of women. They defined women in line with their cultures: women are bodies for reproduction. The moral principle follows: sex for males with women is moral only if used for reproduction.[29]

The implications of a patriarchal, androcentric worldview are clear. When women are classed as property, questions about sex center on how this property is to be used. As with any equipment or tool, right use has to do with its function. If the function of women is reproduction, the right use of sex is for procreation. The moral question is for males. When is sex with women moral for males? The answer can be taken for granted: sex is moral when it is used for reproduction.

During the modern period, papal declarations continued to presume the hierarchical structure of marriage and the inferiority of women until the secular progress of women rendered the position less tenable. The emancipation of women was thus largely a secular achievement. The Catholic church was not an advocate for women in their struggle to overcome their status as property or in gaining their rightful status as persons, nor has violence against women been made a primary subject for an encyclical. Church teaching took hierarchical gender relations for granted as the order of creation. Catholic theologians spoke confidently of males as the normative human being. The church's preaching and teaching conceived of the social world in terms of separate and unequal gender spheres. The public sphere was a properly male one, and the private domestic sphere of motherhood and childrearing belonged properly to females.

Evidence that authorities are not unaware of their androcentrism is suggested by the disappearance of these formulations in official documents since the mid-1960s. But even if post–Vatican II popes have been silent on the subordination of women, the subordination remains under the cover of a romanticized theme of women's vocation as mothers. In 1971 when John Paul II took up the "problem" of the "dignity and responsibility of being a woman," in *Mulieris dignitatem* (*On the Dignity and Vocation of Women on the Occasion of the Marian Year*), he defined motherhood as "women's vocation." Mary, the mother who is a virgin, is the exemplar of women in *Redemptoris Mater* (1987). While Mary is exemplary, she is oddly not credited for what she is.

The credit goes to a man: "This maternal role of Mary flows, according to God's good pleasure, 'from the superabundance of the merits of Christ; it is founded on his mediation, absolutely depends on it, and draws all its efficacy from it.'"[30] In "Motherhood Is God's Special Gift" (1996), John Paul II celebrated not only women's place in creation as mothers but in particular the barren mothers in the biblical tradition to whom God gave sons. No daughters are mentioned.[31]

What have been the consequences of Catholic theologians' adoption of the ancient world's androcentric, even misogynist, views about women? By accepting the common patriarchal anthropology that women's nature was less fully human than men, theologians undermined women's dignity and status as created. They denied that women are made in the image of God and absolutized masculine language to mean that men are like God. They took feminine and masculine characteristics as essential and unchanging and made separate and unequal gender spheres into "the order of creation." By grounding women's subjection to male rule in God's will, theologians did not see that gender privilege was a fundamental distortion of creation.

The dualist gender anthropology inherited from the ancient world has been justly critiqued as an ideological distortion of human nature. The modern women's movement challenged and, for a significant number of people, eliminated the myth of female inferiority. New ways of understanding persons and sexuality emphasize the intrinsic relation between the two. Biases in the anthropology of the Christian tradition are explicitly rejected—namely, the exclusive identification of women with body and reproduction, masked by the romanticizing of motherhood; and the identification of full humanness with male nature, leaving female nature deficient.

RECOVERING TRADITIONAL INSIGHTS FOR FUTURE CATHOLIC THEOLOGY

While the *magisterium* expects its understanding of natural law to be taken as normative and binding, widespread rejection of this teaching by both married couples and theologians has resulted in several decades of critique. Contemporary moral theologians call not only for a change in the prohibition against birth control but a radical transformation of the method and presuppositions of the church's sexual ethics. Yet it is also incumbent on theologians to recover insights from the tradition that can be further developed and promoted. One theologian long accepted as an authority for Catholic theology and church teaching is Thomas Aquinas. Despite the weaknesses in his own teaching about women, his understanding of morality is a valuable resource to include in the work of transforming the church's whole approach to sexual morality.

In my opinion, the various failures of *HV* and of the church's teaching in the area are compounded by the failure to ground sexual morality in moral consciousness itself and the ultimate understanding of persons themselves and in their relationship to each other and to God. There can be no moral act without the moral process itself. *HV* allows the marital couple only one question: Should we have sex? With their yes or no, the rest is settled—the biological act must be open to children whether or not the couple is ready emotionally or financially, whether their family is large enough, or whether they are capable of taking on the challenges of parenthood. In reality, however, sex is only one aspect of their marriage, and marriage is one dimension of their larger personhood within the world. What is missing in the church's teaching on sex is what people should do with their freedom. Further, by insisting that procreation is the sole purpose of sex and marriage, the church has, in effect, denigrated the marriage itself and sustained the bias that women are created for reproduction.

Aquinas, by contrast, puts human morality into a cosmic and teleological framework. God is the beginning and end of all creatures. In their very creation, things act purposefully for an end. Aquinas identifies the end proper to human beings as happiness. It is through their moral acts that persons become fully who they are.[32] The moral process leading up to the decision and act has ultimate significance. Human beings are unique among created beings in that their self-actualization takes place through moral acts. If Aquinas had been writing in the twentieth century rather than the thirteenth, he would have described human beings as "self-constituting." Still, the idea of self-constitution is there in the dynamism suggested by self-actualization. Humanness is not finished at birth but is open and unfinished. For Aquinas, all things come from God and return to God. "Each creature returns to God by becoming ever more completely itself." It is human potentiality becoming actual. In desiring their own good, human beings desire God. "Creatures are said to desire or love God in exactly the same way in which they are said to desire or to love the good which is their complete actuality."[33] For Aquinas, morality bears ultimate significance for who and what we are. It is through deliberation, evaluation, choices among courses of action, decisions, and acts that we become fully ourselves. This is our way back to God. "To be a person, to be made in the 'image of God,' is to act freely and intelligently as the principle of one's own acts."[34]

By emphasizing authority and an absolute principle derived from the body, the church's teaching on sexual ethics has failed to engage believers in their own capacity to bring about the human good—for themselves, their families, and the larger human family. Without questions, there are no choices; without alternatives, there is no moral agency; without decisions, there are no judgments of value. Further, in appropriating the cultural gender anthropology, the status of women as property, and a male ideology of superiority, the church cut short the possibility of self-actualization on the part of women. By considering women legally property of their fathers or husbands, the church denied women genuine moral agency. To judge moral failure as a sin of property is a contradiction in terms. Without freedom, there can be no sin, as Augustine emphasized: "Where there is no free exercise of will, there is no sin. . . ." Or, again, "Sin, to be sin must be voluntary."[35]

Aquinas's identification of happiness as the end of human existence is a much-needed reminder to the church that its purpose in moral teaching must be in the service of helping believers discover that they themselves become who they are before God by virtue of the decisions they make. What Aquinas identified as happiness might be called, in a more dynamic anthropology, authenticity. When we affirm something to be worthwhile, we move beyond the immediacy of personal satisfaction to acknowledge objective value. However, this is only the first step toward authentic human existence. Authenticity is realized "when judgments of value are followed by decision and action, when knowing what is truly good leads to doing what truly is good."[36] Because authenticity is realized when judgments of value are the product of responsible choices and actions, locating that responsibility in the couple's own complex discernment of authentic value may prove a promising a starting point for a future Catholic theology of sexuality.

The Roman Catholic insistence that only marital sex open to procreation is moral has been the source of much suffering. It disregards all the factors that have immediate import in a family—whether there is money to care for children, whether the family is already large, whether both parents are emotionally, psychically, and physically able to care for the existing children. By defining procreation as the purpose of sex and marriage, the church's teaching in effect sustained the view of women in patriarchal cultures as created solely for reproduction. Finally, in *HV* and other papal documents, morality as a means of self-actualization has been closed to them as Roman Catholic couples.

If happiness is indeed the purpose of human existence, then pregnancy must itself be a choice. For there to be choice, there must be the freedom to ask the question: Should we have a child? So the crucial moral question about contraception is not about whether to have marital sex. Inasmuch as sexual intimacy is a primary expression of marital commitment and love, relations should not themselves be the moral issue. Rather, deliberation should consider the many relevant factors that are at issue in creating a family. The decision should reflect intelligent and responsible consideration of these factors. The yes or no to having a child is one judgment of value in a couple's lifelong search for responsible self-actualization. That principle might be a good starting point for renewed Roman Catholic thinking about not only contraception but the whole range of issues, questions, and conflicts over sexuality and sexual morality.

Further Suggested Readings

Cahill, Lisa Sowle. *Sex, Gender and Christian Ethics*. Cambridge: Cambridge University Press, 1996.

Curran, Charles E. *Catholic Moral Theology in the United States: A History.* Washington, D.C.: Georgetown University Press, 2008.

Lonergan, Bernard J. F. *Method in Theology*. Chaps. 2, 4. New York: Herder & Herder, 1972.

Mahoney, John. *The Making of Moral Theology: A Study of the Roman Catholic Tradition.* Oxford: Clarendon, 1987.

Ruether, Rosemary Radford. *Women and Redemption: A Theological History.* Minneapolis: Fortress Press, 1998.

CHAPTER 7

Reformation Views on Celibacy:
An Analogy for Gay Protestants Today

Paul E. Capetz

A THEOLOGICAL PERSPECTIVE IS SHAPED, to a large extent, by a person's experience of life. It is also the case that a well-articulated theological framework can inform the interpretation of experience by providing religious categories that enable us to make sense of our lives. This double-sided relationship between experience and theology is pivotal to the following attempt to interpret my existential predicament as a gay man in the church in the light of my religious convictions as a Protestant theologian. I was an ordained minister in the Presbyterian Church (U.S.A.) until circumstances forced me to make a choice I wish could have been averted. In 1997, the Presbyterians amended their constitution to require of gay people a vow of celibacy as a condition of ordination.[1] It then became apparent to me that I could no longer be an official representative of an institution that treats people like me with such suspicion, even hostility, in its dismissal of our lives as unnatural and immoral. My resignation from the ministry was thus a protest against the church for causing so much suffering in the lives of gay people by opposing our efforts to love one another in the name of the gospel.

It is a terrible thing to have to choose between one's vocation and the elemental human need for loving intimacy, but that is precisely the choice the church has forced upon me. Although I am single, fidelity to my ordination vow to abide by the church's discipline would have meant ruling out the possibility of a committed relationship with another man. In a letter addressed to my colleagues in the ministry I explained: "A vow of lifelong celibacy is an unrealistic expectation for the church to ask of me. I fear that the prospect of having to face the future without hope of ever finding someone with whom to share my life in a loving relationship would result in unspeakable despair." Now that I have relinquished the ministerial office, I need not worry about a potential conflict between professional and personal life, not to mention ecclesiastical discipline for violation of moral standards. Of course, there is no guarantee that I will ever find a partner with whom to share my life, but at least I can be genuinely open to that possibility without feeling caught between the rock of integrity and the hard place of loneliness. While I have resolved for myself what had been a terrible bind of conscience, the church continues to be torn apart by its own crisis of conscience.

Sometimes I wonder why I remain in the church at all. Many, if not most, of my gay friends have severed their ties to whatever religious tradition nurtured them from earliest childhood. There are good reasons for disaffiliation: people know when they're not welcome. I suppose my reasons for staying are, in part, because I am professionally engaged in theological education. Though I am not considered morally qualified to be a minister, I earn my living by teaching others who are preparing for this vocation. Besides, my roots are planted too deeply in the church's heritage for me to uproot myself completely. I know in my gut that even if I tried to sever my ties to the church, it would never let go of me. I am so deeply grasped by its religious and moral substance that I remain in the church, even committed to it in a measured sort of way, albeit with a heavy heart.

This very personal reflection upon my own experience is by way of introduction to the theological point I want to make. As a professor of historical theology, my task is to open up the classical Christian traditions for tomorrow's religious leaders. In our ahistorical culture, this is not an easy task, but it is vitally important, nonetheless. I am convinced that it is only by appreciative yet critical engagement with the theological heritage that the church has any real hope of orienting itself responsibly in the present situation. This is not to say that the tradition has all the answers to our contemporary questions, if we would only submit to its wisdom. Sometimes it is necessary to recognize that the tradition itself is deeply flawed and the only faithful response is to revise it, "to put it in the form we think will prove best," as John Calvin (1509–1564) once said of his own reforming work.[2] To dismiss the historical tradition as though it has nothing of import to say to us is quite clearly shortsighted. If we can learn to converse with the tradition, to pose our questions to it all the while letting it pose its challenges to us, the church may find unexpected resources in the most unlikely of places.

It is just this sort of open-ended engagement with the Protestant tradition that I want to exemplify here. This essay argues that there is an important analogy to be explored between one aspect of the Reformation initiated by Martin Luther (1483–1546) and the contemporary plight of gay people in those churches that trace their history back to that sixteenth-century event. There is a striking parallel between the Protestant Reformation polemic against clerical celibacy and the contemporary objection on the part of gay people to the insistence by most Protestant churches upon a vow of celibacy as a condition of our ordination to ecclesial office. Of course, in every analogy there are dissimilarities as well as similarities to be taken into account, so I cannot make the anachronistic claim that Luther has already solved the problem facing us today. Still, I do think that considering the analogy could prove potentially fruitful for Protestant churches if, indeed, they are truly committed to taking seriously both their own theological traditions and the lived experience of their gay members. By looking at the distant past through our own lens, we may see the immediate present refracted in an unfamiliar, though very illuminating, light.

THE REFORMATION POLEMIC AGAINST CELIBACY

While the issue of clerical celibacy was only one facet of the Protestant polemic against the medieval church, its relation to the center of the Lutheran Reformation is clear and unambiguous. There was a widespread perception in the late Middle Ages that the infidelity of priests, monks, and nuns to their vows of chastity was certainly one of the most telling indications that the church stood in need of reform. In the view of those we now call "forerunners" of the Reformation as well as reform-minded contemporaries of Luther who deemed his teachings to be heretical, the sexual indiscretions of persons committed to the religious life (in distinction from the secular life of ordinary Christians who married and reared children) was a moral problem calling for a moral and administrative solution. Reform of the church would require that ecclesiastical discipline be tightened up so as to enforce the strict observance of celibacy. This was also the approach eventually adopted by the reforming Council of Trent of the Roman Catholic Church (1545–1563). In striking contrast, Luther advocated that vows of celibacy be abolished altogether. Behind this opposing strategy for dealing with a very real practical matter affecting the life of Christendom was a divergent diagnosis of the situation needing to be addressed. Unlike his Roman Catholic counterparts for whom the problem was one of lax morality in the ranks of the clergy, for Luther the problem was fundamentally religious and theological: the church taught a false gospel.

Luther's critique was directed primarily at the church's doctrine and defined the distinctively "Protestant" approach among other late medieval programs for reforming the church. Whereas they called for a reform of moral and administrative practices, Luther located the source of all ecclesiastical abuses in a corrupted doctrine taught by the Scholastic theologians under papal auspices.[3] Historian Heiko Oberman gets at the profound difference between the Protestant notion of "reformation" and other earnest appeals for "reform." Referring to fourteenth-century reformer John Wycliffe and his younger contemporary, John Hus, Oberman writes: "Luther criticizes Wycliffe and Hus for having directed their attacks at the moral sins of the Pope. He calls for a true reformation, and this has to be not primarily a reform of morals but rather a reformation of doctrine."[4] For Luther, the underlying root of the malaise of the church was a defection from, even a distortion of, the essential message of the gospel concerning God's grace. Although the theologians of the church talked a lot about grace, their doctrine, Luther charged, was nothing other than a subtle form of the Pelagianism against which Augustine had fought a thousand years earlier.[5] Technically speaking, the Roman church never officially taught such pure Pelagianism, and so Luther's claim seemed preposterous to a church that boasted of Augustine as its *doctor gratiae* ("teacher of grace"). Yet to Luther's mind, Scholastic disputations on the question of merit, whether condign or congruous, were only refined and sophisticated versions of the more brazen teaching of Augustine's foe, since grace and merit are antithetical terms allowing for nothing but opposition.[6] With the historical perspective opened up by hindsight, it is now possible for Catholic and Protestant scholars to take a more impartial view of the sixteenth-century polemics, which enables us to recognize that Luther and his papal opponents were operating out of two distinct models for interpreting what grace means and how it is appropriated by the sinful soul. Nonetheless, in order to understand Luther's polemic against religious celibacy, it is necessary to grasp the logic of his distinctive doctrine of grace, which underlay all his criticisms of the Roman church and informed each particular reform undertaken by the Protestants.

In the Lutheran recasting of the Augustinian insistence upon salvation *sola gratia* ("by grace alone"), justification (i.e., one's standing as righteous before God) is said to occur *sola fide* ("by faith alone").[7] Faith, in this framework, is defined as trust in and wholehearted reliance upon the freely given promise proclaimed in the gospel that God mercifully accepts sinners as righteous on account of Christ's merit. This Protestant conception of soteriology involved a significant departure from the traditional Catholic interpretation of grace. Whereas Catholicism likened grace to a supernatural medicine that, infused through the sacraments, heals the soul of its spiritual sickness and makes possible a new love for God (Rom. 5:5), Protestantism understood grace to denote God's character as merciful, which is revealed in the proclamation of forgiveness. Similarly, faith is no longer the intellect's assent to the truth of Catholic doctrine as defined by the church's *magisterium* (teaching office); it is, rather, the assurance of forgiveness evoked and sustained by God's word as heard in the sermon (Rom. 10:17). Implicit in these contrasts are alternative conceptions of the relation of justification to sanctification.

For Catholics, sanctification was the premise of justification: one would be justified before God only after the process of sanctification had been completed. Since sanctification (literally: "to be made holy") does not occur without the infusion of sacramental grace, this doctrine is not technically a form of Pelagianism. The grace that sanctifies is *gratia gratum faciens* (literally: "grace making pleasing"): grace makes the sinner acceptable to a holy and righteous God. The end of this sanctifying process is that the sinner is transformed by grace into a saint—that is, someone who loves God above all things and loves the neighbor as self. For that reason, faith (belief) is not sufficient, since love is the chief theological virtue (1 Cor. 13:2, 13).[8]

By contrast, Protestants taught that justification is not dependent upon sanctification so that they affirmed the paradoxical idea that we are simultaneously righteous and sinful (*simul iustus et peccator*), which was a contradiction in terms given the premises of Catholic theology. Justification, which concerns our relation to God, is by faith alone. There are no merits based on loving deeds performed on the neighbor's behalf of which to boast before God. This is not antinomian, either; since faith is inherently active, love for the neighbor flows spontaneously as the disinterested expression of gratitude for the free forgiveness God has given the sinner through Christ.

Differing formulae served to express these two variants on the Augustinian tradition. Catholics affirmed that justification is through "faith formed by love" (*fides caritate formata*) and not by faith alone. Protestants denied that faith needs to be formed or supplemented by works of love and affirmed that "faith works through love" (Gal. 5:6)—that is, only the heart which confides completely in God's mercy for justification is capable of bringing forth genuinely disinterested acts of love directed toward the neighbor. To Protestants, the Catholic doctrine taught the need for meritorious works, while Catholics saw in the Protestant doctrine intellectual belief devoid of love. Needless to say, both sides talked past one another given their distinctive use of terms and the internal coherence of these terms within their respective systematic frameworks.

Unlike traditional apologists for Protestantism, I do not believe that the New Testament gives unambiguous support to the Protestant doctrine of justification. From my reading of the scriptural evidence, the Catholic and Lutheran paradigms are equally plausible formulations of what it means to be a Christian. Both insist upon salvation by grace alone, though the meanings of grace and faith differ, as do the understandings of the relations between justification and sanctification. In our ecumenical age, it is important to affirm and appreciate this sort of theological pluralism within the church at large, rooted as it is in the diversity of the biblical witnesses. This means, of course, that today one's reasons for subscribing to the Protestant view have to be defended on theological, rather than strictly exegetical, grounds. Yet it is important to stress that the Catholic and Protestant interpretations of the gospel are different and there is simply no way to harmonize them in the name of ecumenism without doing violence to their doctrinal integrity. Each one brings in its train a distinctive pattern of thinking about practical issues in the Christian life, including religious vows to lifelong celibacy.[9]

From the earliest period of Christianity's history, celibacy had been upheld as a religious ideal embodied by the saints and venerated by the less saintly faithful. Celibacy was considered instrumental in the process of sanctification since it assisted in weaning the Christian pilgrim from attachment to earthly and temporal loves for the sake of a heavenly and eternal love.[10] The religious celibate continues to enjoy a place of honor in both the Roman Catholic and Eastern Orthodox traditions even today.[11] In its categorical rejection of this religious ideal, Protestantism broke new ground and charted a different course from the ancient tradition by consistently drawing forth the implications of Luther's doctrine of justification. To Protestant eyes, the high regard accorded to the celibate life was symptomatic of the false theology corrupting the medieval church, which refused to ascribe salvation to grace alone since it reserved a place for the Christian pilgrim to earn merit before God. Luther looked upon a vow of celibacy as a sign of presumption, even though he himself had once made an earnest attempt to live the monastic life of chastity. After his intense engagement with the Bible led him to his revolutionary conviction that justification, properly understood, is by faith alone, he left the monastery and repudiated the vows he had once made, believing that the monastic religious ideal stood in contradiction to the gospel.

The understanding of Christian life presupposed in the traditional valorization of the celibate ideal had no place in the Protestant framework. Since justification was no longer believed to be contingent upon sanctification, the Christian life was viewed less as a spiritual pilgrimage and more as having its proper context in the secular arena where service to the neighbor is understood as an expression of gratitude for a salvation that is already secured. Accordingly, the vocation to marriage and secular work was no longer deemed as in any way inferior to the life of the so-called religious. From Luther's new perspective, the attempts by ascetics to do good on behalf of the neighbor were corrupted by an ulterior self-love, having their own personal salvation as the final end in view. It is only after the anxiety concerning salvation has been eradicated that one is really free to love without thought of reward.

Indeed, the Protestant theological revolution completely dismantled the distinction between religious and secular that had been at the heart of medieval culture. The doctrine of the "priesthood of all believers" put an end to all sacerdotalism.[12] The Reformation abolished monastic life, and even the calling of the Protestant minister to preach the gospel was not considered to partake of a spiritual significance above and beyond that of the vocation to work as a mason or a maid. Luther's doctrine of justification, in other words, had tremendous social consequences that broke radically with medieval cultural assumptions and societal arrangements. Contemporary scholarship has been greatly exercised to understand the impact of culture and society upon developments in religion and theology, and rightly so. In the case of the Reformation, however, we have a clear example of how new religious sensibilities and their theological interpretation played an important role in reshaping the values of a culture and transforming the institutions of a society.

Marriage became the norm for Protestants. Ministers were encouraged to marry, even if they had hitherto taken vows of celibacy as priests or monks. Historian Roland Bainton aptly remarks, "a Protestant minister almost had to marry to demonstrate the genuineness of his conviction."[13] Nuns were exhorted to flee the convent for the married life. Luther himself married a former nun named Katherine von Bora (1499–1550). Their married life together became a concrete demonstration of the new understanding of Christian faith pioneered by the Reformation. To be sure, not all Protestants were quite as eager to marry as was Luther, however much they shared his opinions on the matter. Calvin, though firmly opposed to clerical celibacy, had to be talked into marriage by his colleagues who found for him a suitable wife. He soon became very appreciative of the joys of domestic life and, after the death of his wife Idelette de Bure in 1549, remarked that he had been bereaved of the best companion of his life.[14]

Others who would eventually join the Protestant cause were not at all reticent to break with the traditional requirement of clerical celibacy since they had long since ceased to observe it anyway. The case of Ulrich Zwingli (1484–1531) is a striking example of a late medieval cleric struggling to find a compromise between the requirements of holiness, on the one hand, and the demands of the flesh, on the other. Zwingli, usually considered to be the first father of the "Reformed" tradition later to be identified preeminently with Calvin's name, was "living in sin" (some scholars euphemistically call it a "secret marriage") with his concubine, Anna Reinhart (c. 1484–1538), while still serving as a Catholic priest before the implementation of the Reformation in Zurich. After two years of cohabitation, the couple finally made their relationship official in a public ceremony.[15] As one historian of the period comments, "Priestly concubinage was widespread at this time, and Zwingli's behavior was hardly scandalous to his contemporaries."[16]

Zwingli wasn't the only important figure in the formative years of the Reformed tradition who found himself in this predicament. Zwingli's successor, Heinrich Bullinger (1504–1575), noted for his authorship of "The Second Helvetic Confession" included by Presbyterians in their official compendium, *The Book of Confessions*, lived "for decades as a priest . . . unmolested and respected, with his wife and children."[17] For priests living in Zwingli's and Bullinger's predicament, the Reformation provided a resolution to the tensions between religious vocation and sexual intimacy by sanctioning the "marital" relationships that had already been unofficially acknowledged by many people: "The right of clergy to marry legally and live honorably with women and thereby end such illegal fornication and cohabitation became one of the first reforms of the Swiss Reformation."[18] From the Protestant point of view, the truly lamentable corruption of the medieval church was not to be found in what their Catholic opponents regarded as the licentiousness of the clergy but, rather, in the church's official teachings that required of priests a vow of celibacy in the first place.

The distinctively Protestant rationale for this open advocacy of marriage and the abolition of the celibate monastic ideal had initially been forged in the crucible of Luther's own tortuous attempt to live the ascetic life. It was reflection upon his experience of despair that led him to charge that a vow of celibacy is contrary to the gospel, since it is nothing other than an effort to justify oneself by works. The problem with a vow of celibacy, Luther argued, is that the church binds the conscience of a Christian by making a particular religious practice a condition of one's standing before God. If the Christian should find that the effort to keep the vow is doomed to failure, the result is despair. Such spiritual despondency, however, is sufficient to show the vow's contradiction to the gospel, the entire point of which is to liberate the conscience from the guilt and despair induced by the false teaching that leads sinners to seek salvation by their own merits. This is the fatal confusion of "law" with "gospel," which Luther saw in the Scholastic mediations between grace and merit and in the false doctrine that justification depends upon sanctification.

In keeping with his characteristic directness of speech, Luther stated the antimony in no uncertain terms: "a vow of chastity . . . is diametrically opposed to the gospel."[19] A vow is a denial of the freedom that is a Christian's birthright through baptism: "God has made a pact of freedom with you in baptism. Consequently, it is always a matter of free choice whether you marry or not."[20] Luther thus believed that a choice had to be made between compulsory celibacy and the gospel: "If you obey the gospel, you ought to regard celibacy as a matter of free choice: if you do not hold it as a matter of free choice, you are not obeying the gospel."[21] All Christians should be free to decide for themselves whether to marry or to remain single, but there is no religious virtue in the single estate.

Luther's experience as a monk, as well as his observation of the behavior of other monks, led him to an extraordinarily realistic assessment of the ineradicable nature of sexual desire in human life. This assessment, in turn, called for a rather pragmatic approach to the question of what to do with sexual desire since it is not possible to get rid of it.[22] Sexual desire, for Luther, is akin to hunger. When one is starving, it is necessary to eat for the sake of the body's health. If the required food can be obtained only by stealing, then such an act is morally justified. Someone struggling with sexual desire yet bound to a vow of celibacy is like a hungry person who must break the law against theft in order to prevent starvation. "Under the stress of a consuming passion you must interpret the law of the vow as though the vow of chastity were not required, just as under the stress of hunger you would regard the law about stealing as if it did not exist."[23]

The Protestants of the Reformation did acknowledge that the single life was a possibility for those persons who had "the gift of celibacy," but they considered this group to be few in number. Moreover, they pointed out that a vow of celibacy is nowhere commanded in Scripture (1 Tim. 4:3) and that even the apostle Paul, who had the gift of celibacy, did not expect all to live as he did (1 Cor. 7:7-9). Through the institution of marriage God has made provision for those without the gift of celibacy to deal with their sexual desires in a responsible way. With reference to Paul's discussion of these matters, Luther commented:

> According to Christ's own interpretation the vow of chastity means this, "I vow chastity insofar as it is possible to do so without danger to the body or soul." If afterward you feel the surge of passion, then the vow is void and you may safely follow Paul's advice, "If they cannot be continent, let them marry," and again, "It is better to marry than burn."[24]

In the idiom of their day, sixteenth-century Protestants spoke of marriage as "the medicine of incontinency" and even "continency itself" that was "instituted by the Lord God himself."[25] An unmarried lifestyle is approved only on the condition that a person actually has the gift of celibacy. Since God looks upon the heart, celibacy cannot be defined in strictly behavioral terms (Matt. 5:27-28). It has to be a matter of "the heart" or the "whole soul."[26] Someone refraining from genital contact with another person but who, nonetheless, is racked with sexual desire is not to be called celibate or chaste. According to the Puritan theology of the Westminster Confession (1647), no Christian "may vow to do anything . . . which is not in his own power, and for the performance whereof he hath no promise or ability from God. In which respects, monastical vows of single life . . . are superstitious and sinful snares."[27] A vow is here defined as "of the like nature with a promissory oath" and "is not to be made to any creature, but to God alone."[28] Given the seriousness of the matter, a vow of celibacy undertaken by those who have not the gift is condemned as binding the conscience in the sense of backing it into a corner. The vow thus becomes a snare. "The Larger [Westminster] Catechism" goes so far as to expound the Seventh Commandment ("Thou shalt not commit adultery") by insisting that it is the duty of Christians "that have not the gift of continency" to marry.[29]

Historian Steven Ozment gives this final assessment of what the Reformers accomplished in their time: "No institutional change brought about by the Reformation was more visible, responsive to late medieval pleas for reform, and conducive to new social attitudes than the marriage of Protestant clergy. Nor was there another point in the Protestant program where theology and practice corresponded more successfully."[30] While all the practices of the Roman church identified as abuses (from indulgences to the veneration of saints) were diagnosed by the Protestants as having their origin in a false teaching about salvation, religious celibacy provided the Protestants with their clearest and most poignant example of the pernicious existential conse-quences of a distorted theology.[31] The abolition of celibacy, it must be under-stood, was a direct consequence of the Reformers' rejection of the Catholic doctrine about grace in favor of Luther's *sola fide*. This doctrine of justifica-tion was the one indispensable premise *sine qua non* of everything else they said and did. As the Lutheran Philipp Melanchthon (1497–1560) put it, jus-tification is "the chief article of Christian doctrine."[32] This doctrine is essen-tial to the Reformed tradition as well. Calvin proved himself a true follower of Luther when he affirmed that this doctrinal locus is the "main hinge on which religion turns."[33] Shifting the metaphor, he could say that everything else "rests on this foundation."[34] Hence, while the abolition of celibacy was merely one aspect of what the Reformation accomplished by way of reform-ing the Roman Catholic Church of abuses, it was unambiguously related to the central theological convictions of the Reformers.

CELIBACY FOR GAY PROTESTANTS?

The similarity between Luther's description of his anguished struggle to live as a celibate monk and my own dilemma as a gay man in the church first struck me after embarking upon a serious study of the Reformation while in the early stages of graduate school. At that time, I was attempting to discern what to do with my sense of calling to the ministry in the face of the haunt-ing awareness that I was different in a way the church condemned. Actually, my pursuit of further studies after having already completed the professional training required for ordination was, in part at least, an attempt to postpone a decision about vocation and to buy myself more time to think about what to do. I had never intended to become an academic; my interest in theology was always closely tied to understanding the role of the minister. In retrospect, I think that the deep confusion that comes from growing up gay without any guidance and support from parents, school, or church forced me to develop an introspective cast of mind well suited to the solitary life of scholarship. I sought wisdom from books since it was not to be had from people. Upon reading Luther, I discovered someone whose experience, including his inter-pretation of it, made sense to me in light of my own.

In Luther's depiction of his struggles with celibacy I saw reflected my private battle with sexual desire on account of its apparent conflict with commitment to a religious life. Even more importantly, I found in Luther's answer to his own predicament a suggestive possibility for how to resolve my dilemma. Ever since adolescence there was a tug of war within my soul between apparently irreconcilable forces: the ineradicable fact of homosexual desire and a heartfelt faith in Christ. I use the word *ineradicable* intentionally, for if it had been possible to rid myself of sexuality altogether, nothing would have stopped me from doing so. As that has never been a realistic possibility (prayer and therapy notwithstanding!), I have sometimes dreamed of being free of Christianity's firm hold on my heart and mind, since there seemed to be no way to express sexual desire all the while being faithful as a Christian. That was the bind of conscience in which I found myself.

Luther's words released me from this bind of conscience. As his interpretation of the gospel gradually took root in my mind and heart, I learned to accept sexual desire as a natural fact of life that need not drive me to despair of myself as a human being. Moreover, since my sexual orientation was neither chosen by me nor amenable to alteration, it seemed best to focus my anxieties on those aspects of my life for which I could actually be held responsible. I acknowledged that, like Luther, the "gift of celibacy" had not been given to me and thus forcing myself to live an ascetic life as a condition of being a Christian was not in keeping with the thrust of the gospel's message as taught by the Reformers.

If ever there was a Christian theology that could speak directly to the lived experience of gay people today, it is Luther's. It is impossible to read the words of Luther without being impressed by his realistic assessment of human nature. It is also true that one hasn't understood the first thing about the theology of the Reformers if their unequivocal doctrine of grace as the sole basis of salvation is falsified. To accept oneself as a gay person involves both realistically assessing oneself and one's sexual desires as well as relinquishing the internalized expectation of parents, church, and society that all of us will grow up to be heterosexual. The "coming out" process has often been likened to a religious "conversion," and not without good reason.[35] Given my Protestant perspective, I prefer to characterize my experience of it as the deep sense of self-acceptance that comes from having internalized the existential implications of the message that we are justified not through works but by faith alone.

To read Luther through the eyes of a gay Protestant is also to wonder if the church's antigay stance does not, in the final analysis, lead to a betrayal of its own theological heritage. To require celibacy of any Christian stands in direct contradiction to a fundamental tenet of Protestant theology as this was articulated during the Reformation: the church does not have the authority to bind the conscience to a vow of celibacy since the entire purpose of the gospel is to liberate persons from the false burden of works righteousness. In the sixteenth century, the Protestants abolished clerical celibacy and allowed ministers to marry; yet in our time, Protestants demand celibacy of gay people as a condition of their serving in the ministry since marriage is categorically denied them. A gay minister has only two options in contemporary Protestantism: either commit oneself to celibacy or live an "immoral" lifestyle since sexuality is properly expressed only in the marital relation. Why wouldn't the consistent implementation of Reformation principles in the matter of homosexuality lead Protestant churches today to allow, indeed encourage, their gay members to marry, so as not to demand of them an enforced celibacy that the sixteenth-century Reformers rejected for themselves? This would seem to be the logical solution to the problem of the church's inconsistency in its treatment of gay people.

Here, however, the analogy I've suggested breaks down at a crucial point that needs to be addressed forthrightly. No one in the medieval dispute ever questioned whether a marriage between a man and a woman was morally licit. No one doubted that it was possible to lead a Christian life while married. Marriage itself was not a sin. Both Luther and Calvin shared the traditional Christian aversion to homosexuality.[36] It goes without saying that the Reformers had no intention of defining marriage in anything other than a heterosexual manner. This was not even a question in the sixteenth century. The Reformers, like everyone else in their time, simply assumed that same-sex relations were morally wrong, but the morality of a sexual relationship between two men or two women is precisely the question today.

The reason the church refuses to ordain gay people who are not celibate is because homosexual relationships are believed to be morally incompatible with a Christian life. This belief explains why the church opposes expanding the meaning of marriage to include the covenanted relationship between two men or two women. The protest on the part of gay people that the church discriminates in excluding us from ordination is inextricably related to the fact that marriage is denied us as well. If the institution of marriage could be broadened to include gay people, then the question of ordination would fall into place of its own accord.

For those who do not view homosexuality itself as immoral, advocacy of marriage is the obvious answer, but that is not going to convince those for whom homosexuality, by definition, excludes the possibility of a moral relationship. There are two major reasons, both deeply rooted in Christian history, adduced to account for the condemnation of homosexuality. The first, especially favored by conservative Protestants, is that the moral code contained within the Bible is supernaturally revealed.[37] Hence, "faith" requires submission of our intellects to the authority of Scripture.[38] The second reason, characteristic of the Roman Catholic tradition, is the philosophical argument of natural-law ethics, according to which nature itself clearly teaches that all nonprocreative sex is unnatural.[39]

There is not space here to address the moral question in depth. Nonetheless, I have to confess that after thirty years, it has assumed an increasingly hollow ring to me. On intellectual grounds alone, the implications of a historical interpretation of both the Bible and philosophy do not warrant the degree of certainty placed in either "revelation" or "reason" called for by those who base their objections to homosexuality upon the infallibility of these sources.[40] On existential grounds, this debate has become pointless because, for gay people, we have no choice but to be homosexual. The urgent moral question we face is how to live our lives in a responsible way. Unfortunately, we will have to answer this question by ourselves without any help from the church so long as it denies that our sexual relationships can be moral. The ethical void to which the church has consigned us is well captured by Andrew Sullivan, columnist and devout Catholic, who observes "that in over thirty years of weekly churchgoing, I have never heard a homily that attempted to explain how a gay man should live, or how his sexuality should be expressed. I have heard nothing but a vast and endless and embarrassed silence. . . . The teaching I inherited was a teaching that, in the best of all possible worlds, I simply would not exist."[41] For those of us who have gone to church all our lives and have come to terms with our sexual orientation as adults, it is patently clear that the Christian teaching regarding homosexuality is really, as Sullivan says, "an unethic, a statement that some people are effectively beneath even the project of an ethical teaching."[42] Sullivan points out that celibates in his tradition at least had a reason for abstinence that gave meaning to their struggle: "Priests and religious were asked to abandon physical love in order to make themselves more fully able to receive God's love and to give it back to their flock. They were not asked, like homosexuals, to deny themselves human intimacy merely for the sake of self-sacrifice."[43]

Gay people do earnestly ask moral questions, even when relegated by church and society to a state of moral limbo. For me, the most tragic aspect of the current situation is that the church is not available for people who would gladly turn to it for guidance and direction. Before setting aside my ordination, I had been hesitant to reveal to other gay people my ministerial vocation lest I be called upon to defend the indefensible position of the church toward us. These days, when I explain that I *used* to be a minister, people are eager to relate their stories of growing up in the church, to explain how they make religious sense of their lives by drawing selectively on the resources of an internalized Christian tradition, and to share their moral dilemmas with me. I have become more of a pastor than ever before, now that I am no longer identified with a homophobic institution. Gay people are going to keep on trying to live responsibly and to find meaning with or without the churches. The saddest consequence of the church's posture toward gay people is its own missed opportunity for significant involvement in the lives of human beings who are religiously and morally serious people, searching for meaning and purpose by which to make sense of their existence and trying to find ways to navigate their course through a confusing world.[44]

Aside from consigning gay people to a moral nihilism, the church's position on homosexuality entails a religious problem. If the Reformers thought that a vow of celibacy was too much to ask of straight Christians, on what basis do the mainline Protestant churches set up the functional equivalent of a vow of celibacy for gay Christians? The analogy can be taken one step further. In Luther's day, his Roman Catholic opponents interpreted the infidelity of clergy to their vows of chastity as a moral problem calling for a moral solution. They countered Luther's assertion that the monastic life was contrary to the freedom of the Christian by accusing him of antinomianism: "Christian freedom means freedom from sin, not freedom from virtue."[45] By contrast, Luther thought Catholic doctrine was flawed since it put people into such binds of conscience in the first place: there is nothing virtuous in fighting a natural desire that is impossible to eradicate. Today we face a similar conflict. The opponents of homosexuality see in the demand of gay people for equal treatment a telling example of a general moral collapse within our society. The proponents of equality find a flaw in the rules that have backed gay people into the corner. A decision has to be made. Is the problem in the church today one of a lax morality, in which case every effort has to be made to uphold traditional standards in the face of threats to them? Or is the problem a religious issue that requires the church to revise its inherited proscription of homosexuality so that gay persons can have the same opportunity as heterosexuals to conduct their lives in a manner appropriate to a Protestant construal of the gospel?

Unlike Luther, I am not proposing a doctrinal reform of theology. My point, rather, is to ask whether, in the matter of homosexuality, today's churches of the Reformation heritage are truly drawing on that heritage's theological resources to think through the implications of their current position—both for the people immediately involved and for the integrity of the church at large.[46] My argument suggests that the Reformation debate surrounding clerical celibacy provides an important, though admittedly imperfect, analogy to assist contemporary churches in thinking about their deepest commitments in matters pertaining to human sexuality and marriage. My hope for the churches and for their gay members is that sexual orientation will eventually become an irrelevant consideration when reflecting upon what it means to live a moral life in a manner consonant with a Protestant interpretation of the gospel.

CONCLUSION

Luther's significance for gay Protestants today is potentially twofold. First, his theology allows gay Protestants to call their churches into question for requiring of us what would be seen as a form of "works righteousness" by heterosexual persons. If celibacy is the ideal for which gay Protestants are to strive as a condition of our faithfulness as Christians, then the church has relegated us to spiritual despair insofar as we are unable to embody the celibate ideal. For those of us who have chosen to reject celibacy as an ideal, the church provides no guidance on how we might live our lives in a truly moral manner. Second, Luther's doctrine of grace can liberate gay people existentially from the false bind of conscience into which the church has put us, even if that means deciding to live our lives outside of or in peripheral relation to the church. Quite apart from ecclesiastical approbation, the understanding of human existence as determined by faith in God issuing in love toward the neighbor can be creatively adapted to suit our particular circumstances. While the church may reject the proposal that the crisis over homosexuality has an analogy in the sixteenth-century debate regarding clerical celibacy, its potential for those gay persons who have already rejected the church's interpretation of our sexuality is enormous.

In the meantime, I have decided that it is no longer possible to represent the church in an official capacity as one of its ministers so long as my existence as a gay man is a matter of such contention. I need to live my life as best I can within the real constraints and in relation to the realistic possibilities that are truly mine, even if the church officially disapproves. In this respect, too, Luther is a model for me: he left the monastery behind, along with the religious ideal it represented, to embark upon a bold experiment in developing a new ideal for the Christian life that had marriage at its center. In relinquishing the ordained ministry, I am engaging in a slightly different experiment to see whether Luther's religious ideal can be embodied by gay people. I see no other alternative that is faithful to the understanding of life before God *sola fide*. Whether the churches in the Protestant tradition will seize upon these possibilities for revision latent within their theological heritage is a question yet to be decided.

Further Suggested Readings

Bainton, Roland H. *Here I Stand: A Life of Martin Luther.* Nashville: Abingdon, 1950.

Bouldrey, Brian, ed. *Wrestling with the Angel: Faith and Religion in the Lives of Gay Men.* New York: Riverhead, 1995.

Capetz, Paul E. "Defending the Reformed Tradition? Problematic Aspects of the Appeal to Biblical and Confessional Authority in the Present Theological Crisis Confronting the Presbyterian Church (U.S.A.)." *The Journal of Presbyterian History* 79, no. 1 (Spring 2001): 23–39.

Ozment, Steven. *The Age of Reform (1250–1550): An Intellectual and Religious History of Late Medieval Europe.* New Haven: Yale University Press, 1980.

PART II

Culture: Bodies, Desires, and Sexual Identitites

CHAPTER 8

Passing as Male in the Academy:
Dynamics of Performance and Desire

Shannon Craigo-Snell

I FIRST REALIZED I had been passing when I was retrieving luggage from the overhead bin of an airplane. Preparing to race to my connecting flight, I was pulling down my bag in the midst of a crush of passengers. A man touched my arm to prevent my being bashed by another bag descending from the same bin. He then touched my arm again, steadying my carry-on and helping me guide it to the floor in the midst of the crowd. He had done nothing wrong; his touch was both appropriate and helpful. And yet, I was shocked. This man—not a friend or a member of my family—had touched me! Furthermore, the way that he had done so had contained an implicit acknowledgment that I am female. He acknowledged he was stronger than I am, and he was very respectful in how he touched me. My surprise that he had done this made me realize that this rarely happens in my day-to-day life, outside of my own circle of family and friends. In fact, in my professional life, the reality that I am embodied and female is rigorously ignored by my male

135

colleagues and had been downplayed as much as possible by myself. I had been passing as male.[1]

In this chapter, I argue that women often have to pass as male in order to be accepted into academia. Two of the reasons for this are connected to dynamics of desire. The first is age-old and ongoing problematization of women's bodies as spaces of temptation, which hinges on male-focused heteronormative sexual desire. The second is somewhat more complex and involves a desire for certainty in modern Western epistemology. This desire is expressed in a dominant epistemology held in the academy that privileges the kinds of knowing associated most closely with males, problematizes embodiment, and demands uniformity of knowledge. Drawing on the work of seventeenth-century philosopher René Descartes and contemporary French feminist Luce Irigaray, I explore how mainstream modern Western epistemology has gone hand in hand with the oppression of women, and how women who are trained in Western academics participate in a discipline of self-erasure. Within mainstream epistemology, women cannot know as women, but only in so far as they imitate men. The effects of these dynamics of desire include cultural pressures for women in academia to downplay their own embodiment as women or, more provocatively stated, to pass as male.

Christian feminist theologians, such as myself, are caught within multiple iterations of these desires that privilege male knowers and abstract knowledge. I will argue that decreasing the pressure for women to pass as men in the academy requires a shifting of epistemological desire away from disembodied, singular, and certain knowledge and toward embodied, communal, and contextual knowing. Such an expansion of epistemological longings can be funded, I argue, by current theories of performance and performativity. These theories view many different kinds of events as performances and, thus, pay attention to many of the realities that Descartes and the mainstream modern epistemology that follows him intentionally ignore—including social location, community, and embodied action. An epistemology that uses the lens of performance, that claims that we know in and through performing, can serve as a corrective to and contestation of traditional modern epistemology. Such a performance-influenced epistemology would not generate the kind of knowledge Descartes desired. It would not be singular, universal, and stable. Instead, it would be multiple, contextual, and fluid, acknowledging many different ways of knowing and kinds of knowers. An epistemology that draws upon concepts of performance, I argue, might make it easier for women not to pass.

PASSING

When I say I pass as male, I mean this in a metaphoric sense. Everyone knows that I am female. Yet in my professional life, inclusion in the categories of "scholar" and "theologian" requires some level of acceptance within the category of "male." More literal passing—being seen by others as white, male, female, straight, Aryan, and so on—has a long and complicated history. In different instances, it can mean being seen as who you understand yourself to be or as someone who you are not. It can mean disappointment, liberation, or survival. It can be intended as a political act subverting norms, a tacit acceptance of normative identity categories, or an apolitical self-expression. What passing means is so dependent upon particularities that it defies confident generalization. Thus, I want to be clear that I am speaking of a very specific phenomenon within the halls of Western academia and that I am using passing in a metaphoric sense within this context.

Once the rubric of passing entered my mind on the airplane, I looked for evidence to support it and found ample supply. I could see it in myself. Since beginning my academic career, my hair had gotten shorter, makeup had disappeared, and my wardrobe tended toward vests and blazers. I could see it in my male colleagues. I had known my male mentor for over a decade; had we ever actually touched? I searched my memories. Once, after I had aced a comprehensive exam in systematic theology, he shook my hand. I recalled how another senior male colleague had to be told I was pregnant, even though I was waddling around in my eighth month, because he so studiously avoided looking at me below the eyes. I could see it in my female colleagues. I remembered, in my early days of graduate school, a classmate saying, "You write like a girl," as she crossed out the mitigating phrases ("I think," "it seems") in my essay. I recalled the box of unflattering bras passed on to me by another female graduate student before I became a teaching fellow at Yale. She informed me that breast camouflage was useful for young, female teaching fellows.

While I was angry when I realized I had been passing as male, I also realized there was no particular or personal malice involved here. My male mentor and colleagues were trying to do the right thing. We are all educated about the perils of sexual harassment, of unequal power dynamics between men and women in the workplace. We all know the history (unfortunately ongoing) of inappropriate crossing of boundaries between students, professors, and colleagues of differing ranks. Everyone is eager to avoid being harassed and being accused of harassment. If a man acknowledges that I am embodied and female, he runs the risk of enacting, or rousing suspicion of, sexual harassment, or at the very least of making my sex and gender a part of our relationship in a way that could be detrimental in our sexist world. There are thus a number of unspoken rules about the limits of interaction between female students and male professors, and I applaud all those men who abide by them. Thank you for leaving the door ajar while we met in your office, for meticulously meeting my eyes in every conversation, and for never mentioning my personal appearance.

However, the cultural response that attempts to fix the problem of women being harassed by men in the academy is deeply embedded in the culture that created the problem in the first place. The view of masculinity as normative and the image of woman as temptress both are reinscribed in the current social rules for how women in academia should be treated. Male normativity, and the heteronormativity that accompanies it, render female bodies as sites of danger. Quite simply, female bodies are problematized.

WHO KNOWS?

The dynamic of desire in which women's bodies are seen as temptations to the normative male is fairly straightforward, or at least terribly familiar. Women are marked as objects of masculine desire within a heteronormative framework in which men are seen as the primary actors and subjects. The second dynamic of desire that influences women passing in academia and the possibility of feminist theology is a bit more complex. This is a desire for certainty.

To describe this dynamic of desire, I find it useful to look to René Descartes. An author who had a profound influence on modern epistemology, Descartes wrote during a time when Europe was in disarray due to a number of factors, including religious warfare, climate change, groundbreaking scientific discoveries, and increasing awareness of cultural and religious diversity.[2] Europeans of this era were faced with difficult questions just when the traditional forms of knowledge and wisdom that they had inherited seemed to fall apart. This turbulent context formed the background for an emerging desire for certain knowledge that is singular, universally true, and self-evident. Such certainty would provide stability in troubled times, create common ground for negotiating disputes and navigating diversity, and be the foundation for a new edifice of human knowledge that would not be threatened by future discoveries.

In order to know with certainty, Descartes decided to doubt everything he had been taught, everything he formerly believed, and everything his senses told him. He attempted to abstract himself from culture, commitment, embodiment, and community. Descartes understood that our social locations and cultural contexts influence how we see the world around us. He wanted to peel away the layers of cultural prejudice and social influence to find purely rational truth, universal and singular, which could form the foundation upon which new, reliable knowledge could be built. Descartes had a kind of epistemological conversion in 1619, when his method of rigorous doubt revealed the one thing he could not doubt, and which he therefore took to be certain: "I think; therefore I am."[3] Descartes took this as "the first principle of philosophy."[4]

Immediately after reaching this landmark conclusion of indubitable truth, Descartes wrote explicitly about the relationship between the body, mind, and soul:

> I knew from this that I was a substance, the whole essence or nature of which was to think and which, in order to exist, has no need of any place and does not depend on anything material. Thus this self—that is, the soul by which I am what I am—is completely distinct from the body and is even easier to know than it, and even if the body did not exist the soul would still be everything that it is.[5]

While a dualistic view of body and mind can be found in many eras in the West, here it is amplified and reinforced for the new context of modernity. The division of body and soul, followed by an identification of soul with mind and the affirmation that thought is the essence of human nature, is a one-two punch that places the body in a inferior, nonessential, nearly expendable role.

The effects of such dualism are relatively obvious and have been noted by many. It grants privilege to the educated: if to be human is to think, then thinkers are the most human. It denigrates people whose daily activities are more associated with the body: if to be human is to think, then those who are not primarily identified with thinking appear less human. These effects fall out in relation to race and gender, thus providing a measure of justification for the oppression of women and black people in the early modern period.[6]

The circumscribed scope of women's daily activities was not the only reason they were seen as less rational than men. Menstruation, pregnancy, childbirth, and nursing are evidence of involvement in bodily and natural cycles and have often been seen as indications that women are more connected than men to the body and to nature. Thus, women have been viewed as more bodily than men, precisely because of their sex. Eighteenth-century philosopher Jean-Jacques Rousseau wrote: "The consequences of sex are wholly unlike for man and woman. The male is only a male now and again, the female is always a female, or at least all her youth; everything reminds her of her sex; the performance of her functions requires a special constitution. She needs care during pregnancy and freedom from work when her child is born; she must have a quiet, easy life while she nurses her children."[7] This fascinating passage raises numerous questions, among them, What are men when they are not male? Clearly Rousseau did not think they are women, and the concepts of intersexed or transgendered persons were not exactly mainstream in the early modern period. I suspect that Rousseau is not indicating that men take on a sex or gender different from male but, rather, that they often inhabit the kind of disembodied humanity, described by Descartes, wherein the body is unnecessary and thought alone defines what it is to be human. Rousseau suggests that when men are not reminded of their maleness, they not only cease to be gendered, they cease to be embodied. Like Wile E. Coyote running over the cliff, standing on pure air, as long as men do not think about their bodies, the bothersome realities of embodiment can be ignored and almost escaped. Race offers a different analogy: as whiteness becomes invisible in a racist society, such that white people are not people "of color" and have no race, so maleness becomes invisible in a sexist society, such that only women are marked by sexuality and embodiment. There are two sides to this coin: a male can be seen as disembodied and the ideal of the disembodied thinker is inherently male.

The two dynamics of desire that I have described—the male heteronormative desire for women that problematizes women's bodies and the desire for certainty—are intertwined. The view of women as sexual temptresses is part of why women are seen as more bodily than men. Conversely, part of why men fear the temptation of women is because women, in their embodiment and sexuality, remind men that they are men, and thereby threaten masculine rationality and the illusion of the disembodied knower. It is not just the case that women are too embodied to know with certainty. By arousing men's awareness of their own sexuality and embodiment, women interfere with the capacity of men to know with certainty.

THE STUDY OF SELF-ERASURE/
THE SELF-ERASURE OF STUDY

It might be possible to imagine that I first observed and analyzed all of this before I cut my hair short and started to pass. In actuality, I started passing long before I was aware of these dynamics. Learning to pass was part and parcel of my training to be an academic. Luce Irigaray paints a chilling portrait of academic training in her essay "Plato's Hystera." This midrashic retelling of Plato's myth of the cave analyzes and criticizes the foundational assumptions of modern Western culture. In a very broad sense, Irigaray's project can be seen in continuity with that of Descartes. She is questioning the cultural assumptions that shape knowledge, in an attempt to gain a clearer view. In particular, she questions many of the assumptions that Descartes did not acknowledge in his moments of radical doubt, such as the singularity of truth.

Linguistically remapping Plato's cave onto the female body, Irigaray contends that Western ways of knowing exclude women from the revered positions of knower and speaker. Irigaray identifies part of the reason for this in the way that Western culture creates identity through opposition, within a larger framework of sameness that is supported by a view of truth as singular. In Western culture, we know one thing in opposition to its other. Dark is the opposite of light, stop is the opposite of go, no is the opposite of yes, and women are the opposite of men. This binary opposition is how identity is established. Yet ultimately, Western epistemology is committed to a singular and universal "Truth." This singularity grounds a logic of sameness in which all things are judged by one standard, all things can be compared, and hierarchy is vital to stability.[8] Difference—even thoroughgoing binary opposition—would threaten the stability of identity and the logic of sameness that allows hierarchy. Thus, the originary moment of difference must be suppressed, repressed, and forgotten. The apparent oppositions that guarantee identity must be understood as hierarchical gradations.[9] Women are seen not as truly different from men but as lesser, inferior reflections of the masculine norm of humanity. Darkness is the absence of light; stop is the negation of go. Women are the other of men, serving to secure masculine identity without being permitted a feminine identity of our own. All of this is anchored and required by an understanding of truth as singular and stable.

Within this framework, Irigaray presents the process of education as one that does violence to the student, systematically blinding her to diverse ways of knowing and inculcating a singular view of truth. Over time, as all other ways of knowing are denied, this singular view of truth appears self-evident.[10] As that singular vision regards women as inferior reflections of men, for a female student, education is a process in which she interiorizes her own erasure.

Irigaray maps this process as a movement out of the cave that is the womb into the mind above. It is an exodus from the female body, and from matter itself, into the ideal of the pure "Idea," untainted by embodiment or location.[11]

In order to have the stability and unity of knowledge that we desire—that certainty—a system is produced that leads away from the body toward an illusion of disembodied knowing that reinforces masculine dominance. Once the student has arrived at the point of contemplating self-evident ideas, any memory of mother/matter must be repressed and forgotten, understood only as the space of mimicry and reflection.[12]

Throughout this essay, Irigaray refutes the basic epistemological claims made by Descartes and embraced by the modern period. Among these are the singular and universal nature of truth and the denigration of embodiment as an impediment to knowledge. Irigaray does not argue against these views directly but, rather, unmasks them and reveals the ways in which they undergird an epistemology that excludes women from discourse and from knowing. She uses a theatrical metaphor, indicating that she is exposing the "stage setup"[13] within which women are constrained. We cannot know or speak as women but only insofar as we reflect and mirror men. Since knowing and speaking are masculine roles, women can only begin to inhabit them by mimicking men. When the disembodied knower is gendered as male, women striving for disembodied knowledge are appropriating a masculine position. "Plato's Hystera" makes the phenomenon of female academics passing as men seem like the logical option for survival within the Western logic of the same.

FEMALE CHRISTIAN THEOLOGIANS

It might seem that women who are Christian theologians could occupy a friendlier theatre. After all, Christianity centers on a story about bodies: a pregnant woman, a squealing infant, hungry masses, a blind man, a bleeding woman, a dead man whose corpse has begun to reek, prisoners in the midst of execution, a battered man on a cross. Moreover, embodiment in Christian life is deeply communal, involving communal liturgy and worship, communal affirmations of faith, and community service. Christians talk about the whole community being one body in Christ. Surely there is an understanding of knowledge here that is far from the disembodied individuality of modern epistemology. There should be room, in such a tradition, for women to know as women. Yet Christianity falls prey to the same dynamics of desire that encourage women throughout academia to pass as men. The first desire, the male-focused heteronormativity that marks women's bodies as sites of danger and temptation, is inscribed deeply in Christian traditions going back to Eve and continuing in contemporary debates about gay marriage. Christians, including many prominent theologians, have both nourished and partaken of this dynamic of desire throughout the ages.

The second dynamic of desire I have discussed, the desire for certainty, has found fertile ground in modern Christian thought. While the traditions of Christianity extend far beyond the scope of modern Western epistemology, contemporary academic theology is deeply imbued with modern sensibilities. In the early modern period, many thinkers, such as seventeenth-century English philosopher John Locke, attempted to understand and articulate Christianity in ways that conformed to modern standards of knowledge.[14] Communal and embodied rituals were downplayed and faith was understood in terms of intellectual assent.

Irigaray's critique describes the desire for certain, self-evident knowledge as inextricably connected with monotheism and with images of God as male.[15] From this perspective, the assumptions of Christianity are implicated in the production of the epistemology that Irigaray rejects. The modern desire for certainty has thrived in Christian soil, out of which some of its seeds have arisen. Add to this a male savior, church traditions that deny women leadership roles, and theological arguments for the divinely ordained submission of women to men, and female theologians have an uphill battle. The embodied and communal knowledge within Christianity is filtered through patriarchal lenses and modern desires.

For example, last year I was teaching a course on systematic theology, lecturing about the doctrine of the incarnation. I asked the students: "If, as some theologians suggest, Jesus redeems humanity by participating in our embodiment, then what do we do with the limitations and particularities of his life? Are the aspects of human life that Jesus did not experience left unredeemed? What does it mean that Jesus never grew old?" The students listened to this in silence: it was an interesting point to ponder, following logically from previous discussions. I continued with several other questions in this vein, then asked, "What does it mean that he never got his period?" At this last question, there was a loud, communal gasp.

I have used this line many times in lectures, always to the same effect. There are probably several reasons why the students find it shocking. One reason is that because Jesus is male, he participates in that kind of embodiment that can be forgotten, that can become invisible and abstract in modern minds. We can speak of the incarnation as something that makes Jesus like us—like all of us—without recalling that bodies are replete with differences. Menstruation is a characteristic of those bodies that cannot be abstracted into an invisible universal, those that are marked as different, other, and less than the ideal. The mention of menstruation was shocking, conjuring the inescapable embodiment of female existence, reminding the students in the room of their own embodiment and of the almost forgotten reality that I, their teacher, am female. I am not like the ideal of a college teacher in their minds: the gentleman with graying temples wearing tweed. Nor am I like the definitive teacher in the minds of the Christian students: a thirty-something Jewish man in sandals.

BEYOND PASSING

How can we move forward, get beyond the need for women to pass in academia? Given my argument, the logical answer is to alter the dynamics of desire discussed above, to resist heteronormativity, and to embrace new epistemologies. Many theologians are working on this. Queer theologians challenge the heterosexist bias of Christianity and the broader culture.[16] Feminist, womanist, and liberation theologians develop methodologies that do not attempt to gain knowledge via abstraction from embodiment, community, and commitment but, rather, within those very realities.[17] The influx of persons who had been previously excluded from academic theology, including women and people of color, brings new perspectives to the field in which experience is seen as a valuable source for theological reflection. Furthermore, the emergence of postmodernism draws attention to the unacknowledged presuppositions of modernity, including the limitations on knowledge imposed by the desire for certain truth.

With all of this, it would seem that the days of modern epistemology are over or at least numbered. However, the structures and traditions of academia often uphold them in ways that are either too subtle or too blatant to notice. Teachers and students can talk of knowing in embodied ways, but often such discussions happen while everyone is seated at a table, in a room designed not to distract, taking notes in a posture that is deeply associated with intellectual pursuits and bodily abstraction. Talking about learning through our bodies, while we enact the rituals of body-forgetfulness associated with scholarship, reinscribes modern epistemology even as it contests it. Traditional pedagogical methods are simply inadequate for emerging epistemologies that challenge the mainstream modern view of knowledge.

Some teachers and professors do the hard work of enacting new pedagogical approaches. However, this comes at a cost. To embrace—not just in theory but in practice—embodied, communal, committed ways of knowing, is to not pass.[18] It is to mark oneself as embodied and gendered, to diverge from the pattern of what a knower looks like, and to risk conflict with all the deep-seated prejudices of colleagues and institutions with roots in the main-stream epistemology of modernity.

There are challenges to research as well. Requirements for publication go nicely with the goal of certain truth, grounded on solid argument, abstract thought, concrete data. Embodied and communal knowing is hard to put on the page. It must be translated, streamlined, made singular or linear enough to withstand scholarly narration. If the text is written to resist this, it might not be read as appropriately academic. In the day-to-day realities of the class-room, the faculty meeting, and the tenure review, there are still many pres-sures for women to pass.

When Irigaray describes possibilities for resisting the all-encompassing logic of the same and its erasure of women as women, she says that women must begin by occupying the roles to which they have been assigned. We cannot immediately jump into a new reality. However, by occupying these roles with some knowledge of the stage setup, doing it deliberately, and doing it in the extreme, women can resist the system in which they are constrained. Irigaray asserts, "There is, in an initial phase, perhaps only one 'path,' the one historically assigned to the feminine: that of mimicry. One must assume the feminine role deliberately."[19] Through mimesis, women can attempt to "make visible, by an effect of playful repetition, what was supposed to remain invis-ible: the cover-up of a possible operation of the feminine in language."[20] As Irigaray's analysis explains why women have to pass in academia, she also offers the possibility that women can go beyond merely passing into a form of implicated resistance. Women can play their assigned role, repeat their scripted parts, and yet do so with enough awareness and difference to chal-lenge the structure of the ongoing theatrics. This kind of thinking has been developed in current conversations about performance and performativity—conversations that seek not only strategies for survival and resistance but also new ways to understand knowledge itself.

MOVING TOWARD PERFORMANCE AND PERFORMATIVITY

In the last sixty years, the concept of performance has become important in a number of different fields, including anthropology, psychology, linguistics, theatre studies, and—more recently—religious studies.[21] The term *perfor-mance* is used differently in these various fields, so much so that some scholars describe performance as an "essentially contested concept."[22] This means "the disagreement over its essence is itself a part of its essence."[23] In the emerg-ing field of performance studies, this multiplicity of meaning is seen not as an incapacitating drawback but, rather, as an invitation to view numerous realities through the lens of performance in order to understand them in new and multiple ways. Many different realities, from a wedding ceremony to an office conversation to the reading of a book, can be seen as a performance.

One way to think of this is that looking at something as a performance encourages paying attention to particular characteristics. These characteristics include action, interaction, and doubleness. A performance is an action that takes place in a specific time, place, and community. Understanding something as performance therefore requires analysis of its context, as the context is both productive of the performance and part of the performance itself.[24] A performance cannot be understood in abstraction from the time, place, and people involved. Similarly, a performance is an interaction. It is a relational reality that involves a performer, an audience, and the culture than engenders the performance. Understanding something as a performance means paying attention to this relationality. Finally, a performance involves doubleness. This odd term refers to "the peculiar doubling that comes with consciousness and with the elusive *other* that performance is not but which it constantly struggles in vain to embody."[25] Consider an actor, striving to perform the character Hamlet but never actually becoming Hamlet; an athlete, attempting to run a few seconds faster than she ever has before; an academic, trying to sound like a scholar as she writes on the page. Each of these efforts involves a doubleness, such that the action performed is "placed in mental comparison with a potential, an ideal, or a remembered original model of that action."[26]

The doubleness of performance indicates that human actions are modeled on ideal or remembered versions of that action. Our behaviors are repetitions of other behaviors we have learned as standard, appropriate, or useful. Richard Schechner, an influential author in the field of performance studies, points out that we can break down our everyday lives into bits of behavior that are familiar, which we have seen and enacted before and which we rearrange and reshape for particular contexts.[27] Schechner calls this "restored behavior," a phrase that is key to his understanding of performance. He writes:

> Restored behavior is "out there," separate from "me." To put it in more personal terms, restored behavior is "me behaving as if I were someone else," or "as I have learned." Even if I feel myself wholly to be myself, acting independently, only a little investigating reveals that the units of behavior that comprise "me" were not invented by "me."[28]

Such understandings of human behavior lead quickly to appreciation for the plasticity of human identity and the social construction of the self. These issues have been explored by scholars such as Judith Butler, a philosopher and queer theorist. Butler draws on postmodern theories and linguistics, particularly the work of J. L. Austen, to describe performativity. For Butler, performativity refers to the ways in which the repetition of culturally normative gestures and performances (what Schechner would call "restored behavior") generates a sense of an abiding self and, more explicitly, a particular gender and sexual identity. We learn, over time, to act in ways that produce the appearance of a stable self, sex, and gender. This overturns the assumption that a stable gender generates certain behaviors and, instead, asserts that the repetitive performance of these behaviors generates the appearance of a stable gender. Butler claims, "There is no gender identity behind the expressions of gender; that identity is performatively constituted by the very 'expressions' that are said to be its results."[29]

The implications of such a theory of performativity for modern epistemology are manifold. The knowing subject simply cannot, as Descartes so fervently hoped, peel away the effects of cultural influence and find a pure, stable subjectivity upon which a new edifice of human knowledge—replete with certain truth—could be erected. The sense of self is generated by cultural influence, as learned behaviors are repeatedly performed in normative patterns. Thus, the concept of performativity furthers the critique of modern epistemology by destabilizing the knowing subject. This destabilization reveals the social construction and cultural locatedness of knowledge.

Butler's theory also has another effect that is important for feminist theologians dealing with the dynamics of desire that play out in the contemporary academy. Her understanding of the self as performatively constituted destabilizes—even unhinges—the assumed links between physical sex, gender, and desire. The assumptions that support heteronormativity are profoundly challenged by her work. This is seen most explicitly in Butler's discussion of how performativity can be deployed in resisting sexist and heterosexist oppression. Drawing on Irigaray's concept of mimesis, Judith Butler identifies the possibility of agency within a repetition that is also a displacement. She writes, "As the effects of a subtle and politically enforced performativity, gender is an 'act,' as it were, that is open to splittings, self-parody, self-criticism, and those hyperbolic exhibitions of 'the natural' that, in their very exaggeration, reveal its fundamentally phantasmatic status."[30] One of Butler's examples of such subversive exaggerations is drag. She argues that drag effectively mocks the expressivist notion of stable gender identities.[31]

Butler illustrates this with a quote from Esther Newton, who, writing about female impersonators, asserts that drag states both "my outside 'appearance' is feminine, but my essence 'inside' is masculine" and "my appearance 'outside' is masculine but my essence 'inside' is feminine."[32]

Butler's work and the ongoing development of the concept of performativity therefore offers another novel take on epistemology, and one that counters mainstream modern epistemology very well. It offers resources for resisting male normativity and heteronormativity and for contesting the view of the best knower as an individual abstracted from community, embodiment, and commitment. Thus, it might be profoundly helpful in creating a space in academia in which women do not have to pass.

Butler's development of performativity has strong resonances with passing. She has written about passing, and many other scholars who write on the topic use her work as a resource.[33] Can performance and performativity be resources for resisting the pressures for female academics to pass if passing is performative, is performance?

NEW DYNAMICS OF DESIRE

Up to this point, I have discussed two dynamics of desire that, I believe, pressure women in academia to pass (metaphorically) as male. These two dynamics of desire are male-focused heteronormativity and modern epistemology that seeks certainty. Here I want to question desire from a different angle. What is it that I desire in passing? I desire to be accepted into specific categories ("scholar," "theologian") that are gendered as male in our culture. Although I note again that the diversity of passings defies generalization, intentional passing often includes a desire on the part of the one who passes to be accepted into categories acknowledged by the broader culture. Conversely, passing reveals a desire on the part of the larger culture to place people into defined categories—to label and name who and what they are. In colloquial language, passing is passing as something, where that something is a known quantity. Passing moves toward known categories, even as it might sometimes subvert them.

Discussions of performance and performativity highlight the ways in which our actions in the world are repetitions of prior actions. Culturally coded behaviors comprise the grammar of our possible conduct and the lexicon through which it will be interpreted. Our enactments and even our desires can never be unmoored from cultural categories and historical patterns; yet the content of a performer's desire is not limited to a predefined norm. Performances move from and within known categories but not necessarily toward them.

Passing "as" something indicates a desire for participation—in some way or degree—in a reality that already exists: to be granted the privileges of masculinity or the safety of straightness, to enter into white society, to get a job or a visa or an opportunity. The limitation of benefits, opportunities, and freedoms to certain groups constrains multiple desires into desire for inclusion in existing categories. In an essay on Nella Larsen's novel *Passing*, Catherine Rottenberg persuasively argues that "racist discourse attempts to produce desire in the black other to mime the ways of the whites."[34] While passing functions in myriad ways—liberating, subversive, repressive—it often involves such regulation of desire. I understand passing to be a subset of performance. I see it as a type of performance that is marked by desire for known categories: the desire to fit into such categories and the desire to fit others into such categories. The broader concept of performance defies delineation by desire. It does not lay claim to what is to be desired.

Both performance and performativity open up the subversive possibilities of playing an assigned role but doing so with a twist. In the particular type of performance that is passing, the twist—the displacement of repetition, the infidelity of performance—is in who performs the roles. Passing, in my own colloquial understanding of the term, implies playing a different role than previously expected. The roles—the positions to be desired—remain the same. In the larger categories of performance and performativity, where the twist in repetition happens is not fixed. It can happen anywhere—in those who perform, how they perform, what, where, for whom, with whom they perform, and so on. The radical open-endedness of how and where the twist can happen in performance and performativity means that desires can be playfully expanded, altered, and explored. Unruly desires could flourish and performers could act their way into novel, unforeseen roles.

Given the two dynamics of desire within Western academia that I have discussed—male-focused heteronormative sexual desire and the epistemological desire for certainty—my own desire to be a Christian theologian translates into a desire to fit into masculine categories. It is regulated into a desire to pass. In order for the pressure for women to pass as men in academia to abate, our regulative cultural desires must change.

Performance and performativity hold out possibilities of contesting the cultural dynamics of desire that encourage female academics to pass and of funding new epistemologies in which women could know as women. Mainstream modern epistemologies honor certain and singular knowledge as the ultimate desideratum. Epistemologies informed by theories of performance and performativity contest the very possibility of such certain, singular knowledge. If both knowers and knowledge come to be in performing, then the messy negotiations of context and culture, the unruly relationships of embodiment, community, and commitment, are always part of what it is to know. Performance-based epistemologies thus challenge both the possibility and the desirabilty of disembodied, singular, and certain truth. What is to be desired, then, as the pinnacle of knowledge? The discourse of performance does not dictate desire. The desire for certainty, with its concomitant affinity for sameness, singularity, and universality, could give way to a desire for possibilities, difference, multiplicity, and fluidity. The longing for stability to ground a sturdy edifice of knowledge might recede as a desire for fecundity to sustain and renew an ongoing generation of knowledge emerges. The regulated desires of male-focused heteronormativity that render women's bodies as temptation might give way to celebration of multiple desires and sexualities in which all bodies are visible. Perhaps, also, the pedagogical practices consonant with modern epistemology might fade, as new ways of knowing are recognized and performed in the classroom.

Thinking of knowledge and identity in terms of performance and performativity can contest the desires that pressure women to pass and can fund new perspectives on epistemology.[35] The kind of analysis offered by performance studies and by discussions of performativity might help create a space in Western academia where women can know and speak as women. Furthermore, such analyses and discussions might help theologians account for and articulate the knowing that takes place in the community that is the body of Christ.

Further Suggested Readings

Bordo, Susan. *The Flight to Objectivity: Essays on Cartesianism and Culture.* Albany: State University of New York Press, 1987.

Butler, Judith. *Gender Trouble: Feminism and the Subversion of Identity.* New York: Routledge, 1990.

Carlson, Marvin A. *Performance: A Critical Introduction.* 2nd ed. New York: Routledge, 2004.

Ginsberg, Elaine K., ed. *Passing: Identity and Interpretation in Sexuality, Race, and Religion.* New York: New York University Press, 2001.

Irigaray, Luce. *Speculum of the Other Woman.* Trans. Gillian C. Gill. Ithaca: Cornell University Press, 1985.

CHAPTER 9

"Baptizing" Queer Characters

Mark D. Jordan

SINCE THE SECOND WORLD WAR, churchly discourse about same-sex desire has changed remarkably—in its detail and volume, in its varieties of evidence and manners of argument, but above all in its choices to "baptize" certain identities or characters, as I prefer to say.[1] Understanding changes in the chosen names for the characters projected around same-sex desire may help us assess the controversies now rending Christian institutions. It will certainly renew old questions about how Christian ethics can be said to make progress—especially when it appropriates from other expert dis-courses changing names and descriptions for ethical actors. In the last fifty years, church writers baptized at least three new characters: the invert, the homophile, and the homosexual. Each term has seemed to promise theo-logians progress in controversial matters. Did any of them in fact help to recognize or to foster Christian characters that could desire queerly?

THE INVERT

I must begin by stepping back before my announced beginning after World War II. In the 1890s, the self-taught reformer Havelock Ellis popularized for English speakers the awkward noun *invert* to describe a character whose "sexual instinct" had been "turned by inborn constitutional abnormality" toward those of the same sex.[2] Ellis fashioned neither the metaphor nor its implied theory. He copied the noun from Italian and French writers of forensic psychiatry, who had coined it to capture the diagnosis—proposed by Carl Westphal, applied by Richard von Krafft-Ebing—of "contrary sexual feeling," that is, of the feeling's "inborn reversal (*Verkehrung*)."[3] The original term translated in English as "homosexuality" was also coined in German during these years. First a neutral term intended for use in legal reform, Krafft-Ebing fused "homosexuality" with Westphal's notion of contrary sexual feeling. Note three things about Westphal's original notion as Englished by Ellis: sexual inversion is inborn, it is a reversal of feeling across a fixed gender binary, and it is pathological. The reversal need not determine sexual behavior. It is entirely possible to be an invert and to have only heterosexual relations or none at all. The reversal of sexual feeling does invariably indicate a "general pathological condition."[4] It manifests an underlying disorder, such as "moral insanity," which is linked in turn to tainted heredity or failed development.[5] In short, Ellis's term *invert*, like so many terms of early sexology, took its meanings from theories of racial superiority and degeneration.

I now jump to the years immediately following World War II and to my first sample from the archives of church speech. In 1954, a group associated with the Moral Welfare Council of the Church of England published a pamphlet entitled *The Problem of Homosexuality: An Interim Report*. The specific occasion for the pamphlet was news reporting and public discussion leading up to a British Home Office review of criminal laws on prostitution and homosexual acts.

The pamphlet was not meant to be public; it was printed "For private circulation," as the title page cautions.[6] It is an invitation to expert consultation among those who must deal with homosexuality as a social problem. The pamphlet cites the first Kinsey report, but it does not take up Alfred Kinsey's suggestion about naming characters. Kinsey urges his readers not to speak of homosexuals but only of the frequency over a particular period of homosexual desires or acts ("outlets," he famously calls them).[7] The Anglican pamphlet, on the contrary, understands homosexuality not as frequent or infrequent conduct but as a permanent condition. Echoing Ellis, it calls a person who suffers the condition an invert. It distinguishes the true invert from the "pervert," that is, from "a heterosexual who engages in homosexual practices."[8]

The character of the invert appears during adolescence most probably from psychological causes rather than from inheritance. Eugenic theories are tacitly rejected by the pamphlet; institutionalized psychoanalytic ones are endorsed. The pamphlet admits that many normal adolescents feel homosexual tendencies for brief periods. The desires can become abnormally and tragically fixed if there is an "unsatisfactory parental relationship": an absent father, a smothering mother, or the retreat of both parents after divorce. This latent parental damage may then be precipitated by failed attempts to date women, by sexual experiments at boys' school, or by the solicitations of an older man confirmed in his vice. Here it becomes clear how inexorably the pamphlet imagines the character of the invert as male, though it does excuse itself at one moment to consider women, noting the particular problem of schoolgirls who fall in love with their teachers—and teachers who reciprocate. In these exclusions and excuses, the pamphlet agrees with most earlier Christian texts on the sodomite. Indeed, we can appreciate here and elsewhere how the supposedly superseded category "sodomite" operates through its successors.[9]

Inversion cannot generally be altered, either because there is no therapy for it or because therapy is resisted. What then are the ethical implications for inverts? The pamphlet answers clearly: fixation in adolescence "will exempt an invert for responsibility for his homosexual condition *but cannot absolve him from responsibility for immoral homosexual practices*."[10] The phrase is a double tautology: a person is by definition responsible for "immoral" acts strictly speaking, and all "homosexual practices" will turn out to be immoral. It may then come as a surprise that the Anglican pamphlet advocates decriminalizing consensual homosexual acts between adults. The authors insist on the state's obligation to protect the young but contend that the current criminal regime endangers children and adolescents by driving fearful adults to prey on them rather than forming liaisons with adults.[11] Of course, a higher age of consent should still be set for homosexual activities in criminal law since they are unnatural.[12]

The legal echo of an old Christian accusation carried in the word *unnatural* may remind us that the pamphlet's arguments are so far not distinctively Christian. Other pages do offer ethico-theological lessons for the invert—all-too-familiar lessons: "Homosexual acts are sins against God, whether or not they are also crimes against the State."[13] The pamphlet uses the mock-scriptural term *sodomy* when condemning every act that involves the "physiologically unnatural use of non-complementary organs within a relationship which is not that of man and woman."[14] These acts cannot be excused on a plea of love any more than can sexual acts between other unmarried lovers. The only space for erotic life among Christians is within marriage. Since inverts should not attempt heterosexual marriage, and since allowing them to pretend to marry each other would undermine society, the pamphlet advises inverts to follow the example of those unfortunate (heterosexual) women who cannot find a husband: they should *"accept their condition, and by seeking to sublimate their sexual lives in socially useful ways achieve personal fulfillment."*[15] Thus, and more specifically, inverts should avoid dubious bars, cultivate chaste friendships, immerse themselves in good works, and have frequent recourse to the sacraments, while society figures out how best to correct the psychological causes of their condition.

That last counsel captures the central incoherence of the 1954 pamphlet. It adopts a medical theory of inversion to advocate decriminalizing some same-sex relations. Adult inverts should not be punished by the state when they form consensual, monogamous pairs: it is the best they can do, and crueler consequences will follow on trying to stop them. This is an expert plea, at once medical and pastoral, for civil clemency. At the same time, the pamphlet offers only the old penitential advice to believing inverts: carry your cross in chaste solitude. The two-stage rhetorical address—a plea for mercy to the state, an ascetical admonition to believers—reveals the incoherence that results from baptizing the character of the invert into otherwise unchanged churchly rhetoric. The pamphlet wants to repeat traditional Christian judgments on same-sex copulations, while replacing the traditional characters posited behind them. The customary church remedies cannot be derived from the psychiatric narrative of inversion. The same incoherence still appears frequently in church speeches, though perhaps most starkly in the contemporary "ex-gay" movement, which attempts to paste mid-twentieth century psychotherapeutic characters into literalist scriptural exegeses and communal practices of spiritual correction.[16]

The 1954 pamphlet's incoherence was addressed immediately by Derrick Sherwin Bailey, who had championed formation of the group and who drafted part of its pamphlet.[17] When Bailey wrote in his own voice about these questions, he wrote beyond the pamphlet and against it. With his colleagues' knowledge, Bailey published for a general audience in 1955 a monograph: *Homosexuality and the Western Christian Tradition*.[18] He introduces it as a historical supplement to the pamphlet, meant to explore how church tradition has contributed to contemporary attitudes about male-male desire. Bailey is struck by the difference between theological, legal, and cultural reactions to male-male acts and those to lesbianism. He insists both on the relative rarity of mentions of lesbianism in Christian tradition and the churches' much lighter persecution of lesbian acts.[19] Still, Bailey's larger aim is actually to disconnect ethical tradition from the present in order to mitigate pastoral incoherence. Christian tradition about homosexuality "can no longer be regarded as an adequate guide by the theologian, the legislator, the sociologist, and the magistrate."[20] Bailey judges the tradition "defective" so far as it failed to recognize a clinical fact about human beings—namely, and again, the distinction between inversion and perversion. Bailey does strain to find earlier hints of the distinction. For example, he argues that Paul in Romans 1:27 is describing "male perverts" and not inverts. Still, the main Western church tradition regularly confuses perverts with inverts and so has "but an indirect and dubious relevance" to contemporary debates.[21]

Given this critique of tradition, it might come as another surprise that Bailey does not endorse inverted love in this book.[22] He finds it a "mysterious and unfortunate condition," an "abnormality," a "handicap."[23] Even if private acts among consenting adults are decriminalized, inversion itself will remain a social problem and an index of the decay of marriage and family life. Instead of punishing inverts with criminal penalties, society ought to admit its responsibility for the conditions that bring them into existence; it ought to improve marriage and family life in order to reduce their numbers. This is another iteration of the Christian tradition's recurring dream of a world without sodomites—I mean, without inverts.

Bailey's argument deprives traditional Christian condemnations of their scriptural and ethico-legal underpinnings, but he then displaces the tradition in favor of the category of pathological inversion. Traditional damnations are replaced with stigmatizing diagnosis and pessimistic prognosis. We might want to think that Bailey performed this shift only as a temporary stratagem—only in order to advance decriminalization or to open space for churchly debate. These may indeed have been his reserved intentions. Still, his text replaces churchly condemnation all too neatly with clinical prognosis. It resolves the pamphlet's incoherence by baptizing the authority of clinicians.

Despite this recourse to pathology, if not indeed because of it, Bailey's book was received eagerly by queer readers in the United States. It was reviewed within a few months of its publication by One: The Homosexual Magazine and by the Mattachine Review.[24] After wondering whether Bailey tries too hard to exonerate the Christian church, One's reviewer judges his book "perhaps the most important . . . yet published on homosexuality" for "the intelligent religious reader."[25] In the next year, the retiring president of the Mattachine Society urged it as required reading for those who want to pursue "a fuller spiritual life."[26] These reviews, these publications and organizations, bring me to my second character—because they belong to what called itself the homophile movement.[27]

THE HOMOPHILE

The word *homophile* was coined at least twice. It was used first in Germany during the 1920s, as part of a psychoanalytically inflected model of gender polarity meant to replace models of inversion.[28] Then the word was coined again, in Los Angeles soon after 1950, when Harry Hay, who would soon preside over the founding of the Mattachine Society, was trying to describe homosexual community as more than a furtive sexual market. For Hay, it was important to recognize homophiles as a distinct subculture, bound together by political, ethical, and ritual needs. Behind the concealing mask society forces them to wear, through the very roles society compels them to play, homophiles constitute an "androgynous minority." Baptizing them as a subcultural minority, Hay inscribed them, of course, within familiar American narratives of race and ethnicity—as he also found space for them in socialist theory.[29] The "like race" analogy is an essential element in Hay's invention of a homophile character.

The invention authorized homophile organizations to engage in political and educational work. From the beginning, some of their prominent members were also concerned with religion and spirituality. "Spirituality" is their preferred positive term—and it has an interesting genealogy in queer literature.[30] Concern with spirituality was controversial among homophiles, given both the reality of churchly persecution and the ardently antireligious views of other members.[31] Early efforts to connect with churches or to imitate them produced conflicts. Chuck Rowland, one of the founders of both the Mattachine Society and *One*, was expelled from the latter corporation in 1956 for starting queer liturgies in Los Angeles with the advice of a Unitarian-Universalist minister.

Later contacts were more productive, and I want to turn to their section in the rhetorical archive. In 1964, a survey was circulated on behalf of the Mattachine Society's national secretary, Don Lucas. This was a survey only in name (since Kinsey, surveys had seemed the way to prove the truth about homosexuality). Lucas was in fact asking members to testify to their experiences with Christian churches. He planned to compile their testimonies for an upcoming consultation between a group of Protestant clergy and leaders of homophile organizations. This consultation, in May 1964, led quickly to the founding of a Council on Religion and the Homosexual (or CRH), which fostered the most sustained dialogue between churches and homophile networks.

The consultation grew out of the "Urban Center" at Glide Memorial Church in San Francisco's Tenderloin district.[32] The archives reveal that, in their presentations to the group, the attending clergy recommend forgetting the church past in order to look toward the church future. They agree with Bailey in wanting to detach history. The homophile leaders are more stubborn about churches past, which they refuse to describe abstractly. Lucas's forty-three-page summary of responses to his national survey registers intimate and often violent memories of scriptural exegesis, preaching, and pastoral counseling. The most direct challenge to the assumed character of the ministers can be found in the presentation by "Billie Talmij," the regular pseudonym of one of the Daughters of Bilitis, the main organization for lesbians.[33] In it, she invokes homophile claims to minority status and cultural distinctness in order to disrupt the consultation's model of encounter between two social groups.

In her presentation, Talmij circulates a list of seventy numbered statements, which she describes as "demolition fuses" for blowing down the walls of mutual ignorance and prejudice between "the Gay and the Straight."[34] She in fact offers, and in pure 1960s idiom, aphoristic challenges to the imagined opposition of churches and homophiles, even as she claims the ground on which the churches want to stand. Her text ends by calling the clergymen to follow the homophiles into an exodus from organized religion. Homophiles have been compelled to discover "an approach to spiritual things" beyond the official God.[35] Talmij solicits the clergy—sometimes mockingly, sometimes teasingly—on behalf of a divinity that has forsaken the dying churches. She aligns homophiles with the movement of spiritual history and so refuses both to disconnect the past and to repeat it.

In her "fuses," Talmij plays with categories of gender and desire in relation to assigned identities. She wonders whether God is a woman; she jokes about traditional female roles in church.[36] Talmij also explicitly arranges her multiple identities in an "order": human first, then woman, then lesbian.[37] In this she expands on homophile theories of the mask and the role.[38] At times Talmij seems to adopt the consultation's logic of representation, of opposed identities. She speaks self-consciously for homophiles, for lesbians, for the Daughters of

Bilitis, but she adopts the roles precisely to draw their anarchic spiritual lessons.

In Talmij's remarks to the consultation, homophile and Christian interact as alternate and simultaneous spiritual characters. Homophiles make spiritual communities apart from the churches. Theirs is one way toward a truer, less encumbered, more universal spirituality. Just this possibility would be developed in the next years by post-Christian queer religious communities, female and male—not least by Harry Hay, when he convened the delightfully disparate Radical Faeries. However, Talmij's provocation suggests as well the possibility of coordinating homophile and Christian characters within a single person—of one person participating alternately in multiple characters, ethics, ritual spheres. This second possibility would also be explored beginning in the mid-1960s, through the proliferation of queer Christian groups alongside established churches.

The church hosts hoped that the 1964 consultation would end with a common ethical statement like one published a year earlier by some British Quakers. They got instead not only a stubborn memory of historical failures but a gendered critique of the grave-like narrowness of the churchly present. Once homosexuals are permitted to speak as homophiles, as a subcultural minority, through a self-conscious social role, they lead churchly dialogue into more disconcerting issues of spiritual identification. These critical energies immediately spin beyond existing church structures, leaving a space that can be filled again by more internal debates. Which brings me to my last and most compact example, a third character approaching the baptismal font.

THE HOMOSEXUAL

During Labor Day weekend 1973, John McNeill, then a Jesuit of the New York Province, spoke in Los Angeles to the first national meeting of Dignity, an organization for lesbian and gay Catholics founded four years earlier.[39] McNeill summarized for those present his book-in-progress: *The Church and the Homosexual*. Publication of McNeill's book would be delayed by several years for the predictable ecclesiastical reasons, and McNeill would revise parts of it in answer to objections, official and unofficial. When finally published, the book did not retreat from the main claims of the speech to Dignity—a speech that helped Dignity to define and defend its purposes.

McNeill's book is often identified as the first extended affirmation of homosexuality by a Roman Catholic theologian. Certainly he makes a number of distinctively Catholic arguments in it. He invokes a basic principle of casuistry to argue that an uncertain moral conclusion cannot be binding.[40]

He reworks the Thomistic distinction between objective evils and subjective goods.[41] Most significantly, McNeill argues from traditions of natural law for a model of psychosexual development in the direction of mature freedom. For McNeill, homosexuality properly speaking is "a psychic condition of the individual" that determines the capacity for sexual love.[42] Mature human beings are called to express sexual love in responsible freedom.[43] So the true homosexual must be reconceived as a developing erotic agent whose particular sexual desires are justified by the general obligation to find "interpersonal love."[44]

This is, of course, exactly the "plea of love" that the Anglican pamphlet had rejected in 1954 on the grounds that licit sexual activity for Christians must be confined to marriage. McNeill's counterargument might be conceived in several steps. First, he argues from the experience of pastoral counseling that converting to heterosexuality or achieving celibacy is impossible for most homosexuals. What the pamphlet recommends cannot be accomplished—and so cannot be the proper pastoral ideal. Second, McNeill reasons from personalist philosophy that the love of God is inseparable from the mature love of other human beings. He insists, third, from psychology, that mature human love normally finds erotic expression in committed relationships. The psychological conclusion is then corroborated by the Scriptures. The "positive ideal" of the New Testament, McNeill writes, is that "all human beings . . . [must] struggle to integrate their sexual powers into their total personality, so that their sexual drive can be totally at the disposition of their desire to achieve union in love with their fellow human beings and with God."[45]

In this scriptural claim, as in the other arguments, McNeill moves the character of the homosexual from narratives of inherited degeneration or childhood miseducation to the teleology of normal development. He knows and even approves the older distinction between pervert and invert, and he identifies the latter with the true homosexual.[46] McNeill makes his meaning for the character of the homosexual by recoining it with something like its original and neutral meaning—though within a much simplified range of characters. "Homosexuality" was originally coined not in opposition to heterosexuality but as one of a number of departures from "normal" sexuality. According to McNeill's new narrative, the homosexual is not a character of abnormality—of racial decay or Oedipal failure. The homosexual participates fully in the universal human striving for fulfillment through community in divinity. On the other hand, the "true homosexual" is for McNeill a fixed type of person defined as equal and opposite to the heterosexual.

The claim that the homosexual is a regularly occurring variation within human nature allows McNeill to find some support for his arguments within Christian tradition rather than in repudiation of it. He knows that natural law teaching is a corollary of the doctrine of creation. When he presents the true homosexual as a created type, he gains a foothold in natural law—a foothold for the new character of the Christian homosexual. If homosexuals are created by God, then they are called to a share in divine life by their very constitution. The Christian homosexual becomes not just a habitable identity but a commanded one.

McNeill has the confidence to appropriate the tradition in this way not least because of two experiences of divine providence, only one of which he names in the book. Here McNeill explicitly identifies the "Gay Liberation Movement" as a "providential" witness to the created variety of human sexuality and its future possibilities.[47] Ethics cannot ignore this new act of providence. We learn from other texts that McNeill had been for many years before the speech to Dignity a sexually active gay man, driven almost to suicide by his inability to remain celibate. In that moment of despair, and then more intensely in prayer about a committed erotic relationship begun in 1965, McNeill reports discovering an assurance of divine approval. He tested the discovery by applying Ignatian rules for the discernment of spirits.[48] Once assured by discernment, McNeill speaks beyond argument in the most traditional of Christian rhetorical forms—the testimony of God's incarnate love at work in these very days. His testimony is a vivid proof that one can inhabit what was long presumed to be an impossible identity—the identity of the fully erotic Christian homosexual.

I end my sampling of three characters with McNeill's Ignatian tranquility, his testimony, his achieved performance—on the crest of a widely shared hope for church reform that buoyed him up. To go on would be to introduce other characters and less hopeful episodes: Anita Bryant's campaign to "Save Our Children," the figure of the ex-gay, the bitter night of AIDS—hardly ended. I stop on the crest of hope to ask some questions about the progress implied in my story. Progress—I need hardly say this—is one way of thinking about the relation of past to present, one way of fixing and limiting the usefulness of history to ethics.

PROGRESS IN CHRISTIAN ETHICS?

Does the movement from Bailey through the CRH consultation to McNeill—the movement from invert to homophile to homosexual—illustrate progress in Christian ethics? A dozen old controversies lurk behind this question, but

I want to take it for the moment as simply as I can, from the observation that not a few American Christians do in fact believe that this movement counts as progress. Indeed, they believe—we believe—that it is an important and consoling reminder of the possibility of churchly reform. What notions of "progress in ethics" underwrite that judgment?

A quick answer might be that the movement I've sampled undoes a serious mistake in Christian ethics. This is Bailey's main point, of course, but it also figures in the CRH consultation and McNeill's book. I take the point— even at the risk of setting a distressingly low standard for progress. Progress ought presumably to mean more than undoing the harms caused by past mistakes. In any case, this answer only pushes the question back another step: What notions of progress do we have in mind when we speak of correcting a serious mistake in ethical traditions? Where exactly is the mistake located— where is a correction best applied?

Let me name some locations of progress or correction under three headings: ethics as *description*, ethics as *prescription*, ethics as *formation*. Both the notions and the pattern demand more than I can give them in this conclusion. Let me proceed to sketch the possibilities even so. Let me also personify ethics—let me speak of it as a single and stable figure, even though—and of course—it is neither.

Description first. I have told a story about three characters. At one level, a character is a description. Certainly each of these characters combines description with diagnosis. One way to recapitulate my story would be to tell it as movement from stigmatizing diagnosis to more accurate description. Progress in description would then mean refusing false pathology for realistic portrayal. The claim is troublesome. Both "invert" and "homosexual" bear the marks of their early use in the nineteenth-century forensic clinic. Is it really such a simple thing to reform or purify a character with a dubious past? Might some of the old imaginary, the carbolic odor of the clinic, cling still to these characters in contemporary uses, even or especially if we ignore it?

These three terms also share with each other—and with many other terms in our social thinking—a model of identity that deserves sustained scrutiny. Naming ethical agents is the least innocent and the most consequential step in ethics. Indeed, my telling of the story has presupposed that the "long duration" of Christian ethics consists not of analyzed acts or denumerable rules but of characters and the plots around them. Relative progress within a particular set of characters can hide the limits that they share. What does Christian ethics risk when it takes for granted the common plots of identity assumed together by the characters of the invert, the homophile,

and the homosexual? Aren't Christian ethicists also obliged to wonder about
the consequences of adopting such a sequence of disparate characters in the
space of a few decades? Is Christian ethics only a timid collector of descrip-
tive forms pioneered elsewhere—say, in the advancing sciences of psychiatry,
sociology, or sexology?

These questions point to worse trouble in description—trouble about
how to make it persuasive, since every description is also a persuasion to
view things in a certain way. A number of my archival samples are evidently
concerned to resist insulting stereotypes of homosexuality by taking up fairer
accounts, but they worry rarely about the conflicting ideals of description
embedded in those accounts. Nor do they push fundamental questions about
what it is to describe a human life persuasively in prevailing cultural circumstances. The decades in which these characters were invented and passed
on to Christian discourses were also decades of crisis in cultural claims for
description—of quarrels over literary modernism, over portraiture and real-
ism in film and photography, over the very syntax of memory (private and
public, in trauma and memorial). How can ethical projects of more persuasive description not engage these quarrels? What exemption can Christian
ethics claim from a cultural crisis of representation?

The second heading I listed for thinking about progress is ethics as prescription. Seen from another angle, a character is an agent in need of roles
or rules. My samples might seem to make progress by moving from conde-
scending prohibition toward positive instruction about how queer Christians
can live as sexually active adults. Stated so simply, the claim is troubling,
again, both particularly and generally. Particularly, the content of the positive instruction is often assimilation. Despite their asserted polarity, McNeill
subsumes homosexuals under the general rules for heterosexuals. This
assimilation reduces significant differences between same-sex and other-sex
relations—or among types of same-sex relations. More importantly, it hides
contradictions and instabilities in Christian teaching on any sexed body. Far
from generalizing existing rules to include the so-called anomaly of same-sex
love, Christian ethicists might do better to use the anomaly as an occasion
to revisit the adequacy of those general rules—or to challenge demands that
ethics provide such rules in order to settle cases. Indeed, they might use the
occasion to resist the extraordinary prominence given to sexual rule making in churchly discourse. Why is it, after all, that contemporary Christians
spend so much energy fighting about sexual regulation? Is it because those
rules are so central to their gospel—or because they are, as general rules,
so widely and pleasurably ignored, so unreal, so usefully distracting? Asked

urgently for sexual rules, ethicists ought always to begin by interrogating the request.

I end with the third heading: progress in ethics considered as formation. A character is most importantly the issue of an education, the site of a formation. What if the mode of progress in Christian ethics is neither classifying acts, nor framing more comprehensive norms for them, but helpfully experimenting with practices for making characters? What if ethical language is not representational so much as effective, artisanal? Christian ethics ought not to assume—as many of the samples do—that the invert, the homophile, or the homosexual arrives at the church doors fully formed. This is one reason I resist the language of "welcoming and affirming" congregations. To assume that homosexuals are formed elsewhere denies the testimony of many proto-queer children and adolescents who have fashioned themselves inside churches. What is more important, this assumption abandons the largest part of the church's tradition of ethical teaching. There can be no strongly affirmative Christian ethics about homosexuality that does not undertake to form homosexuals within churches. We begin to conceive any progress in my samples adequately when we ask of them: How well do your speeches and practices, your rules and rites, form Christian characters that can desire queerly? And then we ask: How do you teach Christians to inhabit characters without being trapped, reduced, or divided by them? The ethical formation of characters must leave them unfinished, because no one of us *is* an invert, a homophile, a homosexual—not simply, not finally.

Further Suggested Readings

Bailey, Derrick Sherwin. *Homosexuality and the Western Christian Tradition.* London and New York: Longmans, Green, 1955.

Carey, Jonathan Sinclair. "D. S. Bailey and 'the Name Forbidden among Christians.'" *Anglican Theological Review* 70 (April 1988): 152–73.

Gallo, Marcia M. *Different Daughters: A History of the Daughters of Bilitis and the Rise of the Lesbian Rights Movement.* New York: Carroll & Graf, 2006.

McNeill, John J. *The Church and the Homosexual.* Kansas City: Sheed Andrews and McMeel, 1976.

White, Heather Rachelle. "Proclaiming Liberation: The Historical Roots of LGBT Religious Organizing, 1946–1976." *Nova Religio* 11, no. 4 (2008): 102–19.

CHAPTER 10

Eroticized Wives: Evangelical Marriage Guides
and God's Plan for the Christian Family

Rebecca L. Davis

AS THE CLOCK APPROACHES the hour of her husband's return, a
nervous housewife readies herself for his arrival. She checks herself one last
time in the mirror, smoothes her hair, and practices a sultry pout. Hearing
her husband's car in the driveway, she shuffles, penguin-style, to the front
door and waits. After an uncomfortable delay, his key turns in the lock. The
door swings toward her, her husband takes one step into the house, and then
he stops, as if frozen, and gawks. "Welcome home, darling," she says, bat-
ting her eyelashes. He looks at her, blinks, and looks again. His wife stands
in the front hall of their home wrapped in nothing but yards and yards of
plastic wrap, her middle-aged curves visible but distorted through layers of
transparent film. "Oh no," he says, as shock turns to mirth, "not leftovers
again!"[1] Served up like a TV dinner for her husband's consumption, this wife
has become what author Marabel Morgan calls a *Total Woman*, a model of
Christian marital perfection.

Morgan laughs when she tells this story about one woman's humiliating (and perhaps apocryphal) efforts to reignite the matrimonial flame, but she had serious intentions when she popularized her method of marriage improvement in the mid-1970s. Recounting the events that propelled her to international notoriety, Morgan explains that she was living in Miami with two young daughters and a husband who worked long hours as an attorney. They appeared blissfully content to the outside world, but Marabel and Charlie Morgan, both born-again Christians, were on the brink of marital breakdown. A dedicated housewife and mother, Morgan embarked upon saving her marriage as her life's calling. Friends took notice as the Morgans appeared more affectionate, and they asked Marabel to teach them her secrets for reigniting the conjugal spark. Informal gatherings grew into "Total Woman" seminars. Over the course of four two-hour sessions, women learned how to follow the "four A's": adapting to, admiring, appreciating, and accepting their husbands. Morgan compiled these principles in *The Total Woman*, published in a short run of five thousand copies by Fleming H. Revell, an evangelical publishing house. Much to everyone's surprise, the book became the national nonfiction bestseller of 1974, and by 1975 it had sold three-and-a-half-million copies. *The New York Times Book Review* rated *The Total Woman* the ninth most popular nonfiction book of the 1970s. Morgan's company, Total Woman, Inc., employed seventy-seven teachers, who hosted workshops throughout the United States. Morgan appeared on the cover of *Time* magazine in March 1977 and claimed in that article that she received upwards of one hundred pieces of fan mail each day. By the summer of 1978, she had made ten appearances on *The Phil Donahue Show* and had had guest spots on *The Today Show, Good Morning, America*, and *To Tell the Truth*.[2] Although many secular and religious readers panned *The Total Woman* for being either frivolous or dangerously misguided, Morgan and her book became household names, celebrated by grateful followers.

The Saran Wrap anecdote epitomizes the fundamental centrality of the wife's body to Morgan's program to renew the sexual charge between husbands and wives and, in so doing, bring families closer to Christ. The husband's rather cruel quip, as Morgan recounts it, reveals the ethos of bodily critique and transformation at the heart of *The Total Woman*: the wife would modify her body, by measures both mundane and extreme, until it became an object of her husband's erotic fascination. The Saran Wrap costume originated with a participant in one of Morgan's seminars who passed the idea along to Morgan. Morgan shared the suggestion during one of her talk-show appearances in the late 1970s. Broadcast to a national audience, the image of the Total Woman sheathed in plastic wrap was born. The story captured the public's imagination; many critics and historians have since misattributed the Saran Wrap suggestion to *The Total Woman*.[3] Despite the Saran Wrap story's obvious ridiculousness, and beneath Marabel Morgan's cheeky retelling of it, it displayed the power of the wife's eroticized body to create and protect the heterosexual Christian family.

By retelling this story, Morgan did not encourage women to humiliate themselves in exchange for fidelity, as some of her critics alleged, but described a detailed process of embodiment at the heart of her vision of marital salvation. Her book and seminars outline a daily regimen of bodily discipline and performance that will culminate in sexual affirmation as the husband reenters his home each evening. Poised at the threshold between a secular workplace and a Christian home, the wife's body (adorned according to Morgan's numerous recommendations for costumes, makeup, and props) reaffirms the husband's heterosexuality, transforming the home into a castle of male gratification. As Morgan explains in her book, by thus embodying biblical precepts of family hierarchy, the wife encourages her husband to follow her on the path to salvation: the sexier she appears to him during the week, the more likely he will be to join her in church on Sunday. In addition, by sating him sexually, she will save him from the sins of adultery and fornication, sins seemingly more tempting with the appearance in the workplace of increasing numbers of female subordinates, on the one hand, and sexless feminist competitors, on the other. Simultaneously tempted and emasculated, the working man needs his heterosexual desires channeled and his patriarchal authority affirmed by day's end. Children who observe these rituals of heterosexual enactment, Morgan concludes, will grow up to be normatively gendered adults. The wife's body "sexes" (inscribes sexual identities and desires upon) her family members; by enacting her submission, a Christian wife exerts enormous power over the erotic and spiritual fortunes of her husband and children.

This reading of Morgan's method of heterosexual family evangelization benefits from recent philosophical, theological, and historical investigations of the body and embodiment. Theories of embodiment, and the beginnings of a history of bodies, insist upon the conceptual and historical intersections of discourse and experience. Such attention to embodied as well as discursive practices corrects more superficial analyses of Morgan's significance. Scholars have too often evaluated Morgan's work as a discursive effort, attributing to her an antifeminist ideology articulated in evangelical language. This stress on Morgan's words, however, overlooks the behaviors that those words imaginatively produced.[4] Morgan taught women a complex process of bodily preparation in order to attain an ideal of marital happiness, happiness defined according to the traditional interpretation of evangelical Protestantism to which both Morgan and her husband subscribed. Practiced and performed, these acts of material self-scrutiny would enable Christian women to embody God's plan for the family.

HISTORICAL CONTEXT: EVANGELICALS AND SEX DURING THE 1960S AND 1970S

The process of embodiment Morgan described was located within a particular historical moment, as twentieth-century Americans elevated human sexual pleasure to unprecedented heights of theological and psychological importance. By the mid-twentieth century, American evangelicals (a catch-all phrase that refers to an enormous but diffuse segment of the population), particularly those with theologically conservative leanings, adopted a narrow reading of New Testament passages regarding gendered power within the family. During the 1940s and 1950s, the influential fundamentalist preacher and publisher John R. Rice based his widely distributed marital advice on Ephesians 5:22-24, verses that admonished wives to obey their husbands and recognized the husband as the head of the family as Christ was head of the church. In Rice's footsteps, evangelical family seminar guru Bill Gothard "popularized the verses as the basis of God's chain of command . . . , which achieved the status of unquestioned folk doctrine across a wide spectrum of conservative Protestant communities," according to Susan Friend Harding.[5] Belief in absolute gender difference and commitment to family hierarchy became core premises of postwar conservative evangelical culture.[6]

Conservative evangelical ideals of marriage shaped Morgan's worldview. Her own home life in central Ohio had been tragically lonely and dysfunctional: Morgan's mother, Delsa Hawk, was mentally ill, and Delsa's second husband, whom Morgan loved, died when Morgan was in her early teens. From her experiences growing up with a volatile and thrice-married mother, Morgan knew the kind of domestic chaos she wanted to avoid. Born again in her late teens or early twenties, she attended a Bible school in Miami and worked briefly for Campus Crusade for Christ, where she learned to envision the ideal marriage as one in which a wife submitted to her husband's authority.[7] Years later, when Morgan counseled wives to subordinate their needs to their husbands' desires, she spoke not from experience but from the evangelical ideals of family hierarchy she had adopted as an adult.

Evangelical Christians seeking advice about marriage and sexuality could peruse a growing list of book titles by the mid-1960s. The Christian publishing industry (not to mention the secular press) was producing a flurry of marital advice guides that discussed the importance of sexual fulfillment to marital happiness. Herbert Miles's *Sexual Happiness in Marriage* (1967) became the foundational text for Christian sexual advice literature. Incorporating anatomical diagrams as well as step-by-step instructions for foreplay and intercourse, Miles encouraged young couples to seek a sexually as well as spiritually fulfilling marital relationship. Authors of marital advice books for conservative evangelicals often referred readers interested in acceptably "Christian" sexual advice to Miles's book. The publication of *Sexual Happiness in Marriage* signaled a new era in evangelical Christian marital advice, as Christian publishers produced dozens of new paperback guides to marital sex.[8] This genre frankly described human anatomy, the mechanics of sexual intercourse, and sexual pleasure. When the well-known fundamentalist activists Tim and Beverly LaHaye published *The Act of Marriage: The Beauty of Sexual Love* (1976), they included illustrations of male and female genitals and reproductive anatomies, suggestions for how husbands might bring their wives to climax (including manual but not oral stimulation), and recommendations for acceptable forms of birth control.[9] As discussions of sexual intercourse in Christian marital-advice books went from prudish admonishments that there was nothing wrong with it, to diagrammed advice for bringing the wife to orgasm, the books contributed to phenomenal growth in the Christian publishing industry.[10]

Morgan belonged to a cohort of Christian women who created many of the self-help books, seminars, and group support programs for marital improvement that helped drive this publishing boom. The self-help format enabled female authors to carve out a niche for themselves as marriage experts. The author of *Fascinating Womanhood* (1963), Helen Andelin, was a Mormon, but the rest of the authors in Morgan's genre were evangelical Christians who considered their marital advice a kind of witness. Despite some geographic and educational diversity, most of the authors were southern or midwestern conservative evangelicals, many of whom served their communities as ministers' wives. Female-authored paperback guides, targeted to young women, sold tens and hundreds of thousands of copies.[11] While a fuller understanding of how readers interpreted and applied, or rejected, the ideas presented in these marriage guides extends beyond the scope of this essay, the sales figures alone suggest that these books did not languish unnoticed on bookstore shelves.

Christian groups' and commentators' reactions to Morgan's book ranged from cautious praise to disgust. A review of *The Total Woman* in the *Moody Monthly,* an evangelical Protestant family publication, praised Morgan for giving "sound advice" and useful suggestions. University of Chicago theologian Martin Marty, however, trashed *Total Joy,* Morgan's 1976 sequel to *The Total Woman,* as a crass example of "Fundies and Their Fetishes." Marty argued that Morgan portrayed the evangelical husband as "a zombie who would do nothing but stare at televised football—or at the sexpots at his office, any of whom he'll rape unless you service him 365 times a year." Marty found Morgan's recommendations for marital success ludicrous, and he assailed her attempts to premise this advice on biblical texts: "The *Total Woman* crowd, massively evangelical, expects an imminent and literal Second Coming. I want to be around to see the enraptured raptured from their trampolines, he as a dime-a-dance ticket taker and she in raincoat and gorilla-head mask."[12] The *Wittenberg Door,* an evangelical humor magazine, parodied the "Totaled Woman" on its August-September 1975 cover. An older woman with curlers in her hair, her stockings rolled up under her knees, sits in an armchair, her legs ungracefully parted, reading *The Total Woman.* A crumpled copy of *Moody Monthly* lies on the floor.[13] Several Christian bookstores allegedly banned *The Total Woman* from their shelves because of its sexual explicitness.

The secular book market, of course, had recently produced far more graphic sex guides; Alex Comfort's *The Joy of Sex: A Gourmet Guide to Love Making* (1972) eventually sold twelve million copies worldwide.[14] American culture was becoming more openly sexual during the 1960s and 1970s: a "sexual revolution" appeared on college campuses and in communes; states legalized abortion; Congress debated the Equal Rights Amendment; and women's and gay liberation movements demanded an end to oppressive heterosexuality.[15] Evangelicals contributed to this unprecedented "talk about sex" during the 1960s and 1970s.[16] Participants in the culture they criticized, Christian authors integrated a new celebration of marital sexual pleasure into their prescriptions for the religiously based family life.

Popular adaptations of Freudian psychology, filtered through Americans' fascination with personal pleasure and fulfillment, also shaped Morgan's outlook on family harmony. In the years following World War II, Americans encountered psychology in an ever-expanding number of social locations, from schools and employers that now mandated personality or vocational testing, to films and literature that explored Freudian motifs.[17] Americans focused especially on Sigmund Freud's theories of sexual differentiation, reducing his complex analyses of drives and repression to a simplistic emphasis on the sexual basis of human behavior. Ironically, although Freud had refused to pathologize homosexuality, American interpreters used his theories to argue for the psychological health of normative gender roles and sexual desires. As early as the 1940s, adulterated versions of Freudian theory had become the basis of antifeminist and antigay polemic.[18] For Morgan, popular psychology provided another vocabulary, in addition to evangelical language, for describing the benefits of becoming a Total Woman.

THEORIZING THE TOTAL WOMAN'S BODY

In the longer history of Western Christianity, Morgan participated in an ongoing debate over the relationship between mind (soul) and matter (body). Many scholars have identified associations within the Western philosophical tradition between the mind or soul and men, on the one hand, and the body and women, on the other. In an early feminist analysis along these lines, Elizabeth Spelman argues that Plato dichotomized the realms of the "adulterated" body and exalted soul by describing women as creatures incapable of exercising rational control over their undisciplined bodies.[19] Historian Margaret Miles similarly finds that late antique Christian and medieval representations of female nakedness trapped the female body in a system of visual and textual objectification within which "human beings defined by mind [men] should rule those defined by body [women]," thereby limiting the availability of subjectivity for women through public representations of their bodies.[20] Medievalist Caroline Walker Bynum disagrees with these conclusions about sharp distinctions between body and soul in early Christian and medieval sources. Instead, she finds evidence that "religious specialists in the late Middle Ages . . . assumed the flesh to be the instrument of salvation." Medieval Christians celebrated "the cultivation of bodily experience as a place for encounter with meaning, a locus of redemption."[21] Bynum establishes medieval precedents for contemporary Christian fascination with the connections between body, soul, and salvation. Her work in particular inspired scholars of religion to reconsider historical and theological attitudes toward the body.

Studies of embodiment have flourished within the field of American religious history. R. Marie Griffith's *Born Again Bodies* provides the fullest examination of these questions about gendered embodiment in the modern context. She documents Protestant devotional practices that displayed unease about bodily functions but also discovers American Christians who began to see the body as a window into the believer's soul. While followers of Christian Science denigrated the body and hoped to liberate the soul from it completely, the New Thought movement of the late nineteenth century capped decades of interest in bodily perfectibility as a path to salvation. From fasting to fitness, American Protestants in the nineteenth and twentieth centuries prescribed devotional practices that form what Griffith terms a "doctrine of body salvation."[22] Like the practitioners of diet and fitness regimens that Griffith describes, Morgan developed a system of bodily perfection. But rather than save the soul of the woman who disciplined her own body, Morgan's system treats the wife's body as an implement of her husband's salvation. The female body becomes not a vessel of the soul it housed but an instrument of another person's devotionalism and sexual identity.

These historical studies, and the present investigation of Morgan, cite and contest theories of embodiment. Michel Foucault introduced one of the first philosophical investigations of bodily discipline in the 1970s in *Discipline and Punish: The Birth of the Prison*. A historical analysis of the criminal justice system in France, *Discipline and Punish* argues that when late-eighteenth and nineteenth-century nation-states replaced public torture with remote imprisonment and forced labor, they enabled the state to exercise almost limitless disciplinary punishment upon the criminal's body. By mobilizing expert knowledge and creating new forms of architectural surveillance (the modern prison as a "panopticon," with prisoners perpetually visible to authorities but hidden from other inmates), modern prison systems became models for a "disciplinary society," whose institutions regulated both criminal and law-abiding citizens' bodies. In that work and in his multivolume *History of Sexuality*, however, Foucault ultimately proves less interested in the materiality of bodies than in their symbolic or discursive meanings, acted upon by dispersed state powers.[23] Poststructural and postmodern theorizations, particularly those with the greatest debt to psychoanalytic thought, have also tended to consider the body a consequence of discursive production. These theorists have rendered materiality—and thus the possibility of understanding bodily subjectivity—ephemeral, defined more by what it excludes or demarcates than what it constitutes.[24]

Feminist and queer theorists have responded by placing the body, and processes of embodiment, at the center of their analyses. Judith Butler, Elizabeth Grosz, and Moira Gatens simultaneously subvert gender essentialism and insist upon the centrality of embodiment to their feminist philosophies.[25] While Butler's first book, *Gender Trouble*, appears to privilege performance to the degree that it undermines theoretical possibilities for embodiment, she subsequently has advanced the conversation beyond these binary categories. In *Bodies That Matter*, she describes reiterative practices that simultaneously produce the sexed body and enable the body to perform its sex. As Gatens similarly explains, "the sexed body can no longer be conceived as the unproblematic biological and factual base upon which gender is inscribed, but must itself be recognized as constructed by discourses and practices that take the body both as their target and as their vehicle of expression."[26] Historians have further specified the kinds of power that can act upon and be constituted through bodily experience. In her work on the female citizen's body in interwar Germany, historian Kathleen Canning illustrates how it is possible to differentiate between *"bodies as objects of regulation and tutelage* by welfare states and social reformers; and . . . *bodies as sites of experience* like pregnancy, childbirth, illness, overwork, and exploitation that marked them indelibly, shaping subjectivities and self-representations."[27] Theorizations of embodiment, performativity, and materiality help to expose the Total Woman's body as an object of the husband's gaze, a discursive production, and at the same time a site of experience.

In *The Total Woman*, Morgan explains that women can create a happy home life by satisfying their husbands' needs for sex, comfort, and confidence. Morgan predicates a wife's happiness upon the continuance of the marriage; the wife's goal is to keep her husband from leaving. To that end, the book describes rituals of bodily self-transformation that climax in the husband's return home at the end of a workday. The tasks Morgan enumerates require daily practice, through "homework" assignments, rigorous housework and meal preparation, and behavior modification. Grosz's discussion of the body's philosophical location is instructive at this point: "The body can be regarded as a kind of *hinge* or threshold: it is placed between a psychic or lived interiority and a more sociopolitical exteriority that produces interiority through the *inscription* of the body's outer surface."[28] So, too, the Total Woman's body stands in her open doorway, marking the threshold between secular and faith-focused domains, and acting as a powerful intermediary in her family members' sexuality. In *The Total Woman* and other evangelical marriage guides, the husband seeks refuge from the workplace, which these books portray as an emasculating arena of anonymity, feminist competition, and frequent disappointment.[29] As the husband crosses the domestic threshold, therefore, the wife's body reinscribes his masculine authority. The Total Woman's body is Morgan's sculpting clay, a rude form that requires time, attention, and skill to be transformed into the feminine body a Christian husband desires. Her own Pygmalion, the Total Woman both possesses the life-giving power of the artist and serves as an object of the male gaze and a vehicle of his development.

Morgan focuses her self-improvement plan on the wife's physical self, the body at the center of the story. The wife's body enables the husband's masculinization, because her attractiveness reassures him of his manliness:

> This is all your husband asks from you. He wants the girl of his dreams to be feminine, soft, and touchable when he comes home. . . . If you are dumpy, stringy, or exhausted, he's sorry he came. That first look tells him your nerves are shot, his dinner is probably shot, and you'd both like to shoot the kids. . . . The quickest way to spin him around is to change your appearance. Will he be star-struck by the way you look tonight?[30]

Husbands need their wives' bodies, Morgan explains: "In fact, he literally craves it. The outer shell of yours is what the real estate people call 'curb appeal'—how the house looks from the outside. Is your curb appeal this week what it was five years ago?"[31] Morgan warns her readers to stop nagging, allow their husbands to make all important family decisions, and lavish their mates with compliments about their manly physiques. Primarily, though, wives will become eager and attractive sexual partners by transforming their own bodies.

The body the Total Woman presents to her husband requires hours of preparation. To ensure a happy homecoming, Morgan coaches wives to plan their days around a 5 P.M. scented bubble bath, during which they should be careful to "remove all prickly hairs and be squeaky clean from head to toe. Be touchable and kissable." Sounding like a dental hygienist, Morgan further reminds her readers to brush their teeth, floss, brush again, and rinse with mouthwash.[32] Thus antiseptically cleansed, a Total Woman will have strategically modified her body. Her performance might require costumes, lest a standard greeting in casual attire grow tedious. In both *The Total Woman* and *Total Joy*, Morgan offers an array of sartorial ideas, from nothing but pearls to a maid's costume. The suspense builds to the moment of the husband's return, at which point the Total Woman's body would be ready for its close-up.

The Total Woman is quite literally a spectacle: her husband needs her—and, indeed, requires her—as an object of his gaze. Morgan explains that men require visual stimulation for erotic pleasure: "Before a man can care about who a woman is, he must first get past that visual barrier of how a woman looks. So your appearance at 6:00 P.M. should have top priority!"[33] When the Total Woman's body arouses her husband, it also affirms his masculinity. In what Butler calls the reiterative citation of gender roles, the moment of encounter reinscribes the husband's masculinity and the wife's femininity. The wife's body, primed and primped, engenders him. Morgan makes sure her readers appreciate how radically aroused a husband thus greeted might become. As Morgan herself notes in her advice to wives preparing for that momentous doorway encounter, "Remember that the tone for the evening is set during the first four minutes after your husband comes home tonight. His senses will be anticipating food and sex."[34] When this sexually crippled man enters his house, the Total Woman's body affirms his masculinity: her body sexes his.

This transmutation succeeds in large measure because the wife masks her husband's body, cloaking it in compliments (which, Morgan avers, tended to be unearned) and thus creating a protective shield around the fragile male ego. In a chapter entitled "Hero Worship," Morgan updates the idea of biblical reverence: "Tell him you love his body. If you choke on that phrase, practice it until it comes out naturally." This theme recurs in other marriage guides that appeared contemporaneously with *The Total Woman*. In *You Can Be the Wife of a Happy Husband* (1974), Darien Cooper encourages wives to bolster their husbands' masculinity by praising the men's appearance: "Compliment him on his broad shoulders, deep voice, strong hands, and yes, even his beard—though you may feel like saying, 'I wish you'd shave that thing off!'" Morgan and Cooper readily admit that wives might have to lie to their husbands in order to compliment them, but they consider the practice of false praise to be another component of a wife's biblically instructed submission.[35] The male body, more absence than presence, materializes—or, in Butlerian terms, the masculine subject is made intelligible—through the performative power of a wife's fawning compliments and in response to her physicality. Butler's insights about femininity as a recitation offer a model for interpreting Morgan's representations of heterosexual desire and masculinity: "Femininity is thus not the product of choice, but the forcible recitation of a norm, one whose complex historicity is indissociable from relations of discipline, regulation, punishment."[36] The Total Woman's body simultaneously displays and inscribes femininity, restores her husband's masculinity, and thus insures the complementary sex roles at the heart of the conservative Christian marriage.

Morgan portrays heterosexuality as a developmental milestone whereby children learn to assign sexual desire to their own and others' bodies. One of *The Total Woman*'s homework assignments requires wives to be ready for sex every night of the week, part of Morgan's plan to remasculinize Christian husbands, but she thinks those behaviors will sex the couple's children as well. The wife's body functions as a totem of heterosexuality for her children. Her body—and the sexual identities and behaviors it signifies—are an instrument of social organization, a "tutelary spirit and protector," in Freud's words, that establishes the group's (family's) sexual parameters.[37] Praising the body's power to create sexual order, Morgan urges parents to display the erotic rewards of heterosexual marriage. In one of her most infamous chapters, she describes the time she welcomed her husband Charlie at the end of the day wearing pink baby-doll pajamas and white boots. He chased her around the dining room table while their daughters observed: "Our little girls stood flat against the wall watching our escapade, giggling with delight." The effects of a mother's semi-nude costume would be equally as hilarious for sons, Morgan cheers: "Can't you just imagine Junior on the sandlot telling his friends, 'I've got to go now, guys. Got to see Mom's outfit for tonight.'" As critics Barbara Ehrenreich and Deirdre English have noted, Morgan raises heterosexuality to a child-rearing philosophy.[38] Morgan's fantasy about a son's fascination with his mother's sexuality suggests a crudely literal interpretation of the Oedipal drama. By placing her body on display for her husband and her children to see, the wife could restore or instill heterosexual identities and normative gender roles in her family members. Her body transforms her husband into a normatively masculine man and ensures that her children conformed to heterosexual norms.

The acts of sexually empowering husbands and raising heterosexual children thus reflects two sides of the same coin for Total Women in their domestic performances of heterosexual desire. A wife who reinforces her husband's masculinity will keep him close; her children will grow up with a father who comes home at night. By contrast, nagging wives who push their husbands to adultery will have no one to blame but themselves when their children become homosexuals. Morgan warns that a girl with an absentee father (inattentive because his bossy wife had antagonized him) will grow up to hate all men. An overprotective mother inverts the gender-based leadership structure of the family as she takes over family decision making. When "Jean and Tom," one of several sample couples in *The Total Woman,* stopped communicating, Morgan recounts, their son "Jimmy" experienced a gender crisis:

> Subconsciously, Jimmy began to lose respect for his father, and for his own sex as well. He began to feel unworthy. As the years go by, Jimmy may grow up weak in male attributes. . . . He may identify with his mother and begin to develop certain feminine qualities on a subconscious level.

. . . Because of his strong attachment to his mother, the door is open to homosexuality.[39]

Morgan combines psychology and Scripture in her analysis of the mother's role in the creation of homosexual children, suggesting that gender identification is mutable and requires perpetual surveillance. The tension inherent in Morgan's description of how repeated, intentional performances might produce God-given gender roles harkens to Judith Butler's interpretation of subjectivity and power. Butler argues: "there is no power, construed as a subject, that acts, but only . . . a reiterated acting that *is* power in its persistence and instability."[40] In blaming the assertive mother for mutations of the heterosexual norm, Morgan joined other conservative evangelical authors who pathologized feminism in order to explain homosexuality.[41]

Total Woman seminars—as well as the seminars and workshops that accompanied numerous other marriage guidance programs for evangelical Christian women during the 1970s—taught women these practices through the structured recitations of biblically defined femininity. Female-authored marriage guides prescribed exercises, rather than individual therapy or psychological adjustments, to bring wives into spiritual harmony with God and marital bliss with their husbands. Books included quizzes, worksheets, charts, checklists, and step-by-step guides to self-assessment and behavior modification. In "Assignment: Man Alive," Morgan offers instructions for wives on how to accept, admire, adapt to, and appreciate their husbands through a regimen of list making and positive thinking. Darien Cooper structures her book of evangelical marital advice, *You Can Be the Wife of a Happy Husband*, around a series of seminars that use role play, quizzes, dramatic reenactments of biblical scenes, and chalkboard drawings (the sketches for which Cooper provides) to impart the book's lessons. Like the Total Woman, the Wife of a Happy Husband needs to prepare her body to enact its wifely obligations. Cooper suggests that group leaders function as the masters of ceremonies for a "Good Grooming Show," during which participants offer suggestions for "cleanliness, diet, exercise, rest, makeup, hair, hands, clothes, posture." Not every author of evangelical marital advice necessarily conflated bodily appearances with godly virtues, as several favored mental rather than physical enhancements. Affiliated workshops and seminars nevertheless all brought readers together to enact the books' lessons.[42]

Women who invested money in purchasing *The Total Woman* and time practicing its principles described an often painful process of bodily transformation. Dozens of letters in Morgan's possession testify to the extent to which women earnestly tried to follow her advice (though many authors chided Morgan for speaking nonsense). Through these letters emerges a picture of *The Total Woman* as an embodied practice that altered women's bodies according to Morgan's instructions. Women describe their struggles to conform to *The Total Woman*'s rigorous demands. (Morgan herself admits that her own self-transformation was arduous and at times excruciating.) A woman from Kentucky writes that she still "rebelled" and that the "old me" endured as she tried to direct her energies toward pleasing her husband. A Dutch woman who married an American serviceman similarly describes her first attempts at Morgan's wardrobe suggestions: "Very hard, embarrassing, but my husband certainly liked it." A twenty-four-year-old housewife and mother (and, the letter infers, a religious Christian) in Illinois likewise writes about the mortification she felt the first time she abandoned her concealing floor-length nightgowns in an attempt to become a Total Woman: "I now own some nightgowns and pajamas that would not even be allowed in a [sic] X-rated movie. Why? Not for me. I feel very uncomfortable in them but I wear them for him and when it makes him happy, I am more than happy." Morgan must have delighted especially in letters like one from a Pennsylvania woman, who writes that she and her husband had been on the verge of divorce when she read *The Total Woman*: "We are happier now than when we were newlyweds. . . . Your book even helped me with something much more—it helped to lead me to Christ." For other women, however, Morgan's advice came too late. They tell her of divorces, abuse, and abandonment and wonder what they had done to deserve it.[43]

The Total Woman and other, similar books functioned as both text and practice, just as Morgan herself constructed Total Women as simultaneously satiric and substantive, fictive and embodied. Morgan made Christian women's bodies purposefully playful and plastic, breathing Barbies of domestic salvation. She and her book instantiated women's bodies at the center of a Christian drama of heterosexual normalization, parodying and parading the fragility of the heterosexual imperative. Playing the part—becoming a Total Woman—represented a process of self-conscious charade but also a seriously intentioned practice. Morgan encouraged the woman who hit upon the Saran Wrap idea to utilize her body as an instrument of God's plan for the Christian family. Morgan's genius lay in her ability to make this task appear hilarious to her readers and seminar participants. A jesting act possessed serious spiritual and cultural consequences and conferred upon wives an awesome sexual power.

In *The Total Woman* Morgan describes the Garden of Eden as a nudist's delight, where Adam and Eve, adorned with adorable fig leaves, passed the hours "experimenting with their newfangled parts."[44] The Saran Wrap story translates that sense of playfulness and sexual invention to the Christian home, where wives continue God's work of sexing their husbands and their children, ushering them toward God's plan for the Christian family.

Further Suggested Readings

Bynum, Caroline Walker. *The Resurrection of the Body in Western Christianity.* New York: Columbia University Press, 1995.

DeRogatis, Amy. "What Would Jesus Do? Sexuality and Salvation in Protestant Evangelical Sex Manuals, 1950s to the Present." *Church History* 74, no. 1 (2005): 97–137.

Griffith, R. Marie. *Born Again Bodies: Flesh and Spirit in American Christianity.* Berkeley: University of California Press, 2004.

Heller, Jennifer. "Marriage, Womanhood, and the Search for 'Something More': American Evangelical Women's Best-Selling 'Self-Help' Books, 1972–1979." *Journal of Religion and Popular Culture* 2 (Fall 2002). Http://www.usask.ca/relst/jrpc/article-selfhelp.html, accessed August 12, 2009.

Putney, Clifford. *Muscular Christianity: Manhood and Sports in Protestant America, 1880–1920.* Cambridge: Harvard University Press, 2001.

Watt, David Harrington. *A Transforming Faith: Explorations of Twentieth-Century American Evangelicalism.* New Brunswick: Rutgers University Press, 1991.

CHAPTER 11

"Eros," AIDS, and African Bodies:
A Theological Commentary on Deadly Desires

Edward P. Antonio

IN AFRICA TODAY, "eros" and erotic desire are linked to sickness and death. Indeed, there is an important sense in which both "eros" and erotic desire have become agents of sickness and death. This can be ascertained through two simple observations that follow from each other. The first is that in Africa, HIV/AIDS is predominantly transmitted through sex or through "eros" as a representative of erotic desire. The second observation follows from this: understandings of "eros," sexual love, and desire are now mediated through HIV/AIDS or through the death it represents. This means that AIDS is the radical framework within which sex, love, and death have become socially (publicly) thinkable as two sides of the same reality. Thus, HIV/AIDS—through "eros" and sexual desire and their relationship to sickness and death—has become an aspect of the making and remaking of African identities. HIV/AIDS has become a site where the question of the survival of a people, a civilization, and a continent is being negotiated and decided.[1]

This essay has a twofold agenda. The first is to describe and critique some of the ways in which the hegemony of Western discourses about HIV/AIDS in Africa is resulting in serious misrepresentation of African modes of sexuality in the name of foreign value-systems. The second is to call attention to the challenge of HIV/AIDS for theology and to provide a brief theological commentary on "eros," AIDS, and human bodies.

The first thing this essay does is to recognize the idea of "eros" as un-African and as Western, specifically that it originates from ancient Greece. Since most of the proposed solutions to HIV/AIDS are Western, I am interested here in how sex and desire in Africa are framed through Western perspectives that represent a recolonizing logic. Not only does this logic distort, misrepresent, and elide indigenous notions of sex and sexuality, it also masquerades as scientific and universal, thereby serving as the basis for the discursive recolonization of African societies.[2] This essay critically interrogates the status of the idea of "eros" in the non-Western cultures of Africa and its relation to Western cultural understandings. This focus on different cultural understandings of "eros" raises two important questions. It raises, first, the question of "eros" and reason—that is, "sensuality" and "rationality" or the always historically and culturally shaped forms of rationality that structure the organization of sexuality and, through this (for example, through repression and sublimation of sexual energy), of society and civilization.[3] Second, this focus on different cultural understandings of "eros" also raises the issue of the universality of love and desire, which are inextricably bound up with "eros." There is a tendency in some theologies and philosophies to posit Western notions of sex, love, and the erotic as somehow unproblematically universal or necessarily paradigmatic for all understandings of love and sex. If all human practices, including sex and love, are historical (it is hard to think of love and sex being anything else), then surely the historicity of sex, love, and the erotic ought to be a fundamental part of the structure of any adequate account of sexual desire.

Regarding the second agenda item, I want to begin to name some theological challenges of AIDS that academic theology has so far neglected, and which pastoral theology often glosses over in the name of practical immediacy. I do this in relation to the categories of "eros," sex, love, and death. I proceed in this way for several reasons. First, Christian theology makes the love of God central to the very possibility of human redemption and to the ethics of human flourishing. Second, sex and erotic love are, on many theological accounts, regarded as God's gift both to be gratefully enjoyed as such and also to be used for reproductive purposes.[4] Third, and central for my argument, in Africa HIV is most commonly spread through sex where the figure of something like "eros" is at work. Given the devastating nature of HIV/AIDS, is "eros," understood as God-given love, possible? Can we theologically make sense of "eros" as love in the presence of massive social death, especially where the latter is the effect of the former? What religious and theological resources (African and Christian) would render such talk both possible and meaningful?

GREEK AND CHRISTIAN FORMS OF "EROS"

Central to my contention is that discourse on HIV/AIDS is not morally or politically neutral but is rather embedded in certain discursive structures that implicitly propose new social principles modeled on Western social norms reconstituted as mechanisms for the reformation and restructuring of African societies. The question of the universality of "eros" arises here precisely because it is Western. To invoke "eros" is to invoke other cosmogonies (accounts of the creation or birth of the universe). Recall that in Greek mythology, "eros" is an originating and creative force, a force that unites, reconciles, and thus explains the connections by which different cosmogonic elements are bound together. For example, in the thought of the Greek philosopher Empedocles, Eros becomes Aphrodite and, with *philia* (Love), binds the elements.[5] Eros is not only the first to overcome chaos, thus instituting itself as the principle of order, it is also the guarantee of the immortality of the gods and thus of life itself. Furthermore, "eros" starts off as male. Thus, to invoke "eros" is to invoke other theologies of love that cannot be appropriated for Africa, and perhaps not even for modern Europeans and Americans, without extensive discussion of their historical underpinnings and their relevance for modern, let alone African, understandings of love.

The idea of "eros" in modern theology is problematical because it tends to be used in an undeconstructed manner as a word without an originary context or a word whose originary context is irrelevant or the meaning of whose originary context is not transparent. Yet, to talk about "eros" is not the same thing as talking about *agape* or *caritas*. Indeed, the problem of the universality of "eros" becomes compounded once we juxtapose to it Roman theologies of love in which, for example, Cupid is not historically the mythical embodiment of Eros, nor *caritas* necessarily that of *agape*. Use of the term *eros* and its cognates calls for translation across many historical and cultural regions in which the word shows up. In the context of this essay, its use raises important questions such as, How ought we to think of "eros" and desire in the postcolony?[6] Can "eros" and desire be thought in a postcolony characterized by different, sometimes conflicting, meanings of love, sex, and the erotic? In the current discursive climate in Africa, dominated as it is by Christian and Western rationalities, is not any appropriation of the notion of "eros" necessarily an un-African?

In this essay, I use terms such as love, "eros," and sex with great vigilance because I write from within several different coexistent cultures: African (Shona and Tewe) and Western (British and American) in which I more or less simultaneously live and move and where these words are necessarily ambiguous precisely because their meanings depend upon and circulate through the possibility of intercultural hermeneutical coexistence and simultaneity. Yet, the logic of such coexistence and simultaneity always begs the question of translatability. Thus, I cannot take the meanings of words such as "eros," love, and sex for granted. In using them, I am always aware of another meaning, another form of expression, another worldview, another pattern of relationships to which they might point. These difficulties notwithstanding, I proceed with the use of the term *eros* but always in quotation marks. I shall use it as a comparative metaphor in order to allow for some possibility of intercultural translation and analysis. Throughout, the way I write "eros" will stand in for the way I think about love, sex, and desire. The quotation marks around the term signify its ambiguity, its unending susceptibility to varying interpretations, and its analogical resilience that allows it to stand in for terms such as love, sex, and desire, although it is itself not reducible to any of these. Thus, an important question is that of translation. The question of the translation of "eros" is crucial because what is at stake is not just the word but, rather, the fact that the imaginary narratives and theogonic frames of reference which it postulates and recapitulates come to us from a sociotheological order that is limited both by the specificity of its Greek origin and by its many ensuing historical renditions in the cultures of the West.[7] It is a mirror in which many of us (Africans and Westerners) pretend to recognize ourselves when, in fact, the images appearing there belong to someone else. Eros is a Greek god who performs certain functions within the pantheon of many such gods. The exchangeability of meanings that many tend to posit between love understood in terms of "eros" and love as differently understood in modern and ancient vernaculars hides a process of uncritical borrowing of foreign theologies whose relation to Christian theology is not always clear.

RECOLONIZATIONS OF AFRICAN SEXUALITY
IN WESTERN PUBLIC HEALTH DISCOURSES

The problem of failing to attend to the historicity and thus to the cultural differences that always characterize sex, love, and "eros" can be illustrated by examining some of the ways in which African sexuality is treated in certain Western conceptions. An example is public health discourse about HIV/AIDS in Africa. This discourse analyzes the diseases and proposes medical, political, and scientific interventions to control and combat its spread. Because HIV/AIDS in Africa is mostly contracted through sex, public health discourse is also necessarily discourse about sex and love in Africa.

Much of the discussion on HIV/AIDS in Africa (more so there than in the Western world, and this for reasons we shall deal with later) is about safety, safe sex, protected sex, condom use, and abstinence, or put negatively, it is about avoiding risky sexual behavior. The discourse is, on the one hand, linked to assumptions (both cultural and scientific) about the relation between human behavior and the magnitude of the pandemic and, on the other, to assumptions about the magnitude of the pandemic and the link to promiscuity, extramarital sex, sex workers, homosexuality, and disease. The significance of safety and the size of the pandemic depend on assumptions about sex, sexuality, and ethics. The ethical dimension of the discourse is often disguised as policy statements. Here normative assumptions about sex, ethics (policy), and sexuality are the conditions that allow the emergence of a discourse of regulation of sexual desire in terms of vulnerability, safety, and security.

There are at least two overlapping trajectories in which this discourse has been moving. One trajectory is about the representation of African sexuality through analysis of HIV/AIDS and the other is about safety and sex. The first trajectory explains the prevalence of HIV/AIDS in Africa through a largely Western construction of what has been called "a hyper-sexualized pan-African culture" in which Africans are stereotypically depicted as marked by an excessive libidinal complex.[8] An example of this is the work of the three Australian scholars, demographer John Caldwell, his anthropologist wife, Patricia Caldwell, and their research partner Pat Quiggin, also a demographer, who argue that there is a distinctive African sexuality that is different from that of what they call Eurasia. These three researchers propose an African civilization (what they dub "an alternative civilization—very different in its workings, including its patterns of sexual behavior . . .") defined by unrestrained sexual license. This civilization belongs to an order of difference characterized as *Homo Ancestralis*.[9] This characterization inscribes African sexual otherness in some primordial, if not atavistic, imaginary. African women especially are singled out as the bearers of this civilization because, we are told, they engage in promiscuous coitus with little or no moral qualms.[10]

One area in which sex and sexuality are experienced is that of gender. Since gender has become a central category for understanding the epidemiology of HIV/AIDS, to single out African women as promiscuous, which is to say they are the agents of the spread of HIV infection, is hugely problematical. It blames the victim and for the wrong reasons. Quite apart from the untenability of the general thesis about the promiscuous nature of African women, it is well known that the vulnerability of African women to infection is, among other things, due to poverty, powerlessness, and lack of access to economic resources. Surely a demographer such as Caldwell would know this; yet, he and his companions insist that it is female sexual abandon that explains the staggering effect of HIV/AIDS in Africa. By contrast, Eurasia has been spared the scourge of the pandemic largely because of its capacity to practice sexual restraint.

In order to intervene against AIDS effectively, the Caldwells and Quiggin urge understanding of "the role of sexual relations within it [Africa]."[11] To understand the prevalence of AIDS in Africa requires understanding not just the sexual behavior of Africans but the way in which that behavior is part of what it is to be African—the culture and civilization in which Africanness is produced and defined. By making African sex and sexual behavior one of the fundamental distinguishing features of African civilization, Africans are ontologically conceptualized and represented in terms of their sexuality. This conceptualization is organized around premarital and extramarital sexual extravagance, promiscuity, lack of restraint, permissiveness, and sex as transactional (the idea that African women engage in sexual activity inside and outside marriage for material gain or as a form of economic exchange). The result is a view, intended or not, of the African as essentially an aberrant sexual being. This conclusion is unavoidable because these terms are not morally neutral in Western culture where they describe unacceptable or, at least, problematical sexual difference.[12]

The Caldwells and Quiggin describe African cultures as "the African system" whose social characteristics and the social behavior they produce and support "are logically related to one another."[13] Some of these characteristics include a reversal in the relation of the order of virtues such that fertility and reproduction are morally more important than sexual conduct. Thus, "reproduction" is more important than "profligacy."[14] The enervation of the marriage bond inscribed in this reversal itself derives from the way in which "Africans neither placed aspects of sexual behavior at the center of their moral and social systems nor sanctified chastity." Within this scheme the question of love is marginal. Sex can imply love and love can imply sex. The question is left open.[15] (I shall come back to this question later.) Furthermore, African women (married or otherwise) engage in extramarital sex mostly for material gain (the transactional element),[16] reproduction, social networking, or because of self-pimping in order to please their husbands who regard their wives' adultery as a matter of male pride and celebration. Since sexual attitudes are not based on morality nor, outside of reproduction, on religion (sex being very much understood as a worldly everyday activity like working, eating, and drinking),[17] Africans experience no guilt about sexual relations.[18] The dialectical counterpart to this lack of guilt is lack of fear regarding the consequences of sexual promiscuity.

These claims about African sexuality are remarkable for several reasons. The first is the genre and style of thought they represent. Intended or not, they represent a long history of stereotypical Western portrayals of Africans as sexually immoral, exotic, aberrant, and totally other.[19] The role science and scholarship played in generating and perpetuating these stereotypes is represented here by the manner in which the Caldwells and Quiggin largely depend upon secondhand ethnographic data and how their work serves as the representation of the sexuality of the African "other" to official world bodies such as the World Bank for whom they have done research on Africa. The second remarkable thing about these claims is that they are made in the 1980s and 1990s, as if the history of protest against these representations has made no difference. Third, it is striking that while acknowledging that their research is based on "scattered evidence" and that "there are no comparable quantitative surveys—nor for much of the material can there be," these researchers create a whole civilization based on this "paucity of evidence" and generalize their theory to a whole continent. Fourth, as criticism and debate of their work has shown, the influence of their work has been widespread.[20] This popularity justifies using their work as a typical example of one of the trajectories along which discourse on HIV/AIDS in Africa is moving. Given the number of times their work has been cited in journals, books, and policy documents, I suggest that it constitutes a discursive hegemony that uses the crisis of AIDS to recolonize language about African sex and sexuality. In the period between its publication in 1987 and 2008, "The Cultural Context of High Fertility in Sub-Saharan Africa" has been cited 194 times, an average of 8.82 citations per year. Another influential essay by the Caldwells and

Quiggin, "The Social Context of AIDS in Sub-Saharan Africa," has been cited 251 times since its publication in 1989, an average of 11.95 citations per year.[21] This discursive hegemony establishes the authority and canonical status of their work. What concerns me here is the impact it has on intellectuals, missionaries, medical doctors, policy makers, government officials, and aid agencies—that is, on those responsible for the shaping of public discourse in and about Africa. Their appropriation of the claims of these three researchers defines an official, yet distorted, orthodoxy about African sexuality. Such distorted perceptions of African sexuality not only perpetuate old stereotypes about African sexual excess, they also lead to misguided and dangerous policies and practices in the fight against HIV/AIDS. There is also the danger that Africans will internalize distorted notions of their own sexuality and thus end up blaming not just themselves as individuals but blaming themselves as Africans for the tragedy of AIDS.

Finally, it is remarkable that in this discourse, sex is cut off from love. There is no discussion anywhere in these essays of the relationship between love and sex in African culture. There is no discussion of desire, pleasure, "eros," or various types of love and how these might connect with sex and sexuality. The reader is left with the impression that in Africa, sex is essentially a loveless activity. Indeed, the Caldwells and Quiggin claim that Africans are so sexually different that they prefer the sex act itself at the expense of foreplay, thinking of the latter as an act of witchcraft.[22] It is as if Africans are indifferent to love or desire, being driven instead by sheer lust.[23]

I have so far been dealing with the first of the two trajectories of HIV/AIDS discourse in Africa—namely, how representations of African sexuality have developed in public health discourses. I now turn to the second trajectory: safe sex.

THE DISCOURSE OF SAFE SEX

The discourse of safe sex is the dominant of the two trajectories I am discussing here.[24] It is behaviorist in outlook, at least in so far as it focuses on the sexual behavior of individuals in different population groups as the main causal factor in the spread of HIV/AIDS. It is precisely this behaviorism that guides the work of the Caldwells and Quiggin. There is a sense in which these two discursive trajectories converge. By framing discourse about sex and sexuality in Africa in terms of safety and security, this behaviorist approach repeats and reinscribes ideas about African sexual deviance. It is the behavior of Africans—that is, their lack of sexual control—that is behind the AIDS epidemic. Since questions of safe sex and security are discussed by medical doctors and AIDS researchers, the discourse becomes "scientific." In a parallel discourse, priests and social workers provide sanction to talk of abstinence, condoms, fidelity, and so on as the path toward sexual healing and thus conquering HIV/AIDS.

The discourse of safe sex is structured by a binary of safe/unsafe, protected/ unprotected, risk-free/risky sex around which public health policies, medical practices, moral and ethical discourses, and international humanitarian intervention have developed. Safety operates in different discursive domains: the moral-existential, the political, the theological, and the medical domains. Safety serves both as a tool and a strategy for reducing the rate of transmission of the AIDS virus. It seeks to achieve this by emphasizing the need for fewer sexual partners, abstinence, the use of condoms, and fidelity in marriage. In this section, I suggest how this safe sex discourse problematizes sex and love. Notions of safe and unsafe sex suggest that there is something problematical in the usual understandings of sex and love. When sex becomes unsafe in such a way that it becomes the medium, if not the agent, of the death of millions of people, when it has to be made safe again, then the connection between love and sex becomes deeply problematical. Much of what I say here depends on presupposing the importance of this sex-love connection.

There are several layers to the relationship between safety and sex. First, there is a personal dimension. It is the individual subject who places the meaning of his or her own life in danger by engaging in unprotected sex or by being exposed to such danger by a partner who has engaged in unprotected sex. It is at this level that the moral-existential aspect of safety is most immediately encountered. Second, over and above this personal dimension, the question of safety also includes the safety or security of the state and the nation. This pertains to the economic, military, and political integrity of both nation and state.[25] That is perhaps why HIV/AIDS is considered a security issue in international politics.[26] The threat to individual well-being becomes a threat to social and national security. Third, the nature of this threat does not subsist simply in the disease itself but in the connection between the disease and sex or human agency. The disease uses sex to realize its threat just as sex is the means by which the disease is acquired. To the extent that love is somehow hitched to sex, love-as-sex becomes implicated in the threat to human well-being on all sorts of levels, as just indicated. To the extent that sex is hitched to love, sex-as-love becomes existentially threatening. How can love be the medium or agent of threat, danger, and destruction? I want to suggest that given this cluster of issues, there really is no safe—that is, unproblematic—way of talking about sex and love in Africa anymore; there is no straightforward way of connecting "eros" and love. Any such connection faces the challenge of suffering and death of individuals and communities.

"Eros" becomes a threat in three ways. It is a threat when it is detached or separated from moral concern for its subject, when the absence of such concern represents a moral gap between the subjects of erotic involvement. In psychoanalytic terms, it is possible to read this gap as desire but such a reading must also emphasize not only the desire of the subjects that brings them together but desire in the specific sense of a lack of commitment of either or both subjects to each other. It is desire in this second sense that separates the subjects from each other even as they profess erotic love one for the other. This is contradictory in that while two people want to be together and indeed come together, the expression of this togetherness is founded upon a lack of commitment to the very idea of being together, of intimacy and love both at a social and at a personal level. There is lack of commitment at a social level because the norms and value of a society generally provide the framework within which what counts as "eros" and love are understood. Thus, there is no commitment to such social values and norms as individuals simply choose to ignore them. There is lack of commitment at a personal level because undermining these values translates into the possibility of either or both subjects encountering each other outside those norms and values and thus of exploitation or objectification each other.[27] Thus, a twofold threat emerges to the integrity of society and of the self–other relationship.

Second, "eros" as love becomes a threat when it is instrumentalized in such a way that it is regarded simply as a biological function in which two naked bodies exchange nothing more than passionate physical and psychological energy—so-called libido. Both libertarian and some conservative notions of sex have instrumentalized "eros" in this way, the first by stressing free sex as a good in itself and the second by linking it to procreation as its only function. Because of the association of "eros" with intimacy or, to put it more properly, because "eros" is one crucial source of human intimacy, to empty it of any values that might guarantee the integrity of such intimacy is to threaten the source of love and friendship which are themselves expressions of intimacy.[28]

The third threat that "eros" poses in light of HIV/AIDS is bodily: the body in its biological and physical makeup and the body in its social and political composition. By threatening the body, the virus threatens the home where it lives; it threatens the organism that sustains it. In this way, it threatens itself. This means that the threat is total or radical. The virus instigates the double annihilation of human bodies in their visible and most concrete forms and the annihilation of the forms of social and political organization that act as metaphoric extensions of human bodies (e.g., the body politic), thus rendering the value of and relation among any remaining bodies uncertain, unreliable, and precarious since they, too, are henceforth always open to the danger of an intractable disease. This means that all erotic relations, all relations of sexual exchange take on the same uncertain and precarious character. Husbands and wives, partners and lovers literally enter into sexual intercourse with each other with no guarantee that they will not contract the disease. The reverse side to this is that faith and trust, what I characterize as "the bad faith of sex," become crucial to the economy of "eros."[29]

The threat itself is intimate because it is lodged in the body as well as in the very structures of bodily existence. The intimacy of HIV/AIDS and the sexual intimacy that is its source and upon which it depends for its transmission exemplify a profound ambiguity at the very heart of "eros." It is an ambiguity in which the distinction between "eros" and *thanatos* (Greek for "death") is produced and problematized, if not eradicated. Intimacy is simultaneously a source of death and of sexual pleasure, including both the pleasure of procreation and the destruction of procreation.[30] Intimacy as used here has several dimensions: physical and psychological self-intimacy; the interpersonal dimension of two people being copresent to one another; and social intimacy. The latter includes kinship intimacy or the intimacy of affines and the intimacy of social others with whom we share the same cultural space such as friends and coworkers. At all these levels, intimacy is disrupted and threatened by HIV/AIDS. Thus, the emphasis on the intimate nature of HIV/AIDS and of what we might call its erotic face must not be allowed to obscure its alienating effects. Paradoxically, intimacy results in stigmatization, obloquy, social isolation, and ultimately death.[31]

HISTORICIZING, DECOLONIZING, AND THEOLOGIZING "EROS"

It is possible to argue that the effect of HIV/AIDS on "eros" is entirely contingent, historical, and parasitic, that it is not ontological and internal to the makeup of "eros," and that the contingency of AIDS relativizes its challenge to "eros." If this argument is valid then it can be said that these elements of contingency do not in any way alter the ontological structure of "eros." The trouble with this argument is that it locates "eros" outside of history, beyond contingency and temporality. It fails to see that there is no access to "eros" that is not mediated through the relational forces constituting human existence. It is perhaps this Platonic idealizing of "eros,"[32] this understanding of "eros" as pure form, that misleads some Western scholars into privileging "eros" as the basis of all genuine ecstatic love. According to this understanding, which is enshrined in Plato's *Symposium* and *Phaedrus*, there is an upward movement in the structure of "eros" from the sensual/carnal to "eros" realized as pure form.[33] Thus, in some versions of Christian theology, the truly erotic is taken to represent some analog of the beatific vision of God. I want to argue against this view by suggesting a less hyper-Hellenistic and a more historical, demythologized view of "eros." In my view, if "eros" is any ultimate form achieved through hierarchical ascent, that form must also be seen in terms of the powerful residual traces of each of the stages transcended in that ascent so that pure form is always historical, always tethered to its lower forms. In suggesting that we see "eros" as essentially historical, I want to relocate its ontology from the realm of form to that of history.[34]

Historicizing "eros" has several advantages. First, ancient Greek philosophy and, through it, the Western world cease to be the ultimate point of reference for thinking and talking about "eros." This decolonizes "eros" and opens up the possibility of reimagining and renaming "eros" and the erotic in the logics of a multiplicity of global vernaculars. Second, we can begin to take seriously the many ways in which love and "eros," in addition to being positive forces, are nevertheless caught up in the ambiguities of life. Third, it opens the possibility of doing genuine comparative histories of the erotic. Fourth, historicizing "eros" may help us to entertain the possibility that in certain contexts "eros" is not the predominant form of love. One thinks of cultures where, for example, human activities are not reduced to sublimated sexual energy or governed by the demands of excessive desire but genuinely stand for autonomous expressions of other kinds of love which may or may not be served by "eros."

To argue for the historicity of love is to recognize the role played in its very structure by risk and vulnerability because love is apparently not above violence.[35] In this regard, it becomes necessary to point to the problem of the historicity of the violence of the cross as a redemptive moment that displays ultimate divine love. I am interested here in the intimate connection of love to violence, death, and salvation. If Christ is the one who, motivated by ultimate love, came to make possible human flourishing by enabling abundant life, and if his violent death was a condition of possibility for this, what are we to make of the gap between massive death due to HIV/AIDS and this promise of human flourishing? If the love of Christ, whose power is ultimately articulated through the cross, is that which forms and informs, shapes and even directs all acts of genuine loving, including sexual loving, then, when loving becomes the occasion for massive death, the question of love turns into that of theodicy.[36] It is here that millions of dead Africans pose for theologies of love and sex an enormous challenge, an interrogation of the presence of a loving God who promises abundant life but is seemingly not able to deliver. Put another way, the discourses of safety and security, of protected sex or even of risky sexual behavior make "eros" and love a zone of anxiety, anguish, fear, and ultimately death, such that "eros" is turned into a site of dereliction, lamentation, and mourning, a place where the love of God is itself radically called into question.

In the end, such a radical recognition of the existential limits of love, even the love of God, means that we must take seriously the ambiguity of love itself. There are several structures that characterize that ambiguity. First comes the connection between will and desire. Love can never be forced. Its true meaning derives from its being an act of will. However, any such act necessarily takes place in the push and pull of a body and mind teaming with instincts, drives, and forces generated at many levels of human consciousness. Second, the ambiguity of love inheres in a certain intractable carnality. There is our creaturely carnality—the fact of our being flesh, blood, and bones and of our of being embodied beings. In the Christian account of love, this carnality is connected with the drama of human existence at every point. Carnality is: connected with creation, in that humanity is endowed with flesh and embodied right from the start; connected with the fall, in that the consequences of the fall are physical and bodily pertaining as much to the pain of childbearing as to the sweat of hard labor; the occasion for and the mode of the incarnation of Christ; the surface upon which the violence of the cross—so central to what many Christians mean by love—is played out; central to the resurrection, to the story of Easter; and central to the constitution of the church as the body of Christ. There is a persistent ambiguity running through all of this in which carnality historically organizes life and death through the violence of redemption. Both "eros" and love or "eros" as love are located in the ambiguities of human carnality. I do not intend to suggest that desire and love are reducible to or exhausted by our physical experience or that failure to experience love at this level cancels the possibility of love. I am not, in other words, proposing a biological understanding of love. As we have already seen in my critique of the Caldwells and Quiggin on African sexuality, I reject a reduction of sexuality to biology.

"EROS," SAFE SEX, AND SALVATION

I wish to conclude by going back to the question of safe sex. Theologically, one of the troubling features of the discourse about safe sex in Africa is its tendency either to moralize about the evils of condom use or to leave questions about safe sex to the experts. In fact, given the extent of the AIDS pandemic, one surprisingly finds little theological reflection on this whole question. Yet there is a close relationship between safety and the Christian idea of salvation which provides a productive framework for the kind of theological reflection about "eros" and safe sex that I think is possible. The relationship between these two terms enables theological movement in several directions. First, we must remember that the Greek term *soteria*, from which we get soteriology and which means salvation, conceptually incorporates the idea of safety so that it is part of the definition of salvation. Salvation also involves other metaphors such as deliverance, rescue, and refuge that reinforce the idea of safety. Second, there is a fundamental link between Christian notions of salvation and the idea of love. The love of God and the death of Jesus on the cross as an expression of such love are taken by many Christians to be the basis of deliverance and salvation from sin. For many Christians, the death of Christ is an actual bodily event that establishes salvation. Both body and death are crucial to salvation. This connection between love and salvation stands as an invitation for African theology to interrogate both "eros" and Christian notions of love, on the one hand, and, on the other, to locate the problem of HIV/AIDS in relation to safety understood theologically. The point here is not to demonize victims of HIV/AIDS by singling them out as somehow constituting an outlandish category of sinners. The point is, rather, imaginatively and constructively to rethink salvation in a context in which its very meaning is imperiled by Africa's Black Death (AIDS).

A third direction in which safety and salvation beckons us is that of the bond between salvation and health. In the ancient world, salvation meant deliverance from disease, disaster, slavery, or death.[37] Salvation also refers to well-being and wholeness.[38] Safety understood in terms of *soteria* (salvation) has great theological potential for addressing the problem of safe-sex in Africa. How the notions of health, body, love, death, and safety positively coalesce around *soteria* corresponds to the way in which these same notions negatively coalesce around HIV/AIDS. The one cluster represents death and mortality and the other life and salvation.

Another discourse that is fruitful for thinking theologically about safe sex is the discourse about human behavior. Much of this discourse reads such behavior in purely naturalistic terms. Its ethics of human behavior is behavioristic. On the other hand, however, *soteria* grounds safety and thus safe sex in a different ethical register, that of redeemed human relationships in which "eros" itself becomes subject to the dynamics of God's self-giving as salvation and thus rediscovers itself. Here, too, we are dealing with human behavior but understood as Christian discipleship, that form of life character-ized not by the instrumentalization of libido or the reduction of sex to a mere biological act but by responsible, mutual self-giving.

Further Suggested Readings

Cimperman, Maria. *When God's People Have HIV/AIDS: An Approach to Eth-ics.* Maryknoll, N.Y.: Orbis, 2005.

Dube, Musa Wenkosi. *The HIV and AIDS Bible: Selected Essays.* Scranton: University of Scranton Press, 2008.

———, ed. *HIV/AIDS and the Curriculum: Methods of Integrating HIV/AIDS in Theological Programmes.* Geneva: World Council of Churches, 2003.

Hunter, Susan. *Black Death: AIDS in Africa.* New York: Palgrave Mac-millan, 2004.

Iliffe, John. *The African AIDS Epidemic: A History.* Athens: Ohio University Press, 2006.

CHAPTER 12

Queering White Male Fear
in the Mirror of Hip-Hop Erotics

James W. Perkinson

IN HIS 1995 EXPOSÉ entitled *The Rhythms of Black Folk,* Jon Michael Spencer identifies the influence of hip-hop culture among white youth as a kind of return of the repressed—a penetration of vanilla suburbs by the sounds of subjugated blackness—that demands analysis in postmodern America as a profound datum.[1] This essay will sound out that sonic eruption as a theological sign of the times—a kind of erotic insurrection, assaulting the gated community with a vital surfeit of the racialized history of the country, like an army of resurrected bones breaking out of a dried valley.[2] I want to probe beneath the surface of the commodified blackness sold to white voyeurs and "wanna-bes" under the twin logos of "bling" and "booty call" to issue a challenge to Christian pedagogy to step up to a crucial responsibility. The interest here is in reading underneath the visual culture exterior in order to exegete an ongoing pathology in the country that has not ceased to trouble the sexual politics of church and society alike for more than three centuries and elucidate the spiritual potencies of the energies articulated in hip-hop practices outside its commercialization.

The leitmotif of this theological analysis will be the longstanding history of white appropriation of black cultural expression—most recently and ruthlessly pursued in crossover hip-hop marketing—that simultaneously reinforces and belies white fear of things black and queer. The linking of these latter two notions in a single analysis will proceed as a governing hypothesis, tracked through the history begun with slave plantation practices of white male rape of black women, continued through Jim Crow terror of black males imagined as seeking revenge in kind, heightened in white male fear of militant black power in the 1960s and a certain white female fascination with the same, carried forward in contemporary society in a co(mmo)dified packaging of that particular complex of loathing and lure into a sonic amulet sold to ward off white impotence and boredom. The question of "penetration"—fear of such by whom in relation to what body—will anchor the analysis. The essay concludes by challenging Christianity to assume prophetic responsibility for facing its own complicity in authoring and reinforcing this Gordian knot of violent erotic entanglement and by articulating a possible process of exorcism and healing.

SELF-CRITIQUE IN MOTOWN

Sometime in the summer of 2004, while living for a time in Denver to be near my wife (until we could work out teaching jobs for both of us back in my hometown of Detroit), I was reading poetry at an open-mike venue hosted at Brother Jeff's Community Center in the Five Points neighborhood north of downtown. I introduced myself as coming from Detroit, kicked out a few syncopated rhymes, and sat down, whereupon the MC, an accomplished "word-spitter" and well-known hip-hop organizer, expressed his surprise at my fifty-year-old performance by riffing, "a white boy from Detroit with skills! Did you hear that? That, that . . . that was Eminem's daddy! That's who that was!" Although I had already been writing (and performing) academic "art" pieces about hip-hop for a number of years by that time, I had never really paid much attention to Eminem. In my mind, he was one more white "wanna-be"—adopting the style, imitating the manner, and taking his pirated goods to the bank, like so many other pink-skinned pickers of blackberries from the vine of tortured creativity. After being tagged with his ancestry, I decided I had better investigate a bit further. I suddenly remembered being cautioned a few years earlier by an African American spoken-word artist friend in Detroit who had edited my first volume of poetry, that Marshall Mather's lyrics actually commanded a lot of respect in her community.[3]

Since then, Eminem has emerged in my awareness as a mixed bag of white genius—obviously skilled, conscious enough to give "props" to black mentors when due, careful to use the idiom to rap his own "trailer trash" story and not pretend to be an urban "gangsta," savvy enough to send up mainstream culture in Slim Shady (his performance "double") parody rather than in direct attack (even though the media then barraged him with interpretive "ain't it awful-ism" that actually said more about their own simplistic predilections than anything else). Nevertheless, for all that, I would venture he is still caught in the trap of white male privilege that invites multiple levels of misperception about the culture at large and culpable immaturity (or worse) in taking responsibility to work for a more just world. I invoke him here as the kind of public figure who embodies the conundrum that I wish to interrogate theoretically (as a kind of postindustrial "haunt" of American culture writ large) and who reflects something of my own personal odyssey.[4] That odyssey provides the baseline for the analysis subsequently offered and the "off-beat phrasing" that I want to "throw down" at the feet of academic production in general. The personal is indeed, for me, the political. It is also the theoretical. Theory, in my personal politics, sooner or later must be self-critical or risk comporting authoritative in a disingenuous manner.

My own theory begins with analysis of the history that has already shaped me before I could ever lift pen to page to begin the inquiry. White male presumption to rule a world by means of a word and a gun is verse one of my "Genesis." Understanding that such rule has not been merely presumption is the key to understanding everything else. Euro-heritage Christian men of heterosexual persuasion, over five centuries now, have successfully installed a globalizing order of unfettered production and rapacious consumption, legitimized largely by racist ideation, which thus far admits of no apparent limitation. The resulting history of genocide, slavery, plunder, rape, and ecological devastation—despite multiple academic cottage industries detailing such in ethnography and historiography, political economy, and critical theory—arguably has yet to gain a full hearing in most white male ears. Actual hearing is more than mere listening. My own writing here—as indeed most of my work—is merely one small offering toward that goal.

The initiative arises out of more than twenty-five years of living, moving, and having my being in near eastside Detroit, initially, as part of an activist Christian enterprise engaged in neighborhood development projects of various sorts and, more recently, as an educator/artist, teaching in an inner-city seminary and performing as a spoken-word poet on the scene in Motown. Actually, more accurately, I did not so much have my being over those years, as lose it. The "ghetto" streets that became home gradually exposed and summarily exorcised many of my motives for moving to the city in the first place. At first thinking I was on "mission" to help, only hard years of initiation into a different perception of reality (under the sharp eyes and honest words of friends and less sympathetic observers) schooled me in the real deal: I was actually in that context to learn. What I learned about, by way of black culture, was whiteness—specifically my own positioning in a much larger ensemble of relations and privileges, norms and powers, access and habits that, while subject to personal questioning and conscientizing, were not simply amenable to renunciation! I have elsewhere elaborated that experience into critical theological and aesthetic examinations of the broader phenomenon of modern white supremacy that, despite rumors of demise, continues to exercise its prerogatives of military power and economic control largely unabated (if certainly muted in more euphemistic codes of identification).[5] In this writing, I want to begin an interrogation of the psychosexual side of that supremacy.

As an introit into that particular focus, another brief personal admission is apropos: I remember a few years ago, hanging out with friends in a reggae club in Memphis after some national meeting, watching a thirty-something Afro-heritage woman—thin, dreadlocked, unpartnered—slowly responding to the music. Her movements caught my eye by way of subtle evocations hard to put to words. They were not highly demonstrative but very contained and precise, a minute patterning of the body to a rhythmic resonance of immense diminution, that would every so often break out in high leg stomps and angular gesture and then just as quickly return to the more muted attentiveness they expressed. Her concentrated face, her bodily absorption, centered with such nuance in the beat, the aura of trance surrounding her presence on the floor, the "old spirit" timelessness and "African" antiquity that I found myself projecting on her—all these together one more time evoked a feeling of fierce aliveness that exposure to Afro-heritage culture regularly arouses within me. That arousal is fraught—something that erupts within my body as a particular facet of my own inner universe of desire and yet, at the same time, frightens as something that is not simply mine either to name or rightfully to claim. It is at core erotic, and it is one of the ways my own psychological formation belies (and apes) the broader social order. Without question, it is at least partially projection, but it has also provoked a useful discipline of self-discovery and animated an ongoing commitment to political struggle.

It has likewise set the agenda for my academic concentration. As Yale art historian Robert Farris Thompson once confessed regarding his own fascination with mambo, my academic work is in one sense merely a way to continue to live out that love of Afro-mediated rhythm.[6] However, the legitimacy of such work on the part of a white scholar—at least this white scholar—finds its test as a mode of accountability. That accountability includes embracing black culture as also encoding learning about white culture: seeking, among black culture's protean riffs, penetrating commentary upon and provocative critique of my own culture's norms and presumptions in order better to learn how to work toward dismantling its supremacy. In any case, I watched the reggae dancer intently that night, from within the circle of my own friends, and then danced in partial imitation, seeking to find similar response to the sound, letting her moves probe and provoke my own. In many respects, my academic work is a literary effort in kind, sitting long and attentively before black knowledges of things white, and of things not-white, as invocation and conjuration for my own continuing interrogation of this space called "America."

Not least, in that invocation, have been black theology's insistence that religion in this country has ever been racialized and historian of religion Charles Long's contention that race—even in secular form—has been religious.[7] These particular challenges pushed me in an earlier work already mentioned to thematize white supremacy as soteriological in its fetishism and violence, seeking to realize and routinize an identity—on the back of the blackness it projected—for which it was willing to act in an ultimate[8] fashion (to kill or be killed). The argument there traced out supremacy's shift from an explicitly Christian confession (judging indigenous cultures as inferior on the basis of clearly theological categories) to an implicitly soteriological elaboration, after 1776, living out white identity and power as an existential project of "ontological" differentiation and imagination (not less caught up in questions of "wholeness" and "ultimacy" for being only inchoately theological).[9] Here, the turn to questions of white allure and anguish in the register of eros will not yield a different result. The "theologicalness" of white ways of fetishizing blackness remains complexly occulted and apophatically mystified precisely in appearing only secular. Long's reworking of Rudolph Otto's category of the *tremendum* as "colonial Terror" provided the key cipher for that first unpacking of white supremacy and identity; here it is the other side of Otto's compound mystery that anchors analysis and figures the "fascination," in all of its convoluted search for integration and wholeness.[10]

RAPE AND FEAR

In particular, I want to linger before this personal love of black creativity, to entertain Eminem as an emblematic white enigma, to hover in general over hip-hop's crossover appeal, all in the name of an exposé of racism's most tangled secret: the erotic desire and dread that compounds its aggression. The place to begin such a display is with the historical fact of rape. Slavery was a quintessentially commercial enterprise, yielding profits and leisure on a massive scale for propertied white males, jump-starting the economic life of the nascent nation, installing the infrastructure of "democracy" on the backside of bondage, hallowing a White House dome with inscriptions to liberty, carved and erected into place by bound black labor. Slavery was also an erotic economy of no mean complexity. Often enough—as is evident from the multicolored menagerie of folk emerging from the far side of the slavery enterprise—white masters used the slave quarters as their own private harem, raping female slaves with impunity. The exact texture of the aggression undoubtedly varied across a wide range of possibility, from Thomas Jefferson-like quasi-romance to a brutally violent and dehumanizing "taking." But in a social order overdetermined with mythic projections and ritual humiliations, the structure of the power relation would necessarily have warped the attraction with all manner of phantasms and phobias.

The depth dimension of that ongoing ritual of rape can only be pondered as convoluted in the extreme—a white act of violent intimacy carried out on "property" otherwise denigrated as "animal." What might it mean to have sex with a "moveable asset" or with a "beast of burden"? A later age might well have tried to articulate the psychodynamics involved, if confessional archives could have been created, but our imagination, today, of such dark practices can only conjecture from without and in hindsight. We can only read back from the "archives" we do have—the quite evident effects of the profound social anxiety anchoring white male racial imagination and action in the postbellum South. The fixations of that imagination, however, as indeed the excess of the actions, belie the dynamics. Here I cannot do more than suggest, but the evidence is telling. White male identity, in the late nineteenth-century American South, was anchored in terror of an otherwise unmentionable psychosexual comeuppance—a terror arguably constituted in an anticipated rape-in-kind, the return vengeance of a now-free black male population. This terror lies at the root of the hypervigilance with which southern white womanhood was policed by its male "protectors" and the castration and lynching visited on any real or imagined black male attention.[11] It is also palpable in the shrill and recurrent declamation of KKK Grand

Wizards against miscegenation if segregation were ever to be relaxed! The expressed hysteria was not that white males would suddenly be possessed of uncontrollable desires to divorce their mates and seek out black life partners but that white male impotence and unattractiveness might suddenly be revealed if the inverse occurred and white females began exploring the exotica and prowess rumored to be true of black males. The images of southern masculinity sheeted in white prophylaxis, southern belle femininity enfolded in imagined purity, and dark bodies backlit by burning crosses in the recesses of night—these images found immediate intelligibility and uncompromising ramification in a Christian "light" symbology that, arguably, has never ceased to animate the common sense of the country.

In spite of such southern repressions, an inversion of sorts did take place, to an extent, in the 1960s in the North. One of the effects of the black power movement—a moment of potent reversal in the racial calculus of the country, when for the first time ever on a large scale, black pride and beauty in general, and black male intelligence and resolve in particular, went militant and unapologetic in the public square—was an upending of that part of white supremacy's self-certainty which was rooted in an erotic construction of racial perception. Until that moment, black masculinity had been publicly constructed, in and by white cultural production and institutional discipline, as inadequate. Whether in terms of the requirements of Jim Crow obsequiousness in public interaction in the South, or of regulation by public health agencies, educational processes, labor market exigencies, and social service surveillance in the North—black collective existence was, in white imagination and experience alike, imminently violable, subject to penetration by white "concern" at any time (southern nooses and bullets found indirect but effective correlates, in the North, in quotidian social policy and business practice). Black masculinity in the mix was thereby manufactured for white voyeurism and policy planning as something less than manly—a proscriptively and proverbially "female" form of maleness, unable to defend its own physical or familial integrity against assault.[12] However, with the sudden appearance of fist-raising, beret-wearing, California-law-spouting "panther" figures like Huey Newton and Bobby Seale, bearing weapons and taking names of police officers when the latter arrested Oakland ghetto dwellers, the script was flipped. Here, suddenly, finally, epiphany-like, was the quintessential white male nightmare, incarnate: a black male body, armed with a hard round "rod," ready to spit bullets into quivering white flesh, all while quoting chapter and verse! The penetration game was seemingly threatening to come around in reverse, with the "white races" now positioned as "female."[13] That no small number of white females picked up a scent of virility and fawned over the imagined militancy (if not the actual persona underneath the image) only confirmed the darkly terrifying white male dry dream.

This dark apparition of power came equipped with a theological script publicly etched in *New York Times* ink, as "black theology incarnate" (in a full-page ad taken out in July 1966). Books quickly followed in its wake, giving passionate articulation to the claim. From a theological point of view, however, the insurgence of public blackness begs analysis not so much on explicitly doctrinal or ecclesiological grounds, but under Long's more heuristic category of a "terrorizing numinosity" (the *mysterium tremendum*) suddenly erupting from the spiritual underbelly of the nation. "Dread incarnate," in the black power movement, did not draw down immediate theological inspection on the part of white Christians, only repudiation. This newly enfleshed mysteriousness would have its more lasting effect on the white side of the divide of race in music rather than theology. Hip-hop, arguably, is its offspring and enduring textualization—the public ritualization of a simultaneous fear and fascination, in "gangsta" lyrics and "booty" clips, that give emblematic representation to this new incarnation of terror and titillation in the body politic.

The political result was a new ruthlessness in policing black masculinity. Recast in reactionary media as the epitome of a rape waiting to happen, black male identity in the 1970s and '80s became the favorite fetish of the newly emergent prison industrial complex, accomplishing for the second "Reconstruction" era (following the civil rights movement's abolition of Jim Crow segregation) what the original convict lease system had instituted in the first Reconstruction (after slavery had been abolished). The "roll-back" Reagan years—in criminal justice practice—reconstructed with a social vengeance the black male as outlaw organ on the prowl for white softness. Prison populations burgeoned with bodies of color out of all proportion relative to overall U.S. criminality as conservative political administrations wielded drug law like a postmodern whip. Rodney King, for instance, became a veritable "gorilla in the mist"—so "bestial," in his sluggish attempts at self-defense while supine on the concrete, as to be deemed a serious threat to twenty-one armed officers bearing batons and boots and magnums. But then he *had* emerged from his Hyundai, shaking his butt at the husband-wife team of California state police who had pulled him over in the first place! That little dance of innuendo with hands clutching a moving behind confirmed the imagined danger: a direct challenge to the white male order of things.[14] Was he shaking it at her . . . or them? Which was more frightening/titillating? Whatever the actuality, the "uppity-ness" had to be put in its place—made to lie down and stay down! In this case, the LAPD's phallic batons only beat King's exterior. A few years later, at the hands of the NYPD, Nigerian-born (but all black bodies are alike in the dark of imagined threat, aren't they?) Abner Louima would suffer something closer to the real desire/dread. This time around, there was a literal reaming with a plunger handle for merely fingering his wallet "inappropriately"!

The episodic litany of white fear and desire thus far sketched is mere outline. What it tracks is a psychosocial conundrum: a kinked-up white male sexual formation, sadomasochistic in its animation, organizing social structures in defense of its quintessential fantasy-scape. That the great object of dread was/is black and erect cannot be adequately thought about absent of history. Three hundred years of recurrent white male rape of black females—all the while with a foot on the throat of the black male—cannot be simply shrugged off, once the supine black body arises after 1865. There are just too many living signs of the deed. That we now inherit a social order structured in that fear is all but inevitable: from corporate board room to government agency, white male prerogative is concentrated and organized intent on containing black male bodies in the space furthest removed—prison—from those white-male-dominated centers of control and normativity. This northern "text of terror" is structurally similar to that enacted earlier with a more explicit theological symbology by KKK enforcers in the South; in the North, the color semiotics have been bled dry of explicit theology, but the color-coding of good and evil, purity and promiscuity, wholeness and pathology are not far removed from a Puritan imagination of the ultimate valuation of light and dark.

COMMODIFIED BLACKNESS

Black male containment, however, is complex, a postindustrial mode of an older colonial pattern of simultaneous inclusion/exclusion that has characterized European domination of peoples of color across the entire landscape of modernity. Indigenous (African, Asian, and American) peoples' land, resources, and labor were continuously incorporated into white European (and later white American) domains. At the same time, those peoples were personally and materially subject to all manner of exclusionary tactics: genocidal elimination in the case of many native groups; incarceration in the institution of slavery or work gangs for Africans and many Asians; later Jim Crow laws mapping out and restricting social access in the South; wage laws, housing regulations, policing patterns, and prison terms exercising a similar exclusionary effect in creating northern ghettos; and so on. That over time, due to social struggles of all kinds, the domain of access to white societal benefits has been pried open to some measure of nonwhite participation does not negate the basic colonizing structure. In effect, colonialism said, "We want your substance (economically) but refuse your person (socially)."

A similar paradox of inclusion/exclusion can be observed at play in the erotic economy of racialization, now that culture itself has become a primary domain of commodification, offering identity for sale like widgets. In hip-hop culture, as never before, commodified blackness has emerged as the new cache of "cool," gaining globalized purchase among youth populations eager to find idioms of rhythm and vernaculars of belonging adequate to their struggles for meaning and identification. "Gangsta" imagery and street argot offer black male posturing for sale, while "booty" video parades black female-ness as the "freshest" play-scape for fantasies of erotic conquest. So much of the product is answering to white teenage angst as well as leveraging sales at the high end of the market to voyeuristically inclined adults, seeking a "hit" of urban excitement without risk of actually being hit, or worse. Here again the structure is double: a desire for the cultural construct minus the actual body. MTV for the (white) mind, prison for the (black) flesh! White suburbanites get to have their ("devil's food") cake and eat it too. Tupac Shakur perhaps stands as the epitome of the aphorism incarnate in 1995, watching his album climb the charts of popularity from his front-row seat in the penitentiary.[15] Ironically, young black males, showing signs of some of the highest levels of personal esteem in the larger social order, are simultaneously dropping out of school at rates never before seen, completely in thrall to the "cool pose" lifestyle.[16] White boys dance wild to the style of "going ugly" under the skin, without a clue as to the cost or the meaning.[17] The image is assimilated to the white thirst for zest without personal or social cost; the black body, in constantly eroding efforts to survive the nightmare, is constantly thrown into the dungeon—another instant of pirated substance while the community is walled out!

Jon Michael Spencer, in writings dated to the 1990s that yet remain divinatory, keys on the moment of black power reversal of the 1960s to probe the reconstruction of black maleness as insurgent—a sexuality, previously contained in an uninterrogated category, now tilting at the suburb itself and drawing blood.[18] Hip-hop is the transfiguration of the 1960s black power fist of retribution into a stealth bombing texture of the 1970s and after. It becomes a kind of sonic phallus, crashing the gate of suburban exclusivity despite all parental interdictions to the contrary. White parents hear rap as rape, mobilize packaging-label laws and prison systems in defense. Their *ressentiment*-listener-children are not thereby saved,[19] but neither are they dammed to the margins like the ghetto bodies yielding the images that the big label corporations are taking to the market.

Spencer notes the payoff for black male rebels refusing to avoid the trouble the stereotypes bring. Public Enemy, for instance, played the name back into the white cultural hysteria that underlay the tsunami of black incarceration in the 1980s and 90s. There was/is at least the pleasure of touching the secret of white, middle-class business-as-usual without dissimulation. Soliciting Michel Foucault's *History of Sexuality* analysis to articulate an "insurgence of subjugated sexualities," Spencer says black rap griots and break-dance shamans just go straight for the gold.[20] Sex sells in capitalist inveiglements of erotics under the double-sign of the unspoken and ever-speaking (the hidden shamefulness that yet serves as the market's ever-invoked dynamism). Far from being the mere target of repression, in modernity sexuality became, rather, the omnipresent effect (and affect) of a proliferating set of social discourses and public practices that, according to Foucault, surveilled its prodigality, policed its unruly contagion, ensured its ubiquity and loquaciousness, and ever-anew, brought its body into being as a double-installation of power and pleasure—a power that became pleasurable in demanding account of sexuality, a pleasure that became powerful in giving account.[21] Among hip-hop artists, that power/pleasure became aphrodisiac in refusing the typical middle-class embarrassment about sex, where erotic reference is repressed in euphemism even as commerce is driven by its subliminal invocation. What advertising exploited as the great titillating subtext of innuendo, hip-hop simply named straight up, without apology or repentance. In so doing, it sounded out not simply the secret of capitalist commodification but the most intricate entanglement of the history of racialization.

DESIRE AND DREAD

On the white side of the divide of race (and now of scratched vinyl), the question is one of a phantasm possessing a body: the white desire for and dread of the black body that now has white males using black maleness as a sexual prosthesis. Certainly there is a history here dating back to the beginnings of black-face minstrelsy in which early-nineteenth-century white performers blacked-up on stage to play with a certain fetishized idea of freedom (associated with blackness) in front of white audiences (some of whom would then go out to beat up or kill actual black persons to make clear that the theatrical spectacle was just that—only "play"—and should not be mistaken as somehow undercutting the white superiority temporarily occluded in the minstrelsy act).[22]

Certainly the music supplies cover. White boys' love of rhythms black and raw is usually owned insipidly as merely "liking what is cool." Asked why it is cool, what it is that captivates at the level of base-beat assault, why it is beautiful to "get ugly" in the old gospel tradition of grunt, growl, and grimace, now run through a synthesizer and a diss' rap lip, most males of pallor can only prevaricate.[23] They dance the groove, without a clue. This writing does not pretend to map an alternative route forward but, rather, to name the subtext. Things queer and black, white and punk—indeed, pink and yellow and red and brown and gay and sad and butch and bad—in fact, all partake of each other. It is not just that sexual oppression and racial discrimination should be of equal concern in an anti-imperial politics. It is, rather, that they cannot be thought except in each other's terms.[24] They happen together, as the composite coding of an ever-solicited and suppressed formation of desire. What is black as a dark cavity, knowable only in probing—now suddenly, in a historic moment, convolutes, becomes its opposite in a continuing fantasy that is not entirely separate from what we mean by rationality itself, begins to loom as protuberance, frightening and seducing, recasting white as opening to be known in turn. What here is male and what female, what is pleasure and what power, is not finally discrete. Race is both a desire to penetrate and to be penetrated, overrun with economics, fraught with violence, sick with abjection, and yet tender with mystery and summons.

Writing as brief as this can only hint, not engage, archaeological depth. The point here is that transforming history requires first owning it. Before the gyroscope of white desire and dread can be turned, the depths of the contradictoriness must at least be sensed and wrestled with. Foucault proves seminal to think with here:

> The society that emerged in the nineteenth century—bourgeois, capitalist, or industrial society, call it what you will—did not confront sex with a fundamental refusal of recognition. On the contrary, it put into operation an entire machinery for producing true discourses concerning it. Not only did it speak of sex and compel everyone to do so; it also set out to formulate the uniform truth of sex. . . . This discourse on sex . . . set itself up as the supreme authority in matters of hygienic necessity, taking up old fears of venereal affliction and combining them with the new themes of asepsis, and the great evolutionist myths with the recent institutions of public health; it claimed to ensure the physical vigor and

the moral cleanliness of the social body; it promised to eliminate defective individuals, degenerate and bastardized populations. In the name of a biological and historical urgency, it justified the racisms of the state, which at the time were on the horizon. It grounded them in "truth."[25]

It is perhaps apposite to say this even more forcefully—much as Charles Mills has argued about modern social contract theory never existing as not also a form of "racial contract"— modern sexuality not only justifies modern racisms but is racial in its very inception.[26] White male heteronormative sexual formation is itself always already a lived reference to (projection of) black female exotica and to the black male threat arising perpetually out of the continuing history of white male "penetration" of black social existence. The secret that sex-as-discourse is made continually and simultaneously to divulge and dissemble is also a racial secret. Modern middle-class and "white" desire is brought into being as a compound of white-and-black fear and fascination. Such is the general working hypothesis of this essay. Hip-hop crossover experimentation is its latest and perhaps most blatant evidence.

Interesting confirmation of this depth-text is found in the recent work of critical race theorist Michael Hill. Reviewing a far-right conference of groups gathered to sound the tocsin of warning about the coming demographic eclipse of white majoritarian power in the United States, Hill quotes the jeremiad of Jared Taylor, head of the neofascist white supremacist group American Renaissance. Taylor summoned the specter of a postwhite America as "black-on-white male rape."[27] Here was the zeitgeist speaking its quintessential nightmare! However, looking at hip-hop, one would have to counter the panic: "Sorry, Jared, too late—rape becomes something else when wanted!" Hill makes a case for a certain psychodynamic parallel between this sort of neofascist hysteria and the emergence of the evangelical right-wing obsession of the Promise Keepers with racial reconciliation. He argues persuasively that what Promise Keepers author Patrick Means explicitly articulates as "a father-shaped void inside a man . . . which no woman will be able to fill" is actually mobilized quite powerfully in Promise Keepers cross-racial healing gatherings, positioning white males at the feet of black male cohorts, asking forgiveness, seeking wholeness, finding redemption in a "white-racial self-dissolution" accomplished by way of (what I would call) black penetration.[28] Hill laments this convoluted script as gerrymandering homoerotic racial intimacy in service of a resurgent patriarchal reclaiming of dominance in family and nation that also does nothing to address the continuing racist effects of public policy. Citing queer theorist Judith Butler's notion of "the unclaimed object of homosexual love" to query the depth-dimension of evangelical grief over absent fatherhood, Hill presciently underscores the irony. This is a white male fawning over black male embrace that seeks to fill the father-void, all the while abjuring and condemning homoerotica with a vengeance.[29] A convoluted homeopathy, indeed—same-sex abjection cured by same-sex affection masked as racial correction!

PROPHETIC RESPONSIBILITY

With such a historical itinerary of white male desire/fear as background, we turn to the theological ramifications of the profile, beginning with confession of the Christian ambience that incubated racial difference into political importance in the first place. As already indicated, white supremacy's racialization of dark bodies is a bastard child of Christian supremacy—a post-1492 theological "shorthand," visually marking out non-Christian populations as presumptively dangerous and demonic subverters of divine majesty and spiritual probity. Christian supremacy's erotic thematic at the same instant organized white desire into a homophobic structuring of its color investments such that, now, neither racism nor heterosexism can be effectively reworked short of dismantling Christian notions of religious superiority or Western notions of social ascendancy. The violence of the last five hundred years is not likely to abate until and unless global populations begin to recover a more complex vision of human being than what is offered under the reductions of "whiteness" or "masculinity" as packaged and promulgated under the auspices of modern Christianity and Western secularity. Said more directly to my own primary audience, a primal therapeutic task for white male Christians, in our current postcolonial situation, would be committed psychospiritual work toward becoming more than simply white, or male, or Christian.

Strangely, it is hip-hop culture as a now global register of identity that points toward an interesting possibility of such work. As a thirty-year-old pop culture phenomenon, hip-hop has yet to receive sustained pastoral response other than surface appropriation in various domestications as "Christian rap." The challenge that the culture of "bling, booty, and beef" throws down is that the crime of racism demands much more than our usual Sunday morning schism (that hour of the week that remains our most segregated sign of racial contradiction) reinforced by quick-trigger policing the other six days, all while relishing a few bumped-up "gospelized" lyrics. At the least, here is a crossover riff (hip-hop signification compelling white adolescent fascination) already incarnate in pop culture flesh that could animate sustained Christian engagement with the continuing inveiglement of desire around fears and fantasies of color. Beyond what appears in commercialized rap, underground hip-hop in urban centers around the globe offers the closest thing yet seen to an actual realization of Martin King's dream of a beloved community. Cadres of kids gather across lines of ethnicity and race in a frenzied menagerie of camaraderie energized by a shared beat that yet awaits its theology.

In my own classroom pedagogy, after deep work on the biblical text in political context, a recasting of the tradition under revisionist interpretation of the word as anti-imperial code, animating slave liberation in Moses' day and peasant resistance at Jesus' insistence, we tackle the history of race as integral to modernity at every turn, leveraging North Atlantic wealth at the expense of a colonized and plundered South—and this on top of a sustained unpacking of gender, class, and sexual orientation in the mix. Unpacking the way Gospel parables and proverbs deconstruct first-century Palestinian politics proves especially provocative to think with in trying to imagine a similar decoding of the politics of modern white Christian supremacy. I make a case for Jesus as generally abstaining from scribal invitations to engage in "Bible battleship"—I lob a text at you and you lob one back at me until one of us is blown out of the water—in favor of sharp one-liners and conscientizing cartoons (parabolic sketches of everyday life in colonized Palestine) designed to provoke peasant reflection on their own conditions of oppression. In so doing, Jesus immerses himself in the "folk soteriology" of his day to articulate an alternative vision of identity and community for the largely disenfranchised lot who find themselves fascinated with his practice.[30] Far from insisting on a scriptural orthodoxy, the upstart Messiah takes his cue from the local "pop culture" idiom. Jesus had already "baptized" himself in the social movement galvanized by John; he will likewise give himself over to peasant traditions of raucous partying (his "rep" is that of a glutton and drunkard, throwing down with the equivalent of the gangbangers and "underclass outlaws" of his day, Matt. 11:19) and rancorous storytelling (e.g., vignettes of day laborers insidiously manipulated and pink-slipped by vicious landlords, Matt. 20:1-15; or a street-savvy "steward," exposed by peasant rumor, switching allegiance from his rapacious absentee owner to his small farmer clients, by writing down the debt, Luke 16:1-9). Jesus will even go so far, in one notorious instance (the so-called Good Samaritan parable, Luke 10:25-37), as elevating the very archetype of underculture illegitimacy—a "bastard Samaritan"—to iconic status for Jewish practice. Here priestly moral probity and scribal doctrinal purity are pilloried in favor of an "unclean" outcast doubling his reprehensibleness by making common cause with a mugging victim. Indeed, Gentile Gospel writer Luke will offer up his entire version of events under the lyric bombast of teenage Mary, spittin' her hard-hitting "diss rap" in the ear of her kin, Elizabeth—a clear clairvoyance of comeuppance on the part of an underclass adolescent, pregnant before the ceremony, destined to labor lifelong under rumor of illicit concourse with (if not rape by) Roman soldiery seeking local entertainment (or rampaging) in Galilean villages after hours (Luke 1:26-56).[31] In all of this revisionist theological challenge, the chosen idiom is local and "little tradition"—peasant *patois* employed to explode official somnambulance with parody and oral grenades! Hip-hop rhyme today would likely be one of the rhythms of comeuppance such a Messiah would spit like a sonic bullet inside the party line of contemporary Christian imperial chatter!

After lengthy tarrying in the fields of liberationist biblical interpretation, we then face the juggernaut of the season for my white students—the carefully unpacked assertion that up inside the missionary position in bedrooms suburban and city alike, at unconscious levels of desire and decision, between multishaded bodies of pink and cream, there is sandwiched a black incubus not entirely either mythic or real. Here I am deploying Long's historicization of the *mysterium* suggestively—a murky spiritual force, at once fascinating and terrible, writhing like a subtext of fear and desire under the surface of conscious cultural expression that can adequately be figured as neither demon nor charism, neither clear condition of an individual psyche nor certain sediment of any historical community, but, rather, a kind of cultural "haint," a force field of convoluted energy never fully subject to representation or elimination. That "black" haunt—patterned as alluring rhythmic motion or nightmare shade troubling sleep and purveyed by Madison Avenue and prime-time news—is a creature of our joint history, not entirely subject either to psychoanalytic inquiry or critical race theory, which will not transform apart from friendship and politics, sustained intimate work and resolute social combat. The "insurrection of subjugated knowledges"—made notorious in Foucault and named a form of throbbing penetration by Spencer—is finally a form of cognition not simply "out there," under dark skin, demanding white recognition.[32] It is also an eruption of premonition or alarm within the experience of white desire. Underneath its co-optation in service of big-label designs for more dollar signs, this insurgent apperception invites a confrontation that is anything but naïve. Eminem represents both its (cross-racial) possibility and its (homophobic) failure.

Hip-hop is sure to pass as a phenomenon. The insurrectionary power it encodes across the divides of race and class, however, given sharp theological attention, could also be entertained as a mode of prophetic challenge, pointing toward human capacity to exceed dominating limitations and deadening interaction inside merely singular categories of identity or parochial understandings of history. Were the beats ever "climbed upstream," to their core impact as a pelvic refraction of vitality, they could also push toward a modality of the sexual that refuses binaries and reduction and toward an embrace of the ancestral that recaptures the racial singularity of the species. This is a juncture where the notion of "incarnation" not only meets necessary refiguration in female forms but also the possibility of a rewriting—provoked by the peculiar experience of ("black") male penetration of ("white") male identification—of racial signification and, indeed, the evolutionary elaboration of an originally African genome. We might even reconceive trinitarian procession itself: father-love and son-love freed from homophobic assumptions, to flip into mother- and daughter-loves pushing beyond gender binds and sexual grinds to find flourishing in all manner of bodies oriented in all manner of affections, held accountable to justice and made honorable in reciprocation but otherwise freed to serve the Mystery that is beyond naming or containing. Whether hip-hop creativity itself can ever be bent toward such a fantastic significance, that agenda remains the future of theology and Christianity alike.

Further Suggested Readings

Foucault, Michel. *The History of Sexuality*, vol. 1: *An Introduction*. Trans. Robert Hurley. New York: Vintage, 1980.

Hill, Michael. *After Whiteness: Unmaking an American Majority*. New York: New York University Press, 2004.

Mills, Charles. *The Racial Contract*. Ithaca: Cornell University Press, 1997.

Perkinson, James W. *Shamanism, Racism, and Hip-Hop Culture: Essays on White Supremacy and Black Subversion*. New York: Palgrave Macmillan, 2005.

Spencer, Jon Michael. *The Rhythms of Black Folk: Race, Religion and Pan-Africanism*. Trenton, N.J.: Africa World, 1995.

PART III

Reconstruction: Erotic Theology

CHAPTER 13

Creation as God's Call into Erotic Embodied Relationality

Laurie A. Jungling

GOD CREATES. This statement represents one of the central doctrinal claims at the heart of most Christian theology. At the heart of God's creative activity is reflected God's relational essence, love (1 John 4:8). In its rich and multidimensional form, love is both the power and the material by which God constructs creation. According to Protestant systematic theologian Paul Tillich, love is a holistic reality containing eros as one necessary aspect of that love.[1] Hence, one part of God's creating love is eros. For the purposes of this essay, I will define eros as the divine call into life as embodied relationality that has been freely and faithfully given in and through God's ongoing creation.[2] Erotic love is the force that gives life the relational essence that fills and empowers all of creation.

One aspect of God's love is freedom. Life in creation is given by the God who freely loves.[3] Beginning with the claim of God's freedom in the loving creation of all things can lead to making freedom the central component in all erotic relations. In fact, many progressive theoethical discussions of the erotic in recent years, particularly queer theology, have made the freedom to pursue and engage in erotic relationships the preeminent theme in articulations of sexuality.[4] While other principles are important, these advocates argue, freedom is finally the axis upon which all eros spins.[5] I submit that when considering creation as well as the creator God in relation to the erotic, something is missing if only freedom is emphasized. The God of love, who calls all things into being, not only loves freely but faithfully as well. God's faithfulness and God's freedom are inextricably linked to one another in the divine creativity so that faithfulness is as much a part of the erotic vitality of creation as is freedom.

In this essay, then, I explore the interweaving of faithfulness and freedom through the lens of a doctrine of creation. This doctrine of creation views God's vocational call as the divine proclamation that relational humans are created in the image of a loving, free, and faithful God and, through this act of creation, are called to serve and enhance relational and social life in all its diversity and abundance.[6] From this divine calling, Christians today can discern a theoethical call to seek, be, and do life-centered erotic relationships in faith-filled freedom.

FREEDOM AND EROS REVISITED

The nature of the erotic in human existence has been much discussed in theoethics recently and as mentioned above, freedom has been the prevailing theme. Embodied life is essentially erotic, some theologians argue, and therefore humans need, deserve, and even have the right to experience their erotic lives freely and with as few limits as possible. Any limits to this erotic experience emerge from an understanding of justice that seeks fairness, rights, and a guarantee of freedom—namely, the idea that all embodied humans are entitled to experience their unique erotic capabilities equally. The only way to discover the truly erotic in human embodiment, such advocates maintain, is through freedom in justice.

Space prevents a deep discussion of these arguments for freedom, but one example will suffice. In his book *Erotic Justice*, gay theologian and ethicist Marvin Ellison lifts up liberation as the primary focal point of his understanding of erotic justice. Ellison names "body right" as one of the central guiding principles of ethical eroticism: "Body right means freedom from control and manipulation by another, as well as having the power to direct the use of one's body and body space according to context and *one's own choices*."[7] According to Ellison, without an open freedom to explore the rich and diverse relational experiences life has to offer, the erotic nature of humans will be suppressed or even denied to some, if not all, human creatures. Freedom is the necessary aspect of the erotic; without freedom, the vitality of the erotic dies.

This advocacy by many Christians for erotic freedom is hardly surprising, given the extreme regulation and suppression of erotic life throughout much of the Western Christian tradition. (One exception would be the mystical tradition that often pursued an erotic, though a decidedly disembodied, relation with God.) Christian theology has been suspicious of humanity's erotic aspects and has invested its energy and authority in controlling erotic relations in a myriad of ways. The most obvious binding of the erotic has involved regulating the sexual realm of human embodiment. Christian thinkers from Augustine in the fifth century to Anders Nygren in the early twentieth century have negated the acceptance and celebration of the erotic in spiritual, creative, intellectual, emotional, and even moral life lest these facets of human embodiment become corrupted by the so-called animal lusts of sexuality and lead us to social and moral chaos.[8] The erotic has represented to many Christians a chaos and unpredictability that requires boundaries, regulations, and tight control. In the past century, historians and theologians have exposed the pervasiveness of these regulations in Christianity that have been and are still used to confine human sexuality to a small number of controlled practices and acceptable relationships.[9]

Given this devaluation and limitation of erotic life, it is no wonder that the demand for erotic freedom is so vocal among those who have been excluded, damaged, and imprisoned by the oppressive and unjust order being forced upon them. Gay and lesbian persons, transgendered and intersex persons, queer and erotically exploring persons are raising their voices to claim the Christian liberty they have found in the heart of creation itself. This call for freedom liberates the captives from erotic subjugation and makes promises for inclusion and acceptance guaranteed by the divine image borne by every human being. This call for freedom opens doors to the fullness and mystery of creation and new possibilities of pleasure and diversity in experiencing relational embodiment within this creation. This call for freedom takes the body seriously and explores human embodiment with a living and life-serving passion. This call to freedom provides the opportunity and demands the capability for all to live the power of their erotic humanity in ways unique to each embodied person. Finally, this call for freedom demands that the richness of embodied life be available to each person equally as moral agents and choice makers.

In the face of Christian attempts to subjugate and control erotic relationality, I agree that erotic freedom cannot be ignored. Eros is a potent
force, one that poet and essayist Audre Lorde has said can change the world.
It is the "creative lifeforce within" that is "turned outward and informs and
illuminates our actions upon the world around us."[10] Essayist Terry Tempest
Williams defines the erotic as the "magnetic pull in our bodies toward something stronger, more vital than ourselves. Arousal becomes a dance of longing. We form a secret partnership with possibility."[11] Thus, erotic embodied
relationality has the power to restore, reconcile, and enhance the relational
life of all creation.

Like all forces of power, however, eros can be misused and abused. This
is particularly the case for humans who have been estranged from its true
potency and from the one who made it. So often the erotic becomes a tool
used at will in the name of human desires and needs. Freedom becomes its
benchmark and any restriction on that freedom is perceived by those who
would escape restriction, illegitimate or legitimate, as a threat to life itself.
Governed only by freedom and a view of justice designed to preserve that
freedom, eros in the wake of human sin can easily become a free-for-all and
a commitment to none.

Erotic relationality is a potent life force that must be balanced with
other life forces to keep relational life interconnected. It is true that denying
the existence of the erotic or preventing its power from entering the world
extracts the life out of creation. However, abundant life requires an element
alongside erotic freedom, one that is perhaps even more important than freedom. That element, I suggest, is faithfulness. Erotic freedom requires erotic
faithfulness for embodied relationality to reach its full potential in creating,
sustaining, and empowering the abundant life of all of creation.

What role does faithfulness have in erotic freedom? Faithfulness is a concept often ignored, feared, or diminished in erotic freedom. According to
many theological proponents of freedom, faithfulness is too entangled with
heterosexual and patriarchal forms of traditional marriage, and thus would
entail too much limitation or regulation of erotic lives.[12] In one recent exploration of the erotic, faithfulness (and its counterparts "commitment" and "fidelity") is never mentioned as a part of the erotic freedom being sought.[13] When
it is mentioned, faithfulness often is seen as an extraneous add-on, something
unnecessary to the erotic experience—merely one possible choice for those
who want it. Even those who would lift up faithfulness as an important aspect
of the erotic often do so in order to serve freedom. For example, in *Erotic
Justice*, Ellison argues that fidelity is a part of an ethical eroticism that allows

for durable and stable relationships that maintain trust; yet, in his view fidelity must remain negotiable as "needs, desires, and conditions unfold."[14] In his later book entitled *Same-Sex Marriage?*, Ellison defines fidelity as "a commitment to honesty and fairness and an ongoing willingness to renegotiate the relationships to serve the needs of both parties."[15] It seems, then, that fidelity is important as long as it remains open to the many possibilities that freedom allows. Freedom to pursue one's needs seems to be primary in the erotic relation; if fidelity should impinge on that freedom, then it is faithfulness and not freedom that needs to be renegotiated in order to protect freedom. In other words, faithfulness is a tool at freedom's service.[16]

While I would agree with Ellison that renegotiation is crucial within any relationship as persons and circumstances change, freedom and the seeking of it ought not be the sole criterion for such renegotiation. Instead, alongside of freedom stands another power that emerges from the divine call in creation: faithfulness. If both faithfulness and freedom are present in divine creative activity and if both are a part of the erotic call that erupts from creation, then any theological discussion of the erotic must give faithfulness its full due as a primary and necessary aspect of erotic life. I argue that faithfulness is what gives the erotic its direction and foundation; it is what holds the power of the erotic together and drives it toward its full potential. Faithfulness is not simply an option in living out our erotic lives; it is crucial to what it means to be called into embodied relation. I further submit that faithfulness is the ground from which our erotic freedom erupts. This does not exclude freedom from the erotic; instead, faithfulness reinforces freedom as a central component to living as erotic creatures. Far from contradicting each other, erotic faithfulness and erotic freedom need each other in order to inspire the fullest life of embodied relationality possible.

GOD AS FAITHFULLY FREE CREATOR

One theological starting place for why faithfulness is a necessary component of created erotic life, rather than an optional thread in the weaving of the erotic experience, is to consider the one whom Christians believe calls humans into life. A Christian understanding of eros depends on an understanding of what it means to be created in the divine image. Who is the God who calls humans to be, do, and seek that image?

On the one hand, Christians assert that God is the potency of life in its fullest manifestation. God is pure life and the free-reigning power of all life. The God who calls life into being is a living God and the source of all life, and this divinely created life is decidedly immense, intense, dynamic, and intricate. The new possibilities found in the life God has called forth are enormous and vastly diverse. This life in its infinite variety is woven with vitality beyond human comprehension and is the abundant life toward which humans consistently yearn and grasp. The mystery of life in the divine is the horizon that entices humans toward infinitely new possibilities of life beyond the here and now.

In this image celebrating the vitality of the divine nature, not only does the erotic become a means of seeking the divine, but the divine is profoundly free in seeking the creature in erotic relationship. In the most extreme articulations of this freedom, some theologians such as Ellison speak of God as "promiscuous lover" who radically seeks connection with all of creation by moving from one relationship to the next to the next, faithful to no singular person or group but "taking in all of creation" into the divine self.[17] This is a picture of an impersonal God who is radically unfaithful (as the concept of human promiscuity implies) and who presumably leaves behind a trail of broken hearts, bodies, and relationships at the whim of divine desire. Relational freedom of this sort is unpredictable, impersonal, and superficial, never committing to anyone or anything beyond the moment. It is the divine at its most capricious. Despite this extreme image, however, reminders of divine freedom are vital to understanding the erotic call in creation. To deny divine freedom is to deny the erotic as embodied relationality rife with the possibilities for abundant life.[18]

Freedom, however, is not the only aspect of the erotic power by which the divine creates. God is not only free and the fullness of life cannot be found in sheer freedom. Rather, God is essentially relational. From within God's trinitarian relationship with God's self, God creates a relational universe through the same love, including eros, that empowers God's internal relationship. "The life of God—precisely because God is triune—does not belong to God alone. . . . God is said to be essentially relational, ecstatic, fecund, alive as passionate love."[19] God passionately desires relationship with another, both within God's self and with that which lies outside of God's self. Thus, God's relational nature continuously creates, calling relational life into existence through God's erotic love. Through God's erotic desire to create, humans can truly know the fullness of God's love and the eros that is revealed in human relations. As theologian Eugene Rogers writes: "For eros does not move from us up to God, so that because we know eros, we know God, but it moves from God down to us, so that because we read the stories of God's yearning and constancy, God's covenant fidelity and God's covenant promise, we learn for the first time what eros is for and what it means."[20] As this quote highlights, the divine call in creation emerges not from a capricious freedom but from fidelity and promise. God's essential desire is for the fulfillment of diverse, life-enhancing multiplicities of relationship with that which is other than God. Creation is indeed God's free call actively bringing life into existence, but it is first and foremost God's faithful call out of love which emerges from the power of erotic relationality. Only in and through this relational nature can the vitality of life reach its fullness and freedom find its true power. Thus, divine freedom is never freedom alone; it is always driven toward the greater desire for life-centered relations that create, sustain, and empower life: a relation of integrity.

I define the relation of divine integrity as one in which God is intimately interconnected with creation and each individual part of it without consuming creation into God's self.[21] There is a personal presence and interdependence in the relationship of the divine to creation, human and nonhuman, which belies any attempt to turn divine freedom into promiscuity. God creates through divine self-limiting freedom, faithfully committing God's relational life to work on the behalf of creation. God is not free from creation; God is free for creation, faithfully exercising God's freedom to enhance all relational life from within the relation and in service to that relation. God, then, is neither a possessive control freak who desires to consume creation into the divine self nor an absent lover who pops in when the occasion of desire warrants it; rather, God is relational in faithful freedom, working with and for relational life from within and occasionally from outside the relationship to call into creation a life that is abundant for all.

Divine erotic freedom, I would argue, is tempered, directed, and balanced with something even more central to relational incarnation: divine erotic faithfulness. Divine faithfulness is God's promise, commitment, and assurance that God desires to call life into being out of the divine's own life-centered relation with creation and that God's freedom will never consume nor abandon that relational life. God is utterly faithful to creation and desires intimate, life-centered relation with that creation. Such life can only come when all participants practice a relation of integrity that respects, trusts, nurtures, and empowers their fellow participants in the relation and the relation itself. Life, even at its most divine, is fullest only when freedom is bounded and grounded by faithfulness.

Faithful freedom in the divine can be known in part through the Hebrew concept of *hesed*, often translated "steadfastness." According to Hebrew Bible scholar Katherine Doob Sakenfeld, however, no single English word can contain what it symbolizes. She defines *hesed* to mean "God's irrevocable commitment that freely serves the other's needs in relationship."[22] In God's ongoing creating action, *hesed* is communicated through God's promised and committed faithfulness that freely preserves and restores God's creation in the face of rejection and suffering.[23] God's *hesed* is experienced in God's enduring, committed love that never gives up on the relation (Isa. 54:10). Finally, God's *hesed* is experienced in God's commitment to the abundant life of all creation, not simply humans.

In creating life through the erotic call to embodied relationality, God has limited God's self and will keep God's promises, binding God's self to creation "for better or for worse" and committing God's self to nurturing abundant life in creation. In creating this abundant life, then, God promises that divine freedom even in all of its vitality will not reject the partner by either pulling her into a communion where the other is consumed or abandoning her to exist outside life-giving relation with the divine. This promise requires a limitation on divine freedom lest it destroy the very relational life God is creating. Thus, divine freedom requires divine faithfulness and vice versa. Without faithfulness, freedom would consume life; without freedom, faithfulness would leech the life out of creation.

THE EROTIC CALL: HUMANS AS FAITHFULLY FREE CREATURES

From this view of God, we can better understand the call to creation that emerges in the creative act. Created life in its most basic essence is a calling from God. "To be is to be called."[24] In the beginning, God spoke and thus called all of life into existence. This is a call to love, to relate, to live in and through the relational life of creation. It is only through this relational power of life that creation can truly live. To be created is to be called into the very essence of relation itself. It is to be called into erotic life.

Christian theology sees this call as imaging the divine. The call of creation is a call to be, do, and seek the "image of God" in one's relational life (Gen. 1:27). This is not simply an invitation to pursue a freely chosen personal project, although personal freedom is a vital aspect of the call; neither is it a call to destroy the self in confirming only the other. Creation is a call into embodied relational life in which the most abundant experience of life can exist only in and through relationship with God, creation, and self.

The divine call into creation implies two realities for created existence: relationship and embodiment. Human creatures are basically relational. We come into being in and through relationship and are formed as humans through relationship. "We are not only created *with* the other, but God actually gives us life *through* the other," writes process theologian Paul Sponheim.[25]

Humans shape one another, our communities, our societies, and the created environment in which we live through our relationships. A central part of being created as God's image is to participate as co-creators in forming fully human selves and lives through relationship. Freedom from this relationality or its implications is impossible, humanly speaking. Theologically speaking, to claim freedom from relationality would be to deny the *imago Dei* that indwells and inspires every human equally and connects each person to the divine, to each other, and to all of creation.

Human creatures are also dynamically and diversely embodied. Humans image the mystery and aliveness of God as whole and richly dynamic bodies. This embodiment is not simply nature enacting its governing laws; nor is it merely a "blank slate."[26] Humans live as a complex interweaving of body, mind, heart, and spirit in relation with the created and co-created world. The physiological, emotional, spiritual, intellectual, and social systems that form and are formed by human existence are so intricately intertwined and complex that it is impossible to tell where the embodied human begins or ends. To separate the human into dualities, whether spirit over body or body over spirit, is to deny the very nature of embodiment. Each uniquely embodied human is formed as a person whole in heart, mind, body, and spirit only in and through the multiple embodied relationships in which she lives.

Christian theology affirms that God's creating call confers what it means to be an embodied relational human creature—namely, to live out one's interwoven embodiment to life's fullest potential. This call invites all of creation into life-empowering, life-sustaining, and life-enhancing relationships that nourish the abundance of life rather than destroy it. Thus, human embodiment is a call as *imago Dei* to seek life in relationship with others.

Eros empowers this call into life-centered relationality. Eros is buried in the depths of every embodied relation and calls all creation to seek embodied relationality. Erotic life is more than mere desire for another and yearning for union (sexual, emotional, spiritual, etc.), though it may indeed manifest as these. To limit the erotic to yearning for union implies a radical individualism in which the autonomous self exists prior to relation, and relationship becomes an option that one might choose or not. Instead, my approach to embodied relationality insists that while relations may be strained, estranged, or damaged, nevertheless life's inherent relationality still exists and becomes the bearer of the erotic power that holds all creation together. Eros is the divine call in the core of embodiment that insists upon, pushes toward, and cries out for relational life at its most abundant. Without this erotic call, humans and all of creation would eventually cease to exist, for this embodied relationality breathes life into existence and inspires life's dynamic diversity, similarity, and abundance.

From this understanding of God's erotic call into creation, it follows, I argue, that creation does indeed involve the freedom to choose with whom and how the erotic call can and should be followed. To limit the erotic to a small number of human physiological or relational forms (e.g., marriage between one man and one woman) is unacceptable. In so doing, the erotic is robbed of its vital power. Erotic life must not be imprisoned in a cave of ordered and lifeless shadows. Instead, freedom in the erotic call opens the doors to a myriad of possibilities of creative life that sparkle on the horizon before us.

However, to focus only on erotic freedom at the expense of erotic faithfulness is problematic if one accepts that God calls creation into existence through an eros marked by both faithfulness and freedom. Freedom, when pursued blindly, has a weakness—namely, the fear that by committing to a single possibility, one is being denied access to other possibilities. "The breadth of life's possibilities should be available to us!" comes the demand in the face of such perceived denial. Doors to the unknown possibilities beyond slam shut and the oppressive perception that our freedom has been imprisoned bears down.

I submit that such freedom without faithfulness actually threatens the possibilities for discovering the fullness of erotic life; the possibilities sought through pure freedom simply remain on the surface of time and space in our relations and rarely penetrate into their depths. Such freedom may even become a means to escape creatureliness instead of entering fully into it. Erotic life as God calls it into being necessarily includes time, space, ordinariness, finitude, messiness, and risk. Without faithfulness, a life-giving relationship can devolve into an attempt to escape space or time in a search for unencumbered eros, which constitutes, theologically speaking, a suppression of creatureliness and of the human calling as God's image.

Faithfulness, I propose, does not have to exclude freedom; instead, it can open new doors to experiencing it. Queer theology has the potential to free erotic relationships from the confines of suspicion and regulation while at the same time exploring the diverse and life-giving possibilities for erotic life that faithfulness can provide. Faithfulness and freedom are necessary partners and only together will they truly bless the erotic relations into which all humans are called to live.

What should faithfulness imply for erotic relationality? Space prohibits an extended discussion here, but at least three aspects of created life can be named: trust, touch, and time. These aspects of human life signify that as *imago Dei*, humans are called to be free for faithfulness, not from it.

Trust. All relationships, erotic or otherwise, begin with trust. God created human life trusting that people would live in a relation of integrity with God. When the human race turned away from the divine love, that trust was shattered. Consequently, trust in a world injured by sin cannot be considered a given. Nor is it something that can be demanded or forced. "Just trust me" is not a viable command in a world in which trust is mangled every day by blind, narcissistic claims to freedom, power, or control. Trust and its counterparts trustworthiness, fidelity, and commitment are birthed, grown, and enlivened from within faith-filled and faith-worthy relations.

Trust, according to Protestant reformer Martin Luther, is faith. To have faith in someone or something is to "trust and believe in that one with your whole heart."[27] For Luther, such faith is not a capability an individual constructs in him, or herself alone; rather, faith is something that can only emerge through a trust-worthy relation. Trust asks, "Will you be there for me?" and is experienced only as this "being there" is demonstrated to me on my behalf.[28] One way such trust is cultivated is through the making and honoring of promises. Once made, promises are self-limiting. They can be renegotiated—not in a search for freedom to pursue personal needs and desires but in service to nurturing trust.

Christian faith proclaims that God honors the divine promises for abundant life given to creation through the divine passion. On the cross and in the resurrection to new life, God creates the very trust humans need to live in erotic relation with one another. God's faithfulness can expand beyond finitude; however, human faithfulness is limited by conditionality and is centered in the body. By every promise, we commit our body's future to the possibilities inspired by that self-limiting choice.[29] For humans, trust is constructed only in and through faith-filled relationships that respect freedom but are governed finally by freely chosen promises and commitments. Thus, even as it limits freedom, faithfulness is profoundly erotic for it inspires and nurtures the trust that enables creation to follow the vital call into embodied relationality.

Touch. As embodied relational creatures, we must be faithful by respecting touch in our erotic relationships. Inherent in the erotic call is complex embodiment, which includes but is not limited to human biological forms. Holistic embodiment interconnects all aspects of created life into incarnate relationship: minds, hearts, souls, as well as our physical existence in time and space. Human embodiment thinks, feels, acts, chooses, sleeps, imagines, creates, yearns, senses, and knows through experiences of touch that include but are more than physical touch. We cannot help but touch and even shape, for good and for bad, each other's spirits, hearts, minds, and bodies every day through our relations with one another. Thus, humans have a responsibility to touch embodied persons, their communities, and all of creation with respect, compassion, and love so that the erotic call might not be distorted or silenced.

When directed toward the erotic fullness of life, embodiment and the touch that accompanies it can be blessings from God and one another. Touch can bless humans with joy, comfort, pleasure, and strength. It is through touch that each person shares life's power with others. Also, mutual and respectful touch can be a source of trust and can empower relationships. As such, it must be honored. Embodied freedom, then, is not a freedom of the body from erotic relationship; nor is it a permission for the body to pursue all of the erotic possibilities embodied life can provide. Rather, embodied touch is a source of faith-filled freedom for relationship and building trust through time. It is a blessing created by God to be explored in freedom yet nurtured by faith. Respectful, faith-filled touch is necessary to the protection and nurturing of all erotic life.

Time. Unlike God who is only limited by time through free choice, humans are necessarily bound by time (and space). Time matters to creation and creatures for it is in and through time that they live out erotic relations. The first creation narrative in Genesis states that God created time on the fourth day and declared it to be a good part of creation. Hence, the biblical text presents time as a blessing given to creation. Time is often seen by contemporary culture as a threat to be feared and avoided, however. Human attempts to extend life, to speed it up or slow it down, or to escape time altogether are obvious in the visible demand for fast food, for quick and easy answers, for instant communications on so-called smart phones. For much of postmodern culture, time is the enemy, one we resist in favor of a search for an instant and neverending orgasmic existence. However, this attempt to deny time forgets the blessings that time contains. Time layers the beauty of creation, swirls through bodies of water, fills our bodily selves, and steers each person's journey through relationships with God, creation, and each other.

Faithfulness in human erotic relations involves bodies living out the highs, lows, and mundane ordinariness of relations during, through, and in spite of time. Faithfulness respects and honors God's gift of time, and opens doors to discovery inherent in a journey that only time can provide. To seek an escape from time is to seek an escape from the erotic creation, for time is as much a part of creation as the erotic call and must be respected as such. As Rowan Williams, Archbishop of Canterbury, states, "when we bless sexual unions, we give them a life . . . so that they may have a certain freedom to 'take time' to mature and become profoundly nurturing as they can."[30]

Time, then, can be as deeply erotic as trust and touch for inherent in its depths lies the joys of discovery, the enrichment of prolonging, and the tantalizing anticipation of future possibilities even as they may be denied in the present. Often the erotic emerges at its most powerful in a journey through a relationship rather than in a single day experienced by that relation. For instance, dating involves time embodied and shared as two lovers gradually intertwine their desire, love, and yearning for each other through time. Time also matters in other erotic relations outside the sexual. Learning together as teacher and student, making a life as parent and child, delighting in the joys of exploring, playing, working, struggling, and resting with friends—all of these experiences can be deeply erotic and each requires time in order to bear the fullness of their fruit. Thus, as Williams argues, "time must be protected and unlimited. The erotic requires time, a respect for it and its limits" so that human embodiment can fully experience grace-filled delight in relationship with the other.[31]

CONCLUSION

Erotic freedom without erotic faithfulness is the person who states of a sexual partner: "Even though I may not know his name, I know what music he listens to, what food he likes, where he vacations. His name is incidental. He's part of our world, that's all I need to know."[32] Such freedom denies the relational partner the blessings of time, respectful touch, and trust to share his fears, hopes, dreams, and desires, to build faith and faithfulness, and finally to know him beyond the mere objective body into the depths of his soul, heart, and mind. It denies holistic embodiment and reverses the spirit/body dualism to make the body's needs lord over all. Freedom without faithfulness is "radical individualism"—the belief that our relational existence is merely a choice and that humans are free to define and construct our selves using our relationships, erotic or otherwise, as little more than tools.[33] This freedom represents a contempt for my fully embodied self, my embodied partner, and our erotic relation because it "demonstrates a failure to take full responsibility" across time for one who has put her or his trust into my hands.[34]

At the same time, however, the call for freedom in our erotic lives remains a crucial one. Faithfulness without freedom is the demand that erotic relations be confined behind walls of simplistically gendered bodies and abusive social orders. It is the pastor's or partner's command to remain in an abusive or dying marriage no matter the cost. It is the letter of the law minus its true, life-protecting spirit. Faithfulness without freedom is equally guilty of rejection of partner, self, God, and creation for it discards the erotic vitality of the relation in the name of law and order and consigns partners to small, static and supposedly universally approved erotic forms such as the current state- and church-sponsored singular form of marriage that is limited to one male and one female.

Finally, freedom and faithfulness need each other. Together they serve and bless the erotic relationality that enlivens creation as they interweave their complex dance into the fullness of a created and embodied life blessed by trust, touch, and time. The life that God calls into existence in creation is an erotic life that pursues both freedom and faith. In this call to faithful freedom, all of creation is invited and empowered to live out erotic, life-centered relation. As part of this creation and as *imago Dei*, embodied humans are called to reflect the divine image and seek, do, and be embodied relationality at its most abundant. Only in living out this call to faithful freedom will humans truly experience erotic life as the divine has created it to be.

Further Suggested Readings

Burns, Camilla. "The Call of Creation." In *Revisiting the Idea of Vocation: Theological Explorations.* Ed. John C. Haughey, S.J. Washington, D.C.: The Catholic University of America Press, 2004.

Dean, Kenda Creasy. *Practicing Passion: Youth and the Quest for a Passionate Church.* Grand Rapids: Eerdmans, 2004.

Farley, Margaret A. *Just Love: A Framework for Christian Sexual Ethics.* New York: Continuum, 2006.

Jenson, Robert W. "Faithfulness." In *Theology and Sexuality: Classic and Contemporary Readings.* Ed. Eugene F. Rogers, Jr. Oxford: Blackwell, 2002.

Jordan, Mark D. *The Ethics of Sex.* Oxford: Blackwell, 2002.

Williams, Rowan. "The Body's Grace." In *Our Selves, Our Souls and Bodies: Sexuality and the Household of God.* Ed. Charles Hefling. Boston: Cowley, 1996.

CHAPTER 14

Promiscuous Incarnation

Laurel C. Schneider

> *What would it look like to speak the language of incarnation?*
> *What sound would this moral language make?*
>
> —*Darby Kathleen Ray*[1]

INCARNATION AND THE RELATIONSHIP of the body to divinity has long been a theme in feminist, womanist, black, and other liberation concepts of God. The very idea that divine essence and will are somehow located in the struggles of the oppressed focuses incarnation in two related directions: the prosaic, everyday dimensions of bodily existence on the one hand, and liberal concerns about the dignity and equality of every human being on the other. The ancient Christian claim that God chose lowly human flesh as a medium and content of revelation finds particular relevance in these approaches to theology—specifically, in their striving to find in the Christian stories of Jesus and in the doctrines of the Trinity theological bases for opposing the sustained bodily assaults that characterize white supremacy, male dominance, and class structures that relegate whole peoples to deep poverty.

To the extent that on this point liberation theologies are right—namely, that the focus of theological reflection should emphasize a materialist concern with the actual plight of the poor and oppressed—then incarnation as a central Christian doctrine of God (perhaps even *the* distinctively Christian doctrine) must also attend to the matter of the oppressed body and its constitutive relation to divinity.[2] The fleshy divine individual body of Jesus and the fleshy divine communal body of Christ (i.e., the church) suffer some incoherence in traditional Christian theologies that manage to honor incarnation in terms of the body of Jesus but force actual bodies in the church, and outside of it, onto the bottom rungs of a tortured hierarchy of being.[3]

The fact is that for all of the attention that feminist, womanist, queer, and black theologians have directed toward the status of the oppressed human and earthly body, the ancient and controversial question of divine incarnation in terms of the fourth-century Nicean claim of full divinity in the full humanity of Jesus remains controversial and underdeveloped in constructive theology today. Work on the doctrines of incarnation and creation by theologians like Sallie McFague, Rosemary Radford Ruether, Jürgen Moltmann, and Nancy R. Howell has begun to take seriously divinity in the world and the worldly body of God; however, the full implication of incarnation in terms of "full" divinity in the flesh still needs to be worked out in contemporary terms.[4]

As a result of my own foray into the question of incarnation as a basis for thinking about multiplicity beyond the reductive dominance of the logic of the "One," I have, with the help of postcolonial, feminist, queer, and race theories, begun to interpret the history of Christian thought as a gradual and inexorable erosion of the early Christian testimony of incarnate divinity. Over time and with the growth of an imperial, globally aspiring religion, actual bodies—of tax agents, fishermen, soldiers, prostitutes, carpenters, and children, for example—have diminished in favor of immutable souls and the separation of divinity from world. As a result, Christian ideas of "God the Creator" have tended toward brittle abstraction, only occasionally relieved by the fleshy imaginings of mystics. Apart from such lush exceptions, the history of Christian thought is desiccated by rigid dependence on exclusive monotheism or, more accurately, a logic that requires divine truth to be singular and noncontradictory.[5] There has been a "drying up" of Christian theology.[6]

Within such a monologic of noncontradiction, incarnation is a conundrum. The coming to flesh of divinity completely disrupts the smooth otherness of the divine, its separateness from the changeable stuff of earth, its abhorrence of rot, its innocence of death, and its ignorance of life or desire.

Rethinking divinity from the body, on behalf of a mutable and utterly inex-changable world of bodies, is a challenging theological task that puts us toe to toe in contest with a tradition of disembodied divinity. To allow "the flesh to show us the divine," rather than the other way around, requires a certain courage in the face of long-standing theological denials of the flesh that have shaped contemporary cultural assumptions about the relationship of divinity to bodies.[7]

Toward the goal of better understanding the implications of incarnation as flesh showing the divine, there is a deliberate provocation in the title of this essay. "Promiscuous incarnation" links two terms that normally operate at a remove from one another. The adjective commonly refers today to "sexual indiscrimination."[8] The noun refers to "a body, person, or form in which a soul, or deity is embodied," which in Christian-dominated English usage is virtually synonymous with "God in Christ."[9] "Promiscuous" here modifies "incarnation," and so immediately the question arises regarding the nature of that modification. As a term most commonly used in relation to sexual excess, perhaps my use of promiscuous in this sense "sexes" the divinity of Christ in some sort of gratuitous manner. However, thanks to the colorful and varied history of the usage of "promiscuous" in English, in which its more primary meaning of "mixture" and even its rare occurrence as a "third gender" are allowed to come into play, "promiscuous" offers more to the concept of incarnation than sex alone.[10] In fact, it may describe incarnation better than any other modifier. The point of looking to other, older definitions of pro-miscuous is not to avoid its associations with sex, however. Sex represents an important challenge to the idea of incarnation, not only because of the obses-sive disavowals made about it over the years by theologians (just look at the long history of theological battles over Mary's virginity) but also because sex can function rhetorically—and promiscuously—as a cipher for both gender and race.[11]

In the cultures shaped by the Abrahamic religions, female sexuality has long been associated with social order or disorder and complicated with notions of purity and pollution. Strict control of women's sexual lives and of reproduction was tied to the attainment of wealth and status (and still is, in rhetoric about welfare mothers). It defined lines of identity by linking wom-en's bodies—and so sex—to communal ideas of ethnic purity.[12] To the extent that incarnation indicates divine enfleshment, it has never been able fully to escape these complexities, although since the church council at Nicea, Christians have tried to separate incarnation from sex in order to effect just such an escape. The Roman Catholic tradition's insistence on Mary's resilient virginity serves to preserve divinity from the perceived pollution and ethnic dangers of sexual intercourse. It also indicates more clearly than in any other aspect of Christian doctrine a fundamental anxiety about female sexuality and reproductive potential that has been inherited by modern Christianity. This anxiety still needs unpacking, in part because sex is still a source of deep conflict among religious people and in part because sex is only ever partly about sex, as I have indicated. It is also about intercourse of all kinds—intercourse that threatens social, political, and even economic boundaries.

In part because of the huge metaphoric power of sex, "promiscuity" suggests not only sexual excess and indiscrimination but also the dangerous inabilities of the body to conform fully to abstract theological requirements. Promiscuity gestures toward everything that, in the monotheistic traditions at least, must be excised from the body to qualify it as divine or as an acceptable vessel for divinity. Thus, promiscuity refers obliquely to the criminal body, its failures and exuberances that offend ascetical sensibilities, which are the sensibilities that have ruled Christian theology, if not absolutely, then predominantly. Promiscuity also refers to a refusal of exclusivity, an openness to intercourse with others that, as I will discuss later, poses all kinds of interesting challenges to the dominant, patrilineal social systems of the West. Promiscuity also means "mixture of different substances" and so it refers to that which is not pure, that which is porous and multiple. In other words, "promiscuous incarnation" suggests something distinctly nonascetical and impure about the central revelatory claim that Christianity makes about God. Furthermore it suggests, against theologies that make exclusive claims for incarnation, that divinity might be less than discriminating in its intimacies with flesh.

PATERNAL PROBLEMS

Promiscuity has typically been a derogatory word, applied to disparage those people (especially women) who enjoy sex synchronically or diachronically with multiple partners. The implication is that promiscuous persons are morally suspect; they have little or no sexual self-control and so constitute a danger to ordered society. Of course, the relation between sexual activity and societal order depends heavily upon the actual role that sex can play in disordering society. For example, in contemporary societies that have inherited their basic social ideas and traditions from the confluence of patriarchal cultures and religions of the ancient Near East, the traditionally close and even obsessive relationship between sex and social order can be traced at least in part to the patrilineal substructure of those cultures. Patrilineal societies trace descent and, more importantly, property inheritance through the father's name or line.[13] This means that the economic stability of the social order rests largely on the identity of fathers as such. In patrilineal systems, the acknowledgment and accuracy of paternity is therefore a matter of serious concern and historically constitutes no small difficulty. Prior to the advent of DNA testing (and even since then for those without the means to purchase tests), paternal identity depends largely on the word of the mother. Lag times between conception and evident pregnancy, possibilities of multiple sperm donors, and variations in individual maternal gestation patterns that allow for blurry timetables constitute only some of the many difficulties with which patrilineal systems must cope in securing paternal identity for the purposes of economic stability and social order.

Conversely, although subterfuge is possible in any system, the relative ease of accurately establishing the identity of mothers in childbirth is so great that one wonders why or how patrilineality ever took hold in so many societies and for so long. In matrilineal societies, the sexual activities of both women and of men need not be (and generally are not) tightly bound to inheritance and family identity because property and family identity are not primarily affected by the sexual activities and reproductive consequences of either men or women.[14] So long as the identity of the mother can be confidently established, property lines of descent and distribution are clearly delineated and easily verified, regardless of who donates the sperm.

This is not to say that matrilineal societies are without sexual ethics or concerns about sexual practices in terms of health, social welfare, or reproduction. Rather, such concerns are bound to issues other than property inheritance. When money is not involved, in other words, social anxieties tend to soften and diminish. The difficulties inherent in securing paternal identity for purposes of inheritance, even in small communities, means that the only way to be absolutely sure of paternity is to control—absolutely—sexual access to mothers. The sexual purity of married or marriageable women is therefore a matter of public concern in patrilineal systems (while the sexual purity of married or unmarried men is not) because of the economic implications that maternal impurity—or promiscuity—can have on establishing paternal identity and, therefore, on the economic base of whole clans and communities.

Although the issue of property distribution does not account for all of the ways that female identities and sexualities have been traditionally constructed and controlled in ancient and modern patrilineal societies, the simple fact of patrilineality as the dominant traditional form of familial organization in historic Jewish, Christian, and Muslim societies may account for much of the obsession with female sexual purity and impurity in the religious thought and practices in those cultures. Through the material lens of historical property distribution, the close link that patrilineality demands between the sexual activity of women and the ordering of society stands out in bold. Promiscuity and the dangers it poses to confidence in patrilineal descent is thereby a matter of longstanding and deeply rooted anxiety, which echoes in contemporary cries that link sex outside of marriage (thus implicating homosexuality as well) to societal disintegration.

If promiscuous is an anxiety-producing word in social circumstances, it seems to be a panic-inducing word in theological circumstances. When I used the word to describe divine love in the concluding chapter of my book *Re-Imagining the Divine*,[15] readers communicated enthusiasm for my argument that monotheistic concerns about fidelity to one God expose human rather than divine jealousy, but they expressed objections to my suggestion of promiscuous divinity as an antidote. "Can't you use a different word?" one reader wrote, "'promiscuous' is too provocative, it insults God, and people will miss the point." Promiscuity, it would seem, not only degrades God, it distracts people from anything else within range. Perhaps there is an opportunity lurking in that fact. When the forbidden is distracting, the distracting usually has something to teach. It bears investigation, if for nothing else than to discover what is being (unsuccessfully) repressed or denied for the sake of order.

The order that promiscuity threatens may be the inherited structure of family that relies on the identity of the father (mirrored in the image of God "the Father," whose demands for purity from "His Church" reflect patrilineal anxiety), but it may also be a habit of anxiety about sex tied to paternal dominance that no longer dominates the social sphere in contemporary, globalized circumstances. The rigidly patrilineal orders inherited by capitalist societies throughout the modern West are rapidly disappearing as women gain the economic and legal status of men and are no longer compelled to pass their wealth to and through their husbands. Promiscuity holds less and less power to disrupt the social and economic structure of society precisely because women's sexuality is no longer tied to economic stability in fundamental ways, to the extent that women are free to make, retain, and distribute wealth in their own name.

A "pure woman" is increasingly an anachronism, despite conservative religious efforts to revive its importance to faith, as in the "Love Waits" campaign, or in fundamentalist movements that link women's independence with loss of religious integrity. As virginity and sexual abstinence lose their ability to secure wealth and status, their power to hold meaning has eroded among the young for whom such limits are difficult under any circumstances. Theologians and ethicists such as Robert Nelson, Mary Hunt, and Kelly Brown Douglas have long been seeking grounds other than the patrilineal inheritance structure for determining sexual ethics, and most feminist scholars recognize that brittle notions of female purity undermine, rather than encourage, mature and loving relationships.[16] Going further, queer theologian Marcella Althaus Reid has taken up the question of "indecency" (which can claim promiscuity, to be sure) as a grave necessity for theology.[17]

Artists, as usual, are in the forefront of social change. Nelly Furtado, for example, released a hit rap crossover duet with Timbaland in 2007 entitled "Promiscuous" (from her appropriately entitled album *Loose*) that extols the attraction of "promiscuous girl" and of "promiscuous boy" while at the same time suggesting that deceit is bad. Although she never defines the term in her lyrics,[18] Furtado's intent appears to be more than selling songs with a shock-value lyric (though that is clearly part of it). The song is a dialogue between two potential sexual partners who are testing each other for honesty "without games." What is significant here is that, depending upon how one interprets the repeated chorus of longing for "promiscuous girl" and "promiscuous boy," the whole song models a navigation of desire in a way that respects sexual desire and the necessity of a process that disallows coercion or harm. Of course, such navigation in the face of desire is never easy, and the lyrics indicate frustration on both sides at different points throughout the song. Perhaps in acknowledgment of and as an answer to the difficulties of living out new sexual norms, the whole song pivots around a single central stanza made up of "Don't be mad. Don't get mean."[19] Tempering promiscuity with a disavowal of meanness suggests the edge of a sexual ethical platform that could easily and cogently challenge traditional religious sexual norms that remain rooted in anachronism.

Of course, it is easy to read too much into one hit song, but it is easy to read too little there as well. I am suggesting that the artwork of popular music is pushing back on religiously grounded sexual norms, as it has done for decades and is succeeding now not only in shocking the system but in proposing new ethical norms in part because the economic structures that once propped up the religious governance and sexual control of women is truly waning in many societies around the world. Religious traditions and what they believe to be divine legitimation of patrilineal governance and sexual control remain, however, like a hardened shell that cannot seem to expand to accommodate the changing life within.

Certainly sexual anxiety is high in many religious communities precisely because the deep cooperation between economic structures and religious beliefs has stumbled so dramatically on the political and economic changes that have taken place over the past two hundred years, changes that continue to shift the structure of social relationships as well. It is perhaps too soon to expect millennia-old doctrines regarding sex to accommodate to such a brave new world in which women can control their own wealth, let alone their own sexual lives. Fears about promiscuity as a threat to economic security are too deeply rooted to die in a few decades of challenge. Indeed, the notion of divine promiscuity as a positive view of God's relation with the world is not a notion that would "preach" in conservative or liberal Christian churches, although it might fly in a few brave, progressive settings.

The distress that divine promiscuity evokes may be merely an indicator of the slowness and inconsistency of cultural change, with pop music at one end of the spectrum of change and religious congregations on another. Perhaps the notion of divine promiscuity represents a stumble in the painful demise of a once-powerful image of God. Dying behemoths may be nearing the end of their power, but in falling they can still cause a lot of damage. When the behemoth is a long-reigning image of God, the theological challenge is both hospice and midwifery, which in each case requires strong doses of patience and the capacity to translate pain into passage. Female sexual self-determination directly depends upon the shift away from the outmoded strictures of patrilineality. However, it should not surprise us that because patrilineality also describes the central incarnational relationship in traditional Christian theology, shifts there may be the most painful to navigate in the long run.

In traditional Christian theology, divinity itself is an inheritance of the "Son" through the "Father." According to doctrine, not only is Jesus the "begotten Son of God," he is the "only-begotten Son," which makes him the sole heir. Mary's virginity assures the identity of God as the father rather than any human male donor (a sort of DNA test of God, which is funny when you think about it) and so assures the identity of Jesus as God's son in classic patrilineal terms via the purity of the mother. The exclusivity of Jesus as God's heir is presumably the province of God's action alone, or rather lack of action in relation to any other opportunity for intercourse elsewhere in the universe.

The contemporary erosion of patrilineality in favor of more egalitarian structures of inheritance and identity is, in the end, a serious threat to latent patrilineal ideas of God, even among those who understand the limitations and anachronisms of male dominance today.[20] Promiscuity understood as sexual indiscrimination stands in direct opposition to divine lines of inheritance that place "God the Father" securely in a place of absolute paternity, not only over Jesus but over all of creation as well. Only in this frame is creaturely fidelity, the lack of which is decried by prophet after prophet, understandably essential to the very identity and honor of God. Only in this frame is God's forgiveness of creaturely infidelity required, because only in this frame does creaturely infidelity threaten the very paternity of God. What is more, promiscuity understood as a quality of distinctly impure hybridity stands in opposition to divinity understood as the pinnacle and epitome of purity and immutability. In incarnation "God chooses to entrust the Divine desire for whole-making self-actualization to the warp and woof of the finite realm."[21] Because it explicitly claims that the finite realm reveals God, the Christian doctrine of incarnation directly dismantles the purity, immutability, and simplicity of divinity, undoing both its oneness and its innocence of complex flesh. Incarnation is therefore the principle of promiscuity, in divine terms at least. So why is it such a shocker to say so?

INCARNATION, THE CHRISTIAN CONUNDRUM

Unlike "promiscuous," "incarnation" is not normally a derogatory term. It is typically applied to the miracle of (chaste) divine love for the world in whose becoming-flesh sex plays no role, or so the story goes. The adjective and noun therefore seem to mean opposite things, sexually speaking, and might even cancel each other out. Placed together in dependent relation—promiscuous incarnation—they form a kind of crass nonsense, a puzzle of contradiction. Like many supposed oppositions, however, the contradiction is misleading; it runs surface-deep only. Incarnation and promiscuity have much more to do with each other than the purveyors of divine chastity would have it—that is, if incarnation means anything at all in terms of actual bodies.

In reality, questions of incarnation and actual bodies are inseparable from Christian thought. Flesh-showing-the-divine lies at the heart of Christianity's complicated origins, which is why questions of incarnation are fundamental to its theology. What is Christian theology, after all, without the person of Jesus, the person who, Christians have claimed since the councils of Nicea and Chalcedon, is, or was, "fully divine and fully human"? As Paul announced in his first-century letter to the Philippians, Christ's equality with God makes all the more imperative an understanding of his human likeness (2:7). Paul insisted, in other words, that there are lessons to be learned from this flesh that reveals divinity. He crafted the flesh-revelation into a lesson of humility and service, though his conclusions have never been the only ones possible. Later on, the writer of the Gospel of John penned the gorgeously memorable line that "God so loved the world that he gave his only son, so that everyone who believes in him may not perish but may have life continuous" (3:16),[22] making incarnation not only a distinctive feature of Christian faith, but an unveiling (an "apocalypse") of intimate and passionate divine love.

In various ways, Christians claim that God, the divine power that created and creates the cosmos, not only has the capacity to become small, particular, and partial in the flesh of a human being, but has done so in history. God became a colonized man under the reigns of the Caesars Augustus and Tiberius of Rome, a man who died the ignominious death of a criminal against the state. That God has such a capacity for temporality and smallness, and can become the incarnate divine, is a fundamental claim shared by Christian communities who in almost every other aspect of experience and belief share little else. God takes on flesh and flesh reveals God, not in a ubiquitous or indistinguishable sense of all flesh all of the time but in the most particular sense of flesh experienced by, in this case, a human being in a particular time and place, which is how flesh is experienced by all human beings. Namely, God takes on this man's flesh, in this first-century Palestinian time-being, under the press and inspiration of these Roman colonial conditions.

It is the very particularity of divine flesh that vexed theological reflections on incarnation in the christological debates of the first three centuries after Jesus' death, and the challenge of that particularity haunts many contemporary theologies today.[23] To give assent to the idea that the God of all the heavens and the earth becomes small and particular in the occurrence of a single man in a particular historical context appears to limit incarnation too much ("Why him?") and, at the same time, threatens to open up incarnation too much ("What's to keep anyone from claiming to be God incarnate?"). Theologians then and now have had to answer the problem of too much and too little flesh in the central claim of divine incarnation.

Early Constantinian theologians and hymnwriters supplied the answer, with which contemporary theology still must contend, by limiting divine mingling with human flesh to one man, one time, one place. In doing so they attempted to answer the question of "Why him?" by focusing on his miraculous virgin birth and thereby establishing his essential distinction in kind from all other human beings. This must have seemed easier than attempting to answer the question of "Why not others?" In the third, fourth, and fifth centuries C.E., when the doctrine of incarnation was first hammered out, church unity was at stake and multiple incarnations could easily have fueled further internal dissension. At the very least Constantine, Christianity's first sponsoring emperor, benefited from a theory of incarnation that mirrored his own claims to exclusive status as sole ruler, raising the political currency of his likeness to a divine incarnate image. The imperial church leaders went to great lengths to crown the man from Nazareth with every trapping of royalty and exclusivity, in part, I suggest, because that raised the status and appeal of their faith as well.

In effect, by limiting divine incarnation to a single historical occurrence in the form of Jesus of Nazareth, the council bishops made of Jesus and his mother Mary a beneficent model of dynastic imperial rule. Whatever uncertainties persist about the actual faith of Emperor Constantine in his life or at his deathbed, his ruthless and bloody drive to become the sole ruler of the known world is well documented.[24] The development by his bishops of a clear Christology that declared Jesus to be the "only-begotten" son of God certainly gave a divine nod, if not blatant legitimation, for the emperor's own goals. Jesus' exclusive filial claim to divinity was made all the more intelligible across the Roman church by widespread patrilineal assumptions about the nature of inheritance.

Despite the clear and easily documented acquiescence of theological integrity to imperial aspiration in Christian doctrines of incarnation, it is important to remember that such aspirations have never fully determined the course of Christian theology. In contrast to the emergent imperial theology of the post-Constantinian church, the rhetoric of Paul's early Philippian letter centers around amazement that equality with God actually seems equal to human failure. Paul suggests that divinity revealed in the flesh of Jesus is divine equality with the slave, the servant, or (in more contemporary language) the day laborer or undocumented worker (Phil. 2:6-8). Liberation theologians have argued strenuously that this revelation of divinity from the fleshy stories of Jesus, not the gilt exclusivity of kings and emperors, is the proper guide to the meaning of incarnation.

What makes equality with God significant here is not just the revelation of divinity in the flesh of a man from Nazareth, at the Augustan pinnacle of the Roman Empire, but the revelation of flesh in divinity. I insist upon both sides of this equation, not only in pursuit of healing for reviled bodies but in addressing the conundrum posed by Christianity's traditional, albeit arbitrary, claim of exclusivity in incarnation.[25] The conundrum is this: If the Christian doctrine of incarnation insists upon God actually becoming flesh (as it does), then it obliterates both the radical and abstract otherness of God and the absolute oneness of God upon which it also insists. Flesh is indiscriminate in its porous interconnection with everything, and it is never, at any level, absolutely unified. To insist upon a solitary incarnate moment is to betray the very fleshiness of flesh, its innate promiscuity, pesky shiftiness, and resilient interruptions of sense. A solitary incarnation is, in other words, not incarnation at all but a disembodiment: a denial of the flesh that in its very cellular structure of integration, disintegration, and passage is always re-forming, dispersing, and returning. The ancients couldn't really know the atomic structure of living flesh or the physics of elemental biology, although some, like the Roman philosopher Democritus, had some pretty good ideas about it.[26] Christians today, however, do not have the excuse of ignorance about the fundamental promiscuity of bodies, their mixtures, in-between genders, and indiscriminate interconnections. Incarnation, if it is about divinity revealed in flesh, should at least attempt to be accurate in its dealings with the latter despite the fact that becoming accurate about flesh changes everything about divinity too.

INCARNATION AS DIVINE EXCESS AND INDISCRIMINATION

Lisa Isherwood, a proponent of "body theology," points out that the

> "struggle for embodiment is a hard fought one, and simply being alive is not enough because we have been subjected to alienation within our own skin for far too long. In a desperate attempt to claim our embodiment as positive, feminists have to face the hard questions about their traditions, and within the Christian tradition we have to realize that we may have to move on beyond the neatly packaged Christ to a place of uncertainty, a place of new imaginings."[27]

To claim outsider embodiment—embodiment in the form of those excluded from social privilege—as positive through the incarnate divine means that incarnation cannot look like any one thing, but neither can it be abstracted, once again, away from bodies into some kind of principle. If, in a world of embodied differences, one body is not to be elevated above all others, then the image of incarnate God cannot reduce to a single referent or a single body.

Fortunately for those who find my argument worth entertaining, but who require a biblical basis for their theological claims, the Christian doctrine of exclusive embodiment postdates the biblical texts and cannot be justified there. Even a strict reading of the Johannine claim by Jesus that he is the "way, and the truth, and the life" through which no other access to the "Father" may be obtained (John 14:6) does not necessitate interpreting Jesus as the only occurrence of divine incarnation. Indeed, Christians have interpreted this passage quite liberally throughout their history. When I was a child, for example, and asked how I was supposed to go "through Jesus" to arrive at God, my Sunday school teacher explained that my baptism and membership in the church constituted my access to God "through" Jesus. This move and others like it, which equate the church itself with Jesus (as the "body of Christ") and so as the bona fide means to the God whom Jesus called "my Father," actually depend upon prodigious theological manipulation. They necessitate the construction of the doctrine of the Trinity and specifically of the Holy Spirit, which forms the basis of the ongoing presence of Jesus Christ in and as the church community. Together these trinitarian developments in effect undermine the exclusivity of the historical individual Jesus as divine incarnation by expanding the notion of incarnation to a vague claim of Christ's spiritual presence in the church as Christ's body. Even more interesting, they constitute an explicit, if perhaps inadvertent, move away from the logic of oneness that otherwise governs the monotheistic traditions.

The Johannine claim that the Christian way to God is through the incarnation changes its meaning when incarnation takes on a more generous, embodied sensibility. "Through me" in John 14:6 could just as easily mean through the body itself, at least if incarnation means anything close to "in the body." A very different story might have emerged had bodies been the doctrinal point of incarnation, and most certainly different practices of the body might have developed in the church, had its leaders read John 14:6 to mean that the path to God runs through the body.[28] Such a reading does not require hermeneutical contortion. It is a simple rendering of the word *incarnation*.

Viewed from the angle of Christianity's implicit and explicit connection to incarnation, the "place of new imaginings" of which Isherwood speaks may therefore not be so far removed from traditional Christian thought as it might appear at first blush. The results of new imaginings, however, may usher in profound changes to the shape and content of the core doctrines. The problem for such imaginings lies less in limitations posed by biblical and narrative sources for Christian theology (they are in fact rich sources for precisely the kind of new imaginings for which Isherwood and I hope) and more in the intertwining social structures that have legitimated—and ossified— particular interpretations. Ancient anxieties about female sexuality, rooted in economic structures of patrilineality, still course through contemporary interpretations of divine incarnation such that robust sexualities of all kinds are shunned from the body of Christ, the body of the divine, just as that body remains—for many at least—ostensibly male.

How might a notion of promiscuous incarnation shift the lens on divinity enough to open up the already existing places of new imaginings? Promiscuity—whether it refers to mixture, or to sexual openness, or to a third gender between male and female—suggests intercourse and multiplicity, a posture of generosity toward change and of ambiguity toward identity, any of which goes a long way actually to describing the character of Jesus' interactions in the narratives of his life. Incarnation, at least as the stories of Jesus imply and as the long history of the church demonstrates, is neither pure nor unambiguously categorizable. Incarnate divinity consorts with specificity, with individuals under the radar of identity categories, in defiance of identity profiles rather than in obedience to them. It is impossible to say, on the basis of the surviving narratives, that Jesus preferred categories of people to the actual individuals who crossed his path. He simply does not seem to be attentive to identity classifications. He does not seem, for example, to prefer only centurians, or wealthy young politicians (Luke 18:18-25), or even the poor, for he spends a great deal of time with people of means, like Mary of the upper-class Magdalenes. Nor does he seem to prefer only children, or only prostitutes, or only fishermen, or only women. Does he reject anyone on the basis of category? He seems to have tried with the Syro-Phoenician woman (Matt. 15:21-28; Mark 7:24-30), but she quickly set him straight. He does not even avoid Romans, or the agents of Tiberius's endless tax levies for imperial expansion, or friends who he knows will betray him. If anything, the narratives of Jesus of Nazareth suggest that the divinity which his flesh reveals is radically open to consorting with anyone. It follows no rules of respectability or governing morality in its pursuit of connection with others, many others, serially and synchronically, passionately and openly.

It is for this reason that I argue (here and elsewhere) that the claims of exclusivity that Christians place on divine incarnation reveal Christian insecurities about a God who loves too freely, too indiscriminately, and too often, rather than jealousy on the part of God. This kind of excess of intimacy and disregard for propriety is the definition of promiscuity in sexual terms. Jesus is a "promiscuous boy" (to borrow Furtado's phrase) whose entire teachings might be reducible to the refrain "don't get mean." The erasure and vilification of sex in Christian theology and in the canonical narratives about Jesus represent a serious error at the core of the tradition. This error is founded not on theological grounds but on economic grounds and cannot be corrected until the patrilineal economics of Christian sexual morality is fully dismantled. The astonishing revelation of flesh in divinity through the Gospel stories and through the doctrinal affirmations of incarnation cannot fully emerge without that correction, because without it, incarnation is desiccated in abstraction and exclusive isolation, which is the opposite of embodiment. And so, without that correction, ostracized bodies—female bodies, black bodies, queer bodies, disabled bodies, fat bodies, tattooed bodies, diseased bodies, anybodies—can hardly be recognized as the flesh that, if Jesus is the way to God, reveals God.

Promiscuous incarnation suggests excess and indiscrimination in divine love. It puts power and the inexorable pull of gravitational attraction in "God so loved the world." It restores sexual bounty and openness to God, which means that it welcomes the end of racialized hierarchies that depend upon sexualized regimes of control. It dismisses purity as a divine attribute and replaces it with the cacophonous mixture of differences that constitute divine time-being. Promiscuous incarnation refuses the either/or of rigid gender roles in exactly the same way that all bodies rebel against those strictures: it is a third gender, which makes divine incarnation a disruption of every social binary, every structure that would divinize one at the expense of all of the others. It honors the hungers of the body, even to the point of picking grain on the Sabbath (Matt. 12:1).

Promiscuous incarnation implies a God outside of human control and even outside of religious rules but not outside of human life and experience, not outside of human hungers and desires, not ever far away from ecstasy or grief. Somehow, if indeed the stories of Jesus are to be the way to divine incarnation, Christians can claim that God always becomes flesh for a purpose and so can be found wherever that purpose is being pursued. That purpose is radical, compassionate, promiscuous love of the world to such an extent that suffering in any person, any body, is a wound in God's flesh, a diminishment of God's own beloved, a gravitational pull on God to come, again. And again.

Further Suggested Readings

Althaus-Reid, Marcella. *Indecent Theology: Theological Perversions in Sex, Gender, and Politics*. London: Routledge, 2000.

Jung, Patricia Beattie, Mary Hunt, and Radhika Balakrishnan, eds. *Good Sex: Feminist Perspectives from the World's Religions*. New Brunswick, N.J.: Rutgers University Press, 2001.

Lerner, Gerda. *The Creation of Patriarchy*. New York: Oxford University Press, 1987.

Povinelli, Elizabeth A. *The Empire of Love: Toward a Theory of Intimacy, Genealogy, and Carnality*. Durham: Duke University Press, 2006.

Schneider, David M. *A Critique of the Study of Kinship*. Ann Arbor: University of Michigan Press, 1984.

Schneider, Laurel C. "What Race Is Your Sex?" In *Disrupting White Supremacy from Within: White People on What We Need to Do*, ed. Jennifer Harvey, Karin Case, and Robin Hawley Gorsline. Cleveland: Pilgrim, 2004.

CHAPTER 15

Ecclesiology, Desire, and the Erotic

Paul Lakeland

*Eroticism begins where sexual emotion becomes, beyond its procreative
goal, an end in itself or an instrument of the soul.*

—*Denis de Rougemont*

*Our age, which has probably lost the notion of amorous passion,
because the latter is more religious than sexual, considers it childish to
be preoccupied with love, and expends all its efforts on marriage.*

—*Robert Musil*

FROM THE SONG OF SONGS to the present day, images of human
love have been employed, even in sacred Scripture, to characterize the relationship between God and human beings. We love God, and God loves us.
God, indeed, is love. But what kind of love is it that God and we are involved
in together? In Christian theology, it is rare that erotic attraction is used as a
metaphor for love of God, still less for God's love of us. Why is this? What is
wrong with desire, and couldn't the strength and character of human erotic
attraction tell us something about human longing for God? If so, can this

also be helpful in explaining the Christian church as "the spouse of Christ," the object of the love of Christ and the communal subject that loves him in turn?

The following pages seek answers to these questions in three stages. First, we have to attend to the dynamics of human desire or eros, where we shall uncover a dialectic of presence and absence or promise and fulfillment that can easily become unbalanced.[1] Second, we shall examine how this tension might be exemplified in Christian communal desire for God, specifically in the way presence and absence work in Catholic and Protestant traditions. Finally, we shall ask what an ecclesiology of desire might look like, rather than one that has seemed historically to prefer the Pauline "spousal metaphor." While marriage need not and should not be without desire, the use of marital imagery in Christian theology privileges a static rather than a dynamic understanding of divine love. It is human sexual desire that is an analog for love of God. It is the desire in itself, not the biological goal of sexual desire in procreation, that is of theological significance.

EROS, ABSENCE, AND PRESENCE

There are many reasons why eros is rarely invoked in theological reflection upon the nature of the Christian church. Chief among them is the strong sexual connotations of the erotic in our contemporary world. Indeed, most Christians think of eroticism as something outside the purview of Christian theology, except perhaps as something whose power the church seeks to control in the interests of . . . what, exactly? Of love? Of the love of God? Of recognizing God's love for us? Of a sober awareness of our own sinfulness, a reality in which, for many if not most adult human beings, eros is implicated? If we can get beyond this stage, it is still true that eros has not been for most of the Christian tradition the place where discipleship of Christ and the love of God begins, or ends. "Self-giving," thus *agape*, has been the dominant image of Christian love. God, we are told, has nothing to gain in creation, which is a product of the self-expression of the divine reality. As love is of its nature a generous outpouring upon others, so God who is love itself is the perfection of *agape*. Christ is this perfection expressed in human form, one who in faithfulness to his God makes the ultimate sacrifice of suffering and death on behalf of all humankind. The task of Christian discipleship, in consequence, is to mirror that self-giving. Christ on the cross is a figure of *agape*, not eros, and discipleship imitates the self-giving of Christ.

If eros is suspect in Christian theology, however, it is far from unknown in Christian religious life and culture. Religious art, for example, is a prime location of the celebration of eroticism, though there is always ambiguity about its meaning. Much "Christian" painting and sculpture is an excuse for the celebration of eroticism, not the celebration of the erotic within religion. The homoeroticism of the many paintings of St. Sebastian's martyrdom is a clear example of such understandable opportunism. Some religious writing, however, particularly the writings of Christian mystics, testifies to a far deeper implication of the erotic in truly Christian love. What, for example, are we to make of Hadewijch of Antwerp's writing of Christ that "He came himself to me, took me entirely in his arms, and pressed me to him; and all my members felt his in full felicity, in accordance with the desire of my heart and my humanity. So I was outwardly satisfied and fully transported." Bernard McGinn, the great historian of mysticism, quotes this text in the course of contrasting the eroticism of the medieval mystics, in which the desires of the body provide at least strong imagery for those of the soul, with the "passionless passion" of early church theologians Origen or Gregory of Nyssa, in which we encounter an "analogy between the activities of the soul and the sense organs of the body."[2]

While this is an enormously complex field of inquiry, there is no doubt that the medieval Christian mystics chose to use erotic imagery to express the relationship between God and the mystic and that they did not think it inappropriate. Moreover, the "passionless passion" of Origen and Gregory seems to have been as foreign an idea to medieval mystics like Hadewijch or Julian of Norwich as it is to us. But where these women were carried along by the power of their emotions, our distance from the church fathers is more likely a deep-seated unwillingness to consider the body or embodiment in any way negatively. If we are in love with God, the body is an integral part of this movement of the heart. Moreover, the language of desire is not employed in a religious context in some merely metaphorical way. The mystics desire closeness with God, prayer is moved to a high degree by desire, and this desire is literal, if not exactly sexual.

In order to go beyond sexual imagery in identifying the erotic, without ever canceling it, we need to attend to the dialectics of absence and presence that mark the experience of desire. The opposite of desire is not its absence but possession. We cannot desire that which we already possess. At best, we can enjoy what we possess, though if our enjoyment is produced by the mere fact of possession, then we are somehow debased. This is the world of the book collector who cares only to collect, not to read. It is the world of a Don Juan, who makes conquests, not love. Enjoying what we possess because of its own inherent value is not about possession but about taking delight in it. This is a challenging disposition, since it so easily becomes displaced by the lack of enjoyment that grows with time, a mere taking-for-granted if not exactly boredom, and it is often not long before the enjoyment of the possession is overcome by the desire—yes, the eros—for something which we do not yet possess. It is an insight of the Buddha that we could well incorporate into the Christian vision of things that the enjoyment of possessions is only possible if we are detached from those things. When we do not treat our possessions as things we possess, then enjoyment is possible. The moment we begin to possess them, we begin to want to move beyond them. Attachment leads to longing. Because Christianity is not Buddhism, it retains a positive valuation of a certain kind of desire. We desire, says the Christian tradition, because we are incomplete; the foundation of our desire, because it is the source of our completion, is desire for God. If Buddhism proclaims the task of detachment overcoming eros, Christianity suggests the priority of eros over detachment. What Christianity does not always notice is that the human longing for union with another is explicable only as an act of self-transcendence that has its ultimate end in union with God.

If we cannot desire what we possess, we also cannot have eros for what we do not know. We can only desire a particular something or someone. Desire is always a transitive term; if there is no object, there is no direction, no drive, no eros. While this has an obvious application in everyday human experience and makes immediate sense in relation to the things or people we may desire, it is much more interesting and challenging when the object is God. I can desire her or him. I can desire a better life or to get married or a plate of pasta. I can only desire these people or these things because (a) I know what they are or who they are, and (b) I do not presently possess them. But God is different. In the case of the divine, I do not know who or what God is in the sense that I know who William Jefferson Clinton or Sandra Day O'Connor is. Moreover, it might be that if I got to know more about Clinton or O'Connor, I would cease to desire to know or to possess either of them. Knowing God is so much more mysterious a process, so much more subtle, but once there is some knowledge, I cannot stop wanting to know and possess God more and more fully. The difference is that in the case of God, the little knowledge that we possess is not of an object out there, but of a reality who always already possesses us. As traditional Christian spirituality would put it, we can only love God because God has first loved us.

We can perhaps say, with reasonable accuracy, that the erotic depends upon the dialectic of absence and presence, of anticipation and realization, of promise and fulfillment. The challenge of eros is that it is fueled by absence, by lack of possession, by an imagination that is feeding on what is not yet or what has been, but its drive toward satisfaction requires presence that will temporarily erase eros itself. Eros is not satisfied with presence, only with possession. In its turn, however, possession is the anteroom to further absence, the fulfillment that portends renewed wanting, the presence become absence again, the little death out of which eros may again be kindled, but which is in itself at least the temporary end of wanting. In this complex process, the desire may be as delicious as the enjoyment, the anticipation indeed more pleasurable than the capture. The satisfaction of desire, as the myth of Don Juan illustrates so well, is a kind of imprisonment in dissatisfaction.

The loved object or thing must at one and the same time be attainable and not presently taken up, must be supremely attractive to us but not currently enjoyed, must hold out to us the prospect of a transformed future while we are not yet living in that new world. While this may not apply to the desire for a plate of pasta, it does describe well the subterranean longings of erotic attraction. Eros that is not mere lust always wants to know the other, in ways far deeper than simple sexual union. The holding-nothing-back of sexual love is a symbol of the union of souls that is the true objective of erotic attraction, though often enough it masquerades as the objective itself. Clearly, the reality does not require the symbol. You can experience erotic attraction that is not destined to culminate in sexual union, and sexual union can often enough signal the end of erotic attraction.

DIVINE PRESENCE, DIVINE ABSENCE

Wherever there are Christians, there is always "the desire for God," however we gloss that phrase. Whether we are conservative or liberal, modern or premodern or postmodern, what makes a religious or even a spiritual person is the drive toward transcendence. We look beyond the present and into the future, perhaps to the final consummation of all things in the reign of God beyond history. Christians are an expectant, eschatological people, like the Hebrews before them, living in messianic hope, even if sometimes their thirst for God's future leads them to undervalue God's presence in this world. Desire for union with God is the common factor, but it may be framed very differently. We might seek union with God out of distaste for the humanity of this world. We might see signs of God's sacramental presence in this world, drawing us forward to a life with God that is in fundamental continuity with this earthly life. Or we might look for God in the deep-down mystery of this world and this life alone. Each is in its own way a passionate drive to know God, but it is not so clear that the God whom each seeks is in fact quite the same God, for the God whom each seeks seems to value the world in particular ways and, hence, the human beings who populate it.

If the erotic as an element in the relationship between God and the Christian is challenging, then employing the erotic in ecclesiology is at one and the same time both more and less daunting. The problem here resides in the fact that the church is a communal reality, a subject that is made up of countless millions of individual subjects. An erotic ecclesiology is more daunting because neither the love of God for the church nor the love of Christians for God can easily be accommodated within a rhetoric of desire, which seems so much more appropriate to the I-Thou language of a personal relationship with God and Christ. When we are dealing with faith communities, the desire for God is more difficult to parse, because the analogy between desire for the other and desire for God is attenuated in the communal context. People can be passionate about their loves, human or divine, but can churches be passionate? It seems difficult to imagine passionate institutions, even passionate communities, though it may well be the case that in their understandings of the relationship between God and the world or Christ and his church, the dynamics of desire somehow come into play. Different Christian traditions, like different individuals, look very differently at church, some of them stressing an erotics of absence, others an erotics of presence or even fulfillment. Both orientations have their strengths and their weaknesses.

The fact that the church is a subject made up of a multitude of subjects can make the language of desire and the erotic less daunting, too. For one thing, it makes it easier to avoid the heated excesses of the medieval mystics and to reach out even for something of the passionless passion advocated by Origen. If Christ and the church are so frequently explained in the terminology of the nuptial metaphor of bridegroom and bride, might this be an effort to locate the faith community somehow beyond desire? Only this can make sense of Paul's ambivalence about marriage. On the one hand, husbands are enjoined to love their wives "just as Christ loved the church" (Eph. 5:25). On the other, marriage is "a remedy for fornication," and "it is better to marry than to be aflame with passion" (1 Cor. 7:9). Somehow, desire is sublimated in marriage, he seems to think, either converted into a nonsexual form (Christ and the church) or literally domesticated. Or is it? For surely no nuptial metaphor can entirely avoid the erotic. Desire must somehow be present, but where exactly is the locus of desire in the church as a community of faith, and how is it embodied?

The stress in Roman Catholic and other more generally sacramental understandings of church is on the faith community as shaped by real *presence*. Eucharistic theology in sacramental traditions always tends toward communion as the possession, the eating of Christ's flesh and blood by which we become one with Christ and he with us. This takes place only in the church. The individual's unification with God in Christ through reception of the Eucharist is a mutual possession that temporarily suspends desire. Catholics encourage frequent return to the sacrament, and it might be that Protestant suspicion of this fixation on the Eucharist has its origin in a feeling that somehow the desire for God is being downgraded through the frequency of the sacramental encounter. Does desire pale when possessing the object of desire and being possessed by it becomes so routine? Even more challenging is the role of the church relative to the Eucharist. The power of orders in Catholicism means that the church holds fast to the presence of God in Christ (present in the tabernacle on the altar, where the little red lamp burns endlessly), and the dialectic of presence and absence that drives desire threatens to become unbalanced. Much of what goes wrong with and in the Catholic tradition can be traced to the excessive focus on presence. Catholics have a saying, which is true enough, that "the Eucharist makes the church." However, constant dwelling on the fullness of eucharistic presence can lead us to forget that the church exists to evangelize. The Eucharist may make the church, indeed, but it makes the church for mission, and mission of its nature is future oriented, fueled by sacred desire for the reign of God that we do not yet fully possess.

Less sacramentally ordered Protestant traditions postpone fulfillment to the eschaton. Theirs is an indefinitely delayed gratification in which spirituality uses the language of real *absence*. Communion, if it is to occur, is in the hearts of the believers and the community is at best proleptic of the coming of the kingdom. What we have in the here and now is memory made present in a ritual recalling of the Last Supper. Communion in these Protestant traditions cannot be the temporary alleviation of the desire for God, because it is not union with the real presence of God. It is simply a ritually ordered longing for union with God in the eschaton. Here too, however, there is the danger of an imbalance. If the desire for God is not sated and therefore not rendered routine, the presence of God in the community of faith is harder to experience. God is present in the mode of absence, like the anticipated visitor in Rainer Maria Rilke's *Stories of God* or the endlessly awaited Godot in Samuel Beckett's play. God's mysterious acts occur at the other side of a veil made all but opaque by human sinfulness. The desire for God is present, often so much more palpable than in the cozier circles of Catholic worship, but it is a desire almost inevitably frustrated by the vagaries of the human condition.

Catholics, one might then say, have an ecclesiology of fulfilled desire, a happy marriage between Christ and the church, with all the joys of full possession and all the dangers of complacency. However, eros, as the troubadours discovered, is at its most vibrant when the object of desire is unattainable. The challenge of marriage is to maintain desire, a Catholic problem perhaps. Protestants are closer to the courtly love tradition, an exquisitely prolonged courtship, a fencing match of delayed desire in which the bread and wine are symbolic of the Last Supper, itself an anticipation of something promised in the eschaton. You can see the contrast symbolized in the stereotypical architectural styles: the plain, New England Puritan tradition church where absence is pregnant with promise, and the glories of the baroque or neo-Gothic American Catholic church where nothing is left to the imagination. The values of each have much to contribute to one another, and it might be that plain Protestant and the baroque Catholic church buildings should be traded off, if only temporarily, between the two religious groups. Catholics could gain from the clean simplicity of things, while Protestants ought to have the opportunity to give full rein to their senses. Clearly, both need to balance one another. Where is the point of balance to be found in the erotic tensions of presence and absence?

The twin evils of the two extremes of eros might offer us some clues about striking a healthy balance. If in the realm of human relationships, sexual longing that is never reciprocated and never, ever, achieves even temporary fulfillment, is always in danger of leading to bitterness and even hatred, so the concomitant and opposing danger is the taking for granted of the loved one and even the boredom that can come in the end to infidelity. In exactly similar fashion within religious longing, the two extremes are the empty and endless postponement, eschatological or merely asymptotic, of dwelling in the presence of God, and the focus on a routinized possession of the divine that risks the domestication of the object of desire. Possession is static, desire is dynamic. Can we find a way toward a healthier ecclesiality through examining the metaphors of human love?

AN ECCLESIOLOGY OF DESIRE

If the dialectics of presence and absence in the phenomenology of human desire make at least some sense in enlightening the difference between Protestant and Catholic understandings of how God is present to us through the sacrament, might it not be possible to press beyond this particular example to a more comprehensive ecclesiology of desire? That this has largely not been attempted has much to do with the assumption that desire is largely sexual or even genital, and much to do with the Pauline insistence on the spousal metaphor for Christ's relation to the church. Of course, the apostolic authority of Paul requires us to overlook the inconsistency in his understanding of the beauty of the spousal relationship. So, is there some other set of reasons for the church's preference for imagery drawn from marriage rather than from desire? For many centuries the Catholic tradition argued that the primary if not sole purpose of human sexual activity is procreation within marriage, and that a secondary end is "a remedy for concupiscence." In recent decades, this has been reformulated as twin purposes, now described as procreation and "the mutual support" of the spouses. Certainly, there has to be desire of some kind if the conjugal relationship is to be strengthened; however, this is very definitely desire within bounds, which, while it makes good sense in exploring the complexity of the marital relationship, says nothing about the role of desire more broadly. Is there perhaps some fear of the consequences of valuing desire itself as an image of divine love? Desire is, after all, always transgressive; it cannot thrive on mere repetition but moves naturally toward greater intensity or novelty. To call marriage a remedy for concupiscence is certainly to demean it, but to see it as the domestication of desire is not much better. Desire breaks bounds; if it is trangressive, its dynamics intend transcendence.

An ecclesiology of desire must address the three problems with the ecclesial preference for the spousal metaphor and show how desire surpasses spousal language and enriches our understanding of the nature of the church. The three problems with the spousal metaphor as it has been employed in the history of Christian theology are: first, that it is too confining as an image of desire; second, that it is unhistorical; and third, that it does not do justice to the richness of human love, whose desires are not exhausted by the metaphor of sexual union that permeates the spousal metaphor. In order to make better use of human love as a way to encounter the love of God, we need to release it from some of the social constrictions imposed by spousal language. We have to see God and the community of faith as more than spouses. We need to examine how dimensions of love other than the erotic help us to understand better what the church really is. An ecclesiology of desire can address all these issues.

First, the spousal metaphor confines Christ and the church in a stasis that simply overlooks the superabundance of divine love, whereas the "more" inherent in the language of desire captures much more successfully the gratuitous outpouring of divine grace. In Christian theology, the spousal metaphor is mostly simply stated, and the inner dynamics of the spousal relationship are not explored because they do not apply to the vastly imbalanced relationship between Christ and the body of the believers. There are two further problems, one a theological issue and one a matter of spirituality. Theologically, the spousal metaphor is part and parcel of an excessively christological ecclesiology, in which emphasis is placed on the founding of the church by Christ. This inevitably leads to the canonization of historical accidents as if they were meant by Christ—whether the tripartite ministry of bishops, priests, and deacons, the evolution of the papacy, or the exclusion of women from ordination. If "Christ" is not open to development, then the church's relationship to its "bridegroom" is condemned to sterility, and a sterile union cannot bear fruit. The spiritual issue follows, as the members of the believing community are members of a faith community that understands itself so ahistorically that the personal relationship to the living Christ sometimes has to be sought outside or despite the church itself. It is this problematic that so often leads to the claim of contemporary Americans that they are "spiritual but not religious."

An ecclesiology of desire substitutes a dynamic for a static relationship between Christ and the church that, while it certainly can be related to a spousal relationship, is not restricted to one. The attribution to individuals of desire for union with Christ is uncontroversial, and the extension of the idea to the collective desire for union of the whole church is not problematic. However, an ecclesiology of desire requires mutual attraction. Christ does not just love the church (spousal metaphor) but desires a closer union with the church. The assertion of desire, of its nature unfulfilled, suggests a need that is not (yet) satisfied, the dialectic of longing and possession that we already identified as the core of eros. To assert a need in Christ is a much more challenging theological note than the simple, static, love of his bride, the church. Desire suggests a lack of fulfillment in God. At the same time, a trinitarian God is inevitably always in process, and the economic Trinity's processions are ongoing in history. From our perspective, if not God's, there is still work to be done to bring Christ and his church closer together—work in which the dependence of Christ on the cooperation of the faithful suggests that desire and need may not be wholly inappropriate language. Moreover, the language of desire allows a little more pneumatology into the excessively christological emphasis of the spousal metaphor, introducing the Holy Spirit who blows where it wills and who is unconfined by images and metaphors. It also admits a note of mutuality that is not obviously present when we explore the theological use of the spousal metaphor. It is hard to think of Christ and the church as equals, still less Christ and the individual believer, but there has to be a way to incorporate the idea of reciprocity in mutual freedom if the relationship is to be a healthy one. Thus, an ecclesiology of desire will construe the church not so much as the community of faith (static) but as the community of fidelity to hope (dynamic).

Second, the ahistorical interpretation of the spousal metaphor conflicts with the need to allow human experience to enlighten our use of theological metaphors and images. On the other hand, the dynamic character of an ecclesiology of desire means that we open ourselves to developmental perspectives on what—as language about God—has most often been thought of as deductive truths, unchanging and universally applicable. No language about God can be anything other than based upon human experience and will inevitably bear the traces of this or that historical period. This is a particularly problematic dimension of the spousal metaphor, since sexuality and interpersonal dynamics are areas of human life in which social, political, and personal expectations have changed enormously over the centuries. Employing the spousal language even in the loosest analogical way leaves us sailing between the Scylla of a claim for the radical equality of Christ and his church and the Charybdis of declaring that modern beliefs about equality in marriage are mistaken. An ecclesiology of desire sidesteps this tangle of issues. It does not require radical equality, since reciprocity is not necessitated. Christ loves the church even when the church fails in its fidelity to eschatological hope, and modern convictions about marriage as a partnership between equals do not result in clumsy theological reflections or deductive imperatives about complementarity rather than equality between human partners.

Third, an ecclesiology of desire completely avoids the inadequacy of the spousal metaphor to the complexity of human love. There is a great deal of erotic attraction and desire that is unconnected to the spousal union, and some indeed that doesn't have much, if anything, to do with the drive toward sexual union. Indeed, the polymorphous nature of human sexual attraction is not something the church deals with well, and it certainly cannot be contained with the spousal metaphor. While Christian commitment to permanence, fidelity, and fruitfulness is an important testimony to the values of human unions, the church does not know what to do with sexual explorations that—outside of the spousal relationship—do not immediately countenance permanence or fidelity or fruitfulness. Nor is the church in a good pastoral position to address those unions between same-sex couples that strive to be permanent, faithful, and fruitful. When we make desire the dominant motif in the Christ/church relationship, however, our assumption is that desire in itself is a good, regardless of the presence or absence of a sexual, genital, or marital context.

While an ecclesiology of desire imagines Christ and the church each longing for a closer, more perfect union with the other rather than simply resting in the possession of some state or condition of being married, what is at least as significant is that this ecclesiology of desire is arrived at inductively. If human desire is so much more widespread than desire in heterosexual marriage, as it surely is, then the human experience of desire that leads to the postulation of an ecclesiology of desire is also broader and deeper. The language will be of lover and beloved, which while obviously not excluding spousal unions goes beyond them, not only to other partnerships of different kinds, but also into all the realms of human activity in which desire plays a part. To provide just a couple of examples, there is desire—though usually nonsexual—in friendship, and there is desire—frequently nonsexual—in love of beauty.

If failure to have a positive response to human sexuality outside the traditional boundaries of heterosexual marriage is a major issue, it is certainly matched in importance by too much emphasis on eros. While this would commonly be the moment to suggest that eros must be balanced by the generous self-giving of *agape*, it might be more productive to give some attention instead to the third dimension of Christian love, *philia* or friendship. For a theology of friendship we might look at John's Gospel, Thomas Aquinas or Aelred of Rievaulx, the spirituality of Ignatius of Loyola, whose Jesuit companions then and now refer to one another as "friends in the Lord," or, indeed, to the Society of Friends themselves. Friendship both adds to and modifies our understanding of the role of desire in loving relationships. Indeed, friendship is an amalgam of altruism and egoism, of *agape* and eros. Friendship that is only friendship is usually if not always a realm where sexual desire is not present, but there is plenty of eros, just as there is in our desire for truth or our ambition to win the lottery. If friendship is something that we ought to look for and work for in our life partners, it is by no means guaranteed.

So perhaps we can say that an ecclesiology of the erotic that is not going to be hamstrung by the spousal metaphor might want to pay greater attention to the dynamics of *philia*. In friendship as friendship, there is eros without sexual passion and *agape* without deprivation. God's desire for us and our desire for God, theologically speaking, is driven by the dynamics of friendship rather than sexuality. The object, *pace* some of the more overheated mystics, is not possession of the loved one, which in any case always suspends desire and issues in the absence that will rekindle further desire, but delight in the loved one. God delights in the church and the church in God. If it is true friendship it is not possessive, it is not exclusive, and it wills the good of the other. Sometimes our friends will call us to task. Sometimes, perhaps most of the time, they are the only ones who will make us look directly into the mirror and see ourselves as we really are. This is only possible in a faithful mutual love that is free of the calculus of sexual desire. There really is something quite odd, in the end (isn't there?), about making sexual desire a consequence of the fall and then using the spousal metaphor for the relationship between Christ and the church. Surely the prelapsarian state should be the model for the church. Over its door should be the words of John's Gospel: "I do not call you servants any longer. . . . I have called you friends" (John 15:15).

In an ecclesiology of desire, what matters is the longing for more, for a closer union, for a better knowledge, for greater intimacy, and this can aid the search for balance between a focus on presence and a stress on absence. Frequently, as we noted earlier, the Catholic tradition's sacramentalism renders it susceptible to too emphatic a sense of possession and too much focus on presence. In contrary fashion, Protestant traditions seem not to enjoy divine presence except in the mode of eschatological hope, which is presence in the mode of (present) absence. However, the church is surely the space in which fidelity to hope is celebrated, whether sacramentally or not. Sacramental traditions have to see the Eucharist as a "foretaste of the heavenly kingdom," not "the thing itself," or they become complacent possessors. Traditions of "the Word" find in their assemblies not so much real presence in the bread and wine but presence nevertheless—perhaps equally real—in word and fellowship. Possession alone cancels desire. Desire alone denies possession. The union that we experience with Christ in sacrament or in word points forward to the eschaton. Our faith is our fidelity to hope, and desire is the engine of that fidelity.

Further Suggested Readings

Alison, James. *The Joy of Being Wrong: Original Sin through Easter Eyes.* New York: Crossroad, 1998. See esp. pp. 147–56.

Burrus, Virginia, and Catherine Keller, eds. *Toward a Theology of Eros: Transfiguring Passion at the Limits of Discipline.* New York: Fordham University Press, 2006.

D'Arcy, Martin. *The Mind and Heart of Love.* London: Faber & Faber, 1945.

De Rougemont, Denis. *Love in the Western World.* Princeton: Princeton University Press, 1983.

Lewis, C .S. *The Four Loves.* New York: Harcourt, 1991.

McGinn, Bernard. *The Presence of God: A History of Western Christian Mysticism.* Vol. 3: *The Flowering of Mysticism: Men and Women in the New Mysticism (1200–1350).* New York: Crossroad, 1998.

CHAPTER 16

*Sex in Heaven? Eschatological Eros
and the Resurrection of the Body*

Margaret D. Kamitsuka

IS THERE SEX IN HEAVEN? Given the antierotic tendencies of Christianity historically, one might assume a resounding "No!" Nevertheless, various scholars have recently investigated how important theological figures within the Christian tradition of the past (Augustine and Dante Alighieri) might be read as answering: "Maybe." In her article "Sex and the City (of God)," professor of historical theology Margaret Miles argues that Augustine's late-fourth-century accounts of bodily resurrection hold open the notion of what we moderns, living in the shadow of Freud, would call sexuality. Miles explains that Augustine rejected the notion of postresurrection sex because "sexual intercourse can only take place between mortal bodies" for the divinely ordained sole purpose of reproduction to perpetuate a mortal race, which would be moot in paradise where no one dies. Nevertheless, it is possible to read Augustine as suggesting that "a quality and value we name as 'sexuality' will be a feature of resurrected 'spiritual' bodies."[1] In a similar move, romance languages scholar Regina Psaki argues for the possibility of heavenly sexuality in Dante's *Divine Comedy*. Contrary to the consensus of scholars that Dante's romantic desires are purified and transformed during his assent through purgatory and the realms of paradise, Psaki points to the poem's "blatantly amorous language" and imagery. According to Psaki, Dante urges readers of *Paradiso* to imagine many divine unfathomable mysteries, including the possibility of "love that is no less sexual than blessed, no less erotic than salvific."[2] Miles and Psaki are not attributing to Augustine and Dante visions of an "eternal orgiastic empyrean"[3]; however, their scholarship does suggest provocative theological questions. If we are sexual beings in this life—sinfully and imperfectly—what would sexuality mean for resurrected bodies in the next? Should we expect perfect erotic happiness in heaven, and what would it entail?

The way we go about answering questions about eschatological eros, I suggest, reveals much about how we view sexuality and treat bodies in this life.[4] Eschatological questions like this, hence, are relevant because they are not just about the end times but are also very much about the here and now.[5] To help us think about heaven and the present, this essay brings together three very different types of discourse: the discourse of Christian philosophers debating about personal bodily resurrection;[6] the discourse of contemporary feminist and queer theologians debating whether resurrected bodies will be gendered and libidinous; and psychodynamic discourse about the nature of human sexuality.

For most Christian philosophy, the issue of what the blessed will be and "do" in heaven hinges on what logically follows from coming into the presence of God—for example, are physical pleasures congruent with or canceled out by the beatific vision? Despite (typically conservative) Christian philosophers' reticence to speak about sexual bodies, it is possible to extrapolate from their position on God's beneficence that resurrected bodies would, in theory, be allowed to experience erotic fulfillment. Current (more liberal) feminist and queer theologians approach the issue of eschatological eros very differently. They use discourse about gender and sexuality in heaven as eschatological verification for combating discrimination and affirming marginalized aspects of gender and sexuality on earth. That is, if one can make the theological case for God's inclusion in heaven of a particular gender or sexual identity, then it should be so in the Christian community in this life as well.

My position emerges by engaging in critical dialogue with these two above-mentioned groups, in light of feminist psychoanalyst and philosopher

Julia Kristeva's views on psychosexual development. From Christian philosophy I adopt the viewpoint that insists that we carry our individual embodied identities—including our memories—into heaven. The category of memory, when inflected psychoanalytically, brings into play theories of pre-Oedipal desires and pre-Oedipal wounds as a result of the infant's break from the maternal body (which Kristeva calls "abjection"). Christian philosophy deems that the blessed having natural bodily desires is congruent with the beatific vision. Over and above this affirmation of eschatological libido, my Kristevan psychoanalytic theological perspective insists that psychic wounds are not canceled out for the blessed in heaven.[7] I also argue that gendered and sexed identity is not canceled out in heaven—though my reasons differ from those put forth by the feminist and queer theologians who also espouse this view—in part, because I employ a poststructuralist approach that theorizes gendered and sexed identity as discursively constructed, not natural or God-ordained. If psychoanalysts like Kristeva are right, the path to healing psychic scars has to do with bringing the repressed wound to speech in the presence of a caring other. This is an intimate erotic experience that Kristeva calls *"jouissance."* The experience of jouissance, which may or may not involve genital sexual expressions, has roots in deep maternal pre-Oedipal connections.

My bringing together of theological, philosophical, and psychoanalytic elements to speculate on eros in heaven can only be eschatological imagining.[8] I am imagining multifaceted eschatological eros that would encompass perfect "narcissistic" (in nonmoral Freudian parlance) sexual gratification. Heavenly eros would also have to encompass the experience of an other-oriented eros—as yet, for most of us, deeply submerged in our consciousness—a perfect, healing, interpersonal jouissance.

RESURRECTED BODIES AND CHRISTIAN PHILOSOPHY

To set the stage for a Christian philosophical basis for sex in heaven, I will first give a brief overview of the nature of some debates on bodily resurrection. I will discuss two representative contrasting Christian philosophical views: (1) the position of those who affirm the notion of personal immortality but dispute that bodily eternal life is intelligible; and (2) the position of those who defend the intelligibility of bodily resurrection—a position that places divine intentionality at the center of the issue of resurrected bodies. It is important to note that sexuality is not only an unimportant factor in this literature but also is a conspicuous nonfactor in most of these debates.

Hence, it will be necessary to extrapolate a position on sexuality from these debates.

Representing the first position, John Morreall argues that only the soul lives in eternal blessedness and that the traditional Christian notion of bodily resurrection is rife with logical difficulties.[9] If one argues that at death the souls of the blessed go immediately to dwell with God and then receive their bodies back in the general resurrection, then this suggests that those souls' interim communion with God prior to the final resurrection was less than perfect. There have been several attempts to avoid this problem of a less-than-perfect period of communion with God. One might postulate that at death, a person's existence—body and soul—ends completely until the final resurrection when the person is divinely reconstituted. Many Christian philosophers find this to be an unsatisfactory position, and it has been dubbed the replica argument, since the reconstituted person sent to heaven (or hell) is not the same person who died but only a replica.[10] Philosophers argue against the replica proposal because of (1) ethical incongruity—that is, the notion that someone else would be reaping the rewards or paying the price for my deeds; and (2) theological incongruity—that is, while God has the power to reconstitute people after death, doing so would not be congruent with God's nature as "both creator and preserver of all existing contingent things." Continuous identity, from this perspective, is defined as having significant premortem and postresurrection "bodily similarities," so as to be recognizable as the same person, as well as "mental similarities"—namely, the "same memories, the same personality."[11]

Another way of avoiding the problems of the soul's interim existence is to postulate an instant body and soul resurrection upon death—a position that has more philosophical coherence but at the expense of undoing the traditional Christian notion of an eschatological bodily resurrection. Morreall argues that if one is willing to chip away at traditional Christian faith claims for the sake of philosophical intelligibility, then why not go all the way? If one begins with a definition of the beatific vision as a "direct experience of an imperceivable God," then bodies are completely superfluous. Not only would they not add anything, but "it is hard to understand how an embodied person enjoying the beatific vision would even know that he was embodied."[12]

How have Christian philosophers defended the traditional notion of eschatological bodily resurrection against views such as Morreall's? Richard F. Creel's "Happiness and Resurrection: A Reply to Morreall" serves as an example.[13] I will focus on how Creel takes issue with Morreall's position and how Creel's critique forms the basis (however unintentionally) for a Christian philosophical defense of sex in heaven. First, Creel finds that Morreall's definition of the beatific vision as "unsurpassable" happiness (which a resurrected body could not logically make any better) is misleading, because that definition does not distinguish between different possible kinds of happiness. Creel distinguishes between perfect happiness (defined as being "eternally completely satisfied") and unsurpassable happiness, which no creature, even the blessed in heaven, can achieve—only God can experience unsurpassability.[14] If blessedness is defined as perfect (rather than unsurpassable) happiness, there is conceptual room for a number of different heavenly experiences: different degrees of happiness of the saints as well as an increase of happiness after the final resurrection.

Having thus posited the notion of the beatific vision as perfect (rather than unsurpassable) happiness, Creel makes a second distinction between perfect happiness and pleasure. Pleasures, he explains, are bodily experiences that can never give us perfect happiness but can "enhance" or make a "worthwhile contribution to" the perfect happiness of the blessed in heaven. Creel points to Thomas Aquinas's claim that "when the body is reassumed [in the final resurrection] happiness will grow, not in depth but in extent."[15] The depth of happiness is determined by the soul's "vision" of God; however, physical experiences could affect the extent of the happiness of the saints after the final resurrection. That God would allow the blessed corporeal delights is a sign of "God's largesse."[16] Unlike in the mortal world, the saints in heaven would experience desire without frustration, discomfort, or suffering: "Being hungry or thirsty is not incompatible with being happy as long as we can readily secure good food or drink." This brings us to the third distinction Creel posits: between objects "enjoyed by perception or action."[17] Creel agrees with Morreall that the vision metaphor is apt for describing the saints' communion with God; corporeal action verbs are not appropriate metaphors to describe beatitude. Creel speculates that the blessed in heaven "could see and hear and hug and dance and sing. Surely such activities . . . would add to the flavour and fullness of even perfect happiness."[18] However, the actions of hearing, hugging, dancing, and singing, for Creel, apply to what the saints would do among themselves in heaven. One cannot dance with the immaterial God. Nevertheless, bodies in heaven would not be content merely to look at objects of delight. They would wish to touch, smell, taste, and so on. Thus, "because of the body [the saints would] have desires that could be satisfied only by action."[19] Heavenly happiness, according to Creel, must be comprised of more than just joys of perception. Heaven will also be a place of blessed actions, allowing for the experience of perfect "natural pleasures."[20]

So, what about sex? Creel answers obliquely: "Ambrosia anyone? If we are capable of such pleasures after the resurrection, I suggest that they will be of the nature of pure rather than mixed pleasures"—that is, not pleasures in which we are driven to partake and which cause us sadness or "discomfort" when left unfulfilled.[21] Even without Creel's reference to ambrosia, one can extrapolate a heavenly sexuality from the components of his argument for resurrection of the body: the saints in heaven can have different kinds and levels of beatitude; bodily experiences can enhance heavenly happiness; and acting upon bodily desires will be part of the heavenly experience of resurrected bodies. An extrapolated position on sex in heaven would go something like this. While they enjoy communing with God continuously, the saints experience bodily—including sexual—desires with various intensities. When a desire for sex becomes acute, the saints can move effectively to fulfill that natural bodily desire without the discomfort of interruptions or prolonged delay. Playing a bit with Creel's choice of language, I suggest that we can find here the basis for a "narcissistic" view of "libido" (to use psychoanalytic terminology that we will return to below). Without a great stretch of the imagination, the mention of bodies having the ability to move pleasurably, and without the discomfort caused by too much delay or deferral, suggests that resurrected bodies will reach pleasurable, including sexual, climaxes. This description of heavenly genital satisfaction seems to follow logically from Creel's premises.

We can now summarize the main points of various Christian philosophers' objections to arguments like Morreall's for disembodied immortality of the soul. Though it is within God's power to populate heaven with disembodied souls or with replicas, it goes against God's nature not to preserve continuous embodied individuals. Moreover, it is congruent with God's nature to grant resurrected persons enjoyment of physical pleasures, including sexual ones, along with the beatific vision. This discourse of eschatological eros revolves around Christian premises of God's nature as an omnipotent and benevolent creator and preserver.

When we turn to contemporary feminist and queer theological perspectives, we find a different discourse on eschatological eros—one that functions to verify gendered and sexual desires in this life by reading heaven's blessing back on our less-than-paradisiacal earthly existence.

FEMINIST AND QUEER DEBATES ON GENDER AND SEX IN HEAVEN

Any attempt to develop a feminist perspective on sex in heaven has to inquire into whether and to what extent gender assumptions are a factor contributing to one's views. There is no dearth of debate in contemporary feminist and queer writings on the question of gender identity. Not surprisingly, religious scholars are grouped on both sides of the gender-in-heaven issue—some claiming a gendered and others a genderless heaven. What may come as a surprise is that the pro and con divide on the question of gender in heaven does not lead to a similar divide on the question of sex in heaven. That is, some scholars who agree that there will be postresurrection gender differences disagree on whether those gendered bodies will have sexual desires in heaven.

Beth Jones and Ronald Long both argue from very different perspectives in favor of postresurrection gender differences.[22] Jones takes a christological starting point, positing that in Christ, God became human to bring peace and unity to our created goodness, which has become distorted and alienated by sin.[23] Redemption, thus defined for Jones, presupposes natural differences. What differences are intrinsic to our nature? First, we are created with a body and a soul. Jones argues (with Aquinas) that it is unnatural for the soul to be apart from the body; hence, at the final resurrection, the body will be reunited with the soul.[24] Eschatological spiritual blessedness thus includes our materiality. Another difference intrinsic to our created nature is that we are different sexes. Male and female is "God's natural intention for humanity."[25] In heaven, God will maintain this binary male-female sexed difference in order to show unity and peace without gender hierarchy. Jones begins with original created human nature, reads that forward onto the bodies of the saints, and then reads those sanctified bodies back onto the present so that eschatological hope will "transform our present bodily practices." Jones says little about sexuality and seems to take a conservative Augustinian position—that is, this-worldly sexual desire is linked to lust because of the fall. In heaven, "vice will be taken away . . . and nature preserved,"[26] meaning that the blessed will enjoy gendered bodily existence undisrupted by the lusty sexuality of this world.

Long takes a different tack, arguing for eschatological gender differences as a basis for his argument for robust sexual activity in heaven. As a gay man, Long affirms that "desire for other men is something that is sacred" and considers heavenly sex to be a kind of eschatological vindication of this deep human desire.[27] The sexual desire of which he speaks is not undifferentiated insofar as gender is concerned, since "what is 'sexy' is precisely the gender of the person involved, not simply their indiscriminate personhood." Heaven, he argues, would have to be a place of differentiated sexual attraction—a place marked by personal identity, familial recognition, and bodies "inflected by gender."[28] Desire is linked to gender, and gender is linked to bodies (with their complex interplay of hormones, genitalia, and so on). If there will be gay male bodies in proximity to gay male bodies in heaven, Long suggests, there will be gendered erotic desires.

Elizabeth Stuart has a very different philosophical starting point in making a case for a genderless and, presumably, sexless heaven. Relying on post-modern feminist philosopher Judith Butler's views about gender and sex as discursively constructed and "culturally negotiated,"[29] Stuart argues that in heaven, cultural constructions, inevitably distorted by sin, will be erased. The saint's eschatological genderless body is foreshadowed in baptism, when the believer becomes "an ecclesial person."[30] All cultural identity markers—gender, race, kinship, nationality—become relativized and "non-essential."[31] Theologically speaking, the baptized acquire—for all intents and purposes—a genderless body before God and within the church. Stuart thus sets out the eschatological basis for undercutting heteronormative discrimination against gays and lesbians in the church. Note, however, that she does not argue for the sacredness of nonheterosexual desire. Stuart decenters all human desires by insisting, with Augustine (and Jones), that human sexual desires are "disordered by sin."[32] No sexuality is pure or God-given. All believers must strive to bring their sexuality in line with what the church is called to be: one, holy, catholic, and apostolic. Stuart admires Gregory of Nyssa's view that the blessed in heaven will be transformed into a prelapsarian genderless state, purified of all sexed desires.[33] Stuart does not negate outright any possibility of sexual desire in heaven, but it looks unlikely for three reasons: (1) given the genderlessness of the saints, it would not resemble what we know about sexual desire in this world; (2) heaven is about the "perfection and fulfilment of desire in God" where human "[d]esire is refocused on the divine"; [34] and (3) as was the case with Mary and the resurrected Jesus in John's Gospel (20:17), for the saints in heaven "[a]ll clinging is ended" (in the Genesis 2:24 sense of a man clinging to his wife when the two become one flesh).[35]

While there are strengths in each of these three theologians' views, I also see problems. Jones's theological decision to make difference intrinsic to redemption is powerful and deserves theological attention in a world where differences (of race, religion, nationality, sexual orientation, and so on) are often subsumed under the identity of the group in power who then deigns to welcome (or not) those "others" who are different. The weakness in Jones's account is her insistence on the naturalness of binary male-female sex dif-

ference, based on orders of creation. Even though she states that her understanding of human nature is christologically based, she gives no specific
christological arguments for why sex differences must remain rather than
be erased in the eschaton. (Indeed, a strictly christological argument might
support the view that the blessed become male in the eschaton, which was a
popular patristic and medieval viewpoint.) Her prior assumption about God's
intention to create humanity as male and female orders her claim that God
redeems our intrinsic sexed identity as either male or female. I have noted
elsewhere the problematic aspects of appealing to a Genesis-based view of
binary maleness and femaleness, and I have argued for a more fluid, postmodern notion of gendered and sexed identity.[36] To make a postmodern case
for nonbinary sexed identity is not, as Jones worries, to obscure the body but,
rather, to allow all bodies and bodily performances to come into view and
work out their salvation with equal fear, trembling, and hope.

Long, on the other hand, claims that if we have bodies in the final
resurrection, we will have gendered awareness and, hence, desires will be
"triggered."[37] Nevertheless, he is like Jones philosophically (and unlike Stuart
and myself) because he disputes a postmodern, social constructivist approach
to bodies. Long argues for seemingly unavoidable, natural, gendered desires
that arise in human bodies in proximity to each other—including in heaven.
Long's argument is appealing because it lends eschatological verification to
the kind of sexual beings most of us experience ourselves to be in this world
where sexual desires just seem to pop up naturally. However, I do not think
he stands on solid ground when he blithely discounts postmodern views of
the person as "social constructionist extremism" and attributes the phenomenon of sexual arousal to "the effects of hormones."[38] I appreciate his judgment that male genital stirrings originate in a natural, biological realm; yet,
there is something undeniably cultural and discursive in his descriptions of
the erotics of arousal in gay men's rituals of "cruising" and dating.[39]

Stuart presses Butler's postmodern views about gender construction into
service when she calls into question all sexual desires in heaven. My tendencies toward a Butlerian, social constructivist view of how persons perform
their gendered and sexed identities lands me in Stuart's camp philosophically
and would seem to link me with her theologically regarding gender and sex
in heaven (*pace* Long). However, it is important to be clearer on the differences between theological and philosophical claims than I think Stuart is.
When she states the theological imperative that the church should approxi-
mate "life beyond gender" and expose the "non-ultimate nature" of "gender

scripts," these statements function as ecclesial directives.[40] These directives translate problematically into a metaphysical statement—that is, "ultimate, real gender nature exists outside of cultural scripts." Postmodern philosophers have argued extensively (and Stuart seems to agree) that ultimate or real human nature is not epistemically accessible to us. This may, in part, be why Stuart says that the postresurrection body is "essentially mysterious and beyond grasp."[41] If Stuart wants to go beyond apophatic theological statements such as this, while maintaining a coherent social constructivist position, however, she will have to grant that heaven—to the extent that it can be theorized at all—must be theorized as discursively structured for the saints whose gender is "performed."[42] Indeed, since Stuart makes the connection between prelapsarian and postresurrection communities, there is good reason to speak of the blessed performing their discursively constructed gendered and sexed identities in heaven, since the Adam and Eve narrative displays the social fabric within which their bodies and desires are mobilized in discursive interactions (Gen. 2:23; 3:2). My theological hope is that the transformed "spiritual" bodies of the blessed (1 Cor. 15:44) will be able to effect novel and nonhegemonic gendered and sexed performances.[43]

What would contribute to such a state of affairs in heaven? The remainder of this essay presents one answer to this question by engaging Julia Kristeva's psychoanalytic perspectives on the nature of human sexuality, especially its pre-Oedipal and Oedipal developments. I will propose the outlines of heavenly eros that encompass both the narcissistic gratification Creel implies and the healing of psychic wounds within the *jouissance* of other-focused maternal care.

ABJECTION, MELANCHOLY, AND MATERNAL *JOUISSANCE*

A Kristevan view of eschatological eros must take into account three central concepts from Kristeva's theories on psychosexual human development—abjection, melancholy, and maternal jouissance. These will be discussed against the backdrop of a brief sketch of the Freudian theory of infantile sexuality from which her views spring. There is, according to Freudian theorists, a "phallic monism" or "primacy" in early human sexual development, which means that both male and female sexualities become organized around the penis and what it comes to signify libidinally—namely, "narcissistic gratification."[44] This organization of male and female libido at the phallic stage is natural yet, also for that matter, problematic. Male and female eros in a phallic economy is, Freud concluded, "'derived from the capacity of the ego to satisfy some of its instinctual impulses auto-erotically'"; then, in later stages of development, the process "'passes over to objects which have been incorporated into the extended ego.'"[45] Whether autoerotic or erotic with a partner, the process of sexual satisfaction remains, from a Freudian perspective, essentially narcissistic.

Kristeva is in basic agreement with this theory—albeit with some important additions and emendations, based on her work on female sexuality. Freudian theory of phallic desire obscures, Kristeva contends, that we are all beings created out of ruptures, a fundamental "dynamic of splitting in two which makes my being an irreconciled being, a being of desire."[46] Abjection is the term Kristeva uses in her effort to emphasize the impact of the child's violent split from the maternal body at birth and the infant's subsequent gradual separation from the mother's body, which is the primary source of nurture, bonding, nourishment, pleasure, and nascent desire. Even prior to the child's self-awareness of himself or herself as separate from the mother, the child already has the ability intentionally to reach for and push away the breast of the pre-separate-object-mother. The mother is known as object only with the acquisition of language and symbolic thought at the Oedipal stage. Yet there remains, according to Freudian theory of the unconscious, "a deep well of memory" of that early quasi-borderless, maternal experience that cannot rise to the level of object but remains at the level of "primal repression."[47] Relegated to the "ashes of oblivion" of infantile psychosexual development, that repressed and jettisoned experience of borderlessness—now abjection—nevertheless imposes itself on the later autonomous subject. Even as adults, we continue to experience the effects of "what existed in the archaism of pre-objectal relations, in the immemorial violence with which a body becomes separated from another body in order to be."[48] Abjection may be experienced through somatic symptoms, for example, when our bodies are overtaken with experiences of nausea and disgust in the presence of borderless things—things that were inside of bodies that are expelled from bodies (excrement, blood, vomit). These encounters threaten us with the archaic inbetweenness out of which we journeyed with such distress, in order to become a separate and speaking subject.[49]

The subconscious eruption of abjection often manifests itself in melancholy. Melancholy is the term Kristeva uses to describe the mood and state of those suffering from the inability to cope with the largely unarticulated loss of the maternal and with assimilation into the symbolic, phallic world. Transition into the symbolic world of the father is easier for the male child who can identify with the bodily same father and find erotic substitutes for the maternal body. This transition is more difficult for the female child who, in abjecting the mother's body, in some way abjects her own. "The fundamental predicament . . . isn't the preservation of infantile emotional ambivalence felt toward the father in the phallic organization of the libido but that the loss of the mother can't be borne. The archaic mother is lost but the subject has failed to lose her."[50] The female subject carries around the "'living corpse'" of the maternal body and only with great difficulty is she able to overcome the abject mother.[51]

For Kristeva, the melancholic crisis of psychosexual development is captured metaphorically by the Narcissus figure from Greek mythology. The female subject who finds herself without adequate symbolic resources to express the loss of the archaic mother is caught in a narcissistic mute-ness, without the means to "bring the power of speech into [those] ostensibly nameless recesses of meaning."[52] Melancholy seems almost inevitable, because it is not as if we can bypass it: "For man and for woman the loss of the mother is a biological and psychic necessity, the first step on the way to becoming autonomous. Matricide is our vital necessity, the sine-qua-non condition of our individuation." When this matricidal drive process is hindered, what results is an "inversion on the self; the maternal object having been introjected, the depressive or melancholic putting to death of the self is what follows, instead of matricide. In order to protect mother I kill myself."[53] Those who have not faced and addressed this melancholy will, in their sexual encounters, only erotically defer the process of mourning the painful experience of maternal loss.

Maternal jouissance is one of the most controversial of Kristeva's categories. She has been accused of romantically exalting motherhood in reaction to her fellow Francophone theorist Simone de Beauvoir's critique of motherhood.[54] Other readers, rightly I think, argue that Kristeva is not promoting an essentialized motherhood but a kind of maternal function, which is distinct from actual motherhood and femaleness. "A representation of the mother as a subject-in-process, as an open subjectivity which contains alterity, sets up a model of autonomy . . . [and] suggests that the maternal operates as a function that, in principle, can be performed by both men and women."[55] From this perspective, we can read Kristeva as urging feminists to give more attention to experiences of the function of maternity and mothering. Functional mothering becomes a basis for a new ethics because this experience points to (even if it never unambiguously instantiates) a needed form of nonphallocratic love and pleasure—namely, the jouissance of tender care for an other: "the maternal body is in the position to transform the violence of eroticism . . . into tenderness."[56]

A woman in maternity (or anyone in a maternal function) has the possibility of cultivating a nonphallic, nonnarcissistic jouissance marked by an embrace of the alterity and otherness that pregnancy (or functional mothering) imposes upon her.[57] Speaking of her own experience of pregnancy, Kristeva writes: "My body is no longer mine, it doubles up, suffers, bleeds, catches cold. . . . As if what I had given birth to . . . [was] not willing to part from me, insisted on coming back, dwelled in me permanently."[58] Kristeva's elaboration of maternal jouissance, in part, comes from her personal experience but, again, need not be essentialized as literal motherhood. She envisions a desire that does not try to become one with the other—that is, the other "'incorporated into the extended [narcissistic] ego'"[59]—but accepts the alterity of the other. That the other does not, cannot, fulfill my desire leads me to the recognition that I remain a being of desire, not a satisfied being. Kristeva attempts to articulate the complexities of the maternal-child bodily connection, which she describes in one place starkly as a "demented jouissance."[60] That is, when spoken of in a phallic register, maternal pleasures may appear to be ravings and lunacies; however, when explored in more psychoanalytic (and also artistic) depth, one can, if not discover, then at least imagine an embodied experience of jouissance that gives one "the possibility—but not the certainty—of reaching out to the other."[61] Men and women especially miss out on maternal jouissance when they suppress the painful vestigal memory of the lost maternal body and "the jouissance that this body gave."[62] However much one may deny it, Kristeva reminds us, "a vestige of the mother can be found in every passionate relationship."[63]

If a vestige of the mother is part of human sexuality and if everyone's relationship with the maternal body is fraught with violence, abjection, and loss, can we hope for good sex in this life or the next? I submit that to begin to answer this question adequately, we need to rethink heavenly eros and happiness in a multifaceted theological and psychological way.

RETHINKING PERFECT HAPPINESS AND EROS

What is the meaning of perfect happiness if the blessed carry with them primal repressions and subconscious melancholy? Even if God grants the blessed who desire it the ability to achieve phallic gratification, how will they be perfectly happy if still affected—even if only in some deep layers of memory—by losses as violent as the break from the maternal body?

As we saw with Creel's discussion of resurrected bodies, if one defines perfect happiness distinct from unsurpassable happiness and allows for bodily pleasure to contribute to perfect happiness, one leaves room for eros to exist alongside the beatific vision. Creel thus contributes elements for a philosophical defense of heavenly sexual gratification—a very important message for the antierotic Christian tradition. We can speak of bodily pleasure contributing to perfect happiness in heaven because those acts would be sinless and never unpleasantly interrupted or deferred. If Kristeva is correct, however, there are not just physical impediments to perfect sex; there are psychic ones, too. Someone suffering from deep melancholy will likely (if not unavoidably) play out those psychic problems in sexual relationships, resulting in less-than-perfect erotic encounters. Though I am no psychoanalyst, the assumption here is that the most gratifying sex happens when one is not projecting one's psychic wounds onto one's partner, even unintentionally.

My contention that psychic wounds are carried over into the afterlife in resurrected bodies is based on the argument about memory, with memory interpreted psychoanalytically. Theologically, the blessed are sinless, but there is nothing definitive in the Christian tradition about them being free of all bodily impediments (as noted above, disability theologies suggest this). Abjection is not sin; it is a repression-turned-psychic-wound. We must avoid the banality of saying heavenly communion with God the loving Father or Mother compensates for the break with the maternal body. What is spirit cannot compensate for what has to do with psychosomatic scars—even if those scars are lodged in the repressed memories of the blessed. Unless we are willing to say that God wipes out memories of the blessed, then the blessed will carry with them their wounded unconscious.[64]

Kristeva, as a psychoanalyst, understandably proposes a psychoanalytic response to the ills of psychic suffering. In the ideal psychoanalytic process, "the speaking being opens up to and reposes in the other."[65] Kristeva thus provides an image to help us imagine a heavenly situation where sharing one's melancholy with a caring other becomes part of a journey toward pleasurable openness to the needs of others. From this perspective, the blessed in heaven would require interpersonal community and time to share deeply.[66] We can imagine this heaven as a place of healing "rebirth with and against abjection"—not a reentry into the womb but a willingness to "keep open the wound" of the maternal loss.[67] Freely mourning the loss of the maternal is rarely done in this life. The maternal body, with its fluid boundaries, is reencountered in every nauseous experience of abjection, and, for that reason, we are more apt to turn away and flee from it. This fright-and-flight response then gets played out in our most intimate sexual and emotional relationships. What if, in heaven, the immediate presence of the divine so infuses the blessed that they are able to share deep psychic wounds with each other and thus experience the eros of mutual maternal jouissance? Such eros would reverberate, we can imagine, to other interpersonal erotic pleasures, including phallic sex.

In this life, we mostly pass uneasily, guiltily, messily from one narcissistic sexual encounter to another. If we are lucky, we also catch glimpses of, or ourselves experience, an other-focused maternal *jouissance*. With reference to Kristeva's theories, we can theologically hypothesize an eschatological situation with resurrected bodies experiencing phallic narcissism unencumbered by any lingering psychic wounds. If we reflect theologically on these paradoxes, we may be able at least dimly to imagine what such eros would look (beatifically) like. The degree to which such eschatological imagining might bring the promise of well-being to the imaginer probably depends on the degree to which we are willing to bring to speech, now, with a caring other, our own repressed thoughts and unruly desires and to face the uncertainties and instabilities of who we are as embodied persons.

Further Suggested Readings

Davis, Stephen T., ed., *Death and Afterlife.* New York: St. Martin's, 1989.

Karras, Valerie A. "Eschatology." In *The Cambridge Companion to Feminist Theology,* ed. Susan Frank Parsons. Cambridge: Cambridge University Press, 2002.

Kristeva, Julia. *Powers of Horror: An Essay on Abjection.* Trans. Leon S. Roudiez. New York: Columbia University Press, 1982.

Oliver, Kelly. *Reading Kristeva: Unraveling the Double-bind.* Bloomington: Indiana University Press, 1993.

Walls, Jerry L., ed. *The Oxford Handbook on Eschatology.* New York: Oxford University Press, 2008.

CHAPTER 17

"Flesh That Dances": A Theology of Sexuality
and the Spirit in Toni Morrison's Beloved

Joy R. Bostic

When warm weather came, Baby Suggs, holy, followed by every
black man, woman and child who could make it through, took her great
heart to the Clearing. . . . In the heat of every Saturday afternoon, she sat
in the clearing while the people waited among the trees . . .

It started [this] way: laughing children, dancing men, crying women and
then it got mixed up. Women stopped crying and danced; men sat down and
cried; children danced, women laughed, children cried, until, exhausted and
riven, all and each lay about the clearing damp and gasping for breath. In
the silence that followed, Baby Suggs, holy, offered up to them her great
big heart . . .

"Here," she said, "in this here place, we flesh; flesh that weeps, laughs; flesh
that dances on bare feet in grass. Love it. Love it hard. Yonder they do not
love your flesh. . . . This is flesh I'm talking about here. Flesh that needs
to be loved. Feet that need to rest and to dance; backs that need support;
shoulders that need arms, strong arms I'm telling you . . ." Saying no more,
she stood up then and danced with her twisted hip the rest of what her heart
had to say while the others opened their mouths and gave her the music.
Long notes held until the four-part harmony was perfect enough for their
deeply loved flesh.

—*Toni Morrison,* Beloved[1]

The whole creation has been groaning in labor pains until now; and not only the creation, but we ourselves, who have the first fruits of the Spirit, groan inwardly while we wait for . . . the redemption of our bodies.

—*Romans* 8:22-23

In Toni Morrison's *Beloved*, Baby Suggs "offer[s] up . . . her great big heart" as members of the community gather together for a weekly ritual. The ritual locus is simply known as "the Clearing." The Clearing, an open space in the woods, serves as a place of refuge and solidarity. Black people who had escaped the violence of slavery would come to the Clearing to find solace, healing, and redemption. Baby Suggs, the "unchurched preacher," is herself an ex-slave who has fled north across the Ohio River to Cincinnati. Upon her arrival she takes up residence in the house at 124 Bluestone Road. Situated on the outskirts of the city, 124, as it is called, serves a vital function for the local African American community as well as for blacks passing through on their way farther north. The house is a site for discreet communications as well as for social and cultural exchange for both the local and transient members of Cincinnati's black community before and after the Civil War. Baby Suggs also plays a critical role in the community as a cultural medium and prophetic voice.[2] In the Clearing, she proclaims from her heart to black women, children, and men whose bodies have been used, abused, and violated: "here . . . in this here place, we flesh." Baby Suggs acknowledges and affirms the goodness of the flesh and the body and validates the need to love, touch, and celebrate black flesh. This need is justified by her cautionary words, "Yonder they do not love your flesh." Baby Suggs recognizes that historically the dominant culture has most often devalued and demonized black bodies. Within the context of a world culture shaped by a legacy of conquest—of land and of people—black bodies have often been reviled, and black sexuality and expressions of erotic power have been reduced to mere commodities available for exploitation and exchange. These distortions of black sexuality and the commodification of black bodies have given rise to violence against black people, particularly black women. As a result, both blacks and non-blacks have developed distorted perspectives on black sexuality and African American expressions of the erotic. Baby Suggs's prophetic ministry and the Clearing ritual provide a corrective to this historical inferiorization and its effects.

In this chapter, I explore the ways in which violence against and exploitation of black bodies, and black female bodies specifically, and the racist and sexist views used to justify this violence and exploitation have resulted in a historical and cultural debasement of black bodies, black female sexuality, and black erotic expressions.[3] This debasement has often led to internalized hatred, shame, and fear of the erotic, especially for African American females. Consequently, a profound disconnection often exists between the physical and spiritual self and between the self and other selves in community. Using Toni Morrison's *Beloved* as a source, I offer, in response, a constructive theology of sexuality and the spirit in dialogue with current womanist and feminist reflections on trinitarian pneumatology, or a theology of the Holy Spirit as part of the Trinity.[4] I engage womanist/feminist works that incorporate classical notions of *perichoresis*, a Greek term adopted by fourth-century C.E. Cappadocian theologians to describe the Trinity,[5] and notions of the dance of the divine to explicate the ways in which all of creation participates in the liberating work of the Holy Spirit. Focusing on Baby Suggs's sermon and the community ritual in the Clearing, I propose the Clearing as a prophetic, incarnational space in which decolonization and reclamation of the erotic can lead to a reconnection of body and spirit, liberation and celebration of black female sexual power, and a pneumatological revisioning of radical relationality and deeply loved flesh.

EROS AND ANGLO-COLONIAL DOMINATION

In drawing upon the Clearing as a metaphorical model for radical relationality and redemption of the erotic, it is necessary to begin by defining "erotic," for the word itself is often charged with negative connotations, especially for groups who hold ambivalent attitudes toward sex and the body. The work of black feminist poet and author Audre Lorde is instructive here. As Lorde suggests, "erotic" is often identified within Western culture with pornography and seamy "red light" districts.[6] This identification operates to separate the erotic from the spiritual and to render invisible the power dynamics involved within human sexual relationships. However, in her classic essay "Uses of the Erotic: The Erotic as Power," Lorde presents the erotic as a positive central organizing force for who we are as human beings and how we relate to one another. The erotic is the raw energy that consists of the swirling chaos of our deepest passions and feelings. It is the creative power that arises out of this chaotic, unruly mess that serves as the very assertion of life. Lorde argues that the key to women laying claim to the power of the erotic resides in their capacity to tap into these strong feelings, which represent people's deepest cravings and greatest joys. These feelings, cravings, and joys are sources of knowledge that inform erotic power. In this way, the erotic serves as an internal guide, an epistemological reservoir, if you will, that consistently points to an insistent "yes" that lies within. This "yes" affirms and celebrates the human passion for living, loving, working, and doing. It enables persons to engage one another deeply with a kind of fearlessness that allows for openness and profound joy despite the messy complexities that often characterize human living and relationality.

However, domination, external control, and exploitation lead to the misuse, distortion, and suppression of erotic power and its cultural expressions. Lorde rightly observes that domination is aided and abetted not only by the systematic regulation, control, and exploitation of the bodies and reproductive abilities of the marginalized but also by distorted constructions of the ways in which the bodies and sexualities of the oppressed are perceived. These distortions, and the concomitant co-optation of the erotic power of marginalized populations, act as deterrents to the individual and collective marshalling of the erotic as a force for resistance activity, counteragency, and identity making. Thus, the drive to distort cultural forms of erotic power manifested within marginalized cultures has been an integral part of the colonial domination and postcolonial mystification of human sexuality.

The mystification of human sexuality within Western culture begins with Christian tensions regarding notions of the erotic rooted in Hellenistic culture. Cultural fears associated with the erotic stem from its being associated with the chaotic, unruly stuff of messy, unrecognized, and unexpressed feelings. In Greek mythology, Eros is the offspring of Chaos. Gaia, also born of Chaos, personifies the earth and is a sibling of Eros. Thus, eros or passion, in its varied forms, is related to the earth. While there certainly were aspects of the Greek tradition that affirmed and celebrated eros, classical Western Christianity adopted elements of Greek philosophical traditions that reviled the chaotic and viewed passion and sexuality as related to chaos and, thus, as dangerous to the condition of the human soul. As such, expressions of eros were to be feared and controlled.[7] These antisexual elements within Western philosophical traditions were dependent upon a hierarchy of spirit/mind/soul (higher nature) over the body and its passions (lower nature). The body and sex were viewed as obstacles to the elevation of the soul. Moreover, from a male-centered, patriarchal point of view, women as well as female bodies and sexuality were often identified with the lower nature and held responsible for the sexual temptation of men. Thus, female sexuality needed to be controlled. This body/soul split along with the demonization of women's sexuality set the stage for imperial and colonial powers to justify the conquest of foreign lands and peoples, which were cast as wild and effeminate and, therefore, needed to be conquered and controlled by "masculine" forces in order to advance civilization.

In order for colonialism to thrive, colonial powers also had to develop and implement strategies by which they could support this rationale and, thus, exploit the land, cultures, bodies, and spiritualities of indigenous people. Christian traditions, interpretations, and doctrines provided some of the language, imagery, and concepts that helped to justify, even sanctify, colonial oppression. Anglo-Christians who settled in North America and pushed their way westward from the Atlantic to the Pacific Ocean, decimating indigenous cultures in their wake, were motivated by a religious fervor and sense of mission. For Anglo-Christians, North America was their promised land. They identified themselves with the Israelites and rationalized that just as God had chosen Israel, so God had chosen them to conquer the indigenous people and their gods and take over the land. It was argued that the indigenous people were not exercising dominion over the land, according to what was understood as the biblical mandate of Genesis 1:28, and so had lost their right to their own territories.[8] Anglo-Christians considered themselves to be better equipped to subdue and tame the North American wilderness in a productive manner.

Black Africans were enslaved to work the land, and the continent of Africa was itself exploited for its rich resources. Black women's bodies were used to satisfy the lusts of white men and their wombs were used to reproduce black labor.[9] In this way, the conquest and exploitation of black bodies and black sexuality was central to the rise of European colonial powers and the development of what would become the United States. Womanist theologian Kelly Brown Douglas, in her book *Sexuality and the Black Church*, writes:

> Black people have been absolutely critical to White economic power, initially as free labor and later as cheap labor. The ability to freely exploit Black bodies with relative impunity has been critical to the labor market. To that end, White culture has attacked Black sexuality as a means of dehumanizing Black men and women. Such dehumanization has made it easier to enslave people and to treat them as merely property and labor commodities rather than as human beings. . . . the best way to gain control of non-White people while protecting White hegemonic values has been to attack their sexuality.[10]

The imposition of these hegemonic values and the exploitation of Africa and Africans were further justified on religious and theological ground by the demonization of Africans as so-called immoral heathens. Those seen as heathens were also identified with the lower nature. They were considered primitive and savage and, like the land, needed to be domesticated. Black women were seen as even more morally dangerous; they were viewed as both animalistic and as temptresses. These moral assessments were not only applied to the individuals themselves but also to the cultural forms that expressed the collective memory, values, and identity of those conquered. Most Europeans viewed African cultural values, rituals, and expressions as antithetical to good Christian virtues.[11]

African ways of life were suppressed through coercive measures that included hegemonic religious rhetoric, torture and violence, destruction of social structures, and physical displacement. Womanist theologian Delores Williams refers to this process as a "Western assault upon the spirits of nature."[12] Captured Africans were limited in their participation or prohibited altogether from engaging in cultural forms and expressions such as dancing, drumming, corporate language, and so on. These forms and expressions had historically served as integral aspects of ritual performance and social interactions that allowed for the development and assertion of individual and collective identity, values, and creativity. Most of the traditional cultures in West Africa (which served as the geographical genesis for much of the African slave trade) not only affirmed the body as an integral part of identity and the self but also believed the body to be at the heart of communal relationships—relationships between human beings and the divine and among human beings themselves. For example, in West African traditions, dance was and is a vital part of the social and spiritual lives of the community. Human bodies serve as instruments of divine communication through gesture and other forms of movement. Moreover, sensuality and sexuality are considered normative and important aspects of human life.[13] Literary critic Carol Henderson describes the intended consequence of the Anglo-colonial limitations and prohibitions of these African cultural forms as the "immoral and socially sanctioned disassembling of the African American person, body and soul."[14]

SLAVERY AND SUPPRESSION
OF THE EROTIC IN *BELOVED*

In *Beloved*, the gathered community consists of women, men, and children whose bodies had been brutalized and who had endured individually and collectively the disassembling effects of slavery and colonization. As a coping strategy, members of the community long ago learned to suppress their feelings and to eschew strong attachment to lovers, children, parents, and siblings who might be sold away at any time or raped, beaten, tortured, or killed right in front of them. They or their ancestors had been taken from their homeland and forced to work the land of another. The multiple alienations black people suffered during slavery are especially demonstrated in the stories of Morrison's female characters. Baby Suggs is a primary example. She is well acquainted with the loss and alienation antebellum blacks faced. She comments there is not a black household in the country that is not "packed to its rafters" with grief due to the painful memories of lost loved ones. Baby Suggs had herself given birth to eight children. All of them were either sold away or escaped from slavery. Her son Halle, Sethe's husband, is the last of her children with whom Baby Suggs hopes to reunite. She deals with her loss by suppressing their memories. Sethe, who grew up on the Sweet Home plantation with Halle, Paul D., and the other "Sweet Home men" has few memories of her own mother not because she had attempted to suppress them but because she had so little contact with her mother. Sethe does remember that her mother still spoke her native African language. Sethe is told stories about how her mother had come to the Americas "from the sea" and had endured the Middle Passage.[15] She was raped multiple times and impregnated by one of her white male captors and subsequently by white slaveholders.

According to an older slave who is from the same African village as Sethe's mother, she "threw away" the babies who were products of these rapes. Sethe, who is the offspring of a union between her mother and a black man her mother had chosen, is the only child Sethe's mother kept. After nursing Sethe for only two to three weeks, Sethe's mother is put immediately back to work in the rice fields where she toils from sunup to sundown. Her life of hard labor is cut short when she is hanged. Her body is so mutilated Sethe cannot recognize her. As a young girl, Sethe does not understand the significance of these events. However, as an adult she begins to feel deep-seated anger even though she never quite knows where to direct her rage. Sethe witnesses the ways in which black women's bodies are easily violated and abused. She learns that black women are used and discarded quite easily. She becomes enraged at the conditions under which enslaved women are forced to live. At the same time, Sethe also understands that even though black women are limited in their choices, they can still exercise agency although the consequences in either case would likely be great.

Despite the cruel and violent scenes Sethe experienced as a child, life on Sweet Home plantation is, at least initially, more humane for her and the Sweet Home men. However, under the iron hand of a new slave master, called "schoolteacher," conditions worsen for the slaves, and most of the men are sold away. In response to the increasingly cruel conditions on the plantation, Sethe and Halle plan to escape with their two sons, a daughter Sethe is still nursing, and a baby on the way. On the day of the planned escape, Sethe, who has already sent her children ahead with other slaves heading north, is confronted by schoolteacher's two young sons. While schoolteacher "observe[s]" and takes notes, the boys attack and sexually violate the pregnant and nursing Sethe. Though Halle witnesses the horrific attack, he is powerless to stop it. As a result, he suffers a mental breakdown. After Sethe tells the mistress what the boys had done, schoolteacher orders the boys to whip her until what Morrison describes as a "chokeberry tree" of scars opens up on her back. Beaten and humiliated, Sethe waits for Halle as long as she can. When he does not appear she leaves, reunites with her children, and heads to the Ohio River.

These and other stories Morrison tells of violence, exploitation, and alienation compel the reader to identify with the realities of black life during and after slavery. The stories of physical and sexual assaults and back-breaking work particularly speak to the physical vulnerability of black women and the power white males exercised over black women's bodies, labor, and reproductive capacities. The precarious state of the black people portrayed in Morrison's novel gives rise to mental breakdown, internalized rage, trauma, and the suppression of painful memories and feelings of affection for loved ones. Consequently, they experience spiritual and physical disruption and displacement, which is displayed, for example, in Sethe's character. When Sethe relays the story about the sexual attack to Paul D., she repeats the phrase "they took my milk."[16] While Paul D. focuses on the horror of such an assault on a pregnant woman, Sethe agonizes over the way in which the assault compromises her ability to care for her baby girl. What this violating act reinforces in Sethe is the reality that she herself is vulnerable to white male power and her vulnerability compromises her power to protect and provide for her children. The inabilities of black women and men to protect, provide for, and freely associate with other black relatives, lovers, and friends creates a kind of dissonance between their own sense of humanity and the society's treatment of them.

Black people's recognition of their physical vulnerability and the power of whites to exert control through coercion and brute force over the bodies, creative capacities, and lives of black people resulted in spiritual and psychological alienation. Black women's capacity to work, reproduce, and form relationships was controlled and co-opted by white men to be used in service of their families. Lorde refers to this usurpation of women's reproductive and creative powers as being "psychically milked."[17] In these instances, the oppressor maintains access to the oppressed, albeit "at a distance," and uses their creative capacities in service to the oppressors' needs. Thus, slaveholders and slaveholder-identified Anglos often held on to morally restrictive notions about sex, family, and the body and, at the same time, rationalized the use and violation of black bodies and black sexuality.[18] Whites objectified and commodified black bodies and black sexuality and, in so doing, projected their own sexual proclivities, desires, and fears onto African American women, children, and men.

This reality led to the suppression of the varied forms of the erotic and the internalization of rage and fear in response to alienation, psychological and physical trauma, and limited access to power. In Sethe, Morrison presents a character whose internalized rage, fear, and powerlessness gets played out in death-dealing ways. When schoolteacher arrives at 124 to take Sethe and her children back with him, Sethe takes control the only way she knows how—she kills her daughter and attempts to kill her other children rather than allow the slave master to possess them. The suppressed rage and memories of pain and loss are literally manifested in the flesh as Beloved, the baby ghost of Sethe's dead child, appears as a young woman after Paul D., one of the Sweet Home men, comes to 124. When Paul D. arrives, he and Sethe struggle with conflicted feelings of sexual needs and desire and the fear of past memories and future attachment. Sethe and many other members of the community have for so long suppressed the capacity to feel fully; they often deny themselves the joy and satisfaction of physical pleasure and sensuality and resist physical and emotional attachment to family and community members. Henderson argues that Beloved's appearance represents the embodiment of human yearning, of speaking the "unspeakable" in the flesh. This embodiment "facilitates reconciliation of body and spirit making public the private longings of a people."[19]

THE CLEARING AS A COMMUNAL SPACE FOR HEALING

In spite of the ugly and horrific experience of slavery and continued racism, sexism, and dehumanization, black people who fought for and gained their freedom (and a relatively greater control over their bodies and creative capacities) sought to build and rebuild lives, families, and community bonds long denied them. Toward these ends, members of the community also employed and developed cultural forms, rituals, and strategies in order to counteract the varied alienations they suffered and establish an individual and collective cohesiveness. In Beloved, the Clearing serves as a locale for the working out of some of these remedies. It is a communal site for regeneration and reclamation of selves fractured by the violence of oppression and by the resulting coping strategies of self-denial and self-deprecation. It is a space that allows for reclamation of the human spirit that has been repressed. As a ceremonial or ritual space, the Clearing, and the sacred space Baby Suggs's sermon creates, serve as loci for the reconfiguration, performance, and celebration of individual and collective identity. Henderson describes this performance as moving those gathered through revolutions of emotional and physical tensions that ultimately lead to a healing of the mind/body/spirit split initiated through the coercive and dehumanizing measures of imperial power:

> The ceremonial rituals performed in these places that connect character to space/place in each instance point up the cycle of repression and oppression associated with each character's attempt to reconcile the self with the self. These efforts reinscribe the textures of flesh, unearthing the fundamental codes that hinder the process of resolution between mind/body and flesh/spirit.[20]

In serving as a site for the performance of cultural and ritual forms, the Clearing functions as a kind of hush harbor. Hush harbors were clearings in the woods, for example, where blacks would gather together away from the watchful eye of the slave master or white officials to meet and connect with the sacred. In her essay "The Erotic in Contemporary Black Women's Writings," womanist theologian Karen Baker-Fletcher describes the hush harbor in relationship to sexuality and the erotic as a sacred place marked by boundaries. These boundaries are demarcations of the lines between "peace and violence, life and death, healing and sickness, freedom and captivity, love and hate."[21] For Baker-Fletcher, the hush harbor is metaphorical space that is safe and liberating and that enables community members to relate to the sacred and others in the community in authentic ways. For community members in Morrison's *Beloved*, the Clearing offers direct connection to African cultural memories. Within this ritual space dance functions as the bridge of embodiment "that speaks the unspeakable in rhyme and rhythm so that flesh and spirit become one."[22] Moreover, tears and laughter promote release of pain and give permission to exercise the capacity to feel deeply and fully again, to let loose passion long suppressed. Even as they allowed for liberating action that helped to release pent up anger and passion, however, these Clearing spaces or hush harbors also established boundaries. These boundaries not only shielded the participants from intrusion from debilitating outside forces but also allowed for the exercise of powerful acts of resistance that enabled participants to experience freedom while guarding against annihilation or the complete descent into chaos.

Within the context of the Clearing, Baby Suggs serves not only as a prophetic voice but also a healing presence. She assists the community in its work of establishing safe space as well as the appropriate boundaries that enable the community to exercise freedom and bring community wholeness and justice. Baby Suggs's ministerial role as an unchurched preacher is a departure from traditional roles of clerics sanctioned by institutional bodies. Historically, many of these traditional clerics focused upon "prohibitive forms of morality and spirituality" as well as theological concepts that assume a "separation of flesh and soul."[23] Instead, Baby Suggs's prayer calls the members of the community to "reconnect the flesh" not only to the individual's soul but to what Henderson refers to as "the essence of the ancestral soul" that has been shattered by the blows of centuries of oppression. Henderson describes Baby Suggs as a community activist, spiritual guide, and priestess who facilitates the work of healing by acknowledging "the wounds of the flesh" and by reconnecting the community to its collective memories.[24]

> In re-membering the body one part at a time, Baby Suggs calls forth a complete being that counters the dismembered self created in chattel bondage. In this way, she creates a shared communal experience for the healing of personal pain, whether self-inflicted or genealogically begotten. "Call and response" becomes a collaborative venture in this instance, as those who have been silenced by social fear or intimidation are empowered to "speak" in a language that allows them to make the emotional transition from seeing themselves as objects to seeing themselves as subjects. Moreover, speech itself is rewritten in this space, for participants laugh, cry and sing, and these utterances become their form of communication. These gestures are not empty expressions of protest, but they are liberating acts of empowerment.[25]

Baby Suggs understands the ways in which social fear, intimidation, and shaming were used against black women, particularly with respect to their sexuality to maintain their status as sexual objects. In conversations with her granddaughter Denver, Baby Suggs talks about the ways in which whites and blacks "look down" upon black women who embrace their sexuality and celebrate sensual pleasure. Baby Suggs states: "Slaves not supposed to have pleasurable feelings of their own; their bodies not supposed to be like that, but they have to have as many children as they can to please whoever owned them." Baby Suggs recognizes the cultural stigma attached to black women who embrace the erotic and dare to feel "pleasure deep down." She teaches Denver to reject these cultural impositions and encourages her to assert herself as a sexual subject by always listening to and loving her own body.[26]

SEXUALITY AND THE DANCE OF THE SPIRIT

In contemporary culture, many Christians continue to believe that bodies and human sexuality are at war with who Christians aspire to be spiritually. There is fear and suspicion of the erotic, because in the history of the dominant Western culture, sex and the erotic are often depicted in violent and objectifying ways. This exploitation of sexuality causes many women, particularly women within marginalized cultures, to be protective of their sexuality. The problem is not sexuality and the erotic, in and of themselves; rather, sexuality and the erotic are often presented as disconnected from sacred spirit. Many Christian churches contribute to the problem by primarily addressing sexuality in prohibitive and shaming ways, leaving a void regarding how people can live out their sexualities in concert with their religious convictions. This separation of sexuality from spirituality results in alienation and hinders people from viewing sexuality positively. There are two possible resources for African Americans to draw from for revisioning sexuality and spirituality: one is indigenous and one is doctrinal.

The legacy of colonization greatly compromises the ability of individuals and communities to imagine sexuality and the erotic differently. Nevertheless, marginalized communities that have internalized this legacy of colonization also carry cultural values, traditions, and memories arising out of their own nondualistic religious and cultural heritages. Tension exists within these communities because of the clash between indigenous and Western antierotic cultural norms. For Christianized Latin Americans, Native Americans, and African Americans shaped by traditional religious and cultural worldviews as a legacy of colonization, indigenous practices and adaptations continue to be present. These indigenous worldviews and practices have been so demonized by Western culture and by the Christian church itself that marginalized communities continue to struggle with internal conflict over the value of their own ancestral traditions. Even though members of these communities may maintain certain non-Western practices, they may not be able to reconcile these practices liturgically or theologically with Western Christianity.

For example, in African-based spirituality, the boundaries between the invisible and the visible, the spiritual and the material, the living and the dead, are not rigid; they are quite fluid. Past, present, and future come together in a particular moment when it comes to how one thinks of one's identity and one's destiny. While one has the power to make choices regarding one's destiny, one is never isolated because the ancestors are in attendance. The spirits become incarnate in the midst of community; indeed, members of the community embody the spirits. The body, sexuality, and sensuality are affirmed as good. They, like everything else in our concrete reality, take on a sense of beauty and power that is rooted in spirit.[27]

While many African American Christian churches remain ambivalent if not antagonistic toward many aspects of classical African spiritualities, there are many ways in which these churches act out this sense of beauty and power that may provide linkages between sexuality and what they would call the Holy Spirit. In black worship the body, though still circumscribed in some ways (constricted clothing, the narrow confines of wooden pews, etc.), is very present in the rocking and swaying of the congregants, the marching of ushers, and the clapping of hands and tapping of feet. Women with ample bodies strut with confidence, maintaining a sense of spiritual humility yet expressing the power of their womanhood. Men dance coolly or with absolute abandon. Men, women, and children might "catch the spirit," and with ecstatic convulsions the body is liberated from the pain that has been housed there. The preacher might grip the pulpit or run up and down the aisle in such a manner that "the Word" truly becomes incarnate and the present, past, and future converge in that one moment of ecstasy. In the tradition of call and response, someone might simply wave her or his hand to acknowledge the agreement of the whole self to what is taking place. In these ways, African Americans rearticulate Christian spirituality through the force of their own embodied power.

The sounds of music, the perfume scents, and meticulous dress all contribute to a space of sensual beauty where the embodiment of spirit and the expression of embodied spirituality are highly valued and celebrated as a part of African American spiritual practice. These practices of embodiment rooted in the cultural idioms of African American life can enable persons to both unearth colonizing notions of sexuality, as Henderson suggests, and to reclaim indigenous ways of being and doing.

Feminists such as Molly Marshall and womanists such as Baker-Fletcher draw upon the classical concept of *perichoresis* within a trinitarian pneumatology to capture the ways in which the Holy Spirit enables human beings to participate in the divine work of healing and redemption. It is this notion of *perichoresis* that can provide a doctrinal resource for a revised understanding of sexuality and the spirituality. Marshall argues how she and other feminists have contributed to the recovery of notions of the third person of the Trinity in ways that counter patriarchal concepts of God.[28] The concept of *perichoresis* invites an image of the trinitarian God as a holy company dancing in a mutual, interanimating, participatory relationality that is not insular but pours itself out not only onto and into human beings but also upon and within all of creation so that the whole of life participates in the divine dance of communion. The language of *perichoresis* suggests a God that makes room for all members of the divine and created community.[29]

Baker-Fletcher employs the language of dance in conjunction with the Trinity to counter patriarchal, white supremacist as well as heterosexist notions of the divine.[30] She argues that in the Cappadocian church's view of the Trinity, God was "understood as three relations . . . in one being."[31] Drawing upon the Cappadocian notion of *perichoresis* and God's relationality within a womanist framework, Baker-Fletcher offers a view of the Trinity as the relationship of three dancers or agents participating in "one dynamic dance."[32] She argues that an emphasis on the relationship of three dynamic agents, rather than on the traditional static identifications of the three persons of the Trinity as God the Father, God the Son, and God the Holy Spirit, makes room for a variety of metaphors for God.[33] The use of diverse metaphors for divinity undermines the traditional monopoly of male-dominated, hierarchical images that have often presented a view of God as a white male patriarch. While affirming the need for multiple metaphors for the divine, Baker-Fletcher ultimately recognizes God, the Trinity, as a spirit. The Holy Spirit is the agent of the Trinity that "empowers and encourages" not only the dance among the agents of the Trinity, but also the divine dance with all of creation.[34] What the classical tradition refers to as the dance of the Trinity is for her, then, the dance of the spirit. Baker-Fletcher draws upon the image of the dancing Trinity to reflect not only upon the role of the spirit as the power of divine creativity in the world but also the role that concrete dance plays in healing.[35]

According to Baker-Fletcher, the "word *dance* . . . refers to the dynamic, ongoing movement of God in creation as God continuously creates and recreates, making all things new. God, who is spirit, moves creation to literally and metaphorically dance."[36] The celebration and movement of bodies in the congregations of people of color is a response to the creative and redemptive work of God as well as to the world itself. This response, which involves both singing and dancing in the spirit, reflects the dynamic, mutual, and ongoing relationship between God and the world and reflects the symbiotic relationship between creation and the divine and among members of the created community. The embodiment of the Holy Spirit, the third person of the Trinity, in dancing and singing bodies in the world gives rise to spirit, the power generated from sharing and giving within community. This practice of embodiment brings about healing and transformation:

> The Holy Spirit inspires the dance of God, calling all to participate in the dance of divine love, creativity, healing, justice and renewal. Healing is contagious. It is something that those who have experienced healing share with others. . . . They literally take heart and commit their lives to receiving and participating in the grace of divine healing.[37]

This kind of embodied spiritual practice is expressed in the scene at the Clearing. The ritual in the Clearing can serve as a site for theological reflection on the dance of the Holy Spirit and the created community's giving and sharing of spirit by way of its own cultural productions.[38] Through a collective performance of embodiment, participants in Clearing rituals share in a dynamic, symbiotic relationship that enables them to confront the wounds of the past and experience release, transformation, and liberation.

PROPHETIC, EROTIC JUSTICE

If Christian churches are to heal the wounds of oppression related to sexuality and the body, then it is important to provide the kind of leadership and to create the kind of space (theological and liturgical) in which members of Christian communities can work together to develop and live out a liberative theology of sexuality and the spirit. Baby Suggs's role as prophetic voice and cultural medium provides cues for such leadership. A liberative theology of sexuality and the spirit would involve bringing about what womanist ethicist Katie Cannon refers to as "erotic justice."[39] Erotic justice calls for individuals and communities—marginalized and privileged—to deconstruct notions of the body, sex, and sexuality that have been informed by oppressive ideologies concerning race, gender, and power. In addition, erotic justice calls for affirmations and strategies that enable members of the community to freely exercise a spirituality that is embodied in order to realize and reclaim their erotic power. It is critical that community members are enabled to reimagine who they are as spiritual and sexual beings. This in turn calls for a kind of conversion that is holistic and justice oriented.

Oftentimes when Christians speak of conversion they limit its meaning to an assent to a belief in a Jesus who is detached from the sociopolitical realities of domination and oppression. The struggle to bring about healing and liberation of the oppressed was central to the ministry of Jesus. This is what made his ministry prophetic. Although certain kinds of moral or personal behaviors can be indications of conversion experiences, focusing on personal morality is too narrow of an approach to bring about holistic, liberating change. What is needed to reconcile sexuality and the spirit is a literal breakthrough in cultural consciousness and spiritual worldview. This means that those once influenced by oppressive worldviews no longer see themselves, the world, and one another through the eyes of the colonizer. Theologies of domination and their underlying dichotomies of mind/body, spirit/material, black/white, male/female are rejected so that these categories no longer hold their power as normative, indeed as sanctified, categories by which human beings order the world and their relationships. This decolonization of the mind and the spirit leads to decolonization of the body. As persons experience this process of transformation, they are also compelled to evaluate the ways in which they understand and treat their own and others' bodies. In other words, members of the community are motivated actively to live out this transformation in and through the flesh. This process of decolonization only takes on significant meaning when it is embodied.

Again, Baby Suggs's ministerial role proves instructive here. Rather than focusing upon moral condemnation for individual choices, she confronts the gathered community with their own sociohistorical reality and challenges them to reconfigure that reality and imagine something more. For the Christian context, I am calling this something more the "prophetic church." The prophetic church is not limited by denominational bounds or local church affiliation and is not housed in a particular building or temple. Rather, it is the body of Christ as each of its members works together to bring about God's "kin-dom."[40] Individual prophetic churches are called to institutional accountability, both in their African and Euro-American expressions, to those who are marginalized in society. They are called to reject doctrines and traditions that stand in the way of healing and liberation and to create safe, sacred space in which members of the body come together to work out the meaning of erotic justice in light of their understanding of a loving, gracious, and just God. These churches can serve as Clearing sites as they facilitate processes of decolonization that liberate persons to affirm the flesh and to dance in the spirit.

Baby Suggs refuses to engage in condemnation talk to a community of persons who are already devalued by society and struggling with their own self-worth but encourages them to listen to and love their bodies. Similarly, prophetic decolonizing churches can empower persons by affirming human sexuality as a gift and by enabling faith communities to explore the possibilities of how they can move beyond dualisms and alienation of body and spirit and live life as whole sexual human beings. How can this be done? First of all, churches can try to identify and name those practices and values of nondualistic traditions that are part of their members' cultural legacies. In conjunction with this process of identifying and naming, church communities can work together to build theological frameworks and faith language that can be inclusive of practices and values that affirm sexuality and erotic expression.

This call to be the prophetic church is not only a call to African American Christians and black churches, it is also a call to white Christians and predominantly white churches to work to deconstruct and eradicate views of the erotic and sexuality both in the churches and in the wider society that contribute to the objectification, commodification, and consumption of black erotic power and sexuality. Moreover, it is crucial that white Christians continue to critique and deconstruct their cultural representations of the sacred, bodies, and sexuality rooted in European cultures and histories—representations that have been assumed to be normative for all ethnic and racial groups or assumed to be the only divinely sanctioned expressions of Christian spirituality.

CONCLUSION

Baby Suggs and the Clearing ritual serve as powerful models for the ways in which the created community can participate with the holy company in a mutual, interanimating, participatory dance of radical relationality that brings about healing, justice, and transformation. Within the sacred boundaries of the Clearing, participants are invited to imagine their own freedom: freedom from condemnation and internalized oppression, freedom to love themselves and one another, and freedom to embrace their whole selves. Within the context of the Clearing, oppressed marginalized communities are empowered to exorcise the demons of internalized oppression and to celebrate the beauty and sacredness of flesh. The Clearing represents a site of redemption. Men, women, and children—whose flesh, whose bodies have been exploited, abused, even demonized by a church and a culture in which patriarchy and white supremacy are considered normative—are cleansed by the shedding of tears, healed through the sharing of laughter, and liberated as they exorcise all of the pent-up anger, pain, and frustration through the unfettered, unrestrained movement of their bodies.

In serving as a Clearing, a site of redemption, prophetic decolonizing churches can provide opportunities for believers to move beyond talking about sexuality in terms of sin and condemnation and imagine a community in which persons are sexually whole. In embracing eros, individuals and communities embrace the incarnation, not only in its historical moment when the "Word" was made flesh in the person of Jesus of Nazareth but also in the sense in which the Holy Spirit is made flesh in and embodied through the lives of those struggling, working, and loving every day. To deny the erotic is to deny the incarnation itself and perpetuate the death-dealing effects of systemic evil. To affirm the erotic is to affirm God's creation of human beings made of flesh and enlivened by spirit, who are called to seek loving, just, and mutual relationships with the rest of God's creations.

In a liberating theology of sexuality and the spirit, the erotic is at the center of human life and human aspirations. To be alienated from this source of creativity and passion, this clarifying agent in the construction of identity, this impetus for connection is to be disconnected from the self, from others, and from God. When persons embrace who they are as sexual beings, as animated spirit-filled flesh, they are empowered to reject oppressive notions of sexuality and spirituality. When women and men refuse to conform to the dictates of systemic evil, they are cleansed. A clearing opens. They are enabled to see God's vision of the whole creation and recognize that the human body is joined with the Holy Spirit and that sexuality pervades the whole of human lives and is a means by which persons experience connection with other human beings and with life and by which they are healed.

The prophetic church as Clearing represents a safe harbor, a sanctuary in which everybody is included, regardless of race, gender, age, orientation, or ability. It is participatory space, where everyone is joining together in creating healing, wholeness, and liberation. The church as Clearing becomes incarnational space as participants dance in the spirit and provide holy harmonies that bear each other up. It is a space where the flesh is deeply loved, where the erotic, the "yes" inside of each and every one, is fully affirmed. Within these kinds of spaces, prophetic, decolonizing church communities can facilitate healing by creating and expanding the Clearing space to make room for others in the dance of the spirit. In the final analysis, the healing and redemptive work of the Clearing demands that at some point all talk ceases, for the Word becomes flesh and lives. Just like Baby Suggs, members of the prophetic church community rise up and dance the rest of what the heart has to say!

Further Suggested Readings

Baker-Fletcher, Karen. *Dancing with God: The Trinity from a Womanist Perspective.* St. Louis: Chalice, 2006.

Brown Douglas, Kelly. *Sexuality and the Black Church.* Maryknoll, N.Y.: Orbis, 1999.

Cannon, Katie Geneva. *Black Womanist Ethics.* Atlanta: Scholars, 1988.

―――. *Katie's Canon: Womanism and the Soul of the Black Community.* New York: Continuum, 1995.

Phillips, Layli, ed. *The Womanist Reader.* New York: Routledge, 2006.

Pinn, Anthony B., and Dwight N. Hopkins, eds. *Loving the Body: Black Religious Studies and the Erotic.* New York: Palgrave Macmillan, 2004.

Afterword

Serene Jones

I HAD THE PRIVILEGE of being present at this book's beginning: a Workgroup on Constructive Theology conference convened in Nashville several years ago.[1] Fifty theologians from around the country had gathered, as we do every year, to wrestle with topics pertinent to present-day life. That year, the provocative title of our meeting was "Sex as a Daily Practice." After our understandable (for many of us, middle-aged) chuckles died down, we began talking about this issue with a level of honesty and seriousness that is rare in the theological academy and church today. We were motivated not only by our own varied life experiences but even more by the painfully honest questions some of us have gotten from our students: Should I have sex with so and so? Am I a virgin if I've had oral sex? Can I become a virgin again? Should I hook up? Should I be abstinent if I love Jesus? Is it okay to not know the person with whom you spend the night? Is it okay to like sex? Or not to? Can I love a boy *and* love a girl? At the same time? And same place?

I'm really lonely, really. Very lonely. Can you help? I want to have sex. I don't want to have sex. What is sex? What does God think about all this? Can you give me some guidance, please?

These student questions were both heart wrenching and matter-of-fact, and they were urgently asked, as quite possibly questions about sex have always been. Vulnerable passions provoke vulnerable passions. With their earnest questions in hand, we set before ourselves the very practical task of trying to address sex concretely and theologically at the same time. That not-so-simple task set us on a three-year journey that in the end produced many of these remarkable pages.

From the start, our discussions faced three challenges. The first involved our need to confess a failure. As progressive theologians who are supposedly open to discussions of sexuality, we realized that we had failed to talk explicitly about many of the topics to which our students needed answers. This failure was made painfully evident to us the minute our conversations began. Our group is made up of scholars whose perspectives span the wide left side of the theological spectrum: liberation theologians, queer theologians, womanist and feminist theologians, black theologians, Latina and *mujerista* theologians, process thinkers, progressive evangelical voices, and the list goes on. Given these orientations, it was not surprising that we immediately homed in on sexual ethics and the role of power relations in erotic interactions. We agreed that consent should be the nonnegotiable starting point for any form of faithful sexual intimacy; that sex should take place between rational adults; that race, class, gender, and sexual orientation dramatically affect the nature of that consent; and that many social relations (pastor–parishioner, employer–employee, teacher–student) render consent too complex to be facilely managed and should be prohibited.

We also agreed that throughout history, religious understandings of sexuality have been shot full of exclusions, repressions, silences, and eccentricities that, as theologians, we needed to surface and engage. We similarly shared a view that sexual orientation and identity have been socially constructed across the centuries in ways both destructive and compelling and, as such, should remain for us an open issue. On all these points, there was ardent agreement.

In order to grasp the nature of our agreement, imagine the word *sex* written in bold letters in the middle of a big, blank sheet of paper. Our collective hand could easily draw a very large red circle around it, a good five inches away from the center. The circle symbolically represents the firm, clear limits that our ethical justice-centered theology could place around sex. To be just, you should not have these kinds of relations. The circle marked a border we all agreed on—a line that managed the flow of appropriate and inappropriate relations across it.

After we finished drawing our metaphoric red circle, a strange and awkward silence fell. Okay. Now what? We found ourselves staring at the big open area that filled the space inside the red circle. We weren't quite sure what should go there. Maybe nothing, maybe lots. It was hard to decide how to begin the discussion. How do we actually talk about the sex we *may* have—from a theological perspective? Addressing that question became the task of this book, but not before we confronted a second challenge. Our initial silence, we reflected, was astonishing given our broader culture's media obsession with sex. As soon as children are able to sit before a computer screen or television set or look at a billboard or even the side of bus, they are bombarded with the images and sounds of people on the verge of or engaged in an endless array of sexual encounters. Beautiful, young, desiring bodies are displayed everywhere. They are the largest and most successful vehicles used to market consumer goods globally. The titillation of sex acts sells everything, including, most importantly, a vision of what the good life is—a life led by someone who's thin, fit, always aroused, slightly melancholic, and barely clothed in expensive jeans.

How could we, as a group of academic theologians, take on a cultural force as powerful and all pervasive as this? We did not have ready answers, but one thing was clear: we recognized that conservative churches had eagerly stepped up to the plate and were filling the religious airwaves with a fierce and constant barrage of so-called Christian sex talk. If we were going to engage critically the full range of popular views of sex, our response had to take into account this phenomenon as well as the bare-chested media barrage.

Our reactions to this conservative religious approach were mixed. At one level, it was completely understandable that conservative Christian groups had responded to this hyper-commercialization by setting up alternative rules for appropriate sexual behavior. Christians have done this for centuries, sometime to good ends. In this instance, however, the specific rules many of these communities had constructed seemed both theologically questionable and culturally confusing. At the center of their model of good Christian sex is a not very biblically or theologically defensible image of the heterosexual, married couple—the bright and shining image of faithful erotic relationship. Put next to them is a considerable array of encounters deemed failures or perversions to which there are Christian cures. For those who are tempted to have sex outside of marriage or with same-sex partners, conservative Christians promote abstinence groups, offer vow-keeping classes, and pursue conversion for homosexuals. For those who do conform to their model of "good Christian sex," there are ample programs designed to promote the kind of active sex life that can keep a marriage happy, and oftentimes, these programs are quite sexually explicit. Oddly, this double approach succeeds in publicizing commercialized views of sex at the very moment it is trying to stop them, either through *ad nauseum* descriptions of the practices they refute or by even more explicit accounts of what constitutes great sex in the martial bed. Even more oddly, this truncated version of erotic life finds only slight support in the history of Christian doctrine or in the pages of biblical texts. On both scores, this book attempts a theological correction—culturally and historically.

This correction, however, takes seriously a reality that the religious Right aptly succeeded in naming, something progressive theologians have tiptoed around for far too long—namely, the consumptive, all-consuming, and often twisted shape of sexual desire in contemporary life. In conservative theology, it is assumed that people want to have sex. All the time. Intensely, obsessively, and wantonly. They assume that young people are hormone crazed; that married people are consumed with desire for their spouses (or tempted by desire for their neighbor's spouse); and that anyone may, at any point, fall prey to the evil pull of the varied offerings of a sex industry that has little respect for basic human values. Without proper controls, they argue, sexual havoc is sure to break loose. Faithful believers are told to contain their lust, directing it toward sanctified marital outlets and, above all, directing it toward the most appropriate object of our deepest desires, God.

What this conservative Christian view rightly identifies is the relentless pressure that culturally cultivated versions of sexual desire exert upon every feature of daily life. Whether or not we admit it, erotic desires are coursing through our lives, everywhere, all the time, in every form imaginable. Responding to this reality must be a core part of any good theology. What this conservative account gets profoundly wrong, however, is its predominantly rule-riddled answer. As experience has repeatedly shown, this approach ends up either driving sexual desires so deeply underground that church followers lose track of the wants that actually haunt them, trying desperately to cultivate or fabricate the wants they think they are supposed to have. Or, alternatively, the rules drive the "fallen folks" away from church, landing them squarely in a spiritual never-never land where no direction is provided at all. Some of these young people end up in our classes and offices, many of them confessing they don't have a clue as to what a better view of sex might be.

Reflecting on theological alternatives to justice-based ethics and theologies of the religious Right brought us face-to-face with our third and perhaps most significant challenge. What kind of theological substance were we looking for? To return to my earlier metaphor of the red circle we drew around "sex," what should fill the center? We found answering this much harder than originally anticipated. We had wide-ranging opinions about whether or not to put anything there at all, some arguing that as long as sexual relations are ethical, a endless array of practices is acceptable—the more the merrier. There were others who insisted that something needed to be put there, but exactly what was not easy to see. We needed new categories.

To find those categories, we reached deeply into the well of Christian traditions and pulled out old views that look surprisingly fresh in today's light. Similarly, we reached into the well of Scripture and found guidance that looked shockingly avant-garde when measured against present-day culture values. At every step along the way, we encountered something new and unexpected. For anyone who thinks they know exactly what God thinks about sex, the results offered here are sure to be unsettling. In the end, we concluded that, theologically speaking, sexuality is both less and more interesting than we are usually led to think. This is because it is both a very ordinary and a quite extraordinary feature of human existence.

To say sex is "very ordinary" is to affirm that having strong sexual and erotic desires for others is part and parcel of being a person. Taking pleasure in satisfying those yearnings, in all their diversity, is very, very normal. That's the way God's creation works. We are creatures with creaturely desires. Our bodies want and we desire. To say sex is "quite extraordinary" is to affirm that with intimate erotic relationships, there is range of experiences that stretches beyond our normal cache of social rules and expectations. Erotic intimacy can push the limits of our normal, enfleshed, bounded existence and let us experience the power of being both earthbound animals and skybound lovers. In the midst of sexual encounters, we can feel the pleasures of being the object of another's satisfaction, our flesh affirmed simply for its firm presence. In the throes of erotic embrace, we can explore the edge of reason and delight in the irrational—if only for a moment. We can revel in the all-consuming joy of transgressing another's boundaries and then diminishing, as much as possible, the skinned-line between oneself and another. Sexual intimacy can permit levels of vulnerability, risk, and self-exploration that reach far beyond what appropriately transpires in other social encounters.

In terms of new language, we also faced the challenge of digging up theological images that describe the sexually intimate erotic love we have for others that is about more than particular sex acts. Even more importantly, we faced the challenge of finding theological language sturdy enough to hold the erotic tone and texture of our relation to God and God's relation to us. That God loves human creatures in their fullness and that human beings are called to love God fully is hardly a topic for debate in theology. Scripture makes it clear. Every Christian accepts it. What is more difficult to see is the place of embodied sexual desire and erotic yearning in this relationship. It is surely a part of it—but how? As the pages of this book illustrate time and again, theologians, poets, prophets, and priests from the past have experienced and written about the importance of this dimension of faith—and as such give us marvelous guidelines for managing the complexity of desire as it courses through our here and now.

At the beginning, earnest student questions provoked and motivated this volume. In response, we offer this book to those students, the ones who come to our office hours, sit in our classes, write us e-mails, and stop us in the halls. This book is also offered to the student who still lives inside each of us—the student still searching for better answers to these fundamental human questions than those that were offered to us.

NOTES

INTRODUCTION

1. Ramon Llull, *The Book of the Lover and the Beloved*, trans. Eve Bonner, in *Doctor Illumina-tus: A Ramon Llull Reader*, ed. and trans. Anthony Bonner (Princeton: Princeton University Press, 1993), 194 (versicle 36).

2. The conference was sponsored by the Workgroup on Constructive Theology, a loosely affiliated group that was originally convened under the auspices of Vanderbilt Divinity School in 1975. See Peter Hodgson and Robert King, "The Workgroup on Constructive Theology: A Brief History," unpublished paper.

3. Tertullian, *On Monogamy* Bk. I.1 and *To His Wife* Bk. II.1 in *The Ante-Nicene Fathers: Translations of the Writings of the Fathers down to A.D. 325*, vol. 3, ed. Alexander Roberts, James Donaldson, and Philip Schaff (Peabody, Mass.: Hendrickson, 1994), 59, 44.

4. Jerome, *Against Jovinianus*, I.20, I.7, available at http://www.newadvent.org/fathers/3009.htm, accessed Apr. 24, 2009.

5. Martin Luther, quoted in Scott Hendrix, "Luther on Marriage," *Lutheran Quarterly* 14, no. 3 (2000): 342.

6. See Richard Kearney, "The Shulammite's Song: Divine Eros, Ascending and Descending," in Virginia Burrus and Catherine Keller, eds., *Toward a Theology of Eros: Trans-figuring Passion at the Limits of Discipline* (New York: Fordham University Press, 2006).

7. See Bernard of Clairvaux, *Sermons on the Song of Songs*, trans. Kilian Walsh (Kalamazoo, Mich.: Cistercian, 1976–81). Some contemporary scholars highlight the forbidden yet unavoidable gender-bending homoeroticism in the monks' allegorical interpretations of the Song. See Stephen D. Moore, "The Song of Songs in the History of Sexuality," *Church History* 69, no. 2 (2000): 328–49.

8. See Merry E. Wiesner, *Christianity and Sexuality in the Early Modern World: Regulating Desire, Reforming Practice* (London: Routledge, 2000); Kelly Brown Douglas, *Sexuality and the Black Church: A Womanist Perspective* (Maryknoll, N.Y.: Orbis, 1999).

9. Exodus International, "Who We Are," http://exodus.to/content/category/6/24/57/; accessed March 2, 2009.

10. Exodus International, "What can I do to make a gay person change?" http://exodus.to/content/view/49/25/; accessed March 2, 2009.

11. See "Relationships and Marriage," Focus on the Family Community, http://www.focusonlinecommunities.com/community/marriage; accessed Apr. 25, 2009.

12. Joseph Knable, *Sex and the Single Guy: Winning Your Battle for Purity* (Chicago: Moody, 2005); Louis McBurney and Melissa McBurney, *Real Questions, Real Answers about Sex: The Complete Guide to Intimacy as God Intended* (Grand Rapids: Zondervan, 2004); Emily Parke Chase, *Why Say No When My Hormones Say Go?* (Camp Hill, Pa.: WingSpread, 2003).

13. See *Encyclical Letter* Deus Caritas Est *of the Supreme Pontiff Benedict XVI to the Bishops, Priests and Deacons, Men and Women Religious and All the Faithful on Christian Love* (Libreria Editrice Vaticana, 2005), #7; available at http://www.vatican.va/holy_father/benedict_xvi/encyclicals/documents/hf_ben-xvi_enc_20051225_deus-caritas-est_en.html; accessed April 14, 2009.

14. For an overview of eros and *agape* in twentieth-century theological writings, see Anne Bathurst Gilson, *Eros Breaking Free: Interpreting Sexual Theo-Ethics* (Cleveland: Pilgrim, 1995), esp. chap. 1.

15. Audre Lorde, "Uses of the Erotic: The Erotic and Power," in *Sister/Outsider: Essays and Speeches* (Freedom, Calif.: Crossing, 1984), 55, 56.

16. Ibid., 54.

17. See Rita Nakashima Brock, *Journeys by Heart: A Christology of Erotic Power* (New York: Crossroad, 1988); Carter Heyward, *Touching Our Strength: The Erotic as Power and the Love of God* (San Francisco: HarperSanFrancisco, 1989); Daniel T. Spencer, *Gay and Gaia: Ethics, Ecology, and the Erotic* (Cleveland: Pilgrim, 1996).

18. See Lisa Isherwood, *The Power of Erotic Celibacy: Queering Heteropatriarchy* (London: T & T Clark, 2006); Diana L. Hayes, "A Sexual Ethic—Built upon the Foundation of Celibacy," *The Witness* (April 2000), http://www.thewitness.org/archive/april2000/hayessexualethic.html, accessed April 13, 2009; Michael J. McClymond, "The Last Sexual Perversion: An Argument in Defense of Celibacy, *Theology Today* 57, no. 2 (2006): 217–31; Kathleen Norris, "Celibate Passion," *The Christian Century* 113, no. 10 (March 20–27, 1996): 331–34.

19. One need only look to the current dissention within the worldwide Anglican Church provoked by the election of openly gay bishop, Gene Robinson, in the Diocese of New Hampshire in 2003. See John F. Burns, "Cast Out but at the Center of the Storm, *New York Times*, August 3, 2008, Section WK, Week in Review Desk, 3.

20. Augustine, *Confessions*, trans. R. S. Pine-Coffin (New York: Penguin, 1986), 5.10, 105.

21. Ibid., 11.4, 256.

22. John Calvin, *The Institutes of the Christian Religion*, ed. John T. McNeill, trans. Ford Lewis Battles (Philadelphia: Westminster, 1960), IV.15/11, 1312.

23. See Cheryl Kristolaitis, "From Purification to Celebration: The History of the Service for Women after Childbirth," *Journal of the Canadian Church Historical Society* 28, no. 2 (1986): 53–62.

24. See Joan R. Branham, "Bloody Women and Bloody Spaces: Menses and the Eucharist in Late Antiquity and the Early Middle Ages," *Harvard Divinity Bulletin*, http://www.hds.harvard.edu/news/bulletin/articles/branham.html#5, accessed Feb. 26, 2009.

25. John Climacus, *The Ladder of Divine Ascent*, trans. Colm Luibheid and Norman Russell (Mahwah, N.J.: Paulist, 1982), 185–86.

26. See Athanasius, *Life of Anthony*, in *Selected Works*, vol. 4, *Nicene and Post-Nicene Fathers*, trans. Henry Wace and Philip Schaff (New York: Charles Scribner's Sons, 1907), 197 (chap. 5).

27. See Rudolph M. Bell, *Holy Anorexia* (Chicago: Chicago University Press, 1985). Other scholars have contested this term; see Caroline Walker Bynum, *Holy Feast, Holy Fast: The Religious Significance of Food to Medieval Women* (Berkeley: University of California Press, 1987).

28. For a helpful overview, see Rita M. Gross, *Feminism and Religion: An Introduction* (Boston: Beacon, 1996).

29. Toinette M. Eugene, "While Love Is Fashionable: An Exploration of Black Spirituality and Sexuality," in *Women's Consciousness, Women's Conscience: A Reader in Feminist Ethics*, ed. Barbara Hilkert Andolsen, Christine E. Gudorf, Mary D. Pellauer (Minneapolis: Winston, 1985). The term *womanist*, borrowed from novelist and essayist Alice Walker, has become a prominent designation for an African American feminist. See Stephanie Y. Mitchem, *Introducing Womanist Theology* (Maryknoll, N.Y.: Orbis, 2002).

30. Michel Foucault, *The History of Sexuality*, vol. 1: *An Introduction* (New York: Vintage, 1990), 12.

31. Mark D. Jordan, *The Invention of Sodomy in Christian Theology* (Chicago: University of Chicago Press, 1997), 107.

32. See Owen Thomas, "Theology and Experience," *Harvard Theological Review* 78 (1985): 179–201.

33. See Linda Hogan, *From Women's Experience to Feminist Theology* (London: Sheffield Academic Press, 1995); J. Michael Clark, *Defying the Darkness: Gay Theology in the Shadows* (Cleveland: Pilgrim, 1997); Justin Tanis, *Trans-gendered: Theology, Ministry, and Communities of Faith* (Cleveland: Pilgrim, 2003); Alma Rosa Alvarez, *Liberation Theology in Chicana/o Literature: Manifestations of Feminist and Gay Identities* (New York: Routledge, 2007).

1. THE BIBLE AND SEX

1. Stanley J. Grenz, *Sexual Ethics: An Evangelical Perspective* (Louisville: Westminster John Knox, 1997), 84.

2. See 1 Cor. 6:12-18, where Paul uses the term in relation to prostitution.

3. See also Mark D. Jordan, *The Ethics of Sex* (Malden, Mass.: Blackwell, 2002), 24–31. Jordan claims that Paul's "lists give us very little evidence about the exact meanings of the terms in them. . . . So, too, the Pauline texts may be using *porneia* metaphorically or symbolically, not intending to refer to specific sexual acts at all" (27–28).

4. John Macquarrie, "Fornication," in James F. Childress and John Macquarrie, eds., *The Westminster Dictionary of Christian Ethics* (Philadelphia: Westminster, 1986), 237.

5. Robert A. J. Gagnon, *The Bible and Homosexual Practice: Texts and Hermeneutics* (Nashville: Abingdon, 2001), 138–42. Gagnon's interpretation of this text, moreover, is plagued by a view of "gender complementarity" that is arguably subverted in Paul's letter to the Galatians, which says that in Christ "there is no longer Jew or Greek, there is no longer slave or free, there is no longer male and female" (3:28). In W. Stacy Johnson's words, "The pairing of male *and* female . . . has no ultimate hold on the new community seeking to live out the gospel. Invoking 'gender complementarity' or even 'gender identity' as a fundamental basis for drawing ethical distinctions of status or worth within the body of Christ has no support in the gospel according to Galatians 3:28." *A Time to Embrace: Same-Gender Relationships in Religion, Law, and Politics* (Grand Rapids: Eerdmans, 2006), 150.

6. In Jordan's words: "The prohibition has nothing to do with women and—in 18:22 at least—nothing to do with the 'passive' or receptive partner. It would also not prohibit

same-sex erotic activities other than anal intercourse: the phrase does not include oral sex, or mutual masturbation, or a number of other practices" (Jordan, *Ethics of Sex*, 30).

7. Lauren Winner, *Real Sex: The Naked Truth About Chastity* (Grand Rapids: Brazos, 2005), 124.

8. Jordan, *Ethics of Sex*, 23.

9. The Deutero-Pauline Epistles, those letters that Paul did not write but which are attributed to him (Colossians, Ephesians, 1 & 2 Timothy, and Titus), contain household codes that document a possible compromise between a vision of Christian freedom that questioned rigid gender roles and dominant Greco-Roman understandings of gender, whereby the radical edges of Christian freedom eventually become accommodated to the wider culture. Yet patriarchal assumptions about gender are by no means restricted to post-Pauline developments in the New Testament; in some regards, those assumptions shape the entire New Testament discussion of gender and sex.

10. Adrian Thatcher, *Liberating Sex: A Christian Sexual Theology* (London: SPCK, 1993), 16.

11. Ibid., 21.

12. Anne Bathurst Gilson, *Eros Breaking Free: Interpreting Sexual Theo-Ethics* (Cleveland: Pilgrim, 1995), 96.

13. Ibid., 112.

14. Grace Jantzen, "New Creations: Eros, Beauty, and the Passion for Transformation," in Virginia Burrus and Catherine Keller, eds., *Toward a Theology of Eros: Transfiguring Passion at the Limits of Discipline* (New York: Fordham University Press, 2006), 286.

15. My reading of Genesis 3 differs from interpretations that stress divine punishment, as if God forbids consumption of the fruit, Adam and Eve ignore this prohibition, and God responds with various curses for breaking the divine command. In my reading, desire for possession becomes its own curse. God does not punish so much as allow persons to experience the injustice of possessiveness that leads to alienation in relationships with each other and with the earth.

16. Here I interpret Thomas's disbelief not as skepticism over the resurrection but disbelief over the catastrophic loss of his teacher and beloved, a "love that cannot come to terms with loss." For this reading, and for some of the thoughts related to Thomas and Mary, I am indebted to Graham Ward, "There is No Sexual Difference," in Gerard Loughlin, ed., *Queer Theology: Rethinking the Western Body* (Malden, Mass.: Blackwell, 2007), 77–81.

17. See Leanne VanDyk, "The Gifts of God for the People of God: Christian Feminism and Sacramental Theology," in Amy Plantinga Pauw and Serene Jones, eds., *Feminist and Womanist Essays in Reformed Dogmatics* (Louisville: Westminster John Knox, 2006), 217.

18. The phrase is from Phyllis Trible, *Texts of Terror: Literary-Feminist Readings of Biblical Narratives*, Overtures to Biblical Theology (Philadelphia: Fortress Press, 1984), though Trible does not discuss this particular passage in her now-classic text.

19. For an example of feminist musings on Revelation, see Catherine Keller, *Apocalypse Now and Then: A Feminist Guide to the End of the World* (Boston: Beacon, 1996).

20. As New Testament scholar Dale Martin has noted about Revelation, "Although actual sexual intercourse is *supposed* to be absent from the eschatological community, desire and the erotic, especially the erotic of the eye, is everywhere." Dale B. Martin, *Sex and the Single Savior: Gender and Sexuality in Biblical Interpretation* (Louisville: Westminster John Knox, 2006), 110.

21. Richard Kearney, "The Shulammite's Song: Divine Eros, Ascending and Descending," in Burrus and Keller, eds., *Toward a Theology of Eros*, 312.

22. Bernard of Clairvaux, *On the Song of Songs*, trans. Kilian Walsh, vols. 1–4 (Kalamazoo: Cistercian, 1979).

23. Robert W. Jenson, *Song of Songs*, Interpretation, a Bible Commentary for Teaching and Preaching (Louisville: John Knox, 2005), 13.

24. See Martin, *Sex and the Single Savior*, 116–18.

25. Kearney, "The Shulammite's Song," 339.

26. See George A. Lindbeck, *The Nature of Doctrine: Religion and Theology in a Postliberal Age* (Philadelphia: Westminster, 1984), 117.

2. EARLY CHRISTIAN CONTEMPT OF THE FLESH AND THE WOMAN WHO LOVED TOO MUCH IN THE GOSPEL OF LUKE

1. See Mark D. Jordan, *The Ethics of Sex* (Oxford: Blackwell, 2002); Stephanie Paulsell, *Honoring the Body: Meditations on a Christian Practice* (San Francisco: Jossey-Bass, 2002); Eugene F. Rogers, Jr., ed., *Theology and Sexuality: Classic and Contemporary Readings* (Oxford: Blackwell, 2002); and Virginia Burrus and Catherine Keller, eds., *Toward a Theology of Eros: Transfiguring Passion at the Limits of Discipline* (New York: Fordham University Press, 2006).

2. My convention regarding S/spirit: when referring to the Spirit of God (e.g., the Holy Spirit), I generally use the definite article and capitalize this word, whereas when referring to the innermost aspect of a person or place (e.g., the "spirit of Christianity" or the "spirit of Rome"), I use lower case "s."

3. Daniel Boyarin, *Carnal Israel: Reading Sex in Talmudic Culture* (Berkeley: University of California Press, 1993), 6 n.11.

4. Peter Brown, *The Body and Society: Men, Women, and Sexual Renunciation in Early Christianity* (New York: Columbia University Press, 1988), 160–89.

5. Jordan, *Ethics of Sex*, 48.

6. But see the early Syriac body-affirming alternative to the antibody sensibility in Pseudo-Titus and similar canonical and extracanonical texts, in Susan A. Harvey, "Embodiment in Time and Eternity: A Syriac Perspective," in Rogers, ed, *Theology and Sexuality*: 3–22.

7. "Pseudo-Titus," in Bart Ehrman, ed., *Lost Scriptures: Books That Did Not Make It into the New Testament* (New York: Oxford University Press, 2003), 246.

8. Augustine, *The City of God*, trans. Marcus Dods (New York: Modern Library, 2000), bks. 13, 14.

9. Elaine Pagels, *Adam, Eve, and the Serpent: Sex and Politics in Early Christianity* (New York: Random House, 1988), 109.

10. Ibid., 111.

11. Clayton Sullivan, *Rescuing Sex from the Christians* (New York: Continuum, 2006), 32–33.

12. See I. Howard Marshall, *The Gospel of Luke: A Commentary on the Greek Text* (Grand Rapids: Eerdmans, 1978), 304–14.

13. The argument for the anonymous Lukan woman as a prostitute is made by Elisabeth Schüssler Fiorenza, *In Memory of Her: A Feminist Theological Reconstruction of Christian Origins* (New York: Crossroad, 1984), and François Bovon, *Luke 1: A Commentary on the Gospel of Luke 1:1—9:50*, Hermeneia, trans. Christine M. Thomas, ed. Helmut Koester (Minneapolis:

Fortress Press, 2002), 293–96. Another perspective is found in Barbara E. Reid, "'Do You See This Woman?' A Liberative Look at Luke 7.36-50 and Strategies for Reading Other Lukan Stories against the Grain," in Amy-Jill Levine, ed., with Marianne Blickenstaff, *A Feminist Companion to Luke* (Cleveland: Pilgrim, 2001), 106–20, and Teresa J. Hornsby, "The Woman Is a Sinner/The Sinner Is a Woman," in Levine, ed., *A Feminist Companion to Luke*, 121–32.

14. See Gail Corrington Streete, *The Strange Woman: Power and Sex in the Bible* (Louisville: Westminster John Knox, 1997), and Carla Ricci, *Mary Magdalene and Many Others: Women Who Followed Jesus*, trans. Paul Burns (Minneapolis: Fortress Press, 1994).

15. Of course, so much more could be said about Mary Magdalene than what I have space for here. We know that Mary was very close to Jesus, but how close? On Easter morning, does she go to the tomb in the dark to sit with her friend or her lover? Some exegetes argue that Mary and Jesus regularly touched one another, perhaps sexually (note what Jesus says to Mary in John 20:17, "Do not hold on to me"). This question is sharpened by the portrait of the extracanonical Gnostic Mary Magdalene, who has frequent visions of Christ in which she is identified as his lover and partner, perhaps even his spouse: "[T]he consort of Christ is Mary Magdalene. The Lord loved Mary more than all the disciples and he kissed her on the mouth many times. The others said to him, 'Why do you love her more than all of us?'" ("Gospel of Philip," in Ehrman, ed., *Lost Scriptures*, 42).

16. See Bovon, *Luke 1*, 291.

17. Anne F. Elvey, *An Ecological Feminist Reading of the Gospel of Luke: A Gestational Paradigm* (Lewiston, N.Y.: Edwin Mellen, 2005), 214.

18. Bovon, *Luke 1*, 295.

19. Teresa J. Hornsby, "The Woman Is a Sinner," 122–23.

20. For other such titles for this passage see Reid, "'Do You See This Woman?'," 112. In consulting similar Bibles and titles for this section, I was not able to find any that spoke directly to the woman's great love for Jesus.

21. See D. Harvey, "Book of Ruth," in George Arthur Buttrick, ed., *The Interpreter's Dictionary of the Bible*, 4 vols. (Nashville: Abingdon, 1962), 4:131–34.

22. In this regard, see Amy-Jill Levine, "Ruth," in Carol A. Newsom and Sharon H. Ringe, eds., *The Women's Bible Commentary* (London: SPCK/Louisville: Westminster John Knox, 1992), 78–84.

23. See B. L. Bandstra and A. D. Verhey, "Sex: sexuality," in Geoffrey W. Bromiley, ed., *The International Standard Bible Encyclopedia* (Grand Rapids: Eerdmans, 1988), 430–35.

24. Hornsby, "The Woman Is a Sinner," 129.

25. Valerie Smith, "'Circling the Subject': History and Narrative in Beloved," in Henry Louis Gates Jr. and K. A. Appiah, eds., *Toni Morrison: Critical Perspectives Past and Present* (New York: Amistad, 1993), 346.

26. Toni Morrison, *Beloved* (New York: Knopf, 1987), 88.

27. Barbara Christian, "Fixing Methodologies: *Beloved*," *Cultural Critique* (Spring 1993): 14–15.

28. Morrison, *Beloved*, 17.

29. Ibid., 17–18.

30. See Friedrich Nietzsche, *On the Genealogy of Morals*, trans. Douglas Smith (New York: Oxford University Press, 1996).

3. THE NEW TESTAMENT, EMPIRE, AND HOMOEROTICISM

This is a substantially revised and enhanced version of an argument that appeared in an earlier form as: William Stacy Johnson, "Empire and Order: The New Testament and Same-Gender Relationships," *Biblical Theology Bulletin*, 37, no. 4 (Winter 2007): 161–73.

1. William Stacy Johnson, *A Time to Embrace: Same-Gender Relationships in Religion, Law, and Politics* (Grand Rapids: Eerdmans, 2006).

2. The importance of empire and dominance in New Testament interpretation is now acknowledged by scholars of diverse theological commitments. On the liberal end of the spectrum, see, for example, Richard A. Horsley, *Jesus and Empire: The Kingdom of God and the New World Disorder* (Minneapolis: Fortress Press, 2002), while on the conservative end, see N. T. Wright, *Paul in Fresh Perspective* (Minneapolis: Fortress Press, 2006). For a recent example that takes Roman conquest as a guiding motif of interpretation, see Davina C. Lopez, *Apostle to the Conquered: Reimagining Paul's Mission*, Paul in Critical Contexts (Minneapolis: Fortress Press, 2008).

3. The two prominent examples of this argument are: Robin Scroggs, *The New Testament and Homosexuality: Contextual Background for Contemporary Debates* (Philadelphia: Fortress Press, 1983); and Victor Paul Furnish, *The Moral Teaching of Paul* (Nashville: Abingdon, 1979).

4. See the somewhat similar delineation employed in Stephen O. Murray, *Homosexualities* (Chicago: University of Chicago Press, 2000), 1–21. Murray is adapting a fourfold typology of age-structured, gender-defined, profession-defined, and egalitarian, derived from Barry Adam, "Age, Structure, and Sexuality," *Journal of Homosexuality* 11 (1986): 19–33.

5. James Davidson, *The Greeks and Greek Love: A Radical Reappraisal of Homosexuality in Ancient Greece* (London: Weidenfield and Nicholson, 2007).

6. Two examples from the scholarly literature will suffice. First, in his excellent book, *The New Testament and Homosexuality*, Scroggs rightly argues that the New Testament condemnations were limited to their cultural context. As noted above, however, Scroggs identifies that context primarily as one of age-differentiated pederasty; yet pederasty was not widespread among the Romans in the days of the New Testament. Second, John Boswell's *Christianity, Social Tolerance, and Homosexuality: Gay People in Western Europe from the Beginning of the Christian Era to the Fourteenth Century* (New Haven: Yale University Press, 1980) argues that the apostle Paul had in mind heterosexuals who were engaged in homosexual activity, not persons with a predominantly homosexual orientation. Boswell's book has the merit of paying much more attention to the particularities of the Roman world, but his main focus is to refute the idea that homosexual practices had been outlawed by the Romans. On this point, Boswell is surely right. Yet Boswell does little to inform his readers of the status-defined and often violent nature of much Roman homoerotic behavior. Boswell also seems to assume that egalitarian homoerotic relationships in the Roman world were widespread, which is doubtful. On closer inspection, there is little that was egalitarian about the sexual world of the Romans. Sex was a relationship of dominance and submission.

7. Robert A. J. Gagnon, in *The Bible and Homosexual Practice: Texts and Hermeneutics* (Nashville: Abingdon, 2001), claims that references to Gentile homoeroticism in the New Testament include not just exploitative, one-sided, and hedonistic relationships but even those that are loving and committed. His primary evidence for this is all the well-known ancient literature that extols love between men. What Gagnon ignores is that most of this literature is speaking of love that by definition is not consummated sexually. After all, this is what "Platonic love" is all about. Men who may have had pederastic sexual relationships in the past grow up to continue a love that transcends sexuality. We need

look no further than the quintessential Greek example of bonded male lovers: Achilles and Patroclus in Homer's *Iliad*. Despite their bond, the two are never explicitly portrayed as engaging in sex with one another; and when they are depicted as having sex, it is with women. Gagnon also misses what most classicists take for granted, namely, that there is a vast cultural difference between the same-gender sexuality of ancient Greece and Rome and the covenantal bonds of gay and lesbian couples today. To put it bluntly, there is a difference between a Roman soldier pleasuring himself with his boy slave and two women committed to one another as they raise a child. In all his many writings on the subject, Gagnon offers no way to morally distinguish between the two cases.

8. The classic study, originally published in 1983, is Amy Richlin, *The Garden of Priapus: Sexuality and Aggression in Roman Humor* (Oxford: Oxford University Press, 1992).

9. The speculation is that the Jewish rule of matrilineal descent may have arisen as a response to the widespread rape of Jewish women, especially during the Bar Kokhba rebellion in 132–133 C.E. However, there is no definitive answer concerning the origin of this rule. For a general discussion of the various theories, see Shaye J. D. Cohen, *The Beginnings of Jewishness: Boundaries, Varieties, Uncertainties* (Berkeley: University of California Press, 2001), 283–303.

10. Ibid., 226.

11. Marilyn B. Skinner, *Sexuality in Greek and Roman Culture* (Oxford: Blackwell, 2005), 197.

12. For photographs and analysis of the Warren Cup, see John R. Clarke, *Roman Sex: 100 BC–AD 250* (New York: Abrams, 2003), 77–91.

13. Author's own translation.

14. The word in Greek may have been coined directly from the Septuagint translation of Leviticus 20:13, though this is certainly debatable. It was the Greek Septuagint translation of Hebrew Scriptures that most Jews in Paul's day read. The word *arsenokoitai* combines the Greek words *arsenos*, meaning "male," and *koiten*, meaning "bed," both of which appear side-by-side in Leviticus 20:13.

15. Dale B. Martin, *Sex and the Single Savior: Gender and Sexuality in Biblical Interpretation* (Louisville: Westminster John Knox, 2006), 38–43.

16. Orlando Patterson, *Slavery and Social Death: A Comparative Study* (Cambridge: Harvard University Press, 1982), 13.

17. For example, Gagnon's book, *The Bible and Homosexual Practice*, contains no sustained discussion of the intrinsic relationship between slavery and homoeroticism in the Roman world. Instead, Gagnon's references to slavery are mostly aimed at distinguishing arguments for the abolition of slavery from arguments for a more progressive stance on gay sexuality.

18. Seneca the Elder, *Controversiae* 4, 1:431, in *Seneca: Controversiae, I–VI*, trans. Michael Winterbottom, vol. 1, The Loeb Classical Library (Cambridge: Harvard University Press, 1974).

19. J. Albert Harrill, "The Vice of Slave Dealers in Greco-Roman Society: The Use of a Topos in 1 Timothy 1:10," *Journal of Biblical Literature* 118, no. 1 (1999): 97–122, esp. 108–12. See J. Albert Harrill, *Slaves in the New Testament: Literary, Social, and Moral Dimensions* (Minneapolis: Fortress Press, 2005).

20. The word translated "body" here in the NRSV rendering "that each one of you know how to control his own body" is possible, but the phrase literally reads, "that each one should possess his own vessel [*skeuos*]." Since the term *vessel* was sometimes used in Judaism to refer to a woman as a receptacle of male semen, some translations render it, "each

one should possess his own wife" (a possible meaning reflecting the way in which women were often thought of as mere sex objects even within the context of marriage). From a strictly linguistic viewpoint, the term *skeuos* could even mean any "body" used as a sexual outlet, including a male body used homoerotically. It is possible, at least linguistically, that Paul meant "body" to include sex with slaves, but it is more probable that Paul followed Jewish thinking in believing that all sexual activity should be confined to marriage.

21. Among the many advocates of this position, see Gagnon, *The Bible and Homosexual Practice*, 229–303; and Stanley J. Grenz, *Welcoming but Not Affirming: An Evangelical Response to Homosexuality* (Louisville: Westminster John Knox, 1998), 48–56.

22. Bernadette Brooten, *Love between Women: Early Christian Responses to Female Homoeroticism* (Chicago: University of Chicago Press, 1998), 251–52 n.103.

23. Ibid., 195–302.

24. This observation is found in John Boswell, *Christianity, Social Tolerance, and Homosexuality*, 112. It is picked up and developed constructively by Eugene F. Rogers Jr., *Sexuality and the Christian Body: Their Way into the Triune God* (Malden, Mass.: Blackwell, 1999).

25. For Christian ownership of slaves, see, in addition to Paul's letter to Philemon, Jennifer A. Glancy, *Slavery in Early Christianity* (New York: Oxford University Press, 2002), 9, 46–49, 131–33, 140–47, 150–53.

26. Martha Nussbaum, *Sex and Social Justice* (New York: Oxford University Press, 2000), 184.

4. AUGUSTINE ON EROS, DESIRE, AND SEXUALITY

1. Two important biographies are Peter Brown, *Augustine of Hippo: A Biography* (Berkeley: University of California Press, 1967), and James J. O'Donnell, *Augustine: A New Biography* (New York: Ecco/HarperCollins, 2005).

2. Augustine, *Confessions*, trans. R.S. Pine-Coffin (New York: Penguin, 1961), 171–72 (Bk. 8.8).

3. Augustine, *On Free Choice of the Will*, trans. A. S. Benjamin and L. H. Hackstaff (Indianapolis: Bobbs-Merrill, 1964).

4. Augustine, "To Simplician—On Various Questions," in *Augustine: Earlier Writings*, Library of Christian Classics, trans. J. Burleigh (Philadelphia: Westminster, 1953), 372–406.

5. Augustine, "On Grace and Free Will," in *Saint Augustin: Anti-Pelagian Writings*, vol. 5 of *Nicene and Post-Nicene Fathers of the Christian Church*, ed. P. Schaff, trans. B. B. Warfield (Grand Rapids: Eerdmans, 1978), 461.

6. Augustine, *Confessions*, 21 (Bk. 1.1).

7. Ibid., 24 (Bk. 1.5).

8. Ibid., 59 (Bk. 3.4).

9. Ibid., 44 (Bk. 2.2).

10. Ibid., 55 (Bk. 3.1).

11. Ibid., 129 (Bk. 6.12).

12. Ibid., 164 (Bk. 8.5).

13. Ibid.

14. Elaine Pagels, *Adam, Eve, and the Serpent: Sex and Politics in Early Christianity* (New York: Random House, 1988), 27.

15. Augustine, *City of God*, trans. H. Bettenson (New York: Penguin, 1986), 587. Augustine had already developed this explanation in his commentary *The Literal Meaning of Genesis*, vol. 2, *Ancient Christian Writers*, vol. 42, trans. John Hammond Taylor (New York: Newman, 1982), 80–82 (Bk. 9, chap. 10).

16. Augustine, *City of God*, 577.

17. Augustine, *Literal Meaning of Genesis*, 73–74 (Bk. 9, chap. 3).

18. Augustine, *Confessions*, 75–76 (Bk. 4.4)

19. Ibid., 159–61, 166–68 (Bk. 8.1-2; 6).

20. Ibid., 178 (Bk. 8.12).

21. Brown, *Augustine of Hippo*, 62.

22. Augustine, *Literal Meaning of Genesis*, 75 (Bk. 9, ch. 5).

23. Augustine, *Confessions*, 196–99 (Bk. 9.10).

24. John E. Thiel, *God, Evil, and Innocent Suffering: A Theological Reflection* (New York: Crossroad, 2002), 113.

25. See the thorough discussion in Peter Brown, *The Body and Society: Men, Women, and Sexual Renunciation in Early Christianity* (New York: Columbia University Press, 1988), 387–427.

26. Elizabeth A. Johnson, *Friends of God and Prophets: A Feminist Theological Reading of the Communion of the Saints* (New York: Continuum, 1998), 27–29.

27. Pagels, *Adam, Eve, and the Serpent*, 146.

28. Augustine, *On Free Choice of the Will*, 8.

29. Ibid., 18.

30. Augustine, *Confessions*, 21 (Bk. 1.1).

5. THOMAS AQUINAS ON THE BODY AND BODILY PASSIONS

1. The best introduction to Aquinas's life and thought is Jean-Pierre Torrell, *Saint Thomas Aquinas*, vol.1: *The Person and His Work*, trans. Robert Royal (Washington, D.C.: Catholic University of America Press, 1996). Aquinas's theology is well introduced in Rik Van Nieuwenhove and Joseph Wawrykow, eds., *The Theology of Thomas Aquinas* (Notre Dame, Ind.: University of Notre Dame Press, 2005). Philosophical issues in Aquinas are summarized and discussed in Eleonore Stump, *Aquinas* (New York: Routledge, 2003). A concise and readable guide to key terms in Aquinas is provided in Joseph Wawrykow, *The Westminster Handbook to Thomas Aquinas* (Louisville: Westminster John Knox, 2005).

2. John Giles Milhaven attributes this development to Aquinas's thorough knowledge of Aristotle's *Nichomachean Ethics*. Milhaven, "Thomas Aquinas on Sexual Pleasure," *Journal of Religious Ethics* 5 (1977): 157–81.

3. A few remarks about Scholastic method are in order. Scholastic methodology was first and foremost a pedagogical methodology. Topics were examined through analysis of competing arguments and authorities, resulting in highly structured texts. When faced with an interpretive or intellectual difficulty, Aquinas often noted that the term or concept under investigation admitted of a distinction. This distinction then grounded Aquinas's solution. For all its structure and distinctions, Aquinas's *Summa theologiae* represents an attempt to simplify and streamline theological education. It also requires an engagement from the reader focused on synthesis rather than analysis. The arguments of a Scholas-

tic text are already broken up for the reader; the task then becomes putting the pieces together.

4. For an introduction to medieval philosophy, see John Marenbon, *Medieval Philosophy: An Historical and Philosophical Introduction* (New York: Routledge, 2007).

5. See Torrell, *Saint Thomas Aquinas*, 224–46.

6. This discussion of Aquinas focuses primarily on his *Summa theologiae* (hereafter *ST*), with some references to his *Summa contra gentiles* (hereafter *SCG*). All translations of *ST* are my own from the Latin *Summa theologiae*, 5 vols., cura et studio Instituti Studiorum Medievalium Ottaviensis ad textum S. Pii Papae (Ottawa: Commissio Piana, 1941–1945). For a complete English translation, see *Summa Theologica*, 5 vols., trans. Fathers of the English Dominican Province (New York: Benziger Bros., 1947). All translations of the *Summa contra gentiles* are my own from *Liber de veritate catholicae fidei contra errors infidelium; qui dicitur Summa contra gentiles*, 3 vols., cura et studio P. Marc, C. Pera, P. Caramello (Taurini: Marietti, 1961–1967). For an English translation, see *Summa Contra Gentiles*, 5 vols., ed. A. C. Pegis, J. F. Anderson, V. J. Bourke, C. J. O'Neil (Notre Dame: University of Notre Dame Press, 1975).

7. On the mendicant controversy, see Torrell, *Saint Thomas Aquinas*, 75–95.

8. See Leonard Boyle, "The Setting of the *Summa Theologiae*," in *Aquinas's* Summa Theologiae: *Critical Essays*, ed. Brian Davies (Oxford: Rowman & Littlefield, 2006), 1–24.

9. See Prudence Allen, *The Concept of Woman: The Aristotelian Revolution, 750 B.C.–A.D. 1250* (London and Montreal: Eden, 1985), 385–407; and idem, *The Concept of Woman: The Early Humanist Reformation, 1250–1500* (Grand Rapids: Eerdmans, 2002), 127–52. Allen discusses at length the extent of Aquinas's acceptance and modifications of Aristotle's gender theory and its views on the subordination of women.

10. See Caroline Walker Bynum, "Material Continuity, Personal Survival and the Resurrection of the Body: A Scholastic Discussion in its Medieval and Modern Contexts," in Caroline Walker Bynum, *Fragmentation and Redemption: Essays on Gender and the Human Body in Medieval Religion* (New York: Zone, 1992), 239–97.

11. See Giles Constable, "The Ideal of the Imitation of Christ," in Giles Constable, *Three Studies in Medieval Religious and Social Thought* (New York: Cambridge University Press, 1995), 143–248.

12. Aquinas's understanding of the Platonic conception derived largely from Nemesius of Emesa's *De natura hominis*. For a translation of Nemesius's *De natura hominis*, see William Telfer, trans., *Cyril of Jerusalem and Nemesius of Emesa* (Philadelphia: Westminster, 1955).

13. For Aristotle's views on the human being as a hylemorphic unity, see Richard Sorabji, "Body and Soul in Aristotle," *Philosophy* 49 (1974): 63–89.

14. See Anton Pegis, *St. Thomas and the Problem of the Soul in the Thirteenth Century* (Toronto: Pontifical Institute of Mediaeval Studies, 1934); Norbert Luyten, "The Significance of the Body in a Thomistic Anthropology," *Philosophy Today* 7 (1963): 175–93; Bernardo Bazan, "La corporalité selon saint Thomas," *Revue philosophique de Louvain* 81 (1983): 369–409; Anthony Kenny, "Body, Soul, and Intellect in Aquinas," in *From Soul to Self*, ed. James Crable (London and New York: Routledge, 1999), 33–48.

15. Aquinas argued that "every power of the soul depends upon the soul as its sole principle. Certain powers depend upon the soul as their sole subject, such as intellect and will. This type of power necessarily remains in the soul once the body is destroyed" (*ST* I, q.77, a.8). Aquinas contrasted these powers with powers relating to the conjoined subject, such as the powers of the sensitive appetite.

16. *ST* I, q.76, a.1, *ad* 6.

17. See, for example, *ST* I, q.75, a.4.

18. See Pegis, *St. Thomas and the Problem of the Soul,* 168–80, and Bazan, "La corporalité," 387–400.

19. "It should be said that since form does not depend upon matter but rather matter depends upon form, the reason why matter is of such a type comes from the form, and not vice versa. The intellectual soul, according to the order of its nature, occupies the lowest grade of intellectual substances because it naturally lacks an infused knowledge of the truth, like the angels, but must collect it from divisible things through the senses" (*ST* I, q.76, a.5).

20. See *ST* I, q.85, a.1.

21. "The sensitive appetite in human beings is naturally moved by [particular reasons]. The particular reasons themselves are naturally moved and directed in human beings according to universal reason, as when in syllogisms singular conclusions are derived from universal propositions. It stands that universal reason rules the sensitive appetite . . . , and this appetite is obedient to it" (*ST* I, q.81, a.3).

22. See *ST* I, q.81, a.3.

23. *ST* I, q.1, a.8, *ad* 2.

24. *ST* I, q.95, a.2.

25. McAleer draws out this notion in comparing Aquinas and Rahner. See Graham McAleer, "The Politics of the Flesh: Rahner and Aquinas on *Concupiscentia,*" *Modern Theology* 15 (1999): 355–65.

26. "The [soul's] body was not indissoluble through some vigor for immortality existing in it, but there was a certain divine power supernaturally given to the soul through which it could preserve the body from all corruption as long as it remained subject to God" (*ST* I, q.97, a.1).

27. "It should be said that human beings in the state of innocence had an animal life requiring food. After the resurrection human beings will have a spiritual life that will not require food" (*ST* I, q.97, a.3). Aquinas viewed the bodily passions as provisional since there will be no rational ends relating to the bodily passions in the afterlife.

28. *ST* I, q.98, a.2. Aquinas sided with Augustine over Gregory of Nyssa on this point of sexual reproduction.

29. *ST* I, q.98, a.2, and *ST* I, q.98, a.2, *ad* 3.

30. *ST* I, q.98, a.2, *ad* 3.

31. *ST* I-II, q.17, a.7.

32. See *ST* I-II, q.30, a.2.

33. See *ST* I-II, q.77, a.5.

34. See *ST* I-II, q.77, a.5.

35. "The privation of original justice, through which the will ought to be ordered to God, is formally identical with original sin. Every disorder of a soul's power is in a certain way materially identical with original sin. The disorder of one of the soul's powers is especially noticed in a disordered turning to a mutable good. This disorder is commonly called concupiscence" (*ST* I-II, q.82, a.3).

36. See *ST* I-II, q.85, a.1.

37. See *ST* I-II, q.85, a.3.

38. *SCG* IV.83.9; III.27.2.

39. "The life of the resurrected is ordered to the conservation of perfect beatitude. Beatitude and human felicity do not consist in corporeal pleasures, which are the pleasures of food and sex, as was shown in the third book. It is not necessary, therefore, to posit this type of pleasures in the life of the resurrected" (*SCG* IV.83.10; cf. *SCG* III.27).

40. *SCG* IV.83.11.

41. "From this last argument it can be maintained that all the occupations of the active life, which seem to be ordered to the use of food and sex and to other things necessary for corruptible life, will come to an end. Only the occupation of the contemplative life will remain among the resurrected" (*SCG* IV.83.23).

42. See Joseph Owens, "Thomas Aquinas," in *Individuation in Scholasticism: The Later Middle Ages and the Counter-Reformation, 1150–1650,* ed. Jorge Gracia (Albany: State University of New York Press, 1994), 173–94.

43. See Jean-Luc Nancy, *Corpus,* trans. Richard Rand (New York: Fordham University Press, 2008), esp. "On the Soul," 122–35.

6. *HUMANAE VITAE,* SEXUAL ETHICS, AND THE ROMAN CATHOLIC CHURCH

1. Encyclicals are papal letters addressed to the whole church on particular matters of importance. The Second Vatican Council was convened by Pope John XXIII in 1962 and closed by Pope Paul VI in 1965. The council was intended to bring the church into dialogue with the modern world. It produced four major documents or constitutions of which one of the most significant is *Gaudium et Spes,* the *Pastoral Constitution on the Church in the Modern World.*

2. The papal documents noted here may be found in the five-volume set edited by Claudia Carlen, IHM, *The Papal Encyclicals, 1740–1981* (Ann Arbor: Pierian, 1990). Quotations from *Humanae vitae* are from the Vatican's translation: *Encyclical Letter* Humanae vitae *of the Supreme Pontiff Paul VI to His Venerable Brothers the Patriarchs, Archbishops, Bishops and other Local Ordinaries in Peace and Communion with the Apostolic See, to the Clergy and Faithful of the Whole Catholic World, and to all Men of Good Will, on the Regulation of Birth,* available at http://www.vatican. va/holy_father/paul_vi/encyclicals/documents/hf_p-vi_enc_25071968_humanae-vitae_ en.html, accessed August 11, 2009.

3. *Casti Connubii: Encyclical of Pope Pius XI on Christian Marriage to the Venerable Brethren, Patriarchs, Primates, Archbishops, Bishops, and other Local Ordinaries Enjoying Peace and Communion with the Apostolic See,* #54, available at http://www.vatican.va/holy_father/pius_xi/encyclicals/documents/hf_p-xi_enc_31121930_casti-connubii_en.html, accessed August 11, 2009. In the same year that Pius XI issued *Casti connubii,* the Lambeth Conference, held by the Anglicans in England, approved the use of artificial birth control. These papal texts are discussed by Penelope J. Ryan, *Practicing Catholic: The Search for a Livable Catholicism* (New York: Henry Holt, 1998).

4. See James A. Brundage, *Law, Sex, and Christian Society in Medieval Europe* (Chicago: University of Chicago Press, 1990), 255.

5. Charles E. Curran, *Catholic Moral Theology in the United States: A History* (Washington, D.C.: Georgetown University Press, 2008), 86.

6. John Mahoney, *The Making of Moral Theology: A Study of the Roman Catholic Tradition* (Oxford: Clarendon, 1987), 2–16.

7. Curran, *Catholic Moral Theology*, 45. In the traditional calculus, a mortal sin also requires full knowledge of the gravity of the matter and full consent of the will.

8. The Vatican has also published in 1987 the *Instruction on Respect for Human Life in Its Origin and on the Dignity of Procreation (Donum Vitae*, "gift of life") as a statement on the church's position on reproductive technologies. In general, the principle for these technologies is the inverse of what is it for birth control. Just as sex without openness to children is immoral, so, too, is having children (through reproductive technologies) without sex. See Curran, *Catholic Moral Theology*, 59.

9. On popular Catholic attitudes and response to *HV*, see William V. D'Antonio, James D. Davidson, and Dean R. Hoge, *American Catholic: Gender, Generation, and Commitment* (Lanham, Md..: Rowman Altamira, 2001), 71–73. See poll results reported in Katy Kelly and Linda Kulman, "A Feisty but Loyal Flock," *U.S. News & World Report*, April 18, 2005, available at http://www.usnews.com/usnews/news/articles/050418/18american.htm, accessed August 11, 2009. These sources confirm my own observations and experience.

10. On Augustine's ideas and influence, see Mahoney, *The Making of Moral Theology*, 37–71. See St. Augustine, *The Literal Meaning of Genesis*, ed. and trans. John Hammond Taylor, 2 vols., *Ancient Christian Writers*, vols. 41, 42 (Mahwah, N.J.: Paulist, 1982), 2:147–55.

11. Evident, too, in *HV* are the theological manuals, which also considered sexual desire even in marriage to be sinful. See Curran, *Catholic Moral Theology*, 43–45.

12. See Wilemien Otten, "Augustine on Marriage, Monasticism, and the Community of the Church," *Theological Studies* 89 (1998): 385–405. See also John T. Noonan Jr., *Contraception: A History of Its Treatment by the Catholic Theologians and Canonists* (Cambridge: Harvard University Press, 1965), 151–52.

13. See Curran, *Catholic Moral Theology*, 86, 97.

14. In 1967 the trustees at Catholic University of America voted to rescind Charles Curran's contract, but after campus protests they reinstated him to the faculty. In 1986 the Vatican's Congregation for the Doctrine of the Faith decreed that Curran was not to teach Catholic theology. Curran was removed from the CUA faculty that same year. See Curran, *Catholic Moral Theology*, 121.

15. The critique of the traditional understanding of moral theology is known as revisionist moral theology. Among influential revisionist theologians, the best known are Richard A. McCormick, Charles E. Curran, Timothy O'Connoll, and James Keenan. They were students of two leading European theologians, Josef Fuchs and Bernard Häring. The foundational text for revisionist theologians was Mahoney's *The Making of Moral Theology*. See James F. Keenan, "The Influence of *The Making of Moral Theology*," in Gilbert Meilaender and William Werpehowski, eds., *The Oxford Handbook of Theological Ethics* (New York: Oxford University Press, 2005).

16. Joseph A. Komonchak, "*Humanae Vitae* and Its Reception: Ecclesiological Reflections," *Theological Studies* 39, no. 2 (1978): 221–57, esp. 250–55.

17. Ibid., 255.

18. Moral agency requires that the action taken by the person genuinely count as the person's own. For this to be the case, alternative actions must be available and, importantly, the person must be able to determine which of the alternatives to take. The person must be able to exercise some control over what he or she does. Otherwise the action cannot be considered as the person's own. See William S. Babcock, "Augustine on Sin and Moral Agency," *Journal of Religious Ethics* 16 (1988): 28–29.

19. For Paul himself, by contrast, women were saved by their decision to turn to the God of Israel, by faith, not by acquiescence to a biological function. The Deutero-Pauline writer of 1 Timothy secures the appropriation of patriarchal structures and norms for the *ekklesia* by designating it as "the household of God" (3:15). Just as women had a place in the patriarchal household, so, too, they were reassigned a subordinate place in the household of God.

20. Irenaeus and Ambrose quoted in Alvin John Schmidt, *Veiled and Silenced: How Culture Shaped Sexist Theology* (Macon, Ga.: Mercer University Press, 1990), 43.

21. John Chrysostom, quoted in Kris E. Kvam, Linda S. Schearing, and Valarie H. Ziegler, eds., *Eve and Adam: Jewish, Christian, and Muslim Readings on Genesis and Gender* (Bloomington: Indiana University Press, 1999), 113.

22. Augustine, quoted in ibid., 152.

23. Gratian, quoted in Brundage, *Love, Sex, and Christian Society*, 255.

24. See Thomas Aquinas, *Summa Theologiae* I, q.92, a.1, *ad.* 2; hereafter *ST*. I quote the translation in *Basic Writings of St. Thomas Aquinas*, ed. Anton C. Pegis, vol. 1 (New York: Random House, 1945).

25. See *ST* I, q.99, a.2, *ad.* 2. Unlike Aristotle, Aquinas had God and divine creation to consider as well. Shifting from reason to revelation, in his reply he pointed to Genesis 1 and 2 as confirmation that God intended the diversity of sexes. He placed the defect of the generation of females in "an extrinsic accidental cause," not in God.

26. *ST* I, q.92, a.1, resp.

27. Clement of Alexandria, quoted in Miguel A. De La Torre, *A Lily among the Thorns: Imagining a New Christian Sexuality* (New York: Wiley, 2007), 13.

28. Tertullian, "On the Apparel of Women," I.1, in *The Ante-Nicene Fathers: Translations of the Writings of the Fathers down to A.D. 325*, vol. 4, ed. Alexander Roberts and James Donaldson, and Philip Schaff (Grand Rapids: Eerdmans, 1965–1970), available online at http://www.ccel.org/ccel/schaff/anf04.iii.iii.i.i.html, accessed August 11, 2009.

29. See Barbara Andolsen, "Whose Sexuality? Whose Tradition? Women, Experience, and Roman Catholic Sexual Ethics," in Charles E. Curran, Margaret A. Farley, and Richard A. McCormick, S.J., *Feminist Ethics and the Catholic Moral Tradition* (New York: Paulist, 1996), 207–39.

30. *Redemptoris Mater: On the Blessed Virgin Mary in the Life of the Pilgrim Church*, #22, available at http://www.vatican.va/holy_father/john_paul_ii/encyclicals/documents/hf_jp-ii_enc_25031987_redemptoris-mater_en.html, accessed August 11, 2009. The pope is quoting the Vatican II document *Lumen Gentium* (*Dogmatic Constitution on the Church*), #18.

31. John Paul II, "Motherhood is God's Special Gift," *L'Osservatore Romano*, English edition, March 13, 1996, available at http://www.ewtn.com/library/papaldoc/jp2bvm14.htm, accessed August 11, 2009.

32. See Aquinas's discussion on human ends in *ST* I-II q.1, and on happiness in *ST* I-II, q.2.

33. Jean Porter, "Desire for God: Ground of the Moral Life," *Theological Studies* 47 (1986): 52. Porter is elaborating on *ST* I, q.6, a.1.

34. Stephen J. Pope, *The Ethics of Aquinas* (Washington, D.C.: Georgetown University Press, 2002), 31.

35. Babcock, "Augustine on Sin," 32, 33.

36. Bernard J. F. Lonergan, "The Future of Christianity," *A Second Collection*, ed. William F. J. Ryan and Bernard J. Tyrell (Philadelphia: Westminster, 1974), 152.

7. REFORMATION VIEWS ON CELIBACY: AN ANALOGY FOR GAY PROTESTANTS TODAY

An earlier version of this essay was previously published under the title "Binding and Unbinding the Conscience: Luther's Significance for the Plight of a Gay Protestant," *Theology and Sexuality* 16 (2002): 67–96.

1. See *The Constitution of the Presbyterian Church (U.S.A.)*, Part II: *Book of Order* (Louisville: The Office of the General Assembly, 1999), G-6.0106b.

2. Cited and translated by B. A. Gerrish, *Tradition and the Modern World: Reformed Theology in the Nineteenth Century* (Chicago: University of Chicago Press, 1978), 13.

3. Scholasticism (from the Latin *schola*, meaning "school") refers to a method for resolving theological disputes during the Middle Ages. The premise of the method is that theological clarity on confused issues can be attained through making precise conceptual distinctions. This type of theology was practiced chiefly in the universities. By and large, the Protestant Reformers rejected Scholastic theology.

4. Heiko A. Oberman, "The Tridentine Decree on Justification in the Light of Late Medieval Theology," in *Journal for Theology and the Church*, vol. 3: *Distinctive Protestant and Catholic Themes Reconsidered*, ed. Robert W. Funk (New York: Harper & Row, 1967), 28–29.

5. "Pelagian," a term derived from the name of late-fourth-/early-fifth-century theologian Pelagius, became shorthand for a doctrine of "works righteousness": instead of relying on the grace of Christ alone for salvation, sinners attempt to justify themselves before God through reliance on their own merits.

6. Condign or congruous merit was a Scholastic distinction intended to clarify how one could hold to a theology of salvation by grace alone and at the same time find a place for human cooperation with grace in the process of salvation. Condign or worthy merit means something one has earned. Congruous or fitting merit was an act that, while not truly meritorious in terms of one's actual accomplishment, was nonetheless accepted by God as though it were deserving of reward since it is fitting for God to accept best efforts even when they fall short. All medieval theologians since Augustine rejected the idea that people could perform condign merits in the fallen state of nature prior to the infusion of grace, but there was debate among them as to whether after the infusion of grace it was possible to bring forth condign merits or only congruous merits.

7. See Luther's commentary on Rom. 1:17, the exegesis of which was pivotal to his entire position, in *Luther: Lectures on Romans*, trans. Wilhelm Pauck, *The Library of Christian Classics* (Philadelphia: Westminster, 1961), 18.

8. Thomas Aquinas, *Summa Theologiae*, II-II, q.23, a.6, in *Aquinas on Nature and Grace*, trans. A. M. Fairweather, *The Library of Christian Classics: Icthus Edition* (Philadelphia: Westminster, 1954), 350–52.

9. In the twentieth century, the Lutheran pastor and theologian Dietrich Bonhoeffer (1906–1945) tried to get at the difference between these two understandings of the Christian life with this personal anecdote: "I remember a conversation that I had in America thirteen years ago with a young French pastor. We were asking ourselves quite simply what we wanted to do with our lives. He said he would like to become a saint (and I think it's quite likely that he did become one). At the time I was very impressed, but I disagreed with him, and said, in effect, that I should like to learn to have faith. For a long time I didn't realize the depth of the contrast. I thought I could acquire faith by trying to live a holy life, or something like it. . . . I discovered later, and I'm still discovering right up to this moment, that it is only by living completely in this world that one

learns to have faith." *Letters and Papers from Prison*, ed. Eberhard Bethge (New York: Collier-Macmillan, 1972), 369–70.

10. The important biography of St. Antony (d. 356) by Athanasius played a pivotal role in disseminating the monastic ideal. Antony was described as having "mortified the body and kept it under subjection . . . [since] the soul's intensity is strong when the pleasures of the body are weak." Athanasius, *The Life of Antony and the Letter to Marcellinus*, trans. Robert C. Gregg with a preface by William A. Clebsch, in *The Classics of Western Spirituality* (New York: Paulist, 1980), 36. See also the insightful studies of Peter Brown, *The Body and Society: Men, Women, and Sexual Renunciation in Early Christianity* (New York: Columbia University Press, 1988), 213–16, 387–95; and Margaret R. Miles, *Desire and Delight: A New Reading of Augustine's Confessions* (New York: Crossroad, 1991), 42–43.

11. While the Eastern Orthodox Church ordains married men, bishops are appointed only from the ranks of the celibate clergy. Timothy Ware, *The Orthodox Church* (Harmondsworth, UK: Penguin, 1984), 298–99.

12. Luther wrote: "Injustice is done those words 'priest,' 'cleric,' 'spiritual,' 'ecclesiastic,' when they are transferred from all Christians to those few who are now by a mischievous usage called 'ecclesiastics.'" "The Freedom of a Christian" (1520), in *Martin Luther: Selections from his Writings*, ed. John Dillenberger (Garden City, N.Y.: Anchor/Doubleday, 1961), 65.

13. Roland H. Bainton, *Women of the Reformation in Germany and Italy* (Minneapolis: Augsburg, 1971), 162.

14. David Steinmetz, *Calvin in Context* (New York: Oxford University Press, 1995), 15.

15. Ulrich Gabler, *Huldrych Zwingli: His Life and Work*, trans. Ruth C. L. Gritsch (Philadelphia: Fortress Press, 1986), 57; Oskar Farner, *Zwingli the Reformer: His Life and Work*, trans. D. G. Sear (New York: The Philosophical Library, 1952), 88.

16. Steven Ozment, *The Age of Reform, 1250–1550: An Intellectual and Religious History of Late Medieval and Reformation Europe* (New Haven: Yale University Press, 1980), 321–22.

17. Gabler, *Huldrych Zwingli*, 13.

18. Ozment, *The Age of Reform*, 322.

19. "The Judgment of Martin Luther on Monastic Vows" (1521), in *Luther's Works*, ed. Jaroslav Pelikan and Helmut T. Lehmann, 55 vols. (St. Louis: Concordia/Philadelphia: Fortress Press, 1955–86), 44:262.

20. *Luther's Works*, 44:314–15.

21. Ibid., 44:462.

22. In this respect, Luther's experience was like that of Augustine who continued to be troubled by erotic dreams and nocturnal emissions well into his celibate period. As Peter Brown writes, these "did point, in no uncertain fashion, to a disjunction between his conscious image of himself and a mysterious inability to follow his own will" (*The Body and Society*, 406). Yet Luther could not have been more unlike Augustine in the way each finally chose to address the problem. In his *Confessions*, the converted Augustine would have readers conclude from the story of his life that celibacy is an exemplary way to resolve the sexual problem. As Margaret Miles notes, Augustine "did not . . . press his own resolution on anyone else or describe celibacy as the norm for Christians. . . . Nevertheless, his mastery of language . . . was powerfully affecting, contributing to the subsequent glorification of the sexless life in Catholic Christianity" (*Desire and Delight*, 38). Luther, whose rather happy married life stands in contrast to the torment of his previous life in the cloister, is

sympathetically described by Roland H. Bainton in *Here I Stand: A Life of Martin Luther* (New York: Abingdon, 1950), 286–304.

23. *Luther's Works*, 44:391.

24. Ibid., 44:390–91. Speaking on behalf of the Swiss Reformed, Bullinger expressed the same sentiment: "Those who have the gift of celibacy from heaven . . . let them serve the Lord in that calling. . . . But if, again, the gift be taken away, and they feel a continual burning, let them call to mind the words of the apostle: "'It is better to marry than to be aflame.'" "The Second Helvetic Confession" (1566), in *The Constitution of the Presbyterian Church (USA)*, Part I: *The Book of Confessions*, Study Edition (Louisville: The Office of the General Assembly, 1996 and Geneva Press, 1999), 5.245.

25. Ibid., 5.246.

26. Ibid., 5.245.

27. "The Westminster Confession of Faith," in *The Book of Confessions*, 6.126.

28. Ibid., 6.124–25. 41.

29. "The Larger Catechism," in *The Book of Confessions*, 7.248.

30. Ozment, *Age of Reform*, 381.

31. "Despite the distinction between doctrine and practice that underlay these discussions of abuses, there were certain practices so inseparable from their doctrinal implications that a change in practice now . . . would amount to a doctrinal concession [on the part of Catholics]. Clerical celibacy was one such . . ." (Jaroslav Pelikan, *Reformation of Church and Dogma*, (1300-1700), vol. 4 of *The Christian Tradition: The Development of Christian Doctrine* (Chicago: University of Chicago Press, 1984), 248.

32. "Apology of the Augsburg Confession," 4.2, in *Die Bekenntnisschriften der evangelisch-lutherischen Kirche*, ed. Hans Lietzmann, Heinrich Bornkamm, Hans Volz, and Ernst Wolf (Göttingen: Vandenhoeck und Ruprecht, 1959), 159. For the English translation (rendered as "the main doctrine of Christianity"), see *The Book of Concord: The Confessions of the Evangelical Lutheran Church*, ed. Theodore G. Tappert with Jaroslav Pelikan, Robert H. Fischer, and Arthur C. Piepkorn (Philadelphia: Fortress Press, 1959), 107.

33. John Calvin, *Institutes of the Christian Religion*, ed. John T. McNeill, trans. Ford Lewis Battles (Philadelphia: Westminster, 1960), 3.11.1.

34. The "entire doctrine of piety," Calvin affirmed, "rests on this foundation." *Commentary* on John 20.23, in *Ioannis Calvini opera quae supersunt omnia*, ed. Wilhelm Baum, Edward Cunitz, and Edward Reuss, vols. 29–87 of *Corpus Reformatorum* (Braunschweig: C. A. Schwetschke and Son [M. Bruhn], 1863–1900), 47:440.

35. For stories by gay men about the role of religion in their lives, see *Wrestling with the Angel: Faith and Religion in the Lives of Gay Men*, ed. Brian Bouldrey (New York: Riverhead, 1995).

36. "The Estate of Marriage," in *Luther's Works*, 45:37; *Commentaries on the Epistle of Paul the Apostle to the Romans*, in *Calvin's Commentaries* (Edinburgh: The Calvin Translation Society; reprint ed., Grand Rapids: Baker Book House, 1989), 19:9 (*Calvini opera*, 49:28). In each instance, Luther and Calvin are commenting on Rom. 1:24-27.

37. For a sophisticated version of this sort of biblicism, see Richard B. Hays, *The Moral Vision of the New Testament: Community, Cross, New Creation* (San Francisco: HarperSanFrancisco, 1996).

38. Note that "faith" here is not defined as "trust" or "confidence," as in Luther's usage, but instead as "assent" of the mind to an intellectual proposition, which is precisely the notion of faith rejected by Luther.

39. The classical exposition of this view is found in Thomas Aquinas, *Summa Theologiae*, II-II, q.154, a.11 (London: Blackfriars, 1964), 43:244–45.

40. For alternative interpretations of the biblical and philosophical traditions, see Martti Nissinen, *Homoeroticism in the Biblical World: A Historical Perspective*, trans. Kirsi Stjerna (Minneapolis: Fortress Press, 1998); and Pim Pronk, *Against Nature? Types of Moral Argumentation regarding Homosexuality*, trans. John Vriend (Grand Rapids: Eerdmans, 1993).

41. Andrew Sullivan, *Love Undetectable: Notes on Friendship, Sex, and Survival* (New York: Vintage, 1999), 42–43. That this is no hyperbole is evident from Swiss Reformed theologian Karl Barth's assertion that "homosexuality can have no place in [the Christian] life"; *Church Dogmatics*, vol. 3, pt. 4, ed. G. W. Bromiley and T. F. Torrance (Edinburgh: T. & T. Clark, 1961; German original 1951), 166. In the same place Barth describes homosexuality as a "malady" and calls it an expression of "inhumanity." He made these statements just six years after the end of the Nazi effort to exterminate gay people from society altogether. See the account of Heinz Heger, *The Men with the Pink Triangle*, trans. David Fernbach (Boston: Alyson, 1994); and Martin Sherman's powerful play *Bent* (New York: Avon, 1979).

42. Sullivan, *Love Undetectable*, 45.

43. Ibid., 43.

44. One noted gay writer says of his relation to the church: "I understand that I'll never get around my rage at the tyranny of religion to see if there's anything Higher out there." Paul Monette, *Becoming a Man: Half a Life Story* (San Francisco: HarperCollins, 1992), 34.

45. David V. N. Bagchi, *Luther's Earliest Opponents: Catholic Controversialists 1518–1525* (Minneapolis: Fortress Press, 1991), 149.

46. Paul Tillich raised the disturbing prospect that the Protestant churches of modern times may no longer still be the bearers of the religious and theological insights for which the Reformation was waged. See his collection of essays, *The Protestant Era*, trans. James Luther Adams (Chicago: University of Chicago Press, 1957).

8. Passing as Male in the Academy: Dynamics of Performance and Desire

1. While I have not found a text that discusses this particular kind of passing in academia, excellent work on different forms of passing has been done in a number of books. See, for example, Elaine K. Ginsberg, ed., *Passing and the Fictions of Identity* (Durham: Duke University Press, 1996); María Carla Sánchez and Linda Schlossberg, eds., *Passing: Identity and Interpretation in Sexuality, Race, and Religion* (New York: New York University Press, 2001); Brad Epps, Keja Valens, and Bill Johnson González, eds., *Passing Lines: Sexuality and Immigration* (Cambridge: Harvard University Press, 2005); Nella Larsen, *Passing*, ed. Carla Kaplan (New York: Norton, 2007).

2. In this section, I offer a brief account of Cartesian epistemology and its effects. Many scholars have discussed this in greater depth and detail. See, for example, Susan Bordo, *The Flight to Objectivity: Essays on Cartesianism and Culture* (Albany: State University of New York Press, 1987); and Genevieve Lloyd, *The Man of Reason: "Male" and "Female" in Western Philosophy* (Minneapolis: University of Minnesota Press, 1984).

3. René Descartes, *Discourse on Method, and Related Writings*, trans. Desmond M. Clarke (London: Penguin, 1999), 25.

4. Ibid.

5. Ibid.

6. For an early modern refutation of this logic, see Mary Wollstonecraft, *A Vindication of the Rights of Women*, ed. Deidre Shauna Lynch (New York: W.W. Norton, 2009). See also Lucretia Mott, "Discourse on Woman" and "Declaration of Sentiments," in *Lucretia Mott, Her Complete Speeches and Sermons*, ed. Dana Greene (New York: Edwin Mellen, 1980).

7. Jean-Jacques Rousseau, *Emile*, trans. Barbara Foxley (London: Dent, 1974), 388.

8. Luce Irigaray, *Speculum of the Other Woman*, trans. Gillian C. Gill (Ithaca: Cornell University Press, 1985), 292.

9. Ibid., 275.

10. Ibid., 268–74, 313–15.

11. Ibid., 326, 342.

12. Ibid., 293–95, 307.

13. Ibid., 243.

14. See, for example, John Locke, *The Reasonableness of Christianity: As Delivered in the Scriptures*, ed. John C. Higgins-Biddle (Oxford: Clarendon, 1999).

15. See Irigaray, *Speculum of the Other Woman*, 298, 300, 309, 315, 322.

16. See, for a few examples, Gary David Comstock and Susan E. Henking, eds., *Que(e)rying Religion: A Critical Anthology* (New York: Continuum, 1997); Mark Jordan, *Blessing Same-Sex Unions: The Perils of Queer Romance and the Confusion of Christian Marriage* (Chicago: Chicago University Press, 2005); Eugene F. Rogers Jr., *Sexuality and the Christian Body: Their Way into the Triune God* (Malden, MA: Blackwell, 1999).

17. See, for a few examples among many, James H. Cone, *Black Theology and Black Power* (New York: Seabury, 1969); Gustavo Gutiérrez, *A Theology of Liberation: History, Politics, and Salvation*, trans. and ed. by Sister Caridad Inda and John Eagleson (Maryknoll, N.Y.: Orbis, 1973); Rosemary Radford Ruether, *Sexism and God-Talk: Toward a Feminist Theology* (Boston: Beacon, 1983); Letty M. Russell, *Human Liberation in a Feminist Perspective—A Theology* (Philadelphia: Westminster, 1974).

18. Pamela L. Caughie describes new pedagogical practices that attend to the social construction of knowledge in more embodied ways using the rubric of passing. See *Passing and Pedagogy: The Dynamics of Responsibility* (Urbana: University of Illinois Press, 1999).

19. Luce Irigaray, "The Power of Discourse and the Subordination of the Feminine," in *This Sex Which Is Not One*, trans. Catherine Porter with Carolyn Burke (Ithaca: Cornell University Press, 1985), 76.

20. Ibid.

21. See Marvin A. Carlson, *Performance: A Critical Introduction*, 2d ed. (New York: Routledge, 2004), 9–80. See also Shannon Craigo-Snell, "Theology as Performance," *The Ecumenist* 45, no. 2 (2008): 18–29.

22. Mary S. Strine, Beverly W. Long, and Mary Francis Hopkins, "Research in Interpretation and Performance Studies: Trends, Issues, and Priorities," in *Speech Communication: Essays to Commemorate the 75th Anniversary of the Speech Communication Association*, ed. Gerald M. Phillips and Julia T. Wood (Carbondale: Southern Illinois University Press, 1990), 183. The authors are drawing upon the work of W. B. Gallie, *Philosophy and the Historical Understanding* (New York: Schocken, 1964).

23. Ibid.

24. See Richard Schechner, *Performance Studies: An Introduction* (New York: Routledge, 2002), 1, 24.

25. Carlson, *Performance*, 5. Here Carlson is drawing on comments made by Richard Baumann in "Performance," *International Encyclopedia of Communication*, ed. Erik Barnouw (New York: Oxford University Press, 1989).

26. Ibid.

27. Richard Schechner, *Performance Studies: An Introduction* (New York: Routledge, 2002), 23.

28. Ibid., 28.

29. Judith Butler, *Gender Trouble: Feminism and the Subversion of Identity* (New York: Routledge, 1990), 25. See also idem, "Performative Acts and Gender Constitution: An Essay in Phenomenology and Feminist Theory," *Theatre Journal* 40, no. 4 (1988): 519–31. I group performance and performativity together and do not elide them into one. They are two distinct but related concepts. Further exploration of their relation is beyond the scope of this essay, except to say that my concern for embodiment leads me to foreground performance, as often current conversations about performativity inhabit theoretical and linguistic frameworks. Butler has been criticized for her lack of attention to the body, which she addresses in relation to Descartes in her essay "How Can I Deny That These Hands and This Body Are Mine?" *Qui Parle* 11, no. 1 (1997): 1–20.

30. Butler, *Gender Trouble*, 146–47.

31. In general, expressivist positions understand human speaking and behavior as the external expression of internal states or realities. In the context of Butler's work, an expressivist view would see particular masculine or feminine behaviors as outward expressions of an inner, stable gender identity. In contrast, Butler contends that the behaviors themselves generate the appearance of a stable identity.

32. Esther Newton, *Mother Camp: Female Impersonators in America* (Chicago: University of Chicago Press, 1972), 103, quoted in Butler, *Gender Trouble*, 137.

33. Judith Butler, "Passing, Queering: Nella Larsen's Psychoanalytic Challenge," in *Bodies That Matter: On the Discursive Limits of "Sex"* (New York: Routledge, 1993), 167–85, 274–27. For examples of scholars using Butler's work in their discussions of passing, see Catherine Rottenberg, "*Passing*: Race, Identification, and Desire," in Nella Larsen, *Passing*, ed. Carla Kaplan (New York: Norton, 2007), 489–507. See also Jennifer DeVere Brody, "Clare Kendry's 'True' Colors: Race and Conflict in Nella Larsen's *Passing*," in Larsen, *Passing*, 393–408; and Sara Ahmed, "'She'll Wake Up One of These Days and Find She's Turned into a Nigger,'" *Theory, Culture & Society* 16 (1999): 87–105.

34. Rottenberg, "*Passing*: Race, Identification, and Desire," 496.

35. Author Pamela L. Caughie explores many connections between passing and performativity in *Passing and Pedagogy*. She describes the resonances between the two in ways that also evoke performance, drawing on Jacques Derrida and describing the "double logic" of writing. In writing, the self is both exposed and concealed. Caughie says that this double logic makes "any identity nonidentical with itself" (3). Interestingly enough, she draws on Rousseau at this point. While Caughie relies heavily upon the concept of performativity in her deployment of the term *passing*, she prefers "passing" to "performativity" for a number of reasons, including that "passing is a social practice, not a philosophical or linguistic concept" (5). She warns against interpreting "passing" in her work as "passing as a," that is, against reading it "as an intentional act rather than a performative effect," even while she says that such initial mistakes might be a necessary part of learning what she means (5). While I applaud the pedagogical use Caughie makes of the concept of passing, with an eye to epistemology I am uncomfortable with too closely eliding passing and performativity.

However, I follow the pattern Caughie attempts to avoid with her change in language: I speak of passing as a practice and performativity as a concept.

9. "Baptizing" Queer Characters

1. I use the term *baptize* partly to recall the old idiom for theology's appropriations of secular science (as in "Thomas baptizes Aristotle"), partly to suggest that imposing a new name can have important consequences—as theologians ought particularly to remember. The same holds for names about names. I happen to think that the widespread use of "identity" as a category in theology is problematic. I offer "character" instead to refer to an idealized role or script for organizing, for originating actions that are to be praised or condemned. For more on my scruples or hopes for these terms, see *Blessing Same-Sex Unions: The Perils of Queer Romance and the Confusions of Christian Marriage* (Chicago: University of Chicago Press, 2005), 3 (including n. 9), 37–39. I also return to these questions at the end of this essay.

2. Havelock Ellis and John Addington Symonds, *Sexual Inversion*, vol. 1 of *Studies in the Psychology of Sex* (London: Wilson and Macmillan, 1897; reprint Ayer, 1994), 1.

3. Ibid., *Sexual Inversion*, 27, though it is worth rereading the whole historical summary, 25–35. Cesare Lombroso makes the translation explicit and refers to Krafft-Ebing: "sessualità invertita *(contrāre Sexualemfindung)*." See Lombroso, *L'uomo delinquente in rapporto all'antropologia, alla giurisprudenza ed alle discipline carcerarie*, vol. 2, 5th ed. (Turin: Fratelli Bocca, 1896), 359. For the original diagnosis, see Carl Friedrich Otto Westphal, "Die contrāre Sexualempfindung, Symptom eines neuropathischen (psychopathischen) Zustandes," *Archiv für Psychiatrie und Nervenkrankheiten* II/1 (1869): 73–108. In a regularly misconstrued passage, Michel Foucault refers to Westphal's article ironically as the "birth date" of the psychiatric homosexual in contrast with the sodomite. Foucault is not thinking of the word *homosexual*, but of the diagnosis of inversion. See Michel Foucault, *Histoire de la sexualité*, vol.1: *La volonté de savoir* (Paris: NRF, Gallimard, 1976), 59.

4. Westphal, "Die contrāre Sexualempfindung," 102.

5. On the disorders, see Westphal, 78, 85, and 79, 107; on their links, 79, 96, and 79, 104.

6. Church of England Moral Welfare Council, *The Problem of Homosexuality: An Interim Report* (London: Church Information Board, 1954). Copies I have seen carry the same warning stamped in red on the cover.

7. Alfred C. Kinsey, Wardell B. Pomeroy, and Clyde E. Martin, *Sexual Behavior in the Human Male* (Philadelphia: W. B. Saunders, 1948), especially chap. 21 for "homosexual outlet."

8. Church of England, *Problem of Homosexuality*, 7.

9. For some episodes in the continuing saga of the Christian character of the sodomite, see Mark D. Jordan, *The Invention of Sodomy in Christian Theology* (Chicago: University of Chicago Press, 1997); Helmut Puff, *Sodomy in Reformation Germany and Switzerland, 1400–1600* (Chicago: University of Chicago Press, 2003).

10. Church of England, *Problem of Homosexuality*, 11; italics in original.

11. Ibid., 19, 22.

12. Ibid., 23.

13. Ibid., 15.

14. Ibid., 16.

15. Ibid., 14; italics in original.

16. For the reappearance of older psychiatric models within the genres of evangelical testimony or instruction, see, for example, Tanya Erzen, *Straight to Jesus: Sexual and Christian Conversions in the Ex-Gay Movement* (Berkeley: University of California Press, 2006).

17. In the mid-1950s, Bailey was an officer of the Church of England's Moral Welfare Council. For his role in drafting the pamphlet, see Jonathan Sinclair Carey, "D. S. Bailey and 'the Name Forbidden among Christians,'" *Anglican Theological Review* 70 (April 1988): 152–73, esp. 153.

18. Derrick Sherwin Bailey, *Homosexuality and the Western Christian Tradition* (London and New York: Longmans, Green, 1955).

19. Ibid., 159–65.

20. Ibid., 173.

21. Ibid., 169.

22. Bailey's larger authorship—to say nothing of his private views—is of course more complicated.

23. Bailey, *Homosexuality and the Western Christian Tradition*, 167, 176. Compare Erving Goffman's association of homosexuality with handicap—and the salience of the category "identity"—in his *Stigma: Notes on the Management of Spoiled Identity* (Englewood Cliffs, N.J.: Prentice-Hall, 1963).

24. Lyn Pedersen, review of *Homosexuality and the Western Christian Tradition*, by Derrick Sherwin Bailey, in *One: The Homosexual Magazine* 3, no. 11 (November 1955): 19–21; Donald Norton, "Sex, Religion & Myth: A Book Review in Dialogue Form," *Mattachine Review* 1, no. 6 (November/December 1955): 10–12. See the earlier summary of the Anglican pamphlet in the unsigned note, "A Bold Study by the Church of England," *One: The Homosexual Magazine* 2, no. 6 (June 1954): 17–18.

25. Pedersen, review of Bailey, 21.

26. Ken Burns, "The Homosexual Faces a Challenge" (Summer 1956), reprinted in Robert B. Ridinger, ed., *Speaking for Our Lives: Historic Speeches and Rhetoric for Gay and Lesbian Rights (1892–2000)* (New York: Harrington Park Press, 2004), 47.

27. See, for example, the retrospective remarks by Hal Call in 1962 (Ridinger, ed., *Speaking for Our Lives*, 69).

28. Karl-Günther Heimsoth, *Hetero- und Homophilie: Eine neuorientierende An- und Einordnung der Erscheinungsbilder der "Homosexualität" und der "Inversion" in Berücksichtigung der sogennanten "normalen Freundschaft" auf Grund der zwei verschiedenen erotischen Anziehungsgesetze und der bisexuellen Grundeinstellung der Mannes*, Inaugural-Dissertation zur Erlangung der Doktorwürde der medizinischen Fakultät der Universität zu Rostock (Dortmund: Schmidt & Andernach, 1924), perhaps esp. 14.

29. Hay was not the only one to recognize the power of minority status. See, for example, the 1952 speech by Donald Webster Cory [Edward Sagarin] in Ridinger, ed., *Speaking for Our Lives*, 33–34.

30. See, for example, Richard Meeker [Forman Brown], *Better Angel* (Greenberg, 1933; reprint Boston: Alyson, 1995), 90, on borrowing the French *spirituel*.

31. For example, the June 1954 issue of *One* is devoted to religion. Its essays share a passionate conviction of the evils of churches and the need to move beyond them to a personal mysticism or supportive small groups.

32. If one motive or pretext for much churchly discussion of homosexuality was decriminalization, another—from the 1950s on—was juvenile delinquency. Indeed, from

the nineteenth century on, sexual characters cannot be separated from diseased characters or criminal characters. There are traces of the preoccupation with delinquency in the consultation's archive, but I am more interested in how it frames the encounter between the homophile and the socially conscious minister-activist.

33. It seems to be have been the thinnest of pseudonyms if her legal name was in fact Billye Talmadge. See Marcia M. Gallo, *Different Daughters: A History of the Daughters of Bilitis and the Rise of the Lesbian Rights Movement* (New York: Carroll & Graf, 2006), ix, xv, 9, 16.

34. Talmij, "Talk," 2, from an online exhibit about the CRH at the LGBT Religions Archives Network, http://lgbtran.org/Exhibits/CRH/Room.aspx?RID=1&CID=5&AID=15; accessed August 25, 2008.

35. Talmij, "Fuses," ## 68–69.

36. Talmij, "Talk," 1.

37. Talmij, "Fuses," # 55; see also ## 35–36.

38. Ibid., ## 57, 58, 60. For masks and roles in the strategy of the first Mattachine members, see Martin Meeker, *Contacts Desired: Gay and Lesbian Communications and Community, 1940s–1970s* (Chicago: University of Chicago Press, 2006), esp. 33, 37–39.

39. John J. McNeill, *The Church and the Homosexual* (Kansas City: Sheed Andrews and McMeel, 1976), ix, 5.

40. See ibid., 20.

41. See ibid., 3; compare p. 98 on Thomas as the source for ethical personalism.

42. Ibid., 41. McNeill approves the older distinction between pervert and invert, but he prefers to call the latter the true or real homosexual (42, 55–56).

43. See ibid., 102.

44. Ibid., l, 93.

45. Ibid., 66.

46. See ibid., 42, 55–56.

47. Ibid., 4, 23.

48. See, for example, Robert J. McClory, "Gay Theology Pioneer Trusts 'God's Shrewdness,'" *National Catholic Reporter*, November 11, 2005, http://ncronline.org/NCR_Online/archives2/2005d/111105/111105m.php; accessed August 25, 2008.

10. EROTICIZED WIVES: EVANGELICAL MARRIAGE GUIDES AND GOD'S PLAN FOR THE CHRISTIAN FAMILY

Portions of this essay are adapted and reprinted by permission from "Marriage Under Fire," in *More Perfect Unions: The American Search for Marital Bliss*, by Rebecca L. Davis (Cambridge, Mass.: Harvard University Press, 2010).

1. Marabel Morgan, speech at St. Phillip's Episcopal Academy, Coral Gables, Florida, Thursday, April 29, 2004. Humor author Erma Bombeck famously poked fun at Morgan's set-up with her tale about the time she allegedly waited in costume for her husband, much to the bemusement of the repairman who rang the doorbell first. See Bombeck, "The Sub-Total Woman," *Aunt Erma's Cope Book* (New York: McGraw-Hill, 1979).

2. "1974: The Best Sellers," *Publishers Weekly* (Feb. 3, 1975), 34. Statistics are from the cover of a 1975 paperback edition of *The Total Woman* (New York: Pocket Books, 1975); Ray Walters, "Ten Years of Best Sellers," *New York Times Book Review* (Dec. 30, 1979), 11. See also Russell Chandler, "Conservative Christian Women Resist Feminist Inroads," *Los Angeles Times*, Dec. 29, 1974, 1; Andy Taylor, "Marabel & Charlie Morgan: Being a 'Total

Woman' May Mean Love under the Dinner Table," *People* (Apr. 7, 1975), 44–45; Marabel Morgan, "The Total Woman—Are You One?" *Cosmopolitan* (September 1975), 178–81, 184, 240; Marabel Morgan, "Total Joy!" *Good Housekeeping* (November 1976), 111; "Fighting the Housewife Blues," *Time* (Mar. 14, 1977), 63; Ann Griffith, "Sugar 'N Spice: Champion of Womanhood," *Charleston Daily Mail*, June 2, 1976, section B; "The Total Woman Story," n.d., courtesy of Marabel Morgan.

3. Author's phone interview with Marabel Morgan, Oct. 18, 2002. Historian Ruth Rosen refers to a "widely quoted—and remembered" passage in *The Total Woman* in which "Morgan urged wives to meet their husbands at the door, nude, draped only in Saran Wrap." Rosen derives most of what she knows about Morgan from a 1976 *Redbook* article. See Ruth Rosen, *The World Split Open: How the Modern Women's Movement Changed America* (New York: Penguin, 2000), 318. For the original article, see Claire Safran, "Can the Total Woman 'Magic' Work for You?" *Redbook* (February 1976), 91, 128–30. Rosen cites a reprint of the *Redbook* article, under a different title. For other examples of scholars who mistakenly attribute the Saran Wrap anecdote to *The Total Woman*, see Mark Oppenheimer, "In the Biblical Sense: A Guide to the Booming Christian Sex-Advice Industry," *Slate*, posted November 30, 1999; Andrea Dworkin, *Right-Wing Women: The Politics of Domesticated Females* (London: Women's, 1983), 25–26, 40. The misattribution even appeared in *The New York Times Magazine*; see Jennifer Senior, "Everything a Happily Married Bible Belt Woman Always Wanted to Know About Sex But Was Afraid to Ask," *New York Times Magazine* (July 4, 2004), 37.

4. See Jennifer Heller, "Marriage, Womanhood, and the Search for 'Something More': American Evangelical Women's Best-Selling 'Self-Help' Books, 1972–1979," *Journal of Religion and Popular Culture* 2 (Fall 2002): 7; Kristin Mary Celello, *Making Marriage Work: A History of Marriage and Divorce in the Twentieth-Century United States* (Chapel Hill: University of North Carolina Press, 2009), 128–30; Janice M. Irvine, *Talk about Sex: The Battles over Sex Education in the United States* (Berkeley: University of California Press, 2002), 8–88, 104, 106; Michael Lienesch, *Redeeming America: Piety and Politics in the New Christian Right* (Chapel Hill: University of North Carolina Press, 1993), 67–70, 73, 75; Colleen McDannell, *Material Christianity: Religion and Popular Culture in Modern America* (New Haven: Yale University Press, 1995), 248; Rosen, *World Split Open*, 317–20; David Harrington Watt, *A Transforming Faith: Explorations of Twentieth-Century American Evangelicalism* (New Brunswick: Rutgers University Press, 1991), 131–36, 152–53.

5. Susan Friend Harding, *The Book of Jerry Falwell: Fundamentalist Language and Politics* (Princeton: Princeton University Press, 2000), 169, 171–72.

6. For fuller discussions of these topics, see Brenda E. Brasher, *Godly Women: Fundamentalism and Female Power* (New Brunswick, N.J.: Rutgers University Press, 1998), 129; Watt, *A Transforming Faith*, 124–25; Lienesch, *Redeeming America*, 52–93; R. Marie Griffith, *God's Daughters: Evangelical Women and the Power of Submission* (Berkeley: University of California Press, 2000), 44–45, 169–86; Margaret Lamberts Bendroth, *Fundamentalism and Gender, 1875 to the Present* (New Haven: Yale University Press, 1993), 97–117; Nancy Tatom Ammerman, *Bible Believers: Fundamentalists in the Modern World* (New Brunswick, N.J.: Rutgers University Press, 1987), 134–46.

7. Author's interview with Marabel Morgan, Miami, Florida, Apr. 30, 2004.

8. Herbert Jackson Miles, *Sexual Happiness in Marriage* (Grand Rapids: Zondervan, 1967), 85–86, 89–90.

9. Tim and Beverly LaHaye, *The Act of Marriage: The Beauty of Sexual Love* (Grand Rapids: Zondervan, 1976). See also William Edward Hulme, *Building a Christian Marriage* (Engle-

wood Cliffs, N.J.: Prentice-Hall, 1965); Tim F. LaHaye, *How to Be Happy Though Married* (Wheaton, Ill.: Tyndale House, 1968); Dwight Hervey Small, *Design for Christian Marriage* (Old Tappan, N.J.: Revell, 1971).

10. McDannell, *Material Christianity*, 246–56. Tim LaHaye's *How to Be Happy Though Married* sold, according to its publisher, 180,625 copies, though the paperback cover claims over 800,000 copies in print. Tim LaHaye's *Six Keys to a Happy Marriage* (Wheaton, Ill.: Tyndale House, 1968), which excerpted a section of *How to Be Happy Though Married*, sold 92,422 copies (author's correspondence with the publisher, May 19, 2009).

11. Darien Cooper's *You Can Be the Wife of a Happy Husband—By Discovering the Key to Marital Success* (Wheaton, Ill.: Victor, 1974; reprint, Chariot-Victor, 1996) was reissued in 2005 by David C. Cook in a revised and expanded paperback edition with a forward by Tim LaHaye. According to its publisher, the book's various editions have sold about 80,000 copies since the mid-1990s, but prior sales figures are unavailable; the cover of a reprint from the 1990s claims over 900,000 copies in print (author's correspondence with the publisher, Nov. 7, 2001 and May 20, 2009). Elizabeth Rice Handford's *Me? Obey Him? The Obedient Wife and God's Way of Happiness and Blessing in the Home* (1972) is published by Sword of the Lord, a fundamentalist press that in the 1940s published the works of John R. Rice. Handford's book has sold more than 700,000 copies, has gone through two editions, and currently costs only $3.95 (author's correspondence with the publisher, May 20, 2009).

12. Zeda Thornton, "The Total Woman," *Moody Monthly* (December 1973), reprint, courtesy of Marabel and Charles Morgan; Martin E. Marty, "Fundies and Their Fetishes," *Christian Century* (Dec. 8, 1976): 960–62.

13. *The Wittenberg Door* (August–September 1975), cover.

14. Clare Rayner, "Alex Comfort," *The Guardian*, Mar. 28, 2000; John D'Emilio and Estelle B. Freedman, *Intimate Matters: A History of Sexuality in America* (New York: Harper & Row, 1989), 330.

15. David Allyn, *Make Love, Not War: The Sexual Revolution, an Unfettered History* (Boston: Little, Brown, 2000). As several historians of American politics have demonstrated, those issues helped catalyze a reinvigorated conservative movement centered around "family values." See especially Lisa McGirr, *Suburban Warriors: The Origins of the New American Right* (Princeton: Princeton University Press, 2001); Catherine E. Rymph, *Republican Women: Feminism and Conservatism from Suffrage through the Rise of the New Right* (Chapel Hill: University of North Carolina Press, 2006); Linda Kintz, *Between Jesus and the Market: The Emotions That Matter in Right-Wing America* (Durham: Duke University Press, 1997).

16. I am borrowing this phrase from Janice Irvine, *Talk about Sex: The Battles over Sex Education in the United States* (Berkeley: University of California Press, 2002).

17. Ellen Herman, *The Romance of American Psychology: Political Culture in the Age of Experts* (Berkeley: University of California Press, 1995); Lori Rotskoff, *Love on the Rocks: Men, Women, and Alcohol in Post–World War II America* (Chapel Hill: University of North Carolina Press, 2002).

18. Jennifer Terry, *An American Obsession: Science, Medicine, and Homosexuality in Modern Society* (Chicago: University of Chicago Press, 1999).

19. Elizabeth V. Spelman, "Woman as Body: Ancient and Contemporary Views," *Feminist Studies* 8, no. 1 (1982): 109–31.

20. Margaret R. Miles, *Carnal Knowing: Female Nakedness and Religious Meaning in the Christian West* (Boston: Beacon, 1989), 17.

21. Carolyn Walker Bynum, "Why All the Fuss about the Body? A Medievalist's Perspective," *Critical Inquiry* 22 (Autumn 1995): 15.

22. R. Marie Griffith, *Born Again Bodies: Flesh and Spirit in American Christianity* (Berkeley: University of California Press, 2004), quoted at 239. See also, R. Marie Griffith, "Body Salvation: New Thought, Father Divine, and the Feast of Material Pleasures," *Religion and American Culture: A Journal of Interpretation* 11, no. 2 (2001): 119–53; Amy DeRogatis, "What Would Jesus Do? Sexuality and Salvation in Protestant Evangelical Sex Manuals, 1950s to the Present," *Church History* 74, no. 1 (2005): 97–137; Clifford Putney, *Muscular Christianity: Manhood and Sports in Protestant America, 1880–1920* (Cambridge: Harvard University Press, 2001).

23. Michel Foucault, *Discipline and Punish: The Birth of the Prison*, trans. Alan Sheridan (New York: Vintage, 1979); Michel Foucault, *The History of Sexuality*, vol. 1: *An Introduction*, trans. Robert Hurley (New York: Vintage, 1978).

24. For a useful summary of these debates and trends, see Margrit Shildrick with Janet Price, "Openings on the Body: A Critical Introduction," in *Feminist Theory and the Body: A Reader* (New York: Routledge, 1999), 1–14.

25. See especially Judith Butler, *Gender Trouble: Feminism and the Subversion of Identity* (New York: Routledge, 1990); Judith Butler, *Bodies That Matter: On the Discursive Limits of 'Sex'* (New York: Routledge, 1993); Elizabeth Grosz, *Volatile Bodies: Toward a Corporeal Feminism* (Bloomington: Indiana University Press, 1994); Elizabeth Grosz, "Feminism and the Crisis of Reason," in *Space, Time, and Perversion: Essays on the Politics of Bodies* (New York: Routledge, 1995), 25–43; Moira Gatens, *Imaginary Bodies: Ethics, Power, and Corporeality* (New York: Routledge, 1996); and idem, "Power, Bodies, and Difference," in *Destabilizing Theory: Contemporary Feminist Debates*, ed. Michèle Barrett and Anne Phillips (Stanford: Stanford University Press, 1992), 120–37.

26. Gatens, "Power, Bodies, and Difference," 130.

27. Kathleen Canning, "The Body as Method? Reflections on the Place of the Body in Gender History," in *Gender History in Practice: Historical Perspectives on Bodies, Class, and Citizenship* (Ithaca: Cornell University Press, 2006), 168–69, emphasis in the original.

28. Grosz, "Feminism and the Crisis of Reason," 33, emphasis in the original.

29. Margaret Bendroth cites a Jan. 2, 1942, article from *Sword of the Lord* in which evangelist Robert G. Lee described the home as man's "fortress," "where a woman buckles on his armor in the morning as he goes forth to the battles of the day and soothes his wounds when he comes home at night." See Bendroth, *Fundamentalism and Gender*, 100.

30. Morgan, *The Total Woman*, 113.

31. Ibid., 112.

32. Ibid., 114–15.

33. Ibid., 113–14.

34. Ibid., 152.

35. Ibid., 68; Cooper, *You Can Be the Wife of a Happy Husband*, 39–40. See also Lou Beardsley and Toni Spry, *The Fulfilled Woman* (Irvine, Calif.: Harvest House, 1975), 7, 27; Phyllis Schlafly, *The Power of the Positive Woman* (New Rochelle, N.Y.: Arlington House, 1977), 54–57.

36. Butler, *Bodies That Matter*, 232.

37. Sigmund Freud, *Totem and Taboo: Resemblances between the Psychic Lives of Savages and Neurotics*, trans. A. A. Brill (New York: Moffat, Yard and Co., 1918), 3.

38. Morgan, *The Total Woman*, 116, 118; Barbara Ehrenreich and Deirdre English, *For Her Own Good: 150 Years of the Experts' Advice to Women* (Garden City, N.Y.: Anchor, 1979), 248–49.

39. Morgan, *The Total Woman*, 148–49.

40. Butler, *Bodies That Matter*, 225.

41. Kintz, *Between Jesus and the Market*, 9–10.

42. Darien B. Cooper, *Leader's Guide for You Can Be the Wife of a Happy Husband** (Wheaton, Ill.: SP Publications, Victor, 1974), 34–35; Morgan, *The Total Woman*, 106–07. See also Lois McBride Terry, *By His Side: A Woman's Place* (Fort Worth: Brownlow, 1967), 75.

43. Undated letters, Marabel Morgan's personal collection, Miami, Florida.

44. Morgan, *The Total Woman*, 130.

11. "EROS," AIDS, AND AFRICAN BODIES: A THEOLOGICAL COMMENTARY ON DEADLY DESIRES

1. On the extent and devastation of HIV/AIDS in Africa see "Facts at a Glance," Global HealthReporting.Org, http://www.globalhealthreporting.org/diseaseinfo.asp?id=23#global; and Joint United Nations Programme on HIV/AIDS and World Health Organization, "Sub-Saharan Africa AIDS Epidemic Update Regional Summary" (Geneva: UNAIDS, 2008), http://data.unaids.org/pub/Report/2008/jc1526_epibriefs_ssafrica_en.pdf, both accessed August 13, 2009.

2. I define recolonization as the reintroduction and imposition of foreign colonial patterns of thought, value systems, ideologies, and ways of speaking through which most Europeans represented Africans to themselves in the eighteenth and nineteenth centuries as radically different and other. One of the ways in which European missionaries, explorers, and colonizers represented African cultures was to describe them as immoral, lawless, and godless. Many of these descriptions singled out African modes of sexuality as examples of such immorality. As we shall see below, this discourse is returning in some of the scholarship around HIV/AIDS in Africa. It is this return that I define as discursive recolonization.

3. On sex and reason, see Ning Wang, "Logos-Modernity, Eros-Modernity, and Leisure," *Leisure Studies* 15, no. 2 (April 1996): 121–35; Steven D. Pinkerton and Paul R. Abramson, "Is Risky Sex Rational?" *Journal of Sex Research* 29, no. 4 (Nov. 1992): 561–68.

4. See for example, Eugene F. Rogers, Jr., ed., *Theology and Sexuality: Classic and Contemporary Readings* (Oxford: Blackwell, 2002).

5. See F. E. Peters, *Greek Philosophical Terms: A Historical Lexicon* (New York: New York University Press, 1967), s.v. "eros."

6. By "postcolony" I mean a space (not a place as such) in which different histories and experiences of formerly colonized peoples are recalled and lived out in the light of at least three things: (1) the more or less successful resistance to colonialism itself; (2) acts of cultural and political self-definition that seek to transcend the adverse effects of colonial experience by recalling and reenacting some aspects of a past before the advent of the colonial; and (3) the political and cultural practices that, while still residually grounded in the history of colonialism, are the means in and through which postcolonial subjects define their presence in the world today.

7. Theogony has to do with the genealogy of the gods in Greek mythology.

8. Eileen Stillwaggon, "Racial Metaphors: Interpreting Sex and AIDS in Africa," *Development and Change* 34, no. 5 (2003): 809–32.

9. John Caldwell, Pat Caldwell, and Pat Quiggin, "The Social Context of AIDS in Sub-Saharan Africa," *Population and Development Review* 15, no. 2 (June 1989): 197; and John Caldwell and Pat Caldwell, "The Cultural Context of High Fertility in Sub-Saharan Africa," *Population and Development Review* 13, no. 3 (Sept. 1987): 409–37.

10. Caldwell, Caldwell, and Quiggin, "The Social Context of AIDS," 195–204.

11. Ibid.

12. The second thing that the Caldwells and Quiggin imply is that the goal of intervening against HIV/AIDS is not that of simply changing episodic sexual behavior but ultimately that of transforming a whole civilization. In my view, this is the point at which the recolonization of African societies is instigated.

13. Ibid., 188.

14. Ibid., 194.

15. Ibid., 196.

16. Ibid., 203–4.

17. Ibid. By "worldly" we are meant to understand that for Africans sex has no connection to religion (see 209).

18. Ibid., 195–96.

19. Marijke Steegstra, "'A Mighty Obstacle to the Gospel': Basel Missionaries, Krobo Women, and Conflicting Ideas of Gender and Sexuality," *Journal of Religion in Africa* 32, no. 2 (May 2002): 200–30. See also Diana Jeater, *Marriage, Perversion and Power: The Construction of Moral Discourse in Southern Rhodesia 1894–1930* (New York: Oxford University Press, 1993).

20. Stillwaggon, "Racial Metaphors," 812–13.

21. The figures come from the Social Science Citation (Index SSCI). I have counted both essays from the date of their publication to 2008.

22. Caldwell, Caldwell and Quiggin, "The Social Context of AIDS," 196.

23. On the distinction between love and lust, see Wolfgang Fuchs, "Love and Lust after Levinas and Lingis," *Philosophy Today* 52, no. 1 (Spring 2008): 45–51.

24. On safe sex and risky sexual behavior as problems in the context of HIV/AIDS in Africa, see John Richens, John Imrie, and Helen Weiss, "Human Immunodeficiency Virus Risk: Is It Possible to Dissuade People from Having Unsafe Sex?" *Journal of the Royal Statistical Society,* Series A (Statistics in Society) 166, no. 2 (2003): 207–15; Abigail Harrison, Nonhlanhla Xaba, and Pinky Kunene, "Understanding Safe Sex: Gender Narratives of HIV and Pregnancy Prevention by Rural South African School-Going Youth," *Reproductive Health Matters* 9, no. 17 (May 2001): 63–71; Audrey E. Pettifor, Mags E. Beksinska, and Helen V. Rees, "High Knowledge and High Risk Behaviour: A Profile of Hotel-Based Sex Workers in Inner-City Johannesburg," *African Journal of Reproductive Health / La Revue Africaine de la Santé Reproductive* 4, no. 2 (Oct. 2000): 35–43; Susan Craddock, "Disease, Social Identity, and Risk: Rethinking the Geography of AIDS," *Transactions of the Institute of British Geographers,* New Series 25, no. 2 (2000): 153–68.

25. On the effects of HIV/AIDS on development, see Peris J. Jones, "When 'Development' Devastates: Donor Discourses, Access to HIV/AIDS Treatment in Africa and Rethinking the Landscape of Development," *Third World Quarterly* 25, no. 2 (2004): 383–404; Martha Ainsworth and Mead Over, "AIDS and African Development," *The World Bank Research Observer* 9, no. 2 (July 1994): 203–40.

26. See Joint United Nations Programme on HIV/AIDS, "Report on the Global HIV/AIDS Epidemic 2008" (Geneva: UNAIDS, 2008), 176, http://www.unaids.org/en/Knowl-

edgeCentre/HIVData/GlobalReport/2008/2008_Global_report.asp, accessed August 13, 2009.

27. See Alphonso Lingis, *Libido: The French Existential Theories* (Bloomington: Indiana University Press, 1985), 4ff.

28. On intimacy, see William R. Jankowiak, ed., *Intimacies: Love and Sex across Cultures* (New York: Columbia University Press, 2008); Anthony Giddens, *The Transformation of Intimacy: Sexuality, Love and Eroticism in Modern Societies* (Stanford: Stanford University Press, 1992).

29. Lingis, *Libido*, 34.

30. In referring to procreation here, I have in mind the experience of fecundity, fertility, and reproduction with which sex is bound up in Africa and elsewhere.

31. See Claire Pajaczkowska and Ivan Ward, *Shame and Sexuality: Psychoanalysis and Visual Culture* (London: Routledge, 2008).

32. Jerry Stannard, "Socratic Eros and Platonic Dialectic," *Phronesis* 4, no. 2 (1959): 120–34.

33. Ibid., 122–24.

34. On the idea of the historicity of love or the idea that love has a history, see John Armstrong, *Conditions of Love: The Philosophy of Intimacy* (New York: Norton, 2003), especially the chapter "Why Love Has a History." See also Diane Ackerman, *A Natural History of Love* (New York: Vintage, 1994).

35. Risk and vulnerability are important concepts in thinking about love. Consider the whole notion of risk-taking sexual behavior discussed earlier. Consider also the fact that all acts of self-giving in love involve risk taking. See Faith E. Foreman, "Intimate Risk: Sexual Risk Behavior among African American College Women," *Journal of Black Studies* 33, no. 5 (May 2003): 637–53. Joyce Kloc McClure, "Seeing through the Fog: Love and Injustice in *Bleak House*," *Journal of Religious Ethics* 31, no. 1 (Spring 2003): 23–44; Mark S. Cladis, "Redeeming Love: Rousseau and Eighteenth-Century Moral Philosophy," *Journal of Religious Ethics* 28, no. 2 (Summer 2000): 221–51.

36. This is a huge and interesting topic I cannot go into here.

37. Ramsay MacMullen, *Paganism in the Roman Empire* (New Haven: Yale University Press, 1983). See also Ben Witherington III, *The Acts of the Apostles: A Socio-Rhetorical Commentary* (Grand Rapids: Eerdmans, 1997).

38. Edward Schillebeeckx, *Christ: The Experience of Jesus as Lord*, trans. John Bowden (New York: Crossroad, 1981), 906.

12. QUEERING WHITE MALE FEAR IN THE MIRROR OF HIP-HOP EROTICS

1. Jon Michael Spencer, *The Rhythms of Black Folk: Race, Religion and Pan-Africanism* (Trenton, N.J.: Africa World, 1995), 166, 171.

2. See Ezek. 37:1-14.

3. James W. Perkinson, *Dreaming Moorish* (Detroit: Weightless Language, 2002).

4. Carl Henry Rux, "Eminem: the New White Negro," in *Everything but the Burden: What White People Are Taking from Black Culture*, ed. Greg Tate (New York: Broadway, 2003), 34, 37.

5. See James W. Perkinson, *White Theology: Outing Supremacy in Modernity* (New York: Palgrave Macmillan, 2004); idem, *Shamanism, Racism, and Hip-Hop Culture: Essays on White Supremacy and Black Subversion* (New York: Palgrave Macmillan, 2005).

6. Donald J. Consentino, "Interview with Robert Farris Thompson," *African Arts* 25, no. 4 (Oct. 1992): 54; and Robert Farris Thompson, *Flash of the Spirit: African and Afro-American Art and Philosophy* (New York: Vintage, 1983), xiii–xvii.

7. Charles Long, *Significations: Signs, Symbols, and Images in the Interpretation of Religion* (Philadelphia: Fortress Press, 1986), 7, 9, 137–39.

8. See Perkinson, *White Theology*, 2, 52–85.

9. Ibid., 64–65, 68–71.

10. See ibid., 119–29, 146–47. Long takes up Rudolph Otto's Latin phrase *mysterium tremendum et fascinans*—intended by Otto as a comparative category, facilitating study of religious traditions across the globe—and breaks it open on the anvil of colonial history. See Long, *Significations*, 123, 137–39, 160–63, 196–97; Rudolph Otto, *The Idea of the Holy*, trans. John W. Harvey (London: Oxford University Press). Where the West largely experienced its triumph as confirmation of a presumed superiority of its culture and religion, the "Rest" were decimated in material culture and mythic comprehension alike, forced to reinvent their lifeways and self-understandings in bricolage fashion out of the detritus of colonial conquest and subjugation. In one sense, divinity becomes then a mode of "fascinating" engagement with otherness for Europe, while it assumes an aspect of terrible and inscrutable ultimacy (the *Tremendum*) for those on the underside of modernity.

11. For example, a merely whispered "Bye, bye, baby" directed to a white woman by a naïve and northern-born fourteen-year-old named Emmitt Till while visiting southern relatives in 1954 when leaving a local dime store in Money, Mississippi, was enough to draw down torture and a mortal beating by the woman's husband, aided by a male friend. This incident epitomized white sexual fear and violence and helped launch the civil rights movement.

12. Jon Michael Spencer, "Introduction," in *The Emergency of Black and the Emergence of Rap*, special issue of *Black Sacred Music: A Journal of Theomusicology*, ed. Jon Michael Spencer (Durham: Duke University Press, 1991), 1; idem, *Rhythms of Black Folk*, 165.

13. Spencer, "Introduction," 1; idem, *Rhythms of Black Folk*, 165.

14. Ruth Gilmore, "Terror Austerity Race Gender Excess Theater," and Houston A. Baker, "Scene . . . Not Heard," in *Reading Rodney King, Reading Urban Uprising*, ed. R. Gooding-Williams (New York: Routledge, 1993), 29, 42.

15. Michael Eric Dyson, *Holler if You Hear Me: Searching for Tupac Shakur* (New York: Basic Civitas, 2001), 187, 215–16.

16. Orlando Patterson, "A Poverty of the Mind," *New York Times*, Opinion Page, March 26, 2006, 26.

17. Nelson George, *Hip Hop America* (New York: Penguin, 1999), 75, 138.

18. Spencer, *Rhythms of Black Folk*, 165–66, 169.

19. Spencer, "Introduction," 2, 5.

20. Ibid., 5, 7.

21. Michel Foucault, *The History of Sexuality*, vol 1: *An Introduction*, trans. Robert Hurley (New York: Vintage, 1980), 26–27, 44–45, 72.

22. Some scholars have read this paradoxical behavior as reflecting nostalgia for a precapitalist existence, with blackness relegated to supplying a "pornography of a former self" when life was lived unfettered before the open sky, in contact with other bodies in nature, enjoying sexuality in a mode unbowed by industrial discipline, even if subject to the struggles of a peasant lifestyle. David Roediger, for instance, would argue that the blackface mask allowed a deep and profitable expression of white "emotions of loss and

longing" and of white ridicule of the discrepancies between the American dream and its lived realities. *The Wages of Whiteness: Race and the Making of the American Working Class* (London; New York: Verso, 1991), 124.

23. George, *Hip Hop America*, 75, 138.

24. I am especially indebted for my thinking around these matters to comments made by Laurel Schneider in a panel critiquing my book *White Theology*, and in personal conversations following the "Person, Culture & Religion Group" session at the Annual Meeting of the American Academy of Religion, San Diego, Nov. 16, 2007.

25. Foucault, *History of Sexuality*, 1:54.

26. Charles Mills, *The Racial Contract* (Ithaca: Cornell University Press, 1997), 16–17, 25–27, 46, 138.

27. Taylor, quoted by Michael Hill, *Whiteness*, 5.

28. Hill, *Whiteness*, 98, 119; Raleigh Washington and Glen Kehrin, *Breaking Down the Walls: A Model for Reconciliation in an Age of Racial Strife* (Chicago: Moody, 1993), 186.

29. Hill, *Whiteness*, 131.

30. Aloysius Pieris, *An Asian Theology of Liberation* (Maryknoll, N.Y.: Orbis, 1988), 59, 63.

31. Jane Schaberg, *The Illegitimacy of Jesus: A Feminist Theological Interpretation of the Infancy Narratives*, exp. 20th-anniversary ed. (Sheffield, UK: Sheffield Phoenix, 2006).

32. Under the term "subjugated knowledges," Foucault tracks two forms of knowing that generally do not receive academic valorization but, nonetheless, offer critical challenge to the kinds of knowing the academy normally embraces. These include "erudite knowledges," developed by experts at reading "between the lines" of history or "under the surface" of texts for voices and intuitions otherwise excluded from what gets recorded and authorized; and "naïve knowledges," materializing in the experience of marginalized peoples such as prisoners, the insane, gay and lesbian persons, etc., encoding perceptions gained from suffering adverse power relations, often "conserved" in body language or folk idioms or other covert forms of representation. Michel Foucault, *Power/Knowledge: Selected Interviews and Other Writings, 1972–1977*, ed. and trans. Colin Gordon et al. (New York: Pantheon, 1980), 81–83.

13. CREATION AS GOD'S CALL INTO EROTIC EMBODIED RELATIONALITY

1. See Paul Tillich, *Love, Power, and Justice* (London: Oxford University Press, 1954), 24–34.

2. I thank Mark Jordan for this understanding of the erotic upon which I continue to rely. See also Carter Heyward, *Touching Our Strength: The Erotic as Power and the Love of God* (San Francisco: Harper & Row, 1987), and Annaletvan Schalkwyk, "Heretic but Faithful: The Reclamation of the Body as Sacred in Christian Feminist Theology," *Religion & Theology* 9, nos. 1 & 2 (2002): 135–61.

3. Eugene F. Rogers, Jr., *Sexuality and the Christian Body* (Oxford: Blackwell, 1999), 198–99. See also Nancy Duff, "Christian Vocation, Freedom of God, and Homosexuality," in *Homosexuality, Science, and the "Plain Sense" of Scripture*, ed. David L. Balch (Grand Rapids: Eerdmans, 2000), 261–77.

4. I define "theoethics" as ethics that is overtly and deliberately grounded in theological claims such as ideas of God or creation.

5. Some recent examples include: Marvin M. Ellison, *Erotic Justice: A Liberating Ethic of Sexuality* (Louisville: Westminster John Knox, 1996), and *Same-Sex Marriage? A Christian Ethical Analysis* (Cleveland: Pilgrim, 2004); Dan Spencer, "Keeping Body, Soul, and Earth Together," in *Body and Soul: Rethinking Sexuality as Justice Love*, ed. Marvin M. Ellison and Sylvia Thorson-Smith (Cleveland: Pilgrim, 2003), 319–33; and Robert Goss, "Gay Erotic Spirituality and the Recovery of Sexual Pleasure," in ibid., 201–17; Kathy Rudy, *Sex and the Church: Gender, Homosexuality, and the Transformation of Christian Ethics* (Boston: Beacon, 1997); and queer theorists Janet Jakobsen and Ann Pellegrini, *Love the Sin: Sexual Regulation and the Limits of Religious Tolerance* (Boston: Beacon, 2004), and Ladelle McWhorter, *Bodies and Pleasures: Foucault and the Politics of Sexual Normalization* (Bloomington: Indiana University Press, 1999).

6. Fifteenth-century reformer Martin Luther stated that a Christian's vocations, or callings, are "masks of God" (*larvae Dei*)—masks behind which God continues to create, support, and protect creation. He wrote, "Now the whole creation is a face or mask of God. But here we need the wisdom that distinguishes God from His mask. The world does not have this wisdom. . . . There must be masks or social positions; for God has given them, and they are His creatures." Martin Luther, *Lectures on Galatians* (1535), *Luther's Works*, vol. 26, ed. Jaroslav Pelikan (St. Louis: Concordia, 1961), 95. See also "Commentary on Psalm 147:13," in *Luther's Works*, vol. 14, 112.

7. Ellison, *Erotic Justice*, 82ff.; italics mine.

8. According to Anders Nygren, eros and agape are to be separated into competing forms of love: *agape* (self-giving love) and *eros* (self-serving love). Anders Nygren, *Agape and Eros*, trans. Philip S. Watson (London: S.P.C.K., 1953).

9. Michel Foucault, *The History of Sexuality*, vol. 1: *An Introduction*, trans. Robert Hurley (New York: Vintage, 1978), and Mark Jordan, *The Silence of Sodom: Homosexuality in Modern Catholicism* (Chicago: University of Chicago Press, 2000).

10. Audre Lorde, "Uses of the Erotic: The Erotic as Power," in *Weaving the Visions: New Patterns in Feminist Spirituality*, ed. Judith Plaskow and Carol P. Christ (San Francisco: HarperSanFrancisco, 1989), 212.

11. Terry Tempest Williams, *Red: Passion and Patience in the Desert* (New York: Vintage, 2001), 106.

12. Marvin M. Ellison, "Beyond Same-Sex Marriage," in *Heterosexism in Contemporary World Religion: Problem and Prospect*, ed. Marvin M. Ellison and Judith Plaskow (Cleveland: Pilgrim, 2007), 53ff.

13. For example, see Goss, "Gay Erotic Spirituality," 201–17. Goss does advocate for limits on erotic freedom but faithfulness or fidelity do not seem to be among them.

14. Ellison, *Erotic Justice*, 82.

15. Ellison, *Same-Sex Marriage*, 142.

16. Not all explorers of the erotic deny the importance of faithfulness. See Thomas Briedenthal, "Sanctifying Nearness," in *Our Selves, Our Souls and Bodies: Sexuality and the Household of God*, ed. Charles Hefling (Boston: Cowley, 1996), 45–57; Rowan Williams, "The Body's Grace," in ibid., 58–68; James B. Nelson, *Embodiment: An Approach to Sexuality and Christian Theology* (Minneapolis: Augsburg, 1978); and Margaret Farley, *Just Love: A Framework for Christian Sexual Ethics* (New York: Continuum, 2008).

17. Ellison, *Same-Sex Marriage*, 166.

18. Because of this divine freedom to call forth life in relentless possibility, Christian theological ethics begins not with human freedom but with the "action and freedom of God." Duff, "Christian Vocation, Freedom of God, and Homosexuality," 265.

19. Catherine LaCugna, *God for Us: The Trinity and Christian Life* (San Francisco: HarperSanFrancisco, 1991), 1. See also Rogers, *Sexuality and the Christian Body*, 198, 222; and Elizabeth A. Johnson, *She Who Is: The Mystery of God in Feminist Theological Discourse* (New York: Crossroad, 1992), 200.

20. Rogers, *Sexuality and the Christian Body*, 226.

21. I draw this understanding of integrity from Terence Fretheim, *The Suffering of God: An Old Testament Perspective*, Overtures to Biblical Theology (Philadelphia: Fortress Press, 1987), 35, and *God and World in the Old Testament: A Relational Theology of Creation* (Nashville: Abingdon, 2006), 15.

22. Katherine Doob Sakenfeld, "Love (OT)," in *The Anchor Bible Dictionary*, vol.4, ed. David Freedman (New York: Doubleday, 1992), 377–80.

23. Katherine Doob Sakenfeld, *The Meaning of Hesed in the Hebrew Bible: A New Inquiry* (Missoula: Scholar's, 1978), 238–39.

24. Camilla Burns, "The Call of Creation," in *Revisiting the Idea of Vocation: Theological Explorations*, ed. John C. Haughey, S.J. (Washington, D.C.: The Catholic University of America 2004), 24.

25. Paul Sponheim, *Faith and the Other: A Relational Theology* (Minneapolis: Fortress Press, 1993), 60.

26. Elaine Graham, "Towards a Practical Theology of Embodiment," in *Globalization and Difference: Practical Theology in a World Context*, ed. Paul Ballard and Pam Couture (Cardiff: Cardiff Academic, 1999), 79ff.

27. Martin Luther, "Large Catechism," in *The Book of Concord: The Confessions of the Evangelical Lutheran Church*, ed. T. G. Tappert (Philadelphia: Fortress Press, 1959), 386.

28. Kenda Creasy Dean, *Practicing Passion: Youth and the Quest for a Passionate Church* (Grand Rapids: Eerdmans, 2004), 76–77.

29. Robert Jenson, "Faithfulness," in *Theology and Sexuality: Classic and Contemporary Readings*. ed. Eugene F. Rogers, Jr. (Oxford: Blackwell, 2002), 196.

30. Williams, "The Body's Grace," 63.

31. Ibid.

32. As quoted in Rudy, *Sex and the Church*, 77.

33. Briendenthal, "Sanctifying Nearness," 48.

34. Ibid., 55.

14. Promiscuous Incarnation

1. Darby Kathleen Ray, *Incarnation and Imagination: A Christian Ethic of Ingenuity* (Minneapolis: Fortress Press, 2008), 43.

2. See Jürgen Moltmann's argument for the primacy of the incarnation in Christian theology, *The Trinity and the Kingdom*, trans. Margaret Kohl (Minneapolis: Fortress Press, 1993 [1981]). See also Lisa Isherwood, "The Embodiment of Feminist Liberation Theology: The Spiralling of Incarnation," *Feminist Theology* 12, no. 2 (2004): 140–56.

3. I am referring here especially to the bodies of the nondominant in society—the bodies of people of color, of the homeless, of women, and of sexual minorities. However, a closer study of the "body of Christ" as a euphemism for the church in its explicit ritual

practices of baptism and Eucharist as well as its latent practices of inclusion and exclusion also reveals deep ambivalence about flesh. I cannot attend to these ambivalences in this short essay but hope to do so in a longer treatment of the topic. A good treatment of the hierarchical "chain of being" and its relationship to Christian theology is available online in the University of Virginia's *Dictionary of the History of Ideas*. See Lia Formigari, "Chain of Being," available at http://etext.virginia.edu/cgi-local/DHI/dhi.cgi?id=dv1-45, accessed January 19, 2009.

4. Jürgen Moltmann, *God in Creation: A New Theology of Creation and the Spirit of God*, trans. Margaret Kohl (Minneapolis: Fortress Press, 1993 [1985]); Rosemary Radford Ruether, *Gaia and God: An Ecofeminist Theology of Earth Healing* (San Francisco: HarperSanFrancisco, 1992); Sallie McFague, *The Body of God: An Ecological Theology* (Minneapolis: Fortress Press, 1993); Nancy R. Howell, *A Feminist Cosmology: Ecology, Solidarity, and Metaphysics* (Amherst, N.Y.: Humanity, 2000).

5. Laurel C. Schneider, *Beyond Monotheism: A Theology of Multiplicity* (London: Routledge, 2007).

6. Catherine Keller, *The Face of the Deep: A Theology of Becoming* (London: Routledge, 2003).

7. Isherwood, "Embodiment," 149.

8. *Oxford English Dictionary*, 2nd ed., s.v. "Promiscuous (New York: Oxford University Press, 1989)

9. *Oxford English Dictionary*, 2nd ed., s.v. "Incarnation."

10. *Oxford English Dictionary*, 2nd ed., s.v. "Promiscuous."

11. For more on the co-constitution of sex, race, and gender, see my article "What Race Is Your Sex?" in *Disrupting White Supremacy from Within: White People on What We Need to Do*, ed. Jennifer Harvey, Karin Case, and Robin Hawley Gorsline (Cleveland: Pilgrim, 2004), 142–62.

12. See Judith Romney Wegner, "Leviticus," in *The Women's Bible Commentary*, ed. Carol A. Newsom and Sharon H. Ringe (Louisville: Westminster John Knox, 1998), 40–48. See also Alice Bach, ed., *Women in the Hebrew Bible: A Reader* (London: Routledge, 1998).

13. "Patriarchal" refers to the rule (Gk. *arche*) of the father (Gk. *patria*), while "patrilineal" refers to the paternal line of descent. Societies are patriarchal that place men in ruling positions vis-à-vis women. They are patrilineal when they trace names and inheritance through the father's line. The two most often occur together (as in Roman society) but not necessarily.

14. In the case of the Hopi people, for example, male responsibility for children follows the maternal line, and so individual men are financially and morally responsible primarily for their sisters' children. A mother, therefore, relies for material support on brothers and secures her children's future through them rather than through husband or lovers. As one Hopi friend informed me, "I love my biological son and daughters and am free to dote on them without reserve. But they are my wife's brothers' worry and responsibility for education and proper provision. That is as it should be, since her brothers are their clan elders. My worry is my four nephews, who give me plenty of grey hairs and who will rise up in my clan and carry my name. All of this leaves my wife and me free to enjoy ourselves as English married couples seldom do—we do not fight over how to send our children to college!" Personal correspondence, December, 1999.

15. Laurel C. Schneider, *Re-Imagining the Divine: Confronting the Backlash against Feminist Theology* (Cleveland: Pilgrim, 1999), 171ff.

16. See, among others, James A. Nelson, *Embodiment: An Approach to Sexuality and Christian Theology* (Minneapolis: Augsburg, 1978); Kelly Brown Douglas, *Sexuality and the Black Church: A Womanist Perspective* (Maryknoll, N.Y.: Orbis, 1999); Mary E. Hunt, *Good Sex: Feminist Perspective from the World's Religions* (New Brunswick, N.J.: Rutgers University Press, 2001).

17. See especially Marcella Althaus-Reid, *Indecent Theology: Theological Perversions in Sex, Gender, and Politics* (London: Routledge, 2000).

18. Interestingly, an English-language-testing Web site reported a surge in hits by users who Googled "define promiscuous" directly following the song's release. See http://www.english-test.net/forum/ftopic15620.html, accessed August 17, 2009.

19. Nelly Furtado, "Promiscuous" (featuring Timbaland), written by Tim "Attitude" Clayton, Tim Mosley, Nelly Furtado, and Nate Hills, track from *Loose*, CD B000630002 (Geffen: Universal Music Distribution, 2006).

20. What would have happened, for example, to early Christian configurations of Jesus' identity at Nicea had Israel and Rome calculated descent through the mother's line? The fact that there were serious debates at all about his humanity speaks to the cultural presence (although not dominance) of matrilineal assumptions among the bishops gathered from across the nascent Christian empire.

21. Ray, *Incarnation and Imagination*, 44.

22. I have argued that "continuous" is a better translation than "eternal." See Schneider, *Beyond Monotheism*, 117–20.

23. For example, the particularity of Jesus' maleness vexes contemporary Catholic debates over the ordination of women, as do questions of his sexuality in relation to marriage, homosexuality, and so forth. The idea that "God became flesh" once in history is coming under challenge by feminist, ecological, process, and womanist theologians for whom the revelation of incarnation implicates and imbues all flesh with some dimension of divinity but for whom such worldly divinity remains somewhat abstract. See, e.g., McFague *Body of God*; Howell, *Feminist Cosmology*, and Karen Baker-Fletcher, *Sisters of Dust, Sisters of Spirit: Womanist Wordings on God* (Minneapolis: Fortress Press, 1998). For discussion of the early Christian debates on the nature of Christ, see William Rusch, *The Trinitarian Controversy* (Minneapolis: Fortress Press, 1980).

24. An excellent treatment of this period of doctrinal formation in the Christian church under Emperor Constantine is H. A. Drake, *Constantine and the Bishops: The Politics of Intolerance* (Baltimore: Johns Hopkins University Press, 2002).

25. I follow Lisa Isherwood on this point. See Isherwood, "Embodiment," 149–50.

26. See, for example, David J. Furley, *The Greek Cosmologists*, vol. 1: *The Formation of the Atomic Theory and Its Earliest Critics* (Cambridge: Cambridge University Press, 1987).

27. Isherwood, "Embodiment," 149.

28. A good starting place for thinking about the inherent multiplicity in Christian thought is Moltmann, *The Trinity and the Kingdom*.

15. Ecclesiology, Desire, and the Erotic

1. C. S. Lewis's little book, *The Four Loves* (London: Collins, 1960), is still extremely valuable in distinguishing between eros and plain sexual desire (what Lewis calls "Venus"). But more importantly for our purpose here, Lewis recognizes that eros is not exhausted

by sexual experience and "includes other things besides" (85). "Sexual desire," he writes, "without Eros, wants *it*, the *thing in itself*; Eros wants the Beloved" (87).

2. Bernard McGinn, "The Language of Inner Experience in Christian Mysticism," *Spiritus: A Journal of Christian Spirituality* 1, no. 2 (2001): 157. There is a lengthy and more illuminating discussion of Hadewijch in McGinn's *The Presence of God: A History of Western Christian Mysticism*, vol. 3: *The Flowering of Mysticism: Men and Women in the New Mysticism* (*1200–1350*) (New York: Crossroad, 1998), 200–22.

16. SEX IN HEAVEN? ESCHATOLOGICAL EROS AND THE RESURRECTION OF THE BODY

1. Margaret R. Miles, "Sex and the City (of God): Is Sex Forfeited or Fulfilled in Augustine's Resurrection of the Body?" *Journal of the American Academy of Religion* 73, no. 2 (2005): 309, 310.

2. F. Regina Psaki, "The Sexual Body in Dante's Celestial Paradise," in *Imagining Heaven in the Middle Ages*, ed. Jan Swango Emerson and Hugh Feiss (New York: Garland, 2000), 48, 58.

3. Ibid, 57.

4. Some theologians, especially process, feminist, and ecotheologians raise important theological, moral, and political concerns about how belief in heaven can adversely affect how humans live on earth. For example, an ecotheological perspective would advocate abandoning belief in personal immortality and viewing death as a natural process. This viewpoint emphasizes the interconnectivity of the divine with all that is and points toward an ethic of sustainability. See David Ray Griffin, "Process Eschatology," and Rosemary Radford Ruether, "Eschatology in Christian Feminist Theologies," in *The Oxford Handbook of Eschatology*, ed. Jerry L. Walls (New York: Oxford University Press, 2008); Sallie McFague, *The Body of God: An Ecological Theology* (Minneapolis: Fortress Press, 1993), esp. chap. 7, "Eschatology: A New Shape for Humanity."

5. Eschatology (from the Greek word *eschaton*, meaning "the end") is the doctrine of the end times or consummation of history when the whole cosmos will assume its final destiny—a doctrine that traditionally includes subjects like the last judgment, resurrection of the body, heaven, and hell.

6. Philosophers are also very engaged with the question of whether there is heaven or immortality at all. For an example of a counterargument by an atheist philosopher, see Kai Nielson's essays in *Death and Afterlife*, ed. Stephen T. Davis (New York: St. Martin's, 1989): "The Faces of Immortality," "God and the Soul: A Response to Paul Badham," "God, the Soul, and Coherence: A Response to Davis and Hick," and "Conceivability and Immortality: A Response to John Hick."

7. My claim about the woundedness of the blessed brings up the issue of disabilities. There is a growing literature in theological disability studies regarding how to speak of redemption and physical disabilities. This is beyond the purview of this essay. For one recent set of viewpoints, see "Women with Disabilities: A Challenge to Feminist Theology," *Journal of Feminist Studies in Religion* 10, no. 2 (1994): 99–134.

8. For the notion of eschatological imagination, I am indebted to John Thiel, "For What May We Hope? Thoughts on the Eschatological Imagination," *Theological Studies* 67 (2006): 517–41.

9. John Morreall, "Perfect Happiness and the Resurrection of the Body," *Religious Studies* 16 (1980): 29–35.

10. See ibid., 31.

11. Stephen T. Davis, "Is Personal Identity Retained in the Resurrection?" *Modern The-ology* 2, no. 4 (1986): 333. For a process theological argument for resurrected bodies in which memory is an important factor, see Granville C. Henry, "Does Process Thought Allow Personal Immortality?" *Religious Studies* 31 (1995): 311–21. Other philosophers dispute the importance of the category of memory. See Lynne Rudder Baker, "Material Persons and the Doctrine of Resurrection," *Faith and Philosophy* 18, no. 2 (2001): 151–67.

12. Morreall, "Perfect Happiness," 35. There have been attempts to propose alternatives to the notion of an immortal soul. For example, P. W. Gooch proposes the concept of a resur-rected being as a "disembodied person" ("On Disembodied Resurrected Persons: A Study in the Logic of Christian Eschatology," *Religious Studies* 17 [1981]: 204). Although he insists that this notion is not the same as a soul, the differences seem semantic; Gooch's "disembodied person" seems to be essentially the same as Morreall's concept of a soul—that is, a nonmate-rial being with a personal identity that corresponds to the living earthly being it once was.

13. Richard F. Creel, "Happiness and Resurrection: A Reply to Morreall," *Religious Studies* 17 (1981): 387–93.

14. Ibid., 389.

15. Ibid., 391. The Creel/Morreal debate is modern but not novel. Aquinas and Greg-ory of Nyssa are two classic voices in the tradition that Creel and Morreall echo, respec-tively. Contrary to the logic of Aquinas, Gregory of Nyssa argued that the resurrected bodies in heaven would have no physical needs, make no contribution to the "soul's com-munion with God," and engage in no physical activity all, since the blessed will be involved solely in contemplation of God. J. Warren Smith, "The Body of Paradise and the Body of the Resurrection: Gender and the Angelic Life in Gregory of Nyssa's *De hominis opificio*," *Harvard Theological Review* 92, no. 2 (2006): 226. See n. 33 below.

16. Creel, "Happiness and Resurrection," 394.

17. Ibid., 392.

18. Ibid., 393.

19. Ibid., 392.

20. Ibid. 393.

21. Ibid., 392 n.1.

22. Beth Felker Jones, *Marks of His Wounds: Gender Politics and Bodily Resurrection* (New York: Oxford University Press, 2007); Ronald E. Long, "Heavenly Sex: The Moral Author-ity of an Impossible Dream," *Theology and Sexuality* 11, no. 3 (2005): 31–46.

23. Jones, *Marks of His Wounds*, 102.

24. See ibid., 74.

25. Ibid., 88.

26. Ibid., 113, 95.

27. Long, "Heavenly Sex," 36; see 34.

28. Ibid., 37.

29. Elizabeth Stuart, *Gay and Lesbian Theologies: Repetitions with Critical Difference* (Burling-ton, Vt.: Ashgate, 2003), 108; see 9–11.

30. Elizabeth Stuart, "Sexuality: The View from the Font (the Body and the Ecclesial Self)," *Theology and Sexuality* 6, no. 11 (1999): 15.

31. Ibid., 16. She appeals to Gal. 3:28.

32. Stuart, *Gay and Lesbian Theologies*, 114.

33. See ibid., 110. Or to be more precise, as Sarah Coakley explains, "Gregory holds . . . that the original creation was of non-sexed (that is, non-genitalized) beings" (*Powers and Submissions: Spirituality, Philosophy, and Gender* [Oxford: Blackwell, 2002], 163). For an alternative interpretation of Nyssa, see John Behr, "The Rational Animal: A Rereading of Gregory of Nyssa's *De hominis opificio*," *Journal of Early Christian Studies* 7, no. 2 (1999): 219–47.

34. Stuart, *Gay and Lesbian Theologies*, 112.

35. Elizabeth Stuart, "Turning towards the Tomb: Priesthood and Gender," *Theology and Sexuality* 10, no. 1 (2003): 31.

36. See Margaret D. Kamitsuka, *Feminist Theology and the Challenge of Difference* (New York: Oxford University Press, 2007), 65–71.

37. Long, "Heavenly Sex," 37.

38. Ibid., 36.

39. Ibid., 42.

40. Stuart, *Gay and Lesbian Theologies*, 106; Stuart, "Turning towards the Tomb," 34.

41. Stuart, *Gay and Lesbian Theologies*, 100.

42. The notion of performing gendered and sexed identity is drawn from Judith Butler. See her *Gender Trouble: Feminism and the Subversion of Identity* (New York: Routledge, 1990) and *Bodies That Matter: On the Discursive Limits of "Sex"* (New York: Routledge, 1993). For a concise summary of Butler on these issues, see Kamitsuka, *Feminist Theology*, 70–71.

43. See Anne Daniell, "The Spiritual Body: Incarnations of Pauline and Butlerian Embodiment Themes for Constructive Theologizing Toward the Parousia," *Journal of Feminist Studies in Religion* 16, no. 1 (2000): 522.

44. Julia Kristeva, "Experiencing the Phallus as Extraneous, or Women's Twofold Oedipus Complex," *Parallax* 4, no. 3 (1998): 31. "Phallic primacy is . . . the hallmark of 'infantile genital organization': i.e. it is precisely the factor differentiating infantile genitality from adult genitality, which in principle recognizes the existence of two sexes." That is, the notion of "desire for the other sex" is a post-Oedipal development. "[P]hallic monism . . . remains, for the two sexes, a fundamental datum of the unconscious" (ibid.). That said, there are significant differences in psychosexual development for boys and girls, as Kristeva argues in this essay.

45. Freud, quoted in Julia Kristeva, *Tales of Love*, trans. Leon S. Roudiez (New York: Columbia University Press, 1987), 124.

46. Catharine Clément and Julia Kristeva, *The Feminine and Sacred* (New York: Columbia University Press, 2001), 38.

47. Julia Kristeva, *Powers of Horror: An Essay on Abjection*, trans. Leon S. Roudiez (New York: Columbia University Press, 1982), 6, 11.

48. Ibid., 10.

49. In some of Kristeva's writings, she speaks of this pre-Oedipal experience as prelinguistic and semiotic, in contrast with Oedipal, symbolic meaning. I am critical of this philosophical orientation (see Kamitsuka, *Feminist Theology*, 86–87). However, I have come to believe that Kristeva may be read in a more nuanced manner, as affirming the cultural and linguistic structure of all experience. See Kelly Oliver, *Reading Kristeva: Unraveling the Double-bind* (Bloomington: Indiana University Press, 1993), 103–7.

50. Sara Beardsworth, "Freud's Oedipus and Kristeva's Narcissus: Three Heterogeneities," *Hypatia* 20, no. 1 (2005): 66.

51. Kristeva, cited in Kelly Oliver, "Kristeva's Imaginary Father and the Crisis of the Paternal Function," *Diacritics* 21, no. 2/3 (1991): 50.

52. Kristeva, *Tales of Love*, 7.

53. Julia Kristeva, *Black Sun: Depression and Melancholia*, trans. Leon S. Roudiez (New York: Columbia University Press, 1989), 27–28. Melancholic tendencies toward self-annihilation, Kristeva observes clinically, can also be accompanied by a panorama of sublimating activities—including, for contemporary women especially, an often turbulent search for their own rightful (phallic) gratification. See Kristeva, "Experiencing the Phallus," 38, 41.

54. Linda Zerilli disputes the idea that a stark dichotomy obtains between de Beauvoir and Kristeva on maternity. Linda M. G. Zerilli, "A Process without a Subject: Simone de Beauvoir and Julia Kristeva on Maternity," *Signs* 18, no. 1 (1992): 111–35. For a critique of Kristeva on the maternal body, see Butler, *Gender Trouble*, 79–93.

55. Kelly Oliver, "Kristeva's Feminist Revolutions," *Hypatia* 8, no. 3 (1993): 105. The maternal function can take place in other forms including, importantly for Kristeva, the psychoanalytic situation.

56. Kristeva, "Experiencing the Phallus," 41.

57. Ibid., 43. It is important to clarify that it would be incorrect psychoanalytically to call the phallic narcissism "sexual" and maternal *jouissance* "nonsexual." In Freudian psychology, sexuality has its origins in the early stages of infant and child development and remains a constant datum, at least of the unconscious.

58. Kristeva, *Tales of Love*, 241, 253.

59. Freud, quoted in ibid., 124.

60. Kristeva, *Tales of Love*, 255.

61. Ibid., 259–60.

62. Julia Kristeva, *Julia Kristeva, Interviews*, ed. Ross Mitchell Guberman (New York: Columbia University Press, 1996), 63.

63. Ibid., 62.

64. Some philosophers are willing to speculate that God would wipe out memories of those in heaven—a notion referred to as "blessed ignorance"—but others insist (rightly, I believe) that the blessed would retain their memories (e.g., of loved ones) because "purging the minds of the blessed" would be a divine violation of human autonomy (Eric Reitan, "Eternal Damnation and Blessed Ignorance: Is the Damnation of Some Incompatible with the Salvation of Any?" *Religious Studies* 38 (2002): 444, 445.

65. Julia Kristeva, *In the Beginning Was Love: Psychoanalysis and Faith*, trans. Arthur Goldhammer (New York: Columbia University Press, 1987), 61.

66. The theological topic of temporality and heaven is beyond the purview of this essay. For one defense of this idea, see Bernard P. Prusak, "Bodily Resurrection in Catholic Perspectives," *Theological Studies* 61 (2000): 84–85.

67. Kristeva, *Powers of Horror*, 31, 27. The phrase "rebirth with and against abjection" refers to the therapeutic, clinical "cathartic" process of transference and countertransference that is presumably a pathway to psychic integration and health (31).

17. "Flesh That Dances": A Theology of Sexuality and the Spirit in Toni Morrison's *Beloved*

This chapter is adapted from an essay that was initially written as a section on "Sexuality and the Church" for *Lifelines: Journeys of Sex and the Spirit*, a training manual for community organizers proposed for publication by the Task Force on Sexuality of the Urban-Rural

Missions (URM) of the World Council of Churches. I was a member of this task force, which held several meetings from 1997 to 1999 around issues pertaining to sexuality, spirituality, and colonization. I performed the sermon in the Clearing as a ritual during one of these meetings. I am indebted to Mab Segrest who served as URM Coordinator at the time, the board, and the participants who made room for and helped inform this work.

1. Toni Morrison, *Beloved* (New York: Penguin, 1988), 88–89.

2. When I speak of the prophetic I speak of a position, stance, or action that uncovers and critiques oppressive conditions, yet also presents a remedies or alternative modes of action to bring about a more just, humane, and loving reality.

3. Delores Williams describes this as "the dominating culture's historic abuse and exploitation of African-American women's bodies." Delores S. Williams, "Sin, Nature and Black Women's Bodies," in *Ecofeminism and the Sacred*, ed. Carol J. Adams (New York: Continuum, 2007), 24.

4. Pneumatology refers to the doctrine of the Holy Spirit, including how this third person or agent of the Trinity is understood. See, for example, Molly T. Marshall, "Participating in the Life of God: A Trinitarian Pneumatology," *Perspectives in Religious Studies* 30, no. 2 (2003): 139–50, and Karen Baker-Fletcher, *Dancing with God: The Trinity from a Womanist Perspective* (St. Louis: Chalice, 2006). The terms *womanist* and *feminist* speak to the particular social locations of female scholars in religion. Baker-Fletcher identifies herself as a womanist—a term first coined by Alice Walker to refer to feminists of color in her book *In Search of Our Mother's Gardens* (San Diego: Harcourt Brace Jovanovich, 1983)—meaning, a theologian and scholar who privileges African American female experience and sources in her work. The term *feminist*, as used by Marshall, refers to a broader diversity of female experience (for example, she includes the presentation by Chung Hyun Kyung, an Asian ecofeminist in her discussion of pneumatology). However, historically, "feminist" is a term that has often referred more specifically to the work of white feminists doing scholarship from the perspective of white female experience. Both womanists and feminists have recovered the trinitarian formula as a way of expressing God's multidimensionality.

5. The Cappadocians were a monastic community consisting of early Eastern church "fathers" such as Basil the Great, Gregory of Nyssa, and Gregory Nazianzus. They employed the term *perichoresis* to describe the relationship among the three persons or agents of the Trinity as that of an "ecstatic dance" in which God the Father, Son, and Holy Spirit "stand outside themselves" and yet "evoke the life of their divine counterparts." See Marshall, "Participating in the Life of God," 145.

6. Audre Lorde, "Uses of the Erotic: The Erotic as Power," in *Sister Outsider* (Freedom, Calif.: Crossing, 1984), 54.

7. See David Carr, *The Erotic Word: Sexuality, Spirituality, and the Bible* (New York: Oxford University Press, 2003), 5.

8. See Albert J. Raboteau, "African Americans, Exodus and the American Israel," in *Religion and American Culture*, ed. David G. Hackett (New York: Routledge, 2003); Rosemary Radford Ruether, *America, Amerikkka* (Oakville, Ct.: Equinox, 2007); Andrea Smith, *Conquest: Sexual Violence and American Indian Genocide* (Cambridge, Mass.: South End, 2005).

9. Williams argues that "defilement manifests itself in human attacks upon creation so as to ravish, violate, and destroy creation: to exploit and control the production and reproduction capacities of nature, to destroy the unity in nature's placements, to obliterate the spirit of the created world" ("Sin, Nature and Black Women's Bodies," 25).

10. Kelly Brown Douglas, *Sexuality and the Black Church* (Maryknoll, N.Y.: Orbis, 1999), 23–24.

11. For more on European attitudes toward Africans and the effects white attitudes had on black women's lives in antebellum North America, see Winthrop D. Jordan, *White over Black: American Attitudes Toward the Negro, 1550–1812* (Chapel Hill: University of North Carolina Press, 1995), and Deborah Gray White, *Ar'n't I a Woman? Female Slaves in the Plantation South* (New York: Norton, 1999).

12. Williams, "Sin, Nature and Black Women's Bodies," 27.

13. See Joy R. Bostic, "Taking Hold of the Clouds: Soul Contemplation and the Search for Home" (Ph.D. diss., Union Theological Seminary, New York, 2007), 67–68.

14. Carol Henderson, "Refiguring the Flesh," in *James Baldwin and Toni Morrison: Comparative Critical and Theoretical Essays*, ed. Lovalerie King and Lynn O. Scott (New York: Palgrave, 2006), 150.

15. Morrison, *Beloved*, 17.

16. Ibid., 60–62.

17. Lorde, "Uses of the Erotic," 54.

18. For more on the cultural legacy of slavery and views on black sexuality, see Douglas, *Sexuality and the Black Church*.

19. Henderson, "Refiguring the Flesh," 150.

20. Ibid., 151.

21. Karen Baker-Fletcher, "The Erotic in Contemporary Black Women's Writings," in *Loving the Body: Black Religious Studies and the Erotic*, ed. Anthony B. Pinn and Dwight N. Hopkins (New York: Palgrave Macmillan, 2004), 205.

22. Henderson, "Refiguring the Flesh," 158.

23. Ibid., 155.

24. Ibid., 185.

25. Ibid., 158.

26. Morrison, *Beloved*, 209.

27. See, for example, Elochukwu E. Uzukwu, *Worship as Body Language: Introduction to Christian Worship, An African Orientation* (Collegeville, Minn.: Liturgical, 1997); Peter J. Paris, *The Spirituality of African Peoples: The Search for a Common Moral Discourse* (Minneapolis: Fortress Press, 1995); Kariamu Welsh-Asante, *African Dance: An Artistic, Historical, and Philosophical Inquiry* (Trenton, N.J.: Africa World, 1996).

28. Marshall includes a description of ecofeminist Korean theologian Chung Hyun Kyung's address to the World Council of Churches in 1991 in Canberra as the literal and figurative spark to a radical rethinking of doctrines of the Spirit. See Marshall, "Participating in the Life of God," 143–44.

29. See ibid., 144–45.

30. Baker-Fletcher does so in conversation with process theology. Monica A. Coleman, in *Making a Way Out of No Way: A Womanist Theology* (Minneapolis: Fortress Press, 2008), also uses the language of dance to explore life with God drawing from process and postmodern theology.

31. Baker-Fletcher, *Dancing with God*, 55.

32. Ibid., 56.

33. See ibid., 57–58.

Biblical Reference Index

General Index

abjection, 208, 210, 263, 270–71, 273–74, 342n67
  See also Kristeva, Julia
Adam, 16, 223, 36–37, 74, 76, 103, 178, 270, 306n15
  See also Eve
adultery, 17, 19, 29, 64, 124, 167, 176, 187
Africa, 9, 46, 181–95, 200, 205, 213
African American, 4, 198, 278–79, 282, 285, 288–89, 293, 305n 29, 343n4
afterlife, 83, 96, 274–75, 314n27
  See also heaven
agape, 4, 21, 183, 248, 258, 304n14, 335n8
  eros and, 21, 183, 248, 258, 304n14, 335n8
  See also eros; *philia*
androcentrism, 106, 109–10
Anglican Church, 304n.19, 315n3
  See also Church of England
antigay, 58, 62, 64, 126, 171
anti-Manichean, 5, 70–71, 79–80
anti-Pelagian, 71, 74, 76
appetites, 5, 9, 103
  sensitive, 88–91, 93, 313n15, 314n21
Aquinas, Thomas, 9, 11, 83–97, 109, 111–13, 258, 265, 267, 312nn1, 2, 3, 313nn6, 9, 12, 15, 314nn25,27, 317nn25, 32, 340n15

Aristotelianism, 85–87, 96
Aristotle, 84–85, 87, 109, 312n2, 313nn9, 13, 317n25, 323n1
arsenokoitai, 56–57, 310n14
asceticism, 6, 34, 69–70, 75, 78–79, 81, 86, 123, 126, 154, 234
Augustine, 5, 8, 36–37, 67–81, 83, 85, 100, 103 109, 113, 118, 219, 261–62, 268, 311n15, 314n28, 318n6, 319n22

Baker-Fletcher, Karen, 286, 289, 290, 343n4, 344nn30, 34
Bailey, Derrick Sherwin, 154–55, 157, 160–61, 324nn17, 22
baptism, 5, 63, 69, 76, 123, 241, 266, 336n3
beatitude, 89, 93–95, 265–66, 314n39
Beloved, 10
  Baby Suggs in, 46–48, 277–79, 281, 283–88, 291–94
  Paul D in, 34, 46–48, 283–85
  Sethe in, 34, 45–48, 283–85
Bernard of Clairvaux, 3, 27
Bible, 8, 15–31, 43–45, 52, 69, 121, 128, 211, 223
  See also Biblical Reference Index
birth control, 11, 57, 100, 102, 106, 111, 169, 315nn3, 8